List of Figur

EXPERIENCES OF CHARITY, 1250–1650

This book is dedicated to the memory of Philippa Maddern,

1952–2014

Inspiration and Friend

Experiences of Charity, 1250–1650

Edited by

ANNE M. SCOTT
The University of Western Australia

ASHGATE

Published by
Ashgate Publishing Limited
Wey Court East
Union Road
Farnham
Surrey, GU9 7PT
England

Ashgate Publishing Company
110 Cherry Street
Suite 3-1
Burlington, VT 05401-3818
USA

www.ashgate.com

British Library Cataloguing in Publication Data
A catalogue record for this book is available from the British Library

The Library of Congress has cataloged the printed edition as follows:
Experiences of Charity, 1250–1650 / edited by Anne M. Scott.
    pages cm
    Includes bibliographical references and index.
    1. Charities – Social aspects – England – History. 2. Charities – Social aspects –
France – History. 3. Charities – Social aspects – Benelux countries – History.
    4. Church work with the poor – England – History. 5. Church work with the poor –
France – History. 6. Church work with the poor – Benelux countries – History.
    7. England – Social conditions. 8. France – Social conditions. 9. Benelux countries –
Social conditions. I. Scott, Anne M.
    HV249.E864E86 2015
    361.7094'0802–dc23   2014033505

ISBN   9781472443380 (hbk)
ISBN   9781472443397 (ebk–ePDF)
ISBN: 9781472443403 (ebk–ePUB)

MIX
Paper from
responsible sources
FSC
www.fsc.org   FSC® C013985

Printed in the United Kingdom by Henry Ling Limited,
at the Dorset Press, Dorchester, DT1 1HD

Contents

List of Tables

List of Plates

The colour plate section will fall between pages 140 and 141

1   Pose de la Première pierre de la Chapelle
Source: Cracow, Czartoryski Museum and Library, MS 3092 II, Nicolas Houel, 'Le Manuscrit de la Maison de la Charité chrétienne', 1582, fol. 81.
Reproduced by kind permission of the Princes Czartoryski Foundation, Cracow.

2   Exercices Spirituels
Source: Cracow, Czartoryski Museum and Library, MS 3092 II, Nicolas Houel, 'Le Manuscrit de la Maison de la Charité chrétienne', 1582, fol. 101.
Reproduced by kind permission of the Princes Czartoryski Foundation, Cracow.

3   Le Bureau des Bienfaiteurs
Source: Cracow, Czartoryski Museum and Library, MS 3092 II, Nicolas Houel, 'Le Manuscrit de la Maison de la Charité chrétienne', 1582, fol. 45.
Reproduced by kind permission of the Princes Czartoryski Foundation, Cracow.

4   La Charité ouvre les portes du Ciel
Source: Cracow, Czartoryski Museum and Library, MS 3092 II, Nicolas Houel, 'Le Manuscrit de la Maison de la Charité chrétienne', 1582, fol. 61.
Reproduced by kind permission of the Princes Czartoryski Foundation, Cracow.

5   Festin du Bon Riche
Source: Cracow, Czartoryski Museum and Library, MS 3092 II, Nicolas Houel, 'Le Manuscrit de la Maison de la Charité chrétienne', 1582, fol. 889.
Reproduced by kind permission of the Princes Czartoryski Foundation, Cracow.

6   L'Apothicairerie
Source: Cracow, Czartoryski Museum and Library, MS 3092 II, Nicolas Houel, 'Le Manuscrit de la Maison de la Charité chrétienne', 1582, fol. 69.
Reproduced by kind permission of the Princes Czartoryski Foundation, Cracow.

7   A beggar and a wealthy man
Source: Collégiale Saint-Martin, Champeaux, France. Photograph by Joe Scott, used with permission.

Notes on Contributors

Dr Nicholas Dean Brodie, The University of Tasmania

Nicholas Brodie completed his PhD at the University of Tasmania in 2010. His doctoral thesis addressed 'Beggary, Vagabondage, and Poor Relief: English Statutes in the Urban Context, 1495–1572'. He has other degrees from The Australian National University and Flinders University in History and Archaeology. He publishes on the subject of early modern English poor relief, with a particular interest in the systemic and conceptual mechanics of legislation and poor relief. He has also published on Australian and Colonial History, Indigenous–Settler Contact History and Church History.

Professor Susan Broomhall, The University of Western Australia

Susan Broomhall is Winthrop Professor of Early Modern History at The University of Western Australia. She has published studies on women and gender in early modern Europe, especially France, the Low Countries and more recently England and Scotland. Her research interests include social welfare from 1600–1900, particularly sixteenth-century French poor relief and experiences of the poor, on which she has written a series of articles and book chapters. She has also produced (with David G. Barrie) *Police Courts in Nineteenth-Century Scotland*: (vol. I) *Magistrates, Media and the Masses,* (vol. II) *Boundaries, Behaviours, Bodies* (Farnham: Ashgate, forthcoming). She is currently working on a monograph study, *The Experiences of the Poor in Sixteenth-century France.*

Lisa Keane Elliott, The University of Western Australia

Lisa Keane Elliott is a doctoral candidate at The University of Western Australia working on her thesis 'Poverty, Poor Relief and the *pauvres malades*: A Social History of the Paris Hôtel-Dieu, 1505–1598'. Lisa's previous published papers on charity have appeared in *Governing Masculinities in the Early Modern Period: Regulating Self and Others* (2011) and *Experiences of Poverty in Late Medieval and Early Modern England and France* (2012).

Professor Sharon Farmer, The University of California, Santa Barbara

Professor of History at the University of California, Santa Barbara, Sharon Farmer is the author of *Surviving Poverty in Medieval Paris: Gender, Ideology, and the Daily Lives of the Poor* (2001) and *Communities of Saint Martin: Legend and*

Ritual in Medieval Tours (1991). She is currently completing a monograph on the origins of the silk industry in thirteenth-century Paris.

Dr Dolly MacKinnon, The University of Queensland

Dolly MacKinnon is a Senior Lecturer in History at the University of Queensland. Her research background spans both history and music, and her publications focus on analysing the mental, physical and auditory landscapes of past cultures. Author of *Earls Colne's Early Modern Landscapes* (Ashgate, 2014), she has also co-edited *Exhibiting Madness* (2011), *Madness in Australia* (2003) and *Hearing Places* (2007). Her forthcoming publications include battlefields as emotional landscapes in England and Scotland, and child slavery in early modern Scotland.

Professor Philippa Maddern, The University of Western Australia

Philippa Maddern was Winthrop Professor in Medieval History at The University of Western Australia, and Director of the ARC Centre for the History of Emotions in Europe 1100–1800, until her death in 2014. She published extensively on the social, cultural, family and gender history of England, *c.* 1300–1500. At the time of her death Professor Maddern was working on three projects: on the history of non-nuclear families in England, 1350–1650; on childhood and the lives of English children, 1400–1520; and on the workings of emotion in English households, law courts and devotional practices, *c.* 1300–1520.

Dr Neil S. Rushton

Neil Rushton has a background in archaeology and has been a leading exponent of applying archaeological techniques to complement the analyses of historical data. He has published over twenty articles in both historical and archaeological journals on a variety of subjects and is the recent joint author (with Professor Colin Platt) of *Mont Orgueil and its Guns*, a study of the refortification of the Jersey castle. Neil is a fellow of the Society of Antiquaries and the Royal Historical Society and is currently researching the spatial aspects of remodelling building campaigns in English parish churches.

Associate Professor Anne M. Scott, The University of Western Australia, Editor and Contributor

Anne Scott is an honorary research fellow in English and Cultural Studies at The University of Western Australia. Her field of research is in fourteenth-century English Literature, and she has published a monograph, 'Piers Plowman' *and the poor* (2004), edited four volumes of collected essays, and published several essays on fourteenth- and fifteenth-century English literature. She is Editor of *Parergon*, the journal of the Australian and New Zealand Association for Medieval and Early Modern Studies, available as part of the Project MUSE database.

Dr Lesley Silvester, The University of Western Australia
Lesley Silvester completed her MA in Medieval and Early Modern Studies at The University of Western Australia in 2007 followed by her doctorate in 2012. Her most recent publication was a chapter in the collection *Experiences of Poverty in Late Medieval and Early Modern England and France*, edited by Anne M. Scott (Ashgate, 2012). Her other research interests include the history of emotions associated with music and songs of the sea, the emotional history of genealogy and the symbolic and sentimental significance of museum objects and archaeological artefacts.

Jennifer Stemmle, The University of California, Santa Barbara
Jennifer Stemmle is a PhD candidate at the University of California at Santa Barbara where she works under the supervision of Sharon Farmer. Her dissertation focuses on the leprosarium of Mont Cornillon in the context of ideas about community and the body in the twelfth and thirteenth centuries in the diocese of Liège. Jennifer's work seeks to excavate the activities of people with leprosy and to make their participation in community building and care central to the story of leprosy in the Middle Ages.

Dr Spencer E. Young, The University of Western Australia
Spencer Young is a Research Associate with the Australian Research Council Centre of Excellence for the History of Emotions at The University of Western Australia. He received his PhD in medieval history at the University of Wisconsin-Madison in 2009. He has previously held postdoctoral positions at the University of Notre Dame and the Pontifical Institute of Mediaeval Studies. He is the editor of *Crossing Boundaries at Medieval Universities* (2011) and the author of *Scholarly Community at the Early University of Paris: Theologians, Education and Society, 1215–1248* (2014).

Abbreviations

Actes 1	Elsie Johnston (ed.), *Actes du Consistoire de l'église française de Threadneedle Street, Londres, vol. 1: 1560–65* (London: Huguenot Society of London, 1938)
Actes 2	Anne M. Oakley (ed.), *Actes du Consistoire de l'église française de Threadneedle Street, Londres, vol. 2: 1571–77* (London: Huguenot Society, 1969)
A.D.	Hautes-Alpes Archives départementales des Hautes-Alpes
AEL	Archives de l'État en Belgique à Liège
AP-HP	Archives de l'Assistance publique, Hôpitaux de Paris
BL	London, British Library
BnF	Paris, Bibliothèque nationale de France
EETS	Early English Text Society
NRO	Norwich, Norfolk Record Office
MGH	*Monumenta Germaniae Historica*
Précis	*Précis de l'Histoire de la Ville de Gap* (Gap: Alfred Allier, 1844)
Records	William Hudson and John Tingey (eds), *The Records of the City of Norwich*, 2 vols (Norwich: Jarrold & Son, 1906)
TNA	Kew, The National Archives
Valor Ecclesiasticus	J. Caley and J. Hunter (eds), *Valor Ecclesiasticus temp. Henry VIII, auctoritate regia institutis*, 6 vols (London, 1810–34)
WAM	London, Westminster Abbey Muniments

Preface

This volume follows the 2012 volume of essays, *Experiences of Poverty in Late Medieval and Early Modern England and France*, also published by Ashgate. It is the result of collaboration during a workshop held in February 2013 at the Centre for Medieval and Early Modern Studies at The University of Western Australia, which set out to reconsider the experience and concept of charity. Participants were asked, in the light of their research into the experiences of the poor over the past decade or so, what might they now see differently about how charity was experienced as a concept and in practice, at both community and personal levels in medieval and early modern Europe. The presence of Sharon Farmer and Susan Broomhall as facilitators greatly enriched the deliberations, and the present essay collection is a distillation of the workshop's findings.

Many people have assisted with the production of the volume, and I want to record my gratitude to Lesley O'Brien for sharing her technical knowledge and helping to prepare the manuscript. Stephanie Lassallette, Bruce McLintock and Brett Hirsch also gave generously of their time to ensure that the final product was completed expeditiously, and I am grateful to them. But above all, I want to thank Susan Broomhall who conceived the project, and the authors who responded promptly to all my nagging little emails, and from start to finish, have collaborated enthusiastically in sharing their research.

ANNE M. SCOTT
The University of Western Australia

Chapter 1

Experiences of Charity: Complex Motivations in the Charitable Endeavour, *c.* 1100–*c.* 1650[1]

Anne M. Scott

In this collection we explore the experience of charity, examining the complex motivations that prompt charitable activity, and ask questions about the shared experience of charity that characterised the relationship between paupers, administrators and donors in medieval and early modern Europe. Religion as a motivation has been examined extensively in the historiography of charitable aid, but it is not the only motivation, and in the following chapters we consider, alongside the religious, other impulses arising from civic, familial, personal and political considerations in the provision of various forms of poor relief. How do these motivations change or persist over the period 1100 to 1650 and in response to new religious ideas of the Protestant Reformation and post-Reformation Catholicism? The volume sets out to examine these issues in case studies relating to England, France and the Low Countries.

For a number of recent years scholars who are concerned with issues of poverty and the poor have turned away from the study of charity and poor relief, in order to examine the life of the poor from the standpoint of the poor themselves.[2] This is less difficult to achieve than might appear, even allowing for the fact that records are not comprehensive. Great studies have been conducted resulting in seminal works from scholars such as Sharon Farmer, Marjorie McIntosh, Christopher Dyer, Steve Hindle, Robert Jütte and many others, that have broken new ground in developing methodologies that others have built on.[3] This substantial research has

---

[1] While, in accordance with the title, the main thrust of this volume deals with material from 1250–1650, we have included, in Chapter 3, a valuable study of the experiences of lepers from the twelfth to the fourteenth century.

[2] Recent scholars to engage in such research are Marjorie K. McIntosh, *Poor Relief in England, 1350–1600* (Cambridge: Cambridge University Press, 2012); and the contributors to Anne M. Scott (ed.), *Experiences of Poverty in Late Medieval and Early Modern England and France* (Farnham: Ashgate, 2012). An extensive bibliography of the field is to be found in the last mentioned book, as well as in the well-documented chapters that follow in this volume.

[3] See particularly Sharon Farmer, *Surviving Poverty in Medieval Paris: Gender, Ideology, and the Daily Lives of the Poor* (Ithaca, NY: Cornell University Press, 2002);

enriched our understanding of pauper experiences and the influence and impact of poverty on societies, shifting attention from donors and charitable administration and processes. If we now return our gaze to 'charity' with the benefit of those studies' questions, approaches, sources and findings, what might we see differently about how charity, considered in its multifarious aspects – spiritual, intellectual, emotional, personal, social, cultural and material – was experienced as a concept and in practice, at both community and personal levels?

The chapters that follow engage with the dynamics driving the very real relationships between paupers, administrators and donors. Elsewhere, I have characterised this as a symbiotic relationship between poor and non-poor.[4] The essays here take this idea further, highlighting, often in a very individual and context-specific manner, relationships based on the notions of reciprocity and exchange. To focus on the words 'charity' and 'experiences of' reminds us that the experience is shared by poor and non-poor, each of whom experiences charity in an individual way. Admittedly, the 'exchange' relationship is often unequal, with power largely in the hands of the non-poor. But there is an equation, nonetheless, and the different chapters explore how this exchange in charity operates.

A significant number of these case studies remind us that the relief of the condition called 'poverty', particularly in urban situations, has been regarded as the province of administrators from the Middle Ages through to the early modern period. An equally significant number focus our gaze on poor people and remind us that, in exploring experiences of charity, we are studying the experiences both of poor people and individual donors. Striking, in this regard, is MacKinnon's chapter dealing with the choristers of Christ's Hospital School, which presents us with vivid reconstructions of orphaned children singing psalms of thanksgiving, and traces the subsequent adult life of one of these charity orphans. Striking, too, is Elliott's account of the very personal involvement of the pharmacist, Houel, and the aristocratic ladies he persuaded to sponsor his school to train poor boys as pharmacists. In these, and other relationships described in the chapters that follow, it becomes clear that poor people, far from being a faceless burden on the non-poor, are recognisable individuals who have something valuable they can offer in exchange.

Underlying much scholarship on poverty and charity are assumptions that have suggested either a process of secularisation or the continued strength of religious motivations over the centuries. Some forty or so years ago, the impact of

---

Christopher Dyer, 'The Experience of Being Poor in Late Medieval England', in Scott (ed.), *Experiences of Poverty*, pp. 19–39; McIntosh, especially in *Poor Relief in England*, and her earlier work, *Controlling Misbehavior in England, 1370–1600* (Cambridge; New York: Cambridge University Press, 1998); Steve Hindle, *On the Parish? The Micro-Politics of Poor Relief in Rural England, c. 1550–1750* (Oxford: Oxford University Press, 2004); Robert Jütte, *Poverty and Deviance in Early Modern Europe* (Cambridge: Cambridge University Press, 1994).

[4]   Scott, 'Experiences of Poverty', in Scott (ed.), *Experiences of Poverty*, pp. 1–15 (p. 8).

Protestantism dominated ideas about changes to charity in the sixteenth century. A second thread of the historiography, the role of humanism, uncoupled charity from the confessions. This is the philosophy, which, in a form that translated into day-to-day civic life, prompted organisational responses that led to progressively collective solutions. The suggestion has been that, in contrast to this approach, medieval charity relied heavily on individual responses, and was directly linked to notions of religious devotion, and that the larger organisational effort was, during that period, unusual if not entirely lacking.

Our research sets out to challenge these broad assumptions. In the light of several case studies, and using new sources, we ask 'What do we know now? How differently might we frame the questions about the provision of poor relief in its many forms?' Of seminal interest to our study is the perception of charity. Is charity a religious or a secular term – or does it belong to both orders? Is charity a virtue, or a form of aid? Is it the same as poor relief, or does it vary at different times and in different contexts? Are the poor the same as the needy, and are the poor always considered eligible for assistance? Is there a sense in which the poor can be empowered within the charitable relationship, or are they always subordinate to the administration or donor? The variety of sources used for these studies ensures that the perception of 'charity' as practised within the context of the individual case studies is nuanced and complex.

The Confessional Divide?

One of the obvious findings to spring from the discussions that generated this essay collection is that similar movements in the organisation and practice of poor relief were taking place in both Catholic and Protestant cities of Europe in the sixteenth century. The work of Brian Pullan already, in 1971, made a seminal contribution to our understanding of the way Catholic communities in early modern Europe (particularly the great cities of Italy, and Venice above all) treated poor people and organised poor relief,[5] in this leading the way for many subsequent studies that have acted as a corrective to the belief that Protestantism was responsible for reforms in the organisation of early modern European poor relief.[6] The influence of humanism is also called into question by historians such as Cavallo, who concedes that humanist views created an ideological context in which more sophisticated systems of social organisation and care of the needy could develop, but disagrees that Erasmian humanist principles can be said to have revolutionised the European

---

[5]   Brian S. Pullan, *Rich and Poor in Renaissance Venice: The Social Institutions of a Catholic State, to 1620* (Cambridge, MA: Harvard University Press, 1971); and Brian S. Pullan, *Poverty and Charity: Europe, Italy, Venice, 1400–1700* (Aldershot: Ashgate, 1994).

[6]   For a summary of scholarship relating to this issue, see Sandra Cavallo, *Charity and Power in Early Modern Italy: Benefactors and Their Motives in Turin, 1541–1789* (Cambridge: Cambridge University Press, 1995), pp. 23–33.

welfare reforms.[7] Furthermore, it has been well-documented that the movement towards eradicating vagrancy and begging had already been in train, both in England and France as well as in other European states, since the mid-fourteenth century, when statutes enacted punishments for able-bodied begging.[8] Chapters by Farmer, Silvester, Elliott and Broomhall explore the methods undertaken in sixteenth-century Paris, Norwich and the French city of Gap by civic laymen to control society and remove all begging. While Silvester argues for a Protestant impulse behind the organisation of poor relief in Norwich, and suggests that the writings of Luther and Bucer influenced the leading governors of the city, Farmer and Elliott demonstrate similar outcomes in Catholic Paris, and Broomhall in the Huguenot city of Gap. Farmer acknowledges the humanist milieu of Paris, pointing out that the influential laymen, François du Moulin and Jean Briçonnet, were well connected with the leading humanists in early sixteenth-century France, and that du Moulin was a major intellectual influence in the French royal court.[9] The reforms described in these chapters can be paralleled across Europe in cities of different confessional allegiances.[10]

Elliott's study is based on the treatise *Le Manuscrit de la Maison de la Charité chrétienne* of Houel,[11] an early modern Frenchman, a unique source which she contextualises within the sectarian and civic upheaval in late sixteenth-century Paris. Her analysis invites a reassessment of what she shows to be complex religious motivations in this practical educational endeavour. Elliott leads us away from a militantly Protestant/Catholic divide, by showing how one Catholic man set out to mitigate the excesses of sectarian atrocity in sixteenth-century Paris. He promoted his traditional form of charity as the preferred demonstration of religious allegiance during the contentious period of religious division in late sixteenth-century Paris. Looking at the rhetoric which accompanies the charitable enterprises of Houel and, as Elliott has shown in other instances, Jean Martin and the Duke and Duchess of Nevers, the Catholic doctrine of Good Works is seen to be explicitly promoted as the ideology underpinning their establishment.[12] Yet at

---

[7]   Cavallo, pp. 23–5.

[8]   See for example Bronisław Geremek, 'La Lutte contre le vagabondage à Paris aux XIVe et XVe siècles', in Luigi di Rosa (ed.), *Ricerche storiche ed economiche in memoria di Corrado Barbagallo* (Naples: Edizioni scientifiche italiane, 1970), pp. 213–36.

[9]   Farmer, Chapter 2 in this volume, p. 42.

[10]   See also Natalie Zemon Davis, *Society and Culture in Early Modern France* (Stanford University Press, 1975), esp. 'Poor Relief, Humanism and Heresy'.

[11]   This is preserved in the collections of Cracow's Princes Czartoryski Museum and Library.

[12]   Lisa Keane Elliott, 'Jean Martin, Governor of the *Grand Bureau des Pauvres*, on Charity and the Civic Duty of Governing Men in Paris, circa 1580', in Susan Broomhall and Jacqueline Van Gent (eds), *Governing Masculinities in the Early Modern Period* (Farnham: Ashgate, 2011), pp. 65–83; Lisa Keane Elliott, 'Charitable "Intent" in Late Sixteenth-Century France: The Nevers Foundation and Single Poor Catholic Girls', in Scott (ed.), *Experiences of Poverty*, pp. 159–82.

the same time that civic and aristocratic French men and women were putting their own money into charitable enterprises, in a manner that showed both ideological and practical continuity from the medieval period, the same civic men in Paris were adopting large-scale and sometimes punitive administrative measures to remove beggars from the streets and set them to work in the name of civic order. This scenario, outlined in Farmer's chapter here, has been fully examined recently by Broomhall, exploring what she has called the politics of charitable men.[13]

The Norwich measures described by Silvester are somewhat similar to those adopted in Paris, and similarly founded on politics. Silvester presents arguments that show 'a city oligarchy eager to do what was necessary to rid their city of an annoying problem'. Poor relief is addressed in organisational terms – a census, the establishment of works, punishment for the able-bodied who would not work. Yet the confessional impulse may be present, too, if, as Silvester argues, the Norwich Census of the Poor was undertaken with a view to countering Catholic influences on the poor who were ripe for rebellion. This was a political way of forestalling violence while promoting Protestantism.

A similarly political impulse, according to Broomhall, underlay provision for poor relief in the French city of Gap. Taking as her source document draft notes of the surviving deliberations of the town consulate, Broomhall finds that, in Gap in 1567, civic authorities, for a short period lasting a few years, established systems of poor relief that ignored the sectarian divisions of Catholic and Huguenot, and gave assistance to the needy of both faiths irrespective of their official allegiance. Broomhall calls this an experiment in using poor relief as a 'potential instrument of conciliatory coalition'[14] – a considered response to the national edicts for peace, enjoined from afar upon the municipal governors. Her chapter traces the political vicissitudes of the authorities who struggled to maintain their non-sectarian ideal, and the see-sawing within the municipal council attendant upon dominance in turn by Catholic, then Huguenot ecclesiastics.

Broomhall's chapter on Huguenot charity in London is more concerned with overtly sectarian charitable relief than with politics. This chapter studies the remaining acts of the consistory of Threadneedle Street which shed light on the needs experienced by some of the Huguenot exiles in sixteenth-century London, and the practical steps taken by a close-knit church community to relieve these specific needs.[15] Broomhall's exiled Huguenots were definitely needy, but many were not used to living in straitened circumstances and were ready to complain

---

[13]   See a full discussion of these measures in Susan Broomhall, 'The Politics of Charitable Men: Governing Poverty in Sixteenth-Century Paris', in Scott (ed.), *Experiences of Poverty*, pp. 133–57.

[14]   Broomhall, Chapter 9 in this volume, p. 174.

[15]   Elsie Johnston (ed.), *Actes du Consistoire de l'église française de Threadneedle Street, Londres, vol. 1: 1560–65* (London: Huguenot Society of London, 1938); and Anne M. Oakley (ed.), *Actes du Consistoire de l'église française de Threadneedle Street, Londres, vol. 2: 1571–77* (London: Huguenot Society, 1969).

when the amount of relief left them at a level below the comfort they had been accustomed to enjoy. The Huguenots in exile were a self-contained Calvinist community, intent on maintaining good order among their adherents in a foreign land. Their confessional unity did not make the need of the suppliants palatable to the better-off members, but the elders were able to exert some pressure to raise money for practical and targeted solutions to individual problems. For these exiles, the needy state of some members led to a relationship between donors and suppliants. Broomhall's analysis of the records shows that the recipients of poor relief were treated as their individual needs required, and responded with a full sense of their own personal dignity and worth. The basis may have been the idea of Christian charity towards one's brothers, but the rhetoric dealt with practical, not theoretical, moves towards containment of need and maintenance of good order within the community. The medieval, and by early modern times, Catholic concept of charitable works as justifying the repentant, was not an impulse underlying Huguenot poor relief.

Development or Rupture?

A second thread linking the chapters is the distinction between moves towards the alleviation of poverty, and what Sandra Cavallo, in her 1995 study on Turin, typifies as a naive desire to eliminate the condition.[16] Michel Mollat, whose work is referenced by several of this book's contributors, was an early and influential proponent of the theory that not until the sixteenth century were there any serious moves to eliminate poverty as a condition.[17] Cavallo, disputing this, points to recent scholarship on Europe from the fourteenth to the sixteenth centuries, suggesting that 'provision for the poor adopted in the sixteenth century drew on a wealth of experiences in poor relief administration accumulated over the previous two centuries'.[18] Nicholas Terpstra's most recent work on Italy[19] also cuts across lines of traditional historiography, and proposes that the collective/individual divide exists from medieval times and represents two different constructs of charity working in relation to each other. His Italy-specific study sees approaches to charity as centred on the two notions of 'misericordia' and 'caritas'. Both inform philanthropy, while creating different communities of need. 'Misericordia' represents an attitude that supports the poor and needy in general, leading to the support and development of hospitals, general charitable works such as provision of food for the starving, care of orphans and general infrastructure that underpins a civic society. 'Caritas'

---

[16]   Cavallo, p. 14.
[17]   Michel Mollat, *The Poor in the Middle Ages: An Essay in Social History*, (trans.) Arthur Goldhammer (New Haven, CT: Yale University Press, 1986), p. 1.
[18]   Cavallo, pp. 23–33.
[19]   Nicholas Terpstra, *Cultures of Charity: Women, Politics, and the Reform of Poor Relief in Renaissance Italy* (Cambridge, MA: Harvard University Press, 2013).

leads to vertical connections between individuals and clients – close relations, kin, patronage of donors to individuals, and other connections which create lines of obligation. The essays in the present collection, while not in dialogue with Cavallo or Terpstra, engage with and develop new insights into the issues they have raised, adding fresh findings to the growing number of case studies that seek to understand anew the dynamics of the charitable endeavour in medieval and early modern Europe. Taken as a whole, this collection of essays seeks to test whether there is a continuum exemplifying development rather than rupture over the long period under consideration.

Sharon Farmer addresses this issue in her comparative study of charitable provision in Paris from the thirteenth to the sixteenth centuries. Farmer contends that the roots of the sixteenth-century organisational improvements in rendering poor relief were set down in the thirteenth century. Her chapter traces developments in the organisation of several institutions, such as the Quinze-vingts, the Enfants Rouges, the Hôtel-Dieu and, eventually, the Grand Bureau des Pauvres, and finds that at least five aspects of the organised system of poor relief that developed in sixteenth-century Paris had medieval precedents. Focusing first on the hospital for the blind, the Quinze-vingts, Farmer analyses its organisation, and shows that, while this hospital was a medieval royal foundation, it was managed externally by the Royal Almoner, and internally by lay, preferably married, men. Laymen were also employed by municipal authorities as parish churchwardens, who were responsible for dispensing charitable aid. Then, too, as early as the twelfth century, hospitals were established to become permanent shelters for the city's poor, sick and vulnerable residents, prompting Farmer's comment: 'clearly the founders of these institutions perceived that sustained care was better than one-time handouts'.[20] Anticipating later public poor taxes, provision was made, in the fourteenth and fifteenth centuries, albeit with difficulty, to fund poor relief by the appropriation of fines from a variety of courts. And lastly, the sixteenth-century statutes against beggars and vagabonds, together with systems of forced labour for vagrants set up in Paris, were following traditions that had been established in the mid-fourteenth century.

Another chapter giving evidence of medieval organised poor relief, directed towards specific types of need and managed in a way not unlike early modern initiatives, is that of Stemmle. Her research on the leprosaria of Liège reveals that, not only were charitable institutions formed for specific groups of needy people, but that those people themselves had some agency in the foundation and management of the institutions. When we think of reciprocity, we often reduce the concept to that of needy people being materially supported by donors and, in response, praying for the souls of those who give to them. Stemmle suggests a different way of looking at reciprocity – demonstrating that the lepers had a more personal, practical and gritty involvement in the institutions founded for their benefit, which needed their active participation in order to flourish.

---

[20]   Farmer, Chapter 2 in this volume, p. 39.

Conversely, some of the early modern strategies for dealing with the poor can be found to generate the kind of selectiveness found in the medieval period which can be seen in the two chapters dealing with provision for children, in London (MacKinnon) and in Paris (Elliott). In each case the charitable impulse is specific and potentially limited. The governors of Christ's Hospital in London set out to find and lift from the city slums orphaned or very poor children who were in moral and physical danger. These would be provided with the fundamentals of sustenance – food, shelter, uniforms to wear – in direct exchange for education, and especially musical education. The children gave of their talent, and the community benefited from their singing, which enhanced the religious services. While this strategy definitely answered a need for some children, those who benefited were a limited group taken from the many potential recipients. Similarly, Houel's Parisian initiative to provide education in pharmacy (Elliott), would benefit a select few boys, and while it was designed to provide the boys with a means of sustaining themselves in a career in later life, nevertheless the small numbers meant that the benefit was restricted. This is not in itself a bad thing, but does reflect similarly specific impulses undertaken in the Middle Ages – such as the provision of a maisondieu for a needy elderly person,[21] a hospital for the blind (Farmer), a leprosarium for lepers (Stemmle). Perhaps the big difference is that, in the case of Houel's *Maison*, and Christ's Hospital, the skills learned would give the young people an opportunity to live productive and independent lives, a benefit denied to the medieval inmates of the leprosaria or the Quinze-vingts. Similar movements were to be found in other early modern cities, such as Lyons, where Natalie Zemon Davis has found that an analysis of boys' apprenticeships in the first nine months of the newly formed Aumône shows that the overwhelming majority of them were placed in trades more remunerative or skilled than the work of their fathers.[22] In this, the early modern organisation moved towards structural improvement in the lives of the poor, and in doing so, reflected humanist principles.

Finally, adding support to arguments demonstrating that sophisticated organisation of poor relief existed in the Middle Ages, Rushton takes monastic records and subjects them to quantitative analysis, using more precise sources and tools than those used a century ago by Savine.[23] He offers a cogently argued corrective to Savine's deductions which influenced several generations of scholars to castigate the late medieval monasteries for the paucity and meanness of their poor relief. His conclusions show that, in the two monasteries under consideration, Westminster and Norwich, there was strong organisational support for the needy.

---

[21]   Patricia H. Cullum, '"For pore people harberles": What Was the Function of the Maisonsdieu?', in Dorothy J. Clayton, Richard G. Davies and Peter McNiven (eds), *Trade, Devotion and Governance; Papers in Later Medieval History* (Stroud: Sutton, 1994), pp. 36–54.

[22]   Davis, p. 43.

[23]   Alexander Savine, *English Monasteries on the Eve of the Dissolution*, (ed.) Paul Vinogradoff (Oxford: Clarendon Press, 1909).

Were better records available for other monasteries, he suggests, we would probably find that late medieval English monastic charity across the country was better organised and more generous than historians have allowed. Rushton's important work is a stunning vindication of the charitable importance of the English monastery in the early sixteenth century.[24]

Charity

Religion may provide the underlying ideology of medieval and early modern charity but the practice takes many forms and springs from many motivations, civic, familial, personal and political, as suggested above. This chapter has already pointed towards some of the political, civic and confessional motivations teased out by contributing authors, and now I want to address some of the questions about charity with which I began: is charity a religious or a secular term – or does it belong to both orders? Is charity a virtue, or a form of aid? Is it the same as poor relief, or does it vary at different times and in different contexts? Some of the following chapters examine these distinctions.

Fundamental to the medieval and early modern understanding of the term 'charity' is the idealised love of one person for another following the Gospel precept: 'A new commandment I give unto you: that you love one another as I have loved you'.[25] This love is many-faceted, but importantly, throughout the Middle Ages (and into the early modern period), expresses itself in practical care of the needy, and sees that care as an expression of love for God, who is to be recognised in the needy person. In this volume we define the poor as those who are reliant on others for their support. Inevitably these comprise the traditional Gospel categories, the poor and the feeble, the blind and the lame, the poor of the Gospel parable (Luke 14. 16–24),[26] and those specified in Matthew's account of the Last Judgement,[27] but also those who have been defeated by the unequal battle to maintain a living in difficult circumstances. A pervasive issue in medieval and early modern discussions of charity is the thorny problem of how to identify the poor, a process that inevitably places the needy person in a subordinate position to that of the donor, whether individual or as part of an administration.

---

[24] Professor Peter Cunich, University of Hong Kong, in private correspondence with the Editor.

[25] John 13. 33–5.

[26] The relevant verse (21) says: 'Exi cito in plateas et vicos civitatis et pauperes ac debiles et caecos et claudos introduc huc' ('Go out quickly into the streets and lanes of the city; and bring in hither the poor and the feeble and the blind and the lame').

[27] Matthew 25. 31–46. This scriptural passage is the foundation of the practice of the corporal works of mercy. See fuller discussion in Scott, Chapter 13 in this volume, pp. 261–7.

Of crucial importance to the medieval mind is the concept of good works as a means of attaining remission of sin – a concept dismissed by Protestant reformers. In his chapter, Young teases out distinctions in the motivation for charitable giving during the high Middle Ages. He discusses the rise of the cash economy and the circulation of coinage as bringing new opportunities both for the poor to receive alms and the sinner to give in order to obtain remission of sin. Prostitutes and usurers were much assisted by the rise of the monetary economy, but there were widespread debates about whether such public sinners should be allowed to give alms, and whether the source of the money used in alms would negate the spiritual efficacy of the offering. In another distinction, Young deals with the suggestion that, in the medieval landscape of charity, the relationship between pauper and donor could redound to the secular reputation of the latter, and become prideful and ostentatious. In this scenario, the poor enhance the power of the non-poor, and have little value in their own right. Basing his arguments on those of Brodman,[28] Young advances the idea that religious motives and practical considerations are not so easily separable during this period. Never in doubt, however, is the obligation of those who have material means to relieve the burdens of the poor.

Maddern's chapter examines carefully the practical assistance offered by individual testators to the poor. Her reading of fifteenth-century Norwich wills reveals that 'benefactions' for the good of the testator's soul could as soon describe contributions towards the upkeep of the church fabric, or supplies of candles, as money set aside for the poor. She concludes that, while any assistance in the form of cash, food or clothing was welcome, such testamentary benefactions cannot be considered a reliable form of ongoing relief to the local poor. The correlation between aid given to the poor and merit attributed to the soul of the testator seems to show, in Maddern's analysis, that the balance of benefit was on the side of the donor.

Brodie concurs with the findings of Maddern in asserting that, while the word 'charity' was in use in the Middle Ages, the term 'almsgiving' more frequently characterised the giving of material benefit to the needy. Analysing the use of the term 'charity' by social historians, he points out that 'charity' has come to be 'a catch-all concept for what would more accurately be described as poor relief or welfare'.[29] His chapter cogently argues for continuity over the confessional divide and from medieval to early modern times based on his study of poor boxes. He demonstrates that the poor box which was enjoined by statute in 1547 had already been a church fixture from medieval times. But whereas formerly it had been used for the collection of offerings for a number of good works which, while mentioning care of the poor, also included 'pardons, pilgrimages, trentals, decking of images,

---

[28] James William Brodman, *Charity and Religion in Medieval Europe* (Washington, DC: Catholic University of America Press, 2009), pp. 35–44, 267–85.

[29] Nicholas Brodie, Chapter 11 in this volume, p. 229.

offerings of candles, giving to friars, and ... other like blind devotions',[30] now it was only to be used to help the poor and the needy. Brodie sees the 1547 poor box as 'an indicator of a shift, one where love of God and care for humanity was increasingly to be expressed only in coinage given "in charity" to the poor'.[31]

Experiencing Charity

The place of the poor within society was recognised at all levels, and while, in Scott's terms, the poor were systemic to the social order,[32] generic and faceless in the view of administrators, it was also possible for a relationship to exist between individual poor people and donors. Scott argues that, in a society in which good works led to salvation, the poor were a necessary and structural feature, but she makes a distinction between the anonymous poor appearing in wills, and the poor who are recognised as having emotions, needs and a sense of self-worth. The former appear in the provisions made by the singlewoman, Philippa Russell, for 'poor prisoners in the prisons of Newgate, Ludgate, Fleet, Marshalsea, the King's Bench and the Abbot of Westminster's [prison] of convicted clerks, and also among the sick and other weak and poor people in hospitals within and outside the city of London'.[33] The designation of specific prisons and hospitals suggests that this bequest represented Philippa Russell's targeted compassion, as well as a keen sense of her own spiritual needs: 'to pray especially for my soul'. The poor who are recognised as having a sense of personal worth, and make a clearly defined contribution to society, are exemplified in the work of the fifteenth-century poet, Thomas Hoccleve, who feelingly appeals to Prince Henry, soon to be king, to pay him the annuity he is owed for work done, and not allow him to sink into old-age penury.

These identifiable poor appear in many of the chapters: the Huguenot exiles who challenge as meagre the aid afforded them (Broomhall, 'From France to England'); the leper who himself provides money to fund the leprosarium, and insists on taking part in a local skirmish before being confined within the leprosarium (Stemmle); but perhaps the most appealing are the orphaned choristers of Christ's Hospital (MacKinnon), whose singing of a psalm touched John Evelyn so much that they seemed to him like a vision of angels.[34] MacKinnon aims 'to retune our ears to hear the significance of these psalms sung by the poor as part of

---

[30]   P.L. Hughes and J.F. Larkin (eds), *Tudor Royal Proclamations*, 3 vols (New Haven, CT: Yale University Press, 1964–69), I (1964), no. 287, p. 401.

[31]   Brodie, p. 233.

[32]   Scott, Chapter 13 in this volume, p. 257.

[33]   Judith M. Bennett and Christopher Whittick, 'Philippa Russell and the Wills of London's Late Medieval Singlewomen', *London Journal*, 32 (2007), 251–69 (p. 262).

[34]   John Evelyn, cited in Susi Jeans, 'The Easter Psalms of Christ's Hospital', *Proceedings of the Royal Musical Association*, 88 (1961–62), 45–60 (pp. 54–5).

their role in the public acts of reciprocity that accompanied charitable giving, and that required their vocal articulation of gratitude'.[35] Here, so clearly, the rewards are mutual and instant: to the donor, the immediate and uplifting satisfaction of the children's singing; and to the children, the benefit of a sound and godly upbringing with the promise of future well-being.

In many of the chapters, women figure prominently as providers of the means to relieve poverty. Images in books of hours (Scott) frequently commemorate the role of saintly queens or wealthy benefactresses in giving to the needy. Rushton's chapter gives historical context to such benefaction, analysing the importance of the bequest to Westminster made by Edward I's consort, Queen Eleanor of Castile, which, coupled with further royal foundations such as those of Richard II and Anne of Bohemia, Henry VII and Margaret Beaufort, enabled the monastery to provide regularly and generously for the needy from Eleanor's death in 1290 until dissolution in 1540.[36]

Influential women are carefully nurtured as patrons by Houel, who, as artist and humanist savant, moved in the court circles of King Henri III and Louise de Lorraine. In the aftermath of the violent religious wars of the sixteenth century, Houel consciously invoked the Catholic doctrine of Good Works in his advertisements for the *Maison* he hoped to establish. Elliott suggests that some of the Catholic noble and well-connected women who became his patrons may have felt the need to expiate, by good works, the violent deeds of their husbands in the religious wars. The organisation of the *Maison* with compulsory attendance at the daily celebration of Mass, and the confessional support of the foundation by the Faculty of Theology at Paris, associate these women with Houel's more peaceful, though no less sectarian, profession of Catholicism. While the foundation is by the man Houel, it is the women, and particularly 'the very illustrious and charitable lady Madame de Dampierre' who are depicted in Houel's illustrations and text as taking a leading role in producing material support and thereby gaining heavenly reward. In some respects, the idealised depiction of them in Houel's illustrations reflects similar idealisation of female saintly queens who are depicted giving material help to the needy in medieval illuminations (Scott). Houel's illustrations, in particular, construct the enterprise as a sacred undertaking, idealising the pupils, the Master and the benefactors within a quasi-heavenly context, invoking tropes common to both medieval and early modern visual images. In terms of experiencing charity, it should be noted that, at his death, Houel was almost destitute, having poured his wealth into the school. This was a personal experience of heroic charity.

---

[35]   Dolly MacKinnon, 'Hearing the Poor: Experiencing the Sounds of Charity in Early Modern England', in this volume, p. 240.

[36]   Neil S. Rushton, 'The Forms and Functions of Monastic Poor Relief in Late Medieval and Early Sixteenth-Century England', in this volume, p. 194.

Conclusion

In spite of all the research into experiences and concepts of poverty and charity over the past fifty years, there remains a wealth of source material still to be examined, and in this book we have assembled a range of case studies designed to complement one another and contribute to our understanding of continuities and contrasts over the period.

From Farmer and Stemmle we gain insight into medieval secular provision of institutional care for the needy in Paris (Farmer) and Liège (Stemmle). Scott and Young explore charitable giving and its motivation as evidenced in visual art and literary texts in England and France (Scott), and French *exempla* (Young). Maddern presents evidence of late medieval personal lay responses to needy individuals in eastern England, while Rushton's work on late medieval monastic provision of poor relief to needy individuals in England – Westminster and Norwich – shows that the monasteries at this time were major providers of charitable alms and structurally important within the local economy.

Elliott presents a case study of an early modern Catholic Frenchman's provision for the educational needs of poor boys in Paris; MacKinnon looks at an early modern Protestant English charity school for poor children in London. Broomhall studies a beleaguered early modern religious group, the Huguenots, exploring the records of this church-in-exile's organised provision for its needy in London. Her companion study, of Gap, France, shows municipal authorities setting up civic systems to care for the needy, unusually encompassing both Huguenot and Catholic poor. A significant section of Farmer's chapter examines early modern civic provision for the needy in the Catholic city, Paris, while Silvester's study of Norwich deals with similar movements in an English Protestant city. Brodie's study of the role of poor boxes in the development of systems of urban poor relief in sixteenth-century England draws together many strands of the book's discussions, tracing continuities with medieval practices of almsgiving, and linking early modern poor relief firmly to religious, though not sectarian, motives of charity.

Some of the sources are the well-known genres of wills (Maddern), sermon *exempla* (Young), saints' lives (Stemmle) and monastic and civic records (Farmer, Rushton, Silvester). Stemmle reads saints' lives in a new way, comparing them against a range of other narrative sources from the diocese of Liège in order to search for patterns in the representation of the actions of people with leprosy. Rushton, as has been mentioned, employs a new kind of statistical analysis of monastic records, and revises the long-held historiographical prejudice against the monasteries.

Other types of source are less frequently used in this kind of study – songs (MacKinnon), extant visual representations in buildings and manuscripts (Scott), an early modern poor box (Brodie). These sources create a material record and allow a modern person to interrogate the same material that was available to contemporaries living from the twelfth to the seventeenth centuries. The chapters centring on them seek to achieve some understanding of the relationships between givers and receivers, exploring the dynamic of charity and acknowledging its shifting nature in different time periods, geographical areas and faiths.

The conclusions drawn from these essays suggest that civic operations to eradicate begging and set the poor to work took similar forms in both Catholic and Protestant cities, and are in a direct line of development from the statutes against begging and vagrancy that had been promulgated in France, England and elsewhere in Europe since the fourteenth century. Charitable works, such as those of Houel, or Christ's Hospital founded by the monarch, Edward VI, are in a direct line from medieval enterprises founded for specific purposes by charitable individuals or groups. The medieval monastery, newly reassessed by Rushton, straddles both aspects of poor relief. The monastery was the repository and administrator of charitable gifts given by donors as an act of devotion to God as well as of philanthropy; and by engaging with the poor, the best-run monasteries effectively maintained good civic order.

In the chapters that follow, the approach is a comparative one: across different time periods, nations, faiths. Each chapter considers acts of charity in the context of poor relief, and analyses the impact of acts of charity on the needy themselves as well as on the donors. While the pious rhetoric of the spiritual value of good works diminishes in the Protestant communities, an underlying ethic persists across the centuries in all communities under consideration here: having means above one's own needs entails obligations on the whole community – not just the rich, but everyone.

PART I
The Written Record

Chapter 2

From Personal Charity to Centralised Poor Relief: The Evolution of Responses to the Poor in Paris, c. 1250–1600

Sharon Farmer

In the thirteenth century, Parisian charitable assistance for the involuntary poor, and for those who were considered 'poor' by virtue of their physical or social debilities,[1] was delivered through a confusing hodgepodge of charitable institutions and individual acts of piety. By the end of the century, the city was dotted with at least sixteen charitable institutions addressing the needs of various categories of poor people. At least seven of those institutions provided food and shelter to poor people who were suffering from short term illness; the largest and oldest of those institutions, the main hospital, or Hôtel-Dieu, provided shelter, meals, palliative nursing care and spiritual assistance to as many as 800 sick people, women in labour and orphaned children.[2] Two other hospitals offered temporary lodging to pilgrims; and seven hospices, shelters, convents and leprosaria provided

---

[1] For the argument that the medieval definition of poverty included the weak, vulnerable and disabled see Michel Mollat, *Les Pauvres au Moyen Âge: étude sociale* (Paris: Hachette, 1978), pp. 9–21. Evidence concerning the Parisian hospice for the blind (the Quinze-Vingts) confirms this definition: both the institution and its lay and ecclesiastical supporters referred to the residents as 'the poor blind', despite the fact that they were allowed to retain the usufruct of their personal property, and some of them were relatively wealthy. See 'Testament of Jeanne Haudry, 1309', in Boris Bove, 'Vie et mort d'un couple de marchands-drapiers Parisiens, d'après les testaments de Jeanne et Etienne Haudri (1309, 1313)', *Paris et Ile-de-France, Mémoires*, 52 (2001), 19–81 (p. 64); Léon Le Grand, *Les Quinze-Vingts: depuis leurs fondation jusqu'à leur translation au faubourg Saint-Antoine. XIIIe–XVIIIe siècles*, 2 vols (Paris, 1886–87), II (1887), 67; Mark P. O'Tool, 'Caring for the Blind in Medieval Paris: Life at the Quinze-Vingts 1250–1430' (unpublished doctoral thesis, University of California, 2007), pp. 143–5; see also n. 4 below.

[2] They were the Hôtel-Dieu of Paris, and those of St-Mathurin, St-Marcel, Jean L'Ecuellier, Philippe de Magny, St-Martin-des-Champs and St-Jean-de-Jerusalem: Léon Le Grand, *Les Maisons-Dieu et léproseries du diocèse de Paris au milieu du XIVe siècle* (Paris, 1898), pp. 54, 56, 63, 67, 77; Dorothy-Louise MacKay, *Les Hôpitaux et la charité à Paris au XIIIe siècle* (Paris: E. Champion, 1923), pp. 19, 26.

permanent shelter for people with various needs and disabilities – lepers, blind people, reformed prostitutes and widows.[3]

Despite this impressive array of endowed institutions for the weak, disabled and involuntary poor, outdoor begging was apparently the most important source of alimentary support for those without property who suffered from long term disability. Indeed, institutions and individuals that housed the poor and the disabled often expected them to beg. From the time of its origins, for instance, the well-endowed Congregation of the Quinze-Vingts, founded by King Louis IX in the mid 1250s, sent its blind inmates out on quests for alms in order to augment the income of the institution.[4] The desire to send the blind residents out to beg may have played a major role in the policy concerning marriage within the shelter: it was encouraged, but only if one of the spouses was blind and the other was sighted.[5] At the Hôtel-Dieu of Paris, disabled individuals could receive both shelter and meals, but only for a limited time while they recovered from illnesses or underwent 'physical therapy' in order to enhance their ability to survive on their own. Thus, when Jehanne de Serris, the wife of a carpenter, fell victim to some kind of paralysis in 1276, she stayed in the Hôtel-Dieu for only three months – long enough for the nuns to nurse her back to health and teach her to use crutches. Jehanne's husband then carried her back to their home, and from then on she gained her share of the family income by begging at the door of her parish church.[6]

---

[3]   Temporary shelters: La Trinité and Ste-Katherine. Permanent shelters: leprosaria of St-Lazare, St-Germain-des-Prés and La Roule; Congregation of the Blind of the Quinze-Vingts; Filles Dieu and St-Antoine (convents of reformed prostitutes); Ste-Avoye (shelter of widows): Le Grand, *Les Maisons-Dieu*, pp. 53, 94, 100–102; MacKay, pp. 28–9; François-Olivier Touati, *Maladie et société au Moyen Âge. La Lèpre, les lépreux et les léproseries dans la province ecclésiastique de Sens jusqu'au milieu du XIVe siècle* (Paris-Brussels: De Boeck Université, 1998), pp. 252–3, 261, 265; Sharon Farmer, *Surviving Poverty*, p. 147. On the blind, see discussion below at nn. 60–69.

[4]   Michel Félibien, *Histoire de la ville de Paris*, 5 vols (Paris: Guillaume Desprez and Jean Desessartz, 1725), III, 270. The earliest extant reference to the alms quests of the residents of the Quinze-Vingts is a Papal bull of 1265 encouraging various religious leaders in and around Paris to support the 'domum caecorum pauperum Parisius'. The thirteenth-century poet Rutebeuf complained about these quests: 'Les ordres de Paris', in *Oeuvres complètes*, (ed.) Michel Zink, 2 vols (Paris, 1989), I, 230–32; Mark P. O'Tool, 'The *povres avugles* of the Hospital of the Quinze-Vingts', in Meredith Cohen and Justine Firnhaber-Baker (eds), *Difference and Identity in Francia and Medieval France* (Farnham: Ashgate, 2010), pp. 157–74 (p. 159).

[5]   'Règlement donné aux XV^xx par Michel de Brache, aumônier du roi Jean' (1351–52), in Le Grand, *Les Quinze-Vingts*, II, 154–64 (p. 158); O'Tool, 'Caring for the Blind', pp. 219–20.

[6]   Guillaume de St-Pathus, *Les Miracles de St-Louis*, (ed.) Percival B. Fay (Paris: H. Champion, 1931), pp. 131–4; Sharon Farmer, 'Manual Labor, Begging and Conflicting Gender Expectations in Thirteenth-Century Paris', in Sharon Farmer and Carol Braun Pasternack (eds), *Gender and Difference in the Middle Ages* (Minneapolis: University of Minnesota Press, 2003), pp. 261–87 (pp. 264–5).

In nearby St-Denis, Amelot of Chambly, who suffered for years from a debilitating disease that bent her body in two, was also expected to beg in order to survive. A generous artisan provided Amelot with shelter, but he offered bread only when the weather rendered the streets so muddy that Amelot could not go out.[7]

The institutions and streets of Paris offered a variety of opportunities for needy individuals to 'earn' their daily bread by begging. There were daily handouts at various monasteries, a weekly distribution of alms on the Grand Pont and special distributions on Christian feast days.[8] Disabled beggars with limited mobility could simply wait next to a church door or hold out their hands when aristocratic entourages or wealthy merchants passed by.[9] Those who were more enterprising – or more mobile – could follow a wealthy entourage or show up for distributions at funerals.[10]

It is impossible for us to assess how effective this system was in meeting the needs of the thousands of involuntary poor who populated this city, whose population reached 200,000 around the year 1300. Indeed, as the scholarship on the history of charity and poor relief has emphasised, medieval charity was not construed in terms of efficiency or effectiveness: care for the poor was seen as a pious act, and thus institutions and alms distributions grew out of the personal piety of bishops, kings, nobles and merchants – who hoped that their acts of generosity would enhance their well-being in the afterlife – rather than out of an urge for social planning on the part of municipal or royal authorities. Most hospitals and hospices were viewed as religious institutions: they usually fell under the jurisdiction of local bishops, and they paid as much attention to the health of

---

[7] Henri François Delaborde, *Fragments de l'enquête faite à St. Denis en 1282 en vue de la canonization de Saint Louis* (Paris: H. Champion, 1896), pp. 31–2; discussed in Farmer, *Surviving Poverty*, p. 125.

[8] 'Testament of Etienne Haudri (1313)', in Bove, 'Vie et mort', p. 74; Guillaume de St-Pathus, *Les Miracles de St-Louis*, p. 68; discussed in Farmer, *Surviving Poverty*, p. 34.

[9] Household account books indicate that alms distributions, both planned and spontaneous, constituted a significant portion of aristocratic and royal expenses. See Jules-Marie Richard, *Une petite nièce de Saint Louis: Mahaut comtesse d'Artois et de Bourgogne* (Paris: H. Champion, 1887), pp. 93–7; Xavier de la Selle, *Le service des âmes à la cour: confesseurs et aumôniers des rois de France du XIIIe au XVe siècle* (Paris: École des Chartes, 1995), pp. 161–91. On the locations of princely almsgiving, see Priscille Aladjidi, 'Les Espaces du don au Moyen Âge: l'exemple de la charité princière', in *Construction de l'espace au Moyen Âge: pratiques et représentations* (Paris: Publications de la Sorbonne, 2007), pp. 349–56.

[10] 'Testaments of Jeanne and Etienne Haudri', in Bove, 'Vie et mort', pp. 63, 74; Guillaume de St-Pathus, *Les Miracles de St-Louis*, pp. 51, 68; Farmer, *Surviving Poverty*, p. 34; Sharon Farmer (trans.), 'Charity: A Deaf Mute's Story', in Miri Rubin (ed.), *Medieval Christianity in Practice* (Princeton, NJ: Princeton University Press, 2009), pp. 203–7 (pp. 203–4).

souls as to the health of bodies.[11] The budgets of such institutions, moreover, were sustained, for the most part, by charitable endowments and alms rather than by the use of 'public' funds.

In the sixteenth century, as numerous scholars have observed, this medieval system of ad hoc religious charity – which encouraged outdoor begging, and placed the burden of support of the poor on pious individuals rather than on public institutions – gave way, in municipalities throughout Catholic and Protestant Europe, to centralised programmes of public, or partially public, poor relief. The major turning point occurred in the 1520s, when Protestant towns such as Wittenberg and Nuremberg (1522) and Catholic towns such as Ypres (1525), Lille (1527) and Venice (1528–29) outlawed all public begging and devised centrally administered systems of poor relief.[12] By 1545, 60 towns, including Paris, came up with new centralised poor relief systems; and between 1531 and 1541 central authorities in the Netherlands, France, England, Scotland and Spain passed legislation encouraging similar measures on a national level.[13]

At the core of the new approach to poor relief was a desire to remove *all* begging from the streets and to take a proactive rather than a reactive stance towards poverty and its causes. Begging and the giving of alms to beggars were outlawed, many of the resources supporting charitable institutions were pooled and administered by central municipal governing bodies, the names of those who were considered worthy of assistance were inscribed in carefully monitored registers, and regular censuses enabled the authorities to update the lists. Eventually, in many towns, a public poor tax was established in order to augment the more traditional revenues that supported the poor, such as landed endowments and charitable alms – which were now often collected in parish alms boxes. As part of a programme of rehabilitation and in a manner that was consistent with contemporary humanist thought, moral and practical education was provided, especially for the children of the poor, and some municipalities created new textile industries in order to enhance levels of employment for the poor. By the end of the century, social reformers began to look at the hospitals in a given municipality from a global perspective, with each hospital meeting the needs of a very specific population of people needing assistance or requiring confinement, and they

---

[11] Miri Rubin, *Charity and Community in Medieval Cambridge* (Cambridge: Cambridge University Press, 1987), pp. 148–51.

[12] Carter Lindberg, 'There Should Be No Beggars Among Christians', *Church History*, 46 (1977), 313–34; Carter Lindberg, *Beyond Charity: Reformation Initiatives for the Poor* (Minneapolis: Augsburg Fortress, 1993), pp. 82, 128–51, 200–202; Brian Pullan, *Rich and Poor in Renaissance Venice*, pp. 239–57; Jean-Pierre Gutton, *La Société et les pauvres en Europe, XVIe–XVIIIe siècles* (Paris: Presses Universitaires de France, 1974), pp. 97–105.

[13] Catharina Lis and Hugo Soly, *Poverty and Capitalism in Pre-Industrial Europe*, (trans.) James Coonan (Hassocks: Harvester, 1979), pp. 87–8.

attempted to deal with incorrigible able-bodied beggars by placing them in new institutions of confinement.[14]

Historians of early modern poor relief and modern social welfare systems have justifiably emphasised the radical change in perspective that the new system of early modern poor relief represented. Nevertheless, both they and their medievalist colleagues have acknowledged that there were at least some medieval precedents upon which the new centralised systems drew. Carter Lindberg and Nicole Gonthier have pointed out that the shift to public municipal administration of poor relief had precedents going back to the thirteenth century, when a number of municipalities assumed administrative oversight of hospitals, a responsibility that had once belonged to episcopal administrations. This shift to public administration, Lindberg argues, was closely tied to the confidence gained by secular founders of new hospitals, who had retained the administration of those institutions for themselves and their heirs.[15] Along similar lines, Michel Mollat and Marcel Fosseyeux pointed out that sixteenth-century poor relief in towns of the Low Countries built on the presence in those towns of 'poor tables', first established in the thirteenth century, which administered poor relief on a parish level, keeping lists of recipients and sometimes receiving funds from the urban ruling body.[16] Christopher Dyer and James Brodman have highlighted the ways in which late medieval communities and testators in England and Catalonia began to

---

[14]   For general descriptions, see Lindberg, *Beyond Charity*, pp. 119–27, 200–206; Robert Jütte, *Poverty and Deviance*; Natalie Zemon Davis, *Society and Culture in Early Modern France* (Stanford: Stanford University Press, 1975), esp. 'Poor Relief, Humanism and Heresy', pp. 17–64; H.C.M. Michielse and Robert van Krieken, 'Policing the Poor: J.L. Vives and the Sixteenth-Century Origins of Modern Social Administration', *Social Service Review*, 64 (1990), 1–21. Most aspects of the new reforms were described by Juan Luis Vives, *De subventione pauperum* (1526), in Paul Spicker (ed. and trans.), *The Origins of Modern Welfare* (Bern: Peter Lang, 2010), pp. 1–100. On the introduction or expansion of textile industries in conjunction with efforts to employ the poor, see Davis, *Society and Culture*, p. 43; Nicholas Terpstra, *Cultures of Charity*, pp. 166–83; Pullan, pp. 261–3. A similar proposal for Paris does not seem to have come to fruition, although Paris was successful at creating a residential workhouse for the children of the poor, where they learned a number of crafts. See Henry Heller, *Labour, Science and Technology in France, 1500–1620* (Cambridge: Cambridge University Press, 1996), pp. 39–41. On parochial alms boxes see, in addition to Nicholas Brodie's chapter in this volume, statutes for the poor relief systems in Ypres (1525) and Rouen (1534): 'The Poor Order of Ypres', translated in Carter Lindberg, *Beyond Charity*, p. 204; and 'Les pauvres de Rouen', translated in F.R. Salter (ed.), *Some Early Tracts on Poor Relief* (London: Methuen, 1926), p. 116. On poor boxes in Paris, see Susan Broomhall, 'The Politics of Charitable Men', pp. 133–57 (p. 151).

[15]   Lindberg, *Beyond Charity*, p. 63; Nicole Gonthier, *Lyon et ses pauvres au Moyen Âge (1350–1500)* (Lyon: Éditions L'Hermès, 1978), pp. 213–23.

[16]   Lindberg, *Beyond Charity*, pp. 54–5; Mollat, pp. 171–2; Marcel Fosseyeux, 'Les Premiers Budgets municipaux d'assistance: la taxe des pauvres au XVIe siècle', *Revue d'histoire de l'église de France*, 20 (1934), p. 412. See also Michielse and van Krieken, p.

establish endowments, rather than one-off alms distributions, in order to provide sustained support for those who were incapable of providing for themselves.[17] And A.L. Beier has pointed out that punitive early modern English policies regarding able-bodied beggars had their roots in the period just after the onset of the Black Death of 1348, when legislation mandated the freezing of wages and the expulsion or punishment of able-bodied beggars.[18]

A superficial examination of the history of charity and assistance in Paris would suggest that it was a late-comer both to the medieval drive towards secular oversight of institutions for the poor and to the sixteenth-century transition from personal charity to public poor relief: Paris had no medieval 'poor tables', the financial administration of its major hospital was not transferred to municipal oversight until 1505, and its centralised system of poor relief did not take final shape until 1544, two decades after the appearance of similar systems in Germany and the Low Countries, and a decade after the reform of poor relief in Lyon.

I want to suggest, however, that the roots of the major changes in sixteenth-century Paris reach back to the thirteenth century, and that the transition to a new proactive attitude towards poverty began to take shape there at the very beginning of the 1520s. Because the reform of poor relief took different forms in various municipalities, and we need to understand the specifics of sixteenth-century reform in Paris in order to understand its precedents, I am going to approach this two-pronged argument in reverse chronological order: first I will provide a narrative description of the changes that emerged in sixteenth-century Paris, highlighting some of the early signs of change and some of the specific characteristics. I will then turn to medieval developments that helped pave the way for the specific system of centralised poor relief that emerged in Paris between 1505 and 1544.

Reform in Sixteenth-Century Paris

In 1505 the canons of the cathedral of Notre-Dame in Paris, who were responsible for the oversight of the city's main Hôtel-Dieu, implored the municipality to assume temporal oversight of the hospital, claiming that they were not sufficiently

---

3; and M.-J. Tits-Dieuaide, 'Les tables des pauvres dans les anciennes principautés belges au moyen âge', *Tidjschift voor Geschiedenis*, 88 (1975), 562–83.

[17] Christopher Dyer, 'Poverty and its Relief in Late Medieval England', *Past & Present*, 216 (2012), 41–78 (pp. 67–9); James William Brodman, *Charity and Welfare: Hospitals and the Poor in Medieval Catalonia* (Philadelphia: University of Pennsylvania Press, 1998), pp. 9–14.

[18] A.L. Beier, '"A New Serfdom": Labor Laws, Vagrancy Statutes, and Labor Discipline in England, 1350–1800', in A.L. Beier and Paul Ocobock (eds), *Cast Out: Vagrancy and Homelessness in Global and Historical Perspective* (Athens: Ohio University Press, 2008), pp. 35–63. Marjorie K. McIntosh (*Poor Relief in England*, pp. 17–19) also emphasises continuities in fourteenth- through sixteenth-century negative attitudes towards vagrancy.

qualified to manage its accounts and that it was failing to meet the needs of its inmates.[19] Until recently, historians interpreted this request, and the broader reform that was imposed on the Hôtel-Dieu in the first half of the sixteenth century, as evidence that the internal management of the Hôtel-Dieu had become corrupt and incompetent. Christine Jéhanno has convincingly argued, however, that the Hôtel-Dieu was well managed in the latter part of the fifteenth century and that its sixteenth-century reform was part of a broader effort on the part of municipal and religious elites to impose a stricter religious life on hospitals and religious institutions, especially those housing religious women.[20]

But there was at least one other factor that contributed to the canons' sense of urgency about the well-being of the Hôtel-Dieu: the epidemic of the great pox – or malady of Naples, as it was known in France – which had been raging across Europe for a decade.[21] Although efforts had been made as early as 1496 to establish a new Parisian hospice for poor victims of this disease, the Hôtel-Dieu was still overwhelmed with their presence, and the financial repercussions were considerable: unlike other inmates at the Hôtel-Dieu, these sufferers could remain ill for years; additionally, the oozing pustules that covered their bodies ruined large quantities of linens.[22] Separation of these patients, moreover, was seen as a matter of public health, since the disease was thought to be highly contagious.[23] At the very beginning of the sixteenth century, then, Parisian calls to reform the care of

---

[19]   *Registres des délibérations du bureau de la ville de Paris*, 19 vols (Paris: Imprimerie Nationale, 1883–1958), i: 1499–1526, (ed.) François Bonnardot, 103–6.

[20]   Christine Jéhanno, 'La Réforme de l'Hôtel-Dieu de Paris à la fin du Moyen Âge: remise en ordre nécessaire ou réforme monastique imposée à l'hôpital?', *Revue du Nord*, hors série, collection histoire, 22 (2008), 67–88. For the older view of the reform, see especially Ernest Coyecque, *L'Hôtel-Dieu de Paris au Moyen Âge, histoire et documents, vol. 1* (Paris: H. Champion, 1891), pp. 173–99.

[21]   For general discussions of the 'great pox', see Jon Arrizabalaga, John Henderson and Roger French, *The Great Pox: The French Disease in Renaissance Europe* (New Haven, CT: Yale University Press, 1997); Kevin Siena (ed.), *Sins of the Flesh: Responding to Sexual Disease in Early Modern Europe* (Toronto: University of Toronto Press, 2005); Claude Quétel (*History of Syphilis*, (trans.) Judith Braddock and Brian Pike (Cambridge: Polity, 1990) pp. 12, 24–5, 64–5) discusses the earliest Parisian responses to the epidemic.

[22]   *Registres des délibérations*, i, 103: 'Premierement les malades de la maladie de Naples, appellée la grosse verolle, y sont en grant quantité, et que pour leur ordure y a merveilleusement de linge perdu et gasté … et a ces causes requeroient en ladicte assemblée … de faire delivrer aucun lieu où l'on pourroit faire maisons pour loger les pauvres malades de peste et autre maladie contagieuse'. This was not the first time that managers of the Hôtel-Dieu commented on the linens that were destroyed by patients with the malady of Naples. See Quétel, p. 12 (account from the Hôtel-Dieu of Paris from 1496).

[23]   Quétel, pp. 24–5, 64–5: Concern about the highly contagious nature of the malady of Naples was a constant refrain in Paris as elsewhere; Annie Saunier, 'Gros vérolés à l'Hôtel Dieu de Paris en 1508', *Bulletin d'information de la Société de démographie historique*, 8 (1973), 5–10 (p. 6); *Registres des délibérations*, i, 146; ii (1527–39), (ed.) Alexandre Tuetey, 211. Theories concerning the contagious nature of this disease encompassed not

the poor emphasised not only municipal oversight but also the need for specialised hospitals and a concern for public health in the wake of a new incurable disease.

The municipal authorities of Paris acted immediately on the canons' request for municipal oversight of the Hôtel-Dieu, electing a board of eight governors, who were to be re-elected every three years.[24] Although the dust did not settle on this reform process until 1540, the election of the board of governors marked the end of over eight hundred years of ecclesiastical management of the temporal affairs of the Hôtel-Dieu of Paris, which was the largest hospital in France.[25] Despite numerous efforts, however, it took several decades before the city managed to bring into being sufficient hospital space to isolate those with contagious diseases – including the venereal pox.[26]

The Hôtel-Dieu was not the only hospital to undergo reform in early sixteenth-century Paris. In 1519, King Francis I charged his Grand Almoner, François du Moulin de Rochefort, with the task of reforming all the hospitals of the realm; in turn, du Moulin put Jean Briçonnet, President of the Chambre des comptes, and Pierre du Val, a canon from the cathedral, in charge of reforming the hospitals of Paris.[27] For the Parisian hospital for the blind – the Quinze-Vingts – this push for reform had a profound impact; as was the case with the reform of the Hôtel-Dieu, the reform of the Quinze-Vingts was inspired by monastic ideals.

In 1520, du Moulin, working with Briçonnet, limited the freedom of movement of the residents of the Quinze-Vingts by closing all the entrances to the community except one, where he stationed a porter; he also attempted to impose communal possession of property on the residents, who had enjoyed the right to the usufruct of their personal property since the foundation of the Quinze-Vingts in the thirteenth century. When the inmates resisted these changes, their minister and eight of the brothers were thrown into prison.[28] In 1521, du Moulin went even further, with a set of statutes proposing a radically altered form of community for the Quinze-Vingts: future marriages among the inmates were to be prohibited, the self-governing chapter was to be replaced with a council of six governors, movement in and out of the community was to be strictly controlled, and the brothers were to be compelled to find work. None of these changes was accepted without resistance and, indeed, the inmates continued to marry and to rely, for

---

only sexual transmission but also proximity. See Arrizabalaga, Henderson and French, pp. 121–6.

[24]   Coyecque, *L'Hôtel-Dieu*, p. 181; *Registres des délibérations*, I, 183–6.

[25]   Coyecque, *L'Hôtel-Dieu*, pp. 174–99.

[26]   For efforts in 1508 (hospital for men in the faubourg St-Germain-des-Prés and for women in the faubourg St-Honoré) and 1536 (upper rooms in the Hospital of La Trinité), see *Registres des délibérations*, I, 146; II, 211.

[27]   Jean Imbert, *Le Droit hospitalier de l'Ancien Régime* (Paris: Presses Universitaires de France, 1993), p. 16; Le Grand, *Les Quinze-Vingts*, II, 9.

[28]   Le Grand, *Les Quinze-Vingts*, II, 9–12. On the residents' right to the usufruct of their property, see 'Lettre de fraternité de Raoul l'Assaieur et sa femme' (1290), in ibid., II, 153; and 'Règlement donné aux XV^{xx}', in ibid., II, 160–61.

the most part, on 'quests' rather than on work in order to augment the endowed income of their institution.[29] Nevertheless the effort itself was significant. The next year, in 1522, du Moulin produced an additional set of statutes, which had a lasting impact on the Quinze-Vingts: from then on the inmates were required to attend weekly sermons and daily readings of morally and religiously uplifting texts, and their children were to be given religious instruction and placed in apprenticeships at the age of seven.[30]

Within the broader context of early sixteenth-century changes in systems of poor relief, the reforms at the Quinze-Vingts seem particularly striking. Already, in July 1521 – several months before Wittenberg and Nuremberg implemented their new systems of poor relief, and five years before Juan-Luis Vives published his influential plan for a poor relief system in Bruges, which emphasised that all begging should be eliminated, the poor should receive moral and practical educations, and even the blind could be given useful employment – du Moulin acted on similar principles, attempting to limit the freedom of movement of a community of deserving, disabled poor and to replace their custom of begging for alms with the discipline of gainful employment. A year later, in 1522, du Moulin successfully implemented a programme of moral and religious education for the blind inmates and religious and practical education for their children, again anticipating practices that would be implemented repeatedly in the new poor relief systems of the 1520s, 30s and 40s.[31] Both François du Moulin and Jean Briçonnet were well connected with the leading humanists in early sixteenth-century France, and du Moulin was a major intellectual influence in the French royal court.[32] Their reforms at the Quinze-Vingts suggest that ideas about eradicating begging, putting

---

[29]   Le Grand, *Les Quinze-Vingts*, ii, 12–15.

[30]   Le Grand, *Les Quinze-Vingts*, ii, 13–15; Félibien, v, 748–52. In these statutes, du Moulin conceded that inmates had a right to marry and go out on quests, but he reiterated the need for a porter who would allow the inmates to leave the community only if they had permission. The financial accounts of the community indicate that most of the rules in this collection of statutes were indeed put into practice: Sunday preachers were hired, a book on the life of Christ was bought for the weekday readings, inmates were fined for failure to attend those readings, schoolteachers were hired, and one inmate was fined for failing to place his daughter in an apprenticeship or service position. See Le Grand, *Les Quinze-Vingts*, ii, 66, 91–2, 98–9, 128. There is some evidence, however, that the effort to control the residents' behaviour by guarding the entrance to the community was not entirely successful: in 1523 a male resident was told that he could no longer entertain women in his residence; and in 1525 two women were forced to move because of the 'scandal' they had been causing, see ibid., ii, 32, nn. 1–2.

[31]   'Order of the City of Wittenberg (1522)', translated in Lindberg, *Beyond Charity*, pp. 200–202; Vives, *De subventione pauperum*, pp. 73–6, 79–80, 98; see also Michielse and van Krieken.

[32]   On du Moulin's role as tutor to Francis I and his continuing influence on Louise de Savoy, as well as his connections with Lefèvre d'Etaples, Budé and Erasmus, see Myra Dickman Orth, 'Francis du Moulin and the Journal of Louise de Savoy', *Sixteenth*

the blind to work, and educating the poor were already circulating in Parisian intellectual circles even before various municipalities and municipal reformers began to implement such ideas in 1522.[33]

In the meantime, Briçonnet, who had been named chief administrator of the Hôtel-Dieu in 1511, continued to press for more specialised hospitals. In 1515, he reiterated the idea that the city needed a separate hospital for those with contagious diseases. King Francis I took up that project in 1519, but it was abandoned in 1520.[34] Five years later, Briçonnet again argued that the city was in dire need of a well-organised system of hospitals. The disorder in the Hôtel-Dieu, he suggested, was so great that twelve to fifteen people were being placed indiscriminately in a single bed – those with venereal pox next to those without, plague victims next to non-plague victims, the wounded next to those without wounds.[35]

Until 1535 or so, gestures in the direction of greater hospital organisation in Paris were limited to attempts to fill some of the gaps in the system of care: there were several attempts to open separate hospitals for those with venereal pox, and in 1534 King Francis I and his sister Marguerite of Navarre founded a new hospital for Parisian orphans of legitimate birth, the Enfants Rouges.[36]

Century Journal, 13 (1982), 55–66. On Briçonnet's connections, see Broomhall, 'Politics of Charitable Men', p. 139; and Jéhanno.

[33] As Natalie Zemon Davis (*Society and Culture*, p. 32) points out, John Major, a distinguished professor at the University of Paris, had already suggested in 1516 that secular rulers should prevent all begging. Additionally, du Moulin and Briçonnet would have been familiar, by 1520, with similar ideas promulgated by Erasmus and Thomas More. Erasmus had suggested that young minds needed moral education and strong rulers could eliminate begging; he and More had suggested that rulers could address the structural causes of poverty (such as unfair taxation and wages); and More had portrayed a society in which everyone except the sick worked. See Erasmus, *The Education of a Christian Prince*, (trans.) Neil M. Cheshire and Michael J. Heath, (ed.) Lisa Jardine (Cambridge: Cambridge University Press, 1997), pp. 5, 8, 76, 82–3; and Thomas More, *Utopia*, (eds) George M. Logan, Robert M. Adams and Clarence H. Miller; (trans.) Robert M. Adams (Cambridge: Cambridge University Press, 1995), Book 2, pp. 126–7, 138–9, 242–3. For discussions of More's and Erasmus's impact on the new system of poor relief in England, see Margo Todd, *Christian Humanism and the Puritan Social Order* (Cambridge: Cambridge University Press, 1987); and Paul A. Fideler, 'Poverty, Policy and Providence: The Tudors and the Poor', in Paul A. Fideler and T.F. Mayer (eds), *Political Thought and the Tudor Commonwealth: Deep Structure, Discourse and Disguise* (London: Routledge, 1992), pp. 194–222.

[34] Coyecque, *L'Hôtel-Dieu*, pp. 185–8; Broomhall, 'Politics of Charitable Men', pp. 139–40. On Briçonnet's appointment as manager of the Hôtel-Dieu, see *Registres des délibérations*, I, 163.

[35] Coyecque, *L'Hôtel-Dieu*, p. 334; Le Grand, *Les Quinze-Vingts*, II, 9.

[36] Quétel, pp. 24–5, 65; Susan Broomhall, *Women's Medical Work in Early Modern France* (Manchester: Manchester University Press, 2004), pp. 169–70. Marcel Fosseyeux (*L'Assistance parisienne au milieu du XVIe siècle* (Paris, 1916), p. 88) mentioned a hospice that was founded in the faubourg St-Honoré in 1504, which was intended to house women with the malady of Naples, but he did not cite his source.

The Foundation of the Enfants Rouges took place within the context of a major reform of Paris's poor relief system, which emerged between 1530 and 1534, at a time when the city's hospitals were overwhelmed by a severe outbreak of the plague.[37] These reforms culminated in April, 1534, when Parlement ordered that able-bodied beggars in Paris were to be put to work on public projects, such as repairs of the city's fortifications, non-native beggars were to be expelled from the city, parish lay wardens were to create lists of the deserving disabled poor and they were to conduct regular collections of alms in order to provide for those poor.[38] In 1536 the king legislated that every Parisian poor person who was incapable of working was to receive public assistance at home; around the same time he legislated that the children of those on public assistance were to be placed in apprenticeships.[39] Finally, in 1544, this new system was centralised under a board of commissioners that came to be called the Grand Bureau des Pauvres.[40] It is important to note that while this new commission was organised in response to royal initiatives, and the initiators of the reform were the municipal leaders of the city, its membership included both laymen and members of the ecclesiastical hierarchy. Indeed, throughout the early modern period, poor relief institutions in Paris continued to reflect a partnership between secular and Catholic leadership.[41]

The Grand Bureau des Pauvres (or the *Aumosne Generalle*, as it was called in 1555/7) oversaw a system that identified and eliminated able-bodied beggars and administered relief to the deserving poor – those who were rooted in their parishes and either unable to work or temporarily unemployed. A poor tax, collected from every property owner, augmented by charitable alms, royal munificence and religious quests, funded the new system of poor relief. All of these funds were now

---

[37]   Broomhall, 'Politics of Charitable Men', pp. 141–2.

[38]   *Registres des délibérations*, II, 179, footnote.

[39]   Louis Parturier, *L'Assistance à Paris sous l'Ancien Régime et pendant la Révolution* (Paris: Larose, 1897; Geneva: Mégariotis Reprints, 1978), pp. 70–71; Ernest Coyecque (ed.), *Recueil d'actes notariés relatifs à l'histoire de Paris et ses environs au XVIe siècle, vol. 1* (Paris: Imprimerie Nationale, 1905), p. 274. Occasional documents of practice reveal that even before 1544 the central body in charge of the Parisian poor was taking charge of apprenticeship arrangements for poor children: in 1540, for instance, the commissioner and controller in charge of 'la police générale des pauvres de Paris' arranged for the apprenticeship of a seven year old girl to the wife of a bonnet maker; as part of the arrangement he delivered funds from the common alms chest to help cover the cost of the girl's maintenance.

[40]   *Registres des délibérations*, III (1539–52), (ed.) Paul Guérin, 46–7. The first elected board of directors had three priests, two counsellors of the court, a bailiff, six others, a treasurer and a controller, who was an alderman.

[41]   Matthew Ramsey, 'Poor Relief and Medical Assistance in 18th and 19th Century Paris', in Ole Peter Grell, Andrew Cunningham and Robert Jütte (eds), *Health Care and Poor Relief in 18th and 19th Century Northern Europe* (Aldershot: Ashgate, 2002), pp. 280–308 (p. 283).

distributed through committees working with well-monitored lists of legitimate recipients, rather than on an ad hoc basis.[42]

The implementation of this system of evaluation, distribution and control was carried out at the parish level.[43] Much of the responsibility rested on the shoulders of the *marguilliers* – the lay wardens of the parishes. Within each parish, the lay wardens elected a commissioner who served on the Grand Bureau des Pauvres for a two-year term. The parish commissioners supervised the distribution of alms, evaluated applicants for relief, and conducted regular visitations of the poor to ensure that they were still worthy of relief.[44] The parish wardens assisted their elected commissioners in the distribution of alms to the shamefaced poor of their parishes, and they were charged with the responsibility of capturing and delivering to prison any individuals who were caught begging within the jurisdictions of their

---

[42]   Imbert, p. 278; G. Montaigne, 'La police des paouvres de Paris', in Ernest Coyecque (ed.), 'L'assistance publique à Paris au milieu du xvie siècle', *Bulletin de la Société de l'histoire de Paris et de l'Ile-de-France*, 15 (1888), pp. 105–18. According to Coyecque, this treatise was written between 1555 and 1557. Montaigne (pp. 106, 107) referred to the administrative operation of poor relief in Paris as *la police et aumosne generalle*; Jean Martin (*La police et reiglement du grand bureau des pauvres de la ville & faulxbourgs de Paris* (Paris: Gervais Mallot, 1580)), in his revised version of Montaigne's treatise, arrived at the name *Grand bureau des pauvres*.

[43]   The poor relief systems for Ypres, Bruges, Rouen, Venice and England also depended on administration at the parish level by lay leaders, as did King Francis I's statute of 1536 ordering every parish in France to keep lists of their deserving poor. See Vives, *De subventione*, p. 71; City of Ypres, *Forma Subventionis Pauperum* (1531), in Spicker (ed. and trans.), *Origins of Modern Welfare*, pp. 101–44 (p. 117); Salter (ed.), *Some Early Tracts*, pp. 104, 115; Gary Gibbs, 'New Duties for the Parish Community in Tudor England', in Katherine French, Gary Gibbs and Beat A. Kümin (eds), *The Parish in English Life, 1400–1600* (Manchester: Manchester University Press, 1997), pp. 163–77 (pp. 166, 174); McIntosh, pp. 232–52; Pullan, p. 253. In Lyon, by contrast, the commissioners of the centralised *Grand aulmosne generale*, established in 1531, were to come from the two sides of the Saône River (the side of the Cathedral of St Jean, and that of the parish of St Nizier); for purposes of distribution, the poor gathered at four convents and one hospital. There is no mention of parish lay wardens in a 1539 description of the administration of this system, see *La police de l'aulmosne de Lyon* (Lyon: Gryphius, 1539), esp. pp. 9, 11, 18, 19.

[44]   Martin, *La police et reiglement*, pp. 1v–2, 8v; in his earlier version of this treatise, Montaigne (p. 107) had indicated that, rather than being elected by the parish wardens, the parish commissioners were appointed by the central board of commissioners or by the provost of the merchants and aldermen of the city. However, the parish wardens and local parish notables were already heavily involved in administering the centralised system of poor relief in 1534 (see discussion at n. 38 above), and according to the 1543 royal decree that led to the formation of the newly centralised system, the wardens of each parish were to choose two parish notables to conduct the collection of alms and to elect two 'bons personnages' to make weekly visits of the poor. The wardens, moreover, were to be responsible for keeping a record of the alms that were collected each week and to make a monthly report to the central administrative body. See Félibien, III, 624, 625, 627; Parturier, p. 76.

parishes.[45] Since the terms of the parish wardens could last for a number of years, while the commissioners were elected for two-year terms,[46] it seems reasonable to surmise that the duty of parish commissioner to the Grand Bureau des Pauvres circulated among the parish wardens, or among them and their close associates. In the eighteenth century, parish wardens complained that it was extremely difficult to find anyone who was willing to take on the onerous duties of parish commissioners; such difficulties probably emerged in the sixteenth century as well.[47]

By 1555/7, when G. Montaigne, the abbot of St Germain-des-Prés, wrote a description of the new poor relief system in Paris, the goal of removing all beggars from the streets had given rise to two new hospitals and institutions of confinement, whose functions now complemented those of the Hôtel-Dieu, the Enfants Rouges and the various medieval foundations that continued to serve lepers, widows, blind people and orphans.[48] The hospital of the Trinity had been transformed in 1545 into a residence for the children of those receiving assistance from the *aumosne generalle.* Removed from their parents' homes at as young an age as five, the children were provided with religious and lettered instruction, and then placed in apprenticeships. At first, the children's apprenticeships were arranged in workshops scattered around town, but after observing that many of the children were failing to complete their apprenticeships, the city fathers transformed the Trinity into a residential workhouse, where the offspring of the poor lived and received training in a variety of apprenticeships until their late twenties. Parental access to the children was kept to a minimum.[49]

The second institution that arose in response to the new vision of removing beggars from the street was the Hospital of St-Germain-des-Prés. Founded in 1554 with major financial support from the president of the Chambre des comptes, St-Germain-des-Prés was conceived as an institution of confinement for the incorrigible and incapable poor.[50] Still functioning in 1580, the hospital of St-Germain-des-Prés must have failed in its mission by the early seventeenth century – because new hospitals were founded in 1612 and again in 1656 for similar categories of people who were incapable of earning a living; it is important

---

[45] Martin, *La police et reiglement*, pp. 5v–6, 13v.

[46] Boris Bove, *Dominer la ville: prévôts des marchands et échevins parisiens de 1260 à 1350* (Paris: Éditions du Comité des travaux historiques et scientifiques, 2004), p. 260. In the fourteenth century, the terms of *marguilliers* could last for decades. On the terms of the commissioners, see Martin, *La police et reiglement*, p. 2.

[47] Léon Cahen, *Le Grand Bureau des Pauvres de Paris au milieu du XVIIIe siècle* (Paris: Société nouvelle de librairie et d'édition, 1904), pp. 31–5.

[48] Montaigne, pp. 113–14.

[49] Parturier, pp. 117–23; Heller, pp. 39–41. In his description of the poor relief system in Paris, Montaigne (p. 113) had mistakenly assumed that the children in the Trinity were foundlings.

[50] Montaigne, p. 115; Martin, *La police et reiglement*, p. 15; Parturier, pp. 114–15.

to note, however, that there was a precedent for the seventeenth-century institutions of confinement.[51]

According to G. Montaigne, three additional hospitals were also envisioned in the 1550s: a hospital for poor gentlemen and wounded soldiers, a refuge for poor travellers and a hospital for incurable diseases, such as venereal pox.[52] Also, according to Montaigne, the commissioners of the poor now distinguished between individuals who were merely unemployed, and a criminal element that refused to work: the former were paid for their employment at public works projects; the latter were held in prison and either sent to work in the galleys or banished from town; by 1580, some of those individuals were also led in chains to do forced labour in the city.[53] Montaigne explicitly linked the arrest and imprisonment of street beggars to concern about contagion: the king and Parlement, he explained, forbade all begging in Paris because of the possibility that beggars could introduce the plague or other diseases.[54] A dozen years earlier, concern about crime had also provided a rationale for prohibiting begging on the streets of Paris.[55]

Secular Management, Public Authority and the Poor in Late Medieval Paris

At least five aspects of the organised system of poor relief that developed in sixteenth-century Paris had medieval precedents. First, as was generally the case with the systems of poor relief that took shape in the sixteenth century, and with the hospital reforms that preceded them, secular management and oversight were key, although in Paris, as in the rest of France, such management usually involved a mix of secular and religious participants. In Paris, moreover, perhaps more than in other French municipalities, the agents of secular administrative oversight were both municipal and royal authorities, which often worked in partnership. Second, the new system of poor relief was rooted in the parishes of Paris, where people were likely to know each other face to face. The individuals who engaged in the day-to-day implementation of the programme were the lay leaders of the parish – the *marguilliers*, or lay wardens – and the commissioners whom they elected. Third, ad hoc acts of one-off charity gave way to sustained care of the poor, which

---

[51]   Tim McHugh (*Hospital Politics in Seventeenth-Century France: The Crown, Urban Elites and the Poor* (Aldershot: Ashgate, 2007), pp. 85–6) notes the 1544 establishment of the Grand Bureau des Pauvres as an important precursor to the 'great confinement' of the seventeenth century, but he fails to mention that the hospital of St-Germain-des-Prés provided an important precedent for the seventeenth-century hospitals of confinement.

[52]   Montaigne, pp. 115–16; Martin, *La police et reiglement*, pp. 9, 11–15v, 17, 18v, 20–21. Twenty-five years later, these hospitals had not yet materialised.

[53]   Montaigne, pp. 114, 117; Martin, *La police et reiglement*, pp. 18v, 22.

[54]   Montaigne, p. 109; with similar explanations on pp. 106 and 118.

[55]   Félibien, iii, 622 (royal decree of 1543 mandating the formation of Paris's centralised system of poor relief).

required long-term sources of financial support. The fourth characteristic that drew on medieval precedents was the use of publicly collected funds to support the poor; and the fifth characteristic with medieval precedents was the punitive approach to able-bodied beggars, who were either put to work on the fortifications of the city, sent off to the galleys or confined to special institutions.

I will begin with the medieval origins of the particular forms of secular management that took shape in Paris. The secularisation of charitable institutions and care for the poor took various forms in late medieval Europe. In Northern Italy, lay confraternities played a major role in meeting the needs of the urban poor, especially in the period after the Black Death.[56] In several towns of the Low Countries, lay authorities assumed the responsibility of administering parochial 'poor tables' in the thirteenth century.[57] In other parts of Europe – southern France, Italy and Spain – municipal authorities began to assume direct responsibility for local hospitals at some point between the twelfth and the fifteenth centuries.[58]

In medieval Paris, by contrast, the most important agent of the transition to secular oversight of charitable institutions was the royal administration – working closely with municipal elites.[59] A major turning point occurred in the mid-1250s, when King Louis IX founded the Congregation of the Quinze-Vingts – the Parisian hospice for the blind, which, at the time of its foundation, provided a permanent home for 300 individuals: blind men and women, along with their spouses or other relations.[60] Although the Quinze-Vingts was clearly a charitable institution, and its residents were bound to fulfil certain religious obligations, such as attending mass and praying for their royal founder, King Louis created a system of internal

---

[56]   See Pullan; John Henderson, *Piety and Charity in Late Medieval Florence* (Chicago: University of Chicago Press, 1994); Nicholas Terpstra, *Lay Confraternities and Civic Religion in Renaissance Bologna* (Cambridge: Cambridge University Press, 1995).

[57]   See Tits-Dieuaide.

[58]   Gonthier, pp. 213–23; Brodman, pp. 126–7; Daniel Le Blévec, *La part du pauvre: l'assistance dans les pays du Bas-Rhône du XIIe au milieu du XVe siècle*, 2 vols (Rome: École française de Rome, 2000), I, 290–301; John Henderson, *The Renaissance Hospital: Healing the Body and Healing the Soul* (New Haven, CT: Yale University Press, 2006), pp. 28–31.

[59]   Adam Davis, 'The Economic Power of a Hospital in Thirteenth-Century Provins', in Katherine Jansen, Guy Geltner and Anne E. Lester (eds), *Center and Periphery: Studies on Power in the Medieval World in Honor of William Chester Jordan* (Leiden: Brill, 2013), pp. 121–34 (pp. 123–4); Bernard Delmaire, 'Hôpitaux urbains et hôpitaux ruraux en Artois entre le XIIe et le XIVe siècle', *Histoire médiévale et archéologie*, 17 (2004), 221–40 (p. 224). The situation in Paris and the Ile-de-France had parallels in the counties of Champagne and Artois. In Champagne, the count's almoner, rather than the bishop, took the lead in overseeing charitable institutions. From the thirteenth century on in Artois, the count increasingly assumed the oversight of hospitals.

[60]   Le Grand, *Les Quinze-Vingts*, I, 122–5; Zina Weygand, *The Blind in French Society from the Middle Ages to the Century of Louis Braille*, (trans.) Emily-Jane Cohen (Stanford: Stanford University Press, 2009), pp. 18–23.

management and external oversight that was largely secular. Rather than episcopal oversight, the Quinze-Vingts was placed under the oversight of a royal officer who was also a member of the clerical hierarchy – the Royal Almoner.[61]

Next in line in the management of the Quinze-Vingts was the master of the community, who was appointed by the king, perhaps with the recommendation of the almoner. According to the earliest surviving statutes of the Quinze-Vingts, which were drawn up in the mid-fourteenth century, the master did not reside within its enclosure, but he represented its interests in court and had a close relationship with the community. The statutes indicated that it was preferable that he be married.[62] Documents of practice indicate that even before these statutes were written down, this was the custom: the earliest master of the Quinze-Vingts was, indeed, married.[63]

The mid-fourteenth century statutes of the Quinze-Vingts indicated that the next in line in the hierarchy of authority within the community was the minister, who, like the master, had to be sighted. The minister, however, lived within the community, and he was elected by its members – both blind and sighted – who played an active role in their governance by participating in regular chapter meetings. The statutes also stipulated that the ministers had to be married, because their wives played an active role in caring for the members. Indeed, if the wife of a minister died, he was supposed to remarry within a reasonable amount of time.[64] Again, although we have no surviving statutes from the first century of the Quinze-Vingts' existence, it seems that the earliest ministers conformed to these expectations. Indeed, the first minister was married at least twice, and he may have had a third wife as well.[65]

In the Quinze-Vingts, then, King Louis IX created an institution that was subjected to the external oversight of a member of the royal court – the Royal Almoner – and that was internally managed by a lay master and a lay minister, both of whom were expected to be married, because marriage made them better managers and because their wives played essential roles within the community. In requiring the master and minister of the Quinze-Vingts to be married, the founder and overseers of the institution drew on a trend that had been gaining traction since the twelfth century. Records from hospitals in the Low Countries offer early glimpses of married couples who belonged to, and served, the needy

[61]   O'Tool, 'Caring for the Blind', p. 195; Le Grand, *Les Quinze-Vingts*, I, 124; II, 157. The earliest reference to the almoner's oversight of the Quinze-Vingts dates from 1270. Most of the thirteenth-century almoners were from the order of the Templars. After the suppression of the Templars in the early fourteenth century, most of the Royal Almoners were from the secular clergy. Kings Charles VI and Charles VII tended to favour men from the College of Navarre at the University of Paris. See de la Selle, pp. 98–115.

[62]   'Règlement donné aux XV^{xx}', in Le Grand, *Les Quinze-Vingts*, II, 158–9.

[63]   O'Tool, 'Caring for the Blind', pp. 207–9.

[64]   'Règlement donné aux XV^{xx}', in Le Grand, *Les Quinze-Vingts*, II, 158–9.

[65]   O'Tool, 'Caring for the Blind', pp. 207–10.

inmates of hospitals, and a mid-fourteenth-century source offers similar glimpses of such couples managing hospitals in the diocese of Paris.[66] There was, then, nothing original in the presence, at the Quinze-Vingts, of married administrators. Nevertheless, the Quinze-Vingts was unusual in that it created a statutory requirement that the management be married and in its encouragement of marriage between blind and sighted members.

As far as I know, this aspect of secular management – the use of married couples within a hospital community – was pretty much ignored in early modern France.[67] The Royal Almoner, however, would gain increasing importance as an overseer of charitable institutions and systems of poor relief. By granting oversight of the Quinze-Vingts to his almoner, Louis IX played a pivotal role in facilitating the expansion of the administrative functions of this member of the royal household.[68] By the 1360s, the Royal Almoner claimed the right to appoint the chief administrator of 225 charitable institutions, and his responsibilities extended, as well, to the authorship of statutes and adjudication of disputes for a number of those communities.[69]

Hospitals fell under the jurisdiction of the Royal Almoner in a number of ways. Sometimes, lay founders of hospitals stipulated that when their heirs died out the Royal Almoner should assume the role of overseer.[70] In other cases, the almoner asserted his authority when he suspected internal corruption.[71] In still other cases, a community could fall into the Royal Almoner's hands more by default. Such was the case with the Haudriettes, a Parisian shelter for poor widows that had been founded by one of Paris's most prominent merchants and civic leaders, Etienne Haudri, around 1305. In 1370 Etienne's last descendent died, and the Board of Aldermen of Paris – to which Etienne had belonged – assumed control of the Haudriettes. In 1382, however, after the revolt of the Maillotins, the king suppressed the Parisian Board of Aldermen, and the Royal Almoner assumed the oversight of the Haudriettes.[72]

---

[66]   Sharon Farmer, 'The Leper in the Master Bedroom: Thinking through a Thirteenth-Century Exemplum', in Rosalynn Voaden and Diane Wolfthal (eds), *Framing the Family: Narrative and Representation in the Medieval and early Modern Periods* (Tempe, AZ: Arizona Center for Medieval and Renaissance Studies, 2005), pp. 79–100 (pp. 91–3).

[67]   Broomhall, 'Politics'; Broomhall, *Women's Medical Work*, pp. 156–85. Broomhall has underscored the degree to which laymen and women played an important role in the administrative and palliative work of early modern French hospitals. Nevertheless, I have seen no discussion of married couples playing an important role.

[68]   De la Selle, p. 208.

[69]   De la Selle, pp. 215–17.

[70]   De la Selle, p. 209.

[71]   De la Selle, p. 203.

[72]   Léon Le Grand, *Les Béguines de Paris* (Paris, 1893), p. 350, note; Michael Connally, 'Les "Bonnes Femmes" de Paris: des communautés religieuses dans une société urbaine du bas moyen âge' (unpublished doctoral thesis, Université de Lyon, 2003), p. 47.

We might suspect, given the financial strains that weighed on all fourteenth-century rulers, that one motivation for extending the Royal Almoner's jurisdiction over more and more charitable institutions would have been administrative hunger for the landed incomes that came with endowed institutions. Such motivations seem to have driven both the English royal administration and the Avignon papacy to assert their authority over charitable institutions.[73] However, internal records from several charitable institutions in and around Paris suggest that in the later Middle Ages Royal Almoners exercised a positive influence on the institutional health of those communities.

In the mid-fourteenth century, for instance, Michel de Brache, who served as Royal Almoner from 1350 to 1355, compiled statutes for both the Quinze-Vingts and a second hospice for the blind, in Chartres.[74] De Brache's statutes for the Quinze-Vingts were still highly regarded in the sixteenth century, although a central premise of his statutes – that the blind residents could participate in their own governance – gave way, in the wake of du Moulin's reforms, to a much more authoritarian form of governance.[75]

Although there is no mention of it in de Brache's statutes, the king's sub-almoner also began, at some point in the fourteenth century, to engage in a regular audit of the financial accounts of the Quinze-Vingts. In that capacity, the sub-almoner sometimes refused to allow the minister and other governors of the institution to reimburse themselves for expenses that blurred the line between personal entertainment and professional responsibilities.[76] In so doing, the king's sub-almoner acted in the interests of the long-term financial health of the institution.

Just as they did with the Quinze-Vingts, the Royal Almoners played a positive role in assuring the institutional health of the widows' shelter known as the Haudriettes. Not long after the Royal Almoner took over the supervision of the Haudriettes in 1382, Pierre d'Ailly, who served as Royal Almoner and as governor of the Haudriettes between 1389 and 1395, compiled a set of statutes for that community.[77] Those statutes not only regulated the religious life of the community, but also created wise protocols for the management of its property records, which helped to protect the community's temporal assets. D'Ailly's statutes stipulated that the community's property records were to be locked in a chest with two different keys, one of which was guarded by the mistress of the community, the other by

---

[73] Rubin, p. 139; Le Blévec, II, 638–46.

[74] De la Selle, p. 290.

[75] Le Grand, *Les Quinze-Vingts*, II, 5–17.

[76] Le Grand, *Les Quinze-Vingts*, II, 6: in 1385 the sub-almoner, Jean Faissier, crossed off the books an expense that the minister and procurator had claimed for attending the wedding of a daughter of a royal officer at the Châtelet. Faissier wrote in the margins that they were rich enough to pay for this themselves, especially since the expense involved a meal that they had eaten.

[77] Le Grand, *Les Béguines de Paris*, p. 349, n. 1; Connally, 'Les "Bonnes Femmes"', p. 70.

two of its 'wisest women'. Since the widows of the Haudriettes depended on a male procurator to represent them in court, these statutes allowed the three women jointly to hand over records from the chest to the procurator, but they stipulated that he had to give them written statements describing whatever documents he removed, and he had to return all documents to the three women as quickly as was possible. The statutes also insisted that the procurator immediately hand over to the three women any new documents affecting the institution, and that the seal of the institution had to be locked away with two different keys under the control of the same three women, who were all to serve as witnesses whenever the seal was used.[78] The Haudriette's compliance with these statutes helped to preserve the longevity of the institution: of the ten hospices for widows that dotted the Parisian landscape in the first half of the fourteenth century, only the Haudriettes and one other survived into the seventeenth century; and of those two, only the Haudriettes created a rich archive that has survived to the present day.[79]

In addition to exercising influence over Parisian hospitals through the office of the Royal Almoner, the king intervened on behalf of the Hôtel-Dieu of Paris on a number of occasions in the later Middle Ages. In 1328 King Charles IV established two sworn royal surgeons who were to visit the hospital regularly.[80] And in 1370, when a dispute arose between the master of the Hôtel-Dieu and the chapter of the cathedral, on the one hand, and the prioress of the Hôtel-Dieu on the other, King Charles V intervened, expelling the prioress.[81]

Between the thirteenth and fifteenth centuries, then, the king and his almoner played increasingly important roles in providing secular oversight of Parisian charitable institutions. The early history of the Quinze-Vingts suggests, moreover, that they often worked with the city's merchant elite in order to assure those goals.[82] In Paris, then, the late medieval move toward secular oversight of charitable institutions involved a partnership between the royal administration and municipal elites; in many other towns in France, the process involved only municipal elites.

By extending the role of the Royal Almoner from a mere disperser of alms to an administrator with institutional oversight over the Quinze-Vingts, King Louis IX also set the stage for the expansion of the almoner's influence. Over the course of the later Middle Ages the almoner's oversight extended to a significant number of charitable institutions in and around Paris. In the sixteenth century, either the Grand Almoner, as he came to be called, or his vicar, served as one of the members

---

[78] 'Statuts des Haudriettes', edited in Le Grand, *Les Béguines de Paris*, p. 352; Connally, 'Les "Bonnes Femmes"', pp. 263–4.

[79] Farmer, *Surviving Poverty*, pp. 166–7.

[80] Coyecque, *L'Hôtel-Dieu*, p. 97.

[81] Coyecque, *L'Hôtel-Dieu*, p. 123.

[82] The first masters of the Quinze-Vingts were mercers; the aldermen of Paris in that period included several mercers. See O'Tool, 'Caring for the Blind', p. 197; Le Grand, *Les Quinze-Vingts*, ii, 183; Bove, *Dominer la ville*, pp. 70, 71, 73.

of the board of commissioners of the Grand Bureau des Pauvres of Paris,[83] and in both the sixteenth and seventeenth centuries, Grand Almoners played instrumental roles in broader hospital reform throughout France.[84]

Historians have offered a range of explanations for the broader late medieval trend towards secular oversight of charitable institutions: concern for public health and safety, a desire for greater efficiency, frustration with deteriorating conditions in poorly managed hospitals, concern that the church was accumulating too much tax-exempt property, the desire to prevent the diversion of endowed incomes from charitable institutions to beneficed clergy.[85] In the case of the expansion of the French Royal Almoner's authority, we should add both a general trend favouring the expansion of royal jurisdiction at the expense of the church, and the powerful influence of Christian devotion in the French royal household, which enhanced the king's sense that it was his Christian duty to protect the poor and the weak.[86]

The second characteristic of the sixteenth-century system of Parisian poor relief that had its roots in the Middle Ages was the municipal authorities' dependence on parish church wardens to implement their programme of poor relief. Parish church wardens first appeared in thirteenth- and fourteenth-century France and England as the result of both episcopal legislation and lay pressure: concerned about the decline of the fabric of their parish churches, parishioners sought permission from their bishops to elect, or to have their parish priests nominate, lay wardens to manage resources that were intended for the support of the fabric of their churches.[87] Several Parisian sources from the thirteenth and fourteenth centuries offer glimpses of these lay wardens.[88] For example, a document from

---

[83]   Montaigne, p. 113.

[84]   On the sixteenth century, see discussion above at n. 27; and Imbert, pp. 16–17. On the seventeenth, see Joseph Bergin, *Cardinal de la Rochefoucauld: Leadership and Reform in the French Church* (New Haven, CT: Yale University Press, 1987), pp. 119–24.

[85]   Lindberg, *Beyond Charity*, pp. 62–3; Le Blévec, i, 291–7; ii, 638–47; Gonthier, pp. 213–26; Brodman, p. 138.

[86]   De la Selle, pp. 35–6; 208–11; Priscille Aladjidi, *Le Roi père des pauvres: France XIIIe–XVe siècles* (Rennes: Presses Universitaires de Rennes, 2009), pp. 36–45; Psalm 82; Archives des Quinze-Vingts 1061, edited in Le Grand, *Les Quinze-Vingts*, ii, 2, n. 3. King Francis I's 1519 decree ordering the reform of all of the hospitals of France also demonstrated a keen awareness of the king's responsibility to protect the poor and the weak.

[87]   Paul Adam, *La vie paroissiale en France au XIVe siècle* (Paris: Sirey, 1964), pp. 80–81; Katherine French, *The People of the Parish: Community Life in a Late Medieval English Diocese* (Philadelphia: University of Pennsylvania Press, 2000), pp. 29–30, 45–6. For a rich description of the responsibilities of rural parish wardens in sixteenth-century England, see Eamon Duffy, *The Voices of Morebath: Reformation and Rebellion in an English Village* (New Haven, CT: Yale University Press, 2001), chap. 2. On duties other than poor relief that were imposed on the wardens by the crown, see esp. ibid., pp. 124, 128.

[88]   Bove (*Dominer la ville*, p. 260) lists several archival sources with references to parish *marguilliers*. For surveys of the sources from the fourteenth through eighteenth centuries, see G. Constant, 'Les Registres de marguilliers', *Revue de l'histoire de l'église*

1319 recording the settlement of a dispute between the abbey of St-Magloire and the parish of St-Barthélemy, lists the names of 10 wardens of the parish of St-Barthélemy. The group included a number of Parisian elites, including an alderman, two men who were related to aldermen, and the king's concièrge. Nevertheless, half of the lay wardens of St-Barthélemy were from modest backgrounds.[89] This mixture of parish elites with modest parishioners seems to have been the norm among parish wardens in Paris.[90]

Responsibility for the fabric of a parish did not necessarily include responsibility for the poor of the parish. Nevertheless, a number of Parisian sources from the thirteenth through fifteenth centuries indicate that both private individuals and civic authorities began to expect parish wardens, or their equivalents, to manage resources intended for the poor and to find resources to sustain some categories of the poor. In their testament of 1227, Jehan de Fontenoi and his wife Bauteut indicated that anything that was left over from their various testamentary bequests should go towards providing dowries for poor girls in their parish, who were to be identified by the provost of the parish, along with the three most 'prudent' men of the parish.[91]

In 1316 – the second year of the great famine of the early fourteenth century – the provost of Paris resolved a dispute that had arisen between the Hôtel-Dieu and the parish of St-Christolphe, in which the Hôtel-Dieu was located. The representatives of the Hôtel-Dieu claimed that an infant had been abandoned not on the grounds of the Hôtel-Dieu, but within the jurisdiction of the parish of St-Christolphe; for that reason, the hospital's representatives claimed, the wardens and parishioners of St-Christolphe were responsible for finding care for the infant. According to the representatives of the Hôtel-Dieu, 'throughout France and in Paris as well, both law and custom have established that if a child is left within the limits of a parish, the parishioners of that parish are held responsible for the care of the child'. The wardens of St-Christolphe apparently agreed with the basic principle of the Hôtel-Dieu's argument – they simply wished to dispute on whose territory the infant had been found. The provost of Paris decided in favour of the hospital's claims, and thus he compelled the wardens of St-Christolphe to arrange for care of the child.[92] We need to take note here that, faced with an infant whose survival depended on the care of others, neither the members of the Hôtel-Dieu nor the wardens of St-Christolphe were moved by pious charity, and the issue was resolved not by the

---

de France, 103 (1938), 170–83; Agnès Bos, 'Les Archives des fabriques parisiennes à la fin du Moyen Âge et à l'époque moderne', *Bibliothèque de l'École des Chartes*, 156 (1998), 369–405; Jacques Meurgey de Tupigny, *Histoire de la paroisse Saint-Jacques-de-la-Boucherie* (Paris: H. Champion, 1926).

[89]   Bove, *Dominer la ville*, pp. 259–60.

[90]   Bove, *Dominer la ville*, p. 260; Duffy, pp. 28–30: in the English rural parish of pre-Reformation Morebath, nearly all adults were expected to serve as parish wardens.

[91]   Farmer, *Surviving Poverty*, pp. 34–5, discussing Archives Nationales, L 547, no. 1.

[92]   Coyecque, *L'Hôtel-Dieu*, pp. 289–91.

bishop but by the provost of Paris. It might take a village – or a parish – to raise a child, but in this case it took a royally appointed representative of the state to compel the people of the parish to assume responsibility for the child. In some isolated instances, then, public authorities in Paris assumed ultimate responsibility for ensuring that vulnerable members of the community would be protected.[93] This was consistent with the Biblical injunction to defend orphans and the fatherless.[94]

A third document, a fifteenth-century account book from the Hôtel-Dieu, records the receipt of an annual payment of 10 sous from the lay wardens of the parish of St-Jacques-de-la-Boucherie, in accordance with the testamentary bequest of the well-known Parisian elite, Nicolas Flamel. In this case, the parish wardens were assuming responsibility not only for a testator's bequests to the fabric of their parish, but also for his bequests to a charitable foundation.[95]

The emergence of a new system of centralised poor relief in the sixteenth century added an enormous administrative burden to the duties of the parish wardens of Paris. Nevertheless, it built on two principles that had already been established in the later Middle Ages: first, the duties of parish wardens sometimes included taking charge of poor individuals or the resources intended for poor people and charitable foundations; and, second, it was within the purview of the civic authorities of Paris to impose responsibility for the poor on the wardens.

A third characteristic of the new system of poor relief in sixteenth-century Paris, its emphasis on sustained care for the deserving poor, also had roots in medieval developments – in the foundation of hospitals that were meant to provide permanent shelter and support for long-term residents, rather than providing temporary shelter, meals and palliative nursing care to short-term residents. In Paris, the earliest of those shelters was the leprosarium of St-Lazare, which was founded in the early twelfth century. As is the case with the foundations of hundreds of other leprosaria, the foundation of St-Lazare of Paris can be interpreted as an expression of the 'charitable revolution' that swept across Europe in the twelfth and thirteenth centuries.[96] As this charitable impulse continued to grow, thirteenth-century Paris saw the endowment of two more leprosaria, two convents for reformed prostitutes, a shelter for widows and King Louis IX's hospice for the blind – the Quinze-Vingts. Those diverse institutions were joined, in the fourteenth century, by two

---

[93]   In Montpellier, by contrast, municipal authorities routinely oversaw the care of abandoned children: Leah L. Otis, 'Municipal Wet Nurses in Fifteenth-Century Montpellier', in Barbara Hanawalt (ed.), *Women and Work in Pre-Industrial Europe* (Bloomington: University of Indiana Press, 1986), pp. 83–93.

[94]   Psalm 82. 3; Isaiah 1. 17.

[95]   Coyecque, *L'Hôtel-Dieu*, p. 29, n. 4. For the role of medieval English churchwardens in the distribution and administration of charitable bequests, see Gibbs, p. 174.

[96]   On St-Lazare, see Touati, p. 261; on the leprosaria as manifestations of the 'charitable revolution', see ibid., pp. 242–7, 761–3. For an argument that many leprosaria grew out of the organising impetus of lepers themselves, see Jennifer Stemmle's essay in this volume.

more leprosaria, nine more shelters for widows, two housing blocks (almshouses) for poor householders, and Paris's first orphanage – the St-Esprit.[97] Clearly the founders of these institutions perceived that sustained care was better than one-time handouts, and that there were distinct segments of the city's poor, sick and vulnerable residents that needed their own particular sources of support. Given the limited size of most of these institutions, they must have had only a minor impact on the overall levels of poverty and suffering in the French capital, but they are indicative of an increasingly strategic approach to the problems of urban poverty.

Late medieval developments also provided some precedent for a fourth aspect of sixteenth-century poor relief in Paris: use of public funds to help finance care for the poor. I do not mean to argue that in the Middle Ages the king or municipality actually managed to impose a poor tax on the people of Paris: it was only with difficulty, over the course of the Hundred Years' War, that the French king successfully put into practice the idea that he had the right to tax the people for their common defence even when there was no imminent danger. Nevertheless, in the fourteenth and fifteenth centuries the members of the various courts in Paris – the Châtelet, the Chambre des comptes, the Cour des aides and Parlement – did find ways to direct publicly collected resources to charitable causes, largely by channelling judicial fines to the city's main hospitals. In 1316, for instance, the Parlement of Paris declared that all fines that were collected from its members as a penalty for arriving late at a session would be divided evenly and sent to the Hôtel-Dieu and the Quinze-Vingts.[98] In 1368 the confiscated house of the rebellious Provost of the Merchants, Etienne Marcel, was handed over to the Quinze-Vingts. And throughout the fifteenth century the accounts of the Hôtel-Dieu recorded fines received from the various courts.[99]

The mid-thirteenth-century guild statutes of Paris, compiled by its provost, Etienne Boileau, may have set a precedent for these fourteenth- and fifteenth-century judicial practices: according to the statutes, when members of the poultry-mongers guild were caught buying poultry at unauthorised markets, the poultry was to be confiscated and handed over to the Hôtel-Dieu or to the poor prisoners of the Châtelet. Similar rules applied to confiscated fish.[100] Some scholars have argued that these statutes are indicative of the charitable inclinations of the guilds

---

[97]   On the leprosaria (La Roule and St-Germain in the thirteenth century; St-Hylaire and St-Gervais by the fourteenth), see Touati, pp. 252, 253, 265 and p. 627, n. 146. On the two convents for prostitutes (St-Antoine and the Filles Dieu), the shelter for widows (Ste-Avoye), the almshouses (Ave Maria College and the Hospice Jehan Roussel in the fourteenth century, which were joined by the almshouse of Nicolas Flamel in the early fifteenth century) and the orphanage of the St-Esprit, see Farmer, *Surviving Poverty*, pp. 78, 85–6, 147–8.

[98]   Le Grand, *Les Quinze-Vingts*, ɪ, 141, n. 5.

[99]   Le Grand, *Les Quinze-Vingts*, ɪ, 141; Coyecque, *L'Hôtel-Dieu*, p. 129.

[100]   René de Lespinasse and François Bonnardot, *Le livre des métiers d'Etienne Boileau* (Paris: Imprimerie Nationale, 1879), pp. 149, 215.

themselves. Similarities between the statutes suggest, however, that they were imposed from above, by the provost.

In the thirteenth, fourteenth and fifteenth centuries, then, guild and judicial fines, along with confiscated goods and properties, helped to augment the resources of hospitals in Paris, and those resources reached the hospitals not as a result of charitable acts, but as a result of public policy. Channelling these fines and confiscated goods to charitable institutions helped to ensure that rules and regulations would be enforced for the right reasons, rather than simply padding the incomes of public officials. Nevertheless, there was apparently a perception that the Hôtel-Dieu and the Quinze-Vingts were worthy of receiving those incomes because the services that they provided to the afflicted 'poor' of Paris helped to promote the common good.

The fifth medieval precedent for the system of poor relief in sixteenth-century Paris was the manner of dealing with able-bodied beggars. Bronisław Geremek compiled the standard list of royal and municipal statutes that addressed the issue of able-bodied beggars in late medieval Paris.[101] While there had been earlier precedents, King John the Good's statute of 1351, which tried to address various social and economic problems that arose in the wake of both the Hundred Years' War and the massive mortality of 1348–49, represents a major turn towards a well-defined policy concerning vagrancy.[102] The king directed the criers of Paris to announce that the unemployed and 'lazy' people of the city should either find a job or leave town within three days. Able-bodied beggars who continued to appear on the streets were to face four days in prison for the first offence, time in the pillory for the second offence and branding and banishment for the third offence. Statutes much like this one were repeated again and again well into the sixteenth century.[103]

A second development occurred in 1367: during a period of recovery from a decade of war, the new provost of Paris, Hugh Aubriot, who was eager both to

---

[101]   Bronisław Geremek, 'La lutte', pp. 213–36. For a discussion of criminal records involving the arrest of vagrants, see Esther Cohen, 'Vagabondage à Paris au XIVe siècle', *Le Moyen Âge*, 88 (1982), 293–313. It should be noted, however, that all of the vagrants discussed by Cohen had been arrested for other crimes; there were probably many more vagrants who were expelled from Paris or (after 1367) employed in its public works projects who did not show up in the criminal court records.

[102]   Cohen ('Vagabondage', p. 294) argues that John the Good's statute differed from the English Statute of Labourers because it was shaped as much by social disruptions created by the Hundred Years' War as by the Black Death. For a broader discussion of vagrancy laws, see Trevor Dean, *Crime in Medieval Europe* (Harlow: Longman, 2001), pp. 50–52. For a comparative discussion of royal statutes concerning wages and vagabondage that were promulgated in the wake of the Black Death, see Robert Braid, '"Et non ultra": politiques royales du travail en Europe occidentale au XIVe siècle', *Bibliothèque de l'École des Chartes*, 161 (2003), 437–91.

[103]   Geremek, 'La lutte', pp. 217–18, partial edition of original text on p. 230. For the full text, see René de Lespinasse (ed.), *Les métiers et les corporations de la ville de Paris, vol. 1* (Paris: Imprimerie Nationale, 1886), pp. 2–44.

establish a reputation for ensuring public order and to complete the fortifications on the south side of the capital, declared that the unemployed of Paris should be put to work on its fortifications; those who refused were to be thrown into the prison of the Châtelet. This is the first time that forced labour was proposed as a way of controlling vagrancy in Paris – and, again, as I already explained, it became an integral part of the organised system of poor relief and control that took definitive shape in 1544.[104]

Over the course of the fifteenth century, the French kings added a number of components that would become standard practice in sixteenth-century efforts to control vagrancy and strengthen public order: sending incorrigible vagrants to work in the galleys, conducting weekly searches of Parisian households in order to identify those who were unemployed or otherwise undesirable, and compelling municipal officers to assist the royal officers of the Châtelet in these searches.[105] It was only in the sixteenth century, however, that reformers attempted to remove *all* open air begging from the streets.

There were important differences between medieval and early modern approaches to the poor. Until the end of the fifteenth century open air begging continued to play a major role in the support of the poor, whose care continued to reside, in large part, in the hands of individuals whose concern about their own well-being in the afterlife loomed as large as their concern for the plight of the poor or the good of the community. Over the first half of the sixteenth century, by contrast, poor relief became a matter of social policy driven, in part, by the reformers' perceptions that controlling the poor and removing all beggars from the streets were major preconditions for the safety and health of the entire community. Humanist assumptions that rulers could and should take steps to prevent social ills helped to inspire the new policies; the printing press helped disseminate model plans; and recurrent bouts of plague, along with the virulent spread of a new venereal disease and concerns about social unrest, added impetus as well. Additionally, as a number of historians have argued, there may have been economic motives behind the adoption of new systems of poor relief: in their

---

[104] Geremek, 'La lutte', pp. 219–20, original text edited on p. 232. On Hugh Aubriot, see Antoine Le Roux de Lincy, 'Hugues Aubriot, prévôt de Paris sous Charles V, 1367–1381', *Bibliothèque de l'École des Chartes*, 23 (1862), 173–213. See also *Registres des délibérations*, I, 228–9: in February 1516, the aldermen of Paris proclaimed that all able-bodied beggars had to either find work or leave the city within three days. Those who failed to comply were to be placed in prison, chained up in pairs, and then led out to labour on various public works projects, including work on the defensive walls surrounding the city. By 17 March the programme was in place, and twenty-four prisoners were put to work.

[105] Geremek, 'La lutte', pp. 222–9, 235–6; Bronisław Geremek, 'Criminalité, vagabondage, paupérisme: la marginalité à l'aube des temps modernes', *Revue d'histoire moderne et contemporaine*, 21 (1974), 347–51. On sixteenth-century searches of houses (to search out vagabonds, Protestants and other undesirables), see *Registres des délibérations*, IV (1552–58), (ed.) François Bonnardot, 48, 53, 112, 121, 129, 147; VII (1572–76), (ed.) Bonnardot, 254, 280; IX (1586–90), (ed.) Bonnardot, 377; X (1590–94), (ed.) Paul Guérin, 126.

efforts to gain support for their programmes, reformers argued that by outlawing begging and overseeing job training, municipalities could create a more willing and able labour force and bring down the cost of consumer goods.[106]

There was much that was new in the sixteenth-century municipal plans for eradicating begging and providing work and relief for the poor; but those plans also built on thirteenth-, fourteenth- and fifteenth-century precedents – in the areas of secular management, public funding, sustained support for the needy and anti-vagrancy legislation. In Paris, moreover, the roots of the sixteenth-century reforms involved both a partnership between royal and municipal authorities and a reliance on lay leaders within the parishes. Already in the thirteenth century, the king of France initiated a system of lay oversight and management of a major hospice for disabled individuals, the provost of Paris found ways to channel public fines towards charitable hospitals, the king and municipal elites established endowed institutions to provide sustained care for the poor, and individual testators were asking the lay leaders of the parish to take care of their charitable bequests. Already in the fourteenth century, the provost of Paris imposed his authority upon parish wardens in order to compel them to care for foundlings, and the king of France began to issue harsh legislation concerning able-bodied beggars.

These nascent developments suggest that we sometimes go too far when we emphasise the private, ad hoc, nature of medieval charity, contrasting it sharply with early modern systems of public poor relief. They also help to explain why, in the sixteenth century, not only the municipality but also the royal administration were heavily involved in the development of poor relief in Paris. Indeed, it is instructive to recall that in the early 1520s a partnership between a member of the royal administration and a Parisian municipal elite – the Royal Almoner, François du Moulin de Rochefort, and the President of the Chambre des comptes, Jean Briçonnet – resulted in one of the earliest attempts anywhere in Europe to eliminate mendicancy among a group of the deserving, disabled, poor, insisting that they find work instead. Du Moulin's and Briçonnet's attempt to transform the daily lives of the blind residents of the Quinze-Vingts may have been only partially successful – but the effort itself was symptomatic of new comprehensive approaches to poverty that would soon take hold in many municipalities, including Paris.

---

[106]   On humanist influences, see n. 33 above; Davis, *Society and Culture*, pp. 29–34; and Terpstra, *Cultures of Charity*, pp. 60, 166–7. On concerns about public health and safety, see nn. 54–5 above; Vives, *De subventione*, bk. 2, chap. 1, 2, pp. 66–8; Davis, *Society and Culture*, pp. 26–8; and Pullan, pp. 240–51. On economic motives, see Vives, *De subventione*, bk. 2. 3, pp. 73–4; City of Ypres, *Forma subventionis*, pp. 109, 130, 132; Heller, pp. 39–41; Terpstra, *Cultures of Charity*, pp. 166–78; and Lis and Soly, pp. 88–94. On the impact of the printed versions of municipal poor relief plans from Ypres, Lyon and Paris on policies in other towns and regions, see Salter (ed.), *Some Early Tracts*, pp. 34, 36, 105.

Chapter 3

From Cure to Care: Indignation, Assistance and Leprosy in the High Middle Ages

Jennifer Stemmle

In the mid-thirteenth century, the Cistercian chronicler Gilles of Orval recorded an episode of charitable endeavour on behalf of people with leprosy that renders a dramatic scene of organised lay piety in action.[1] Recounting traditions observed on the anniversary of the martyrdom of Saint Lambert, the patron of Gilles's home diocese of Liège, Gilles described annual celebrations at a church dedicated to Lambert in Würzburg. Here, he wrote, assembled parishioners 'are eager devotedly to offer worldly things to support the spiritual souls of the *leprosi*, and, as for their bodies, they very frequently rejoice to bring back from that place medicines'.[2] The scene in Würzburg speaks of institutionalisation. Some group of people with leprosy knew, it suggests, to arrive at the church on a certain day. A group of pious well-wishers knew to bring medicines and other goods for them. Their exchange took place as part of a public celebration on the liturgical calendar, no doubt under the eyes of ecclesiastical authorities. The scene also speaks to an emphasis on the immediate needs of the body. The pious parishioners had concern for the immortal souls of the *leprosi* and *leprosae*, but their support was material. They did not expect Lambert to perform miracle cures for these sufferers as he was once thought to have done; they brought medicine.

Scholars have told the history of this mid-thirteenth-century configuration of charity for people with leprosy as the story of the pious parishioners. This chapter will reverse the angle of vision and will examine the behaviour of people with leprosy in response to various interlocutors. Using evidence in narrative sources from the medieval diocese of Liège, I will argue that a transformation occurred in

---

[1] Gilles of Orval, *Gesta pontificum Tungrensium, Traiectensium et Leodiensium*, (ed.) J. Heller, in *MGH*, Scriptores 25 (Hannover, 1880), pp. 14–129. The *MGH* texts are available online at <http://www.mgh.de>.

[2] Gilles of Orval, *Gesta pontificum*, p. 42: 'devote student offere carnalia cum spiritualium animarum subsidiis leprosorum quoque corporum sepissime gaudent inde se reportare medicamenta'; see also *The Narrative Sources from the Medieval Low Countries*, (ed.) J. Deploige (Brussels: Royal Historical Commission, since 2009), available online at <www.narrative-sources.be>, number A028 [accessed November 19, 2014]. When I have used *Narrative Sources* entries for information about the texts in question, I refer to their entries in footnotes by their Narrative Sources Identification Number (hereafter NaSo ID).

representations of people with leprosy in such exchanges toward the beginning of the twelfth century and that in this transformation we can see the origins of the kind of institutionalised care represented in the celebration in Würzburg. For much of the medieval period, the dominant theme in such representations is that of penitence and gratitude. Narratives in which people with leprosy evince these attitudes also involve rather striking reversals of the expected flow of charitable giving: saints are as likely to give leprosy as to cure it; *leprosi* and *leprosae* are as likely to be charitable donors as receivers. These narratives emphasise the miraculous cure of leprosy, not the care of its sufferers. In the twelfth and especially thirteenth centuries, these emphases are reversed. Physical care takes priority, and people with leprosy emerge in the narratives with needs beyond that of penitence. This chapter will argue that charity toward people with leprosy that had the character of the scene in Würzburg emerged in part because *leprosi* and *leprosae* moved beyond the pious role that had been assigned to them in a search for dignified care and community.

The historiography of charity as it pertains to people with leprosy in the Middle Ages focuses on the leprosaria, communities of *leprosi* and *leprosae* that emerged in the thousands in western Europe mostly in the twelfth century. This work, and specifically, that which examines the reasons for the existence of the leprosaria, has undergone a series of illuminating revisions in the last fifteen years. An argument that the leprosaria were quasi-monastic communities has broken a generations-long consensus that they were a means of quarantine.[3] This new perspective has come about through two interventions largely undertaken by three historians. First, the careful reading of medical treatises by the historians Luke Demaitre, François-Olivier Touati and Carole Rawcliffe has demonstrated that contagion in the sense of a disease being easily communicable between persons was only rarely considered to be a significant factor in the spread of leprosy until

---

[3]   Elma Brenner, 'Recent Perspectives on Leprosy in Medieval Western Europe', *History Compass*, 8 (2010), 390–92; François-Olivier Touati, *Maladie et société*, pp. 29–51; Carole Rawcliffe, *Leprosy in Medieval England* (Woodbridge: Boydell, 2006), pp. 13–43. Works that argue for fear of contagion as a major influence in the formation of the leprosaria include Albert Bourgeois, *Psychologie collective et institutions charitables. Lépreux et maladreries du Pas-de-Calais (Xe–XVIIIe siècles)* (Arras, 1972); Françoise Bériac-Lainé, *Histoire des lépreux au moyen-âge: une société d'exclus* (Paris: Éditions Imago, 1988); Piera Borradori, *Mourir au monde: les lépreux dans le pays de Vaud, XIIIe–XVIIe siècles* (Lausanne: Université de Lausanne, Faculté des lettres, Section d'histoire, 1992); Saul Brody, *The Disease of the Soul; Leprosy in Medieval Literature* (Ithaca, NY: Cornell University Press, 1974); Simone C. Mesmin (McDougall), 'Du Comté la Commune: La Léproserie de Saint-Gilles de Pont-Audemer', *Annales de Normandie*, 37 (1987), 235–68; Simone C. Mesmin, 'Waleran, Count of Meulan and the Leper Hospital of S. Gilles de Pont-Audemer', *Annales de Normandie*, 32 (1982), 3–19; Peter Richards, *The Medieval Leper and His Northern Heirs* (Woodbridge; Rochester: D.S. Brewer, 2000).

the fourteenth century, long after most of the houses had come into being.[4] Second, in the absence of quarantine as a motivation for the formation of the leprosaria, Touati and Rawcliffe use sermons, hagiography, charters and house regulations to argue that the leprosaria rose on a more generalised tide of twelfth-century charity, that they were an expression of lay piety, one which compared the suffering of people with leprosy to the suffering Christ and that viewed them as privileged penitents capable of efficacious intercessory prayer.[5] People like the parishioners of Würzburg gave material aid and labour to the leprosaria to assist this elect.

The problem with this argument arises in trying to understand why people with leprosy themselves participated in the leprosaria. Understanding this participation is crucial because, while the leprosaria were charitable endeavours in that they attracted and accepted alms from well-wishers, they were also voluntary communities for as much as the first two centuries of their existence. The practice of formal examination for the purpose of placing people with leprosy in institutions was adopted mostly in the fourteenth century and later.[6] Before this, people with leprosy had to find this form of charity attractive or necessary so that they would take it up as a response to the disease. The leprosaria required their participation, just as any monastery required the participation of monks, in order to exist. Indeed, we cannot rule out the presence of people with leprosy themselves in the very origination of the houses, as the 'founding' documents for them often refer to gatherings that were already in place before donations allowed for the construction of chapels and other structures.[7]

The evidence for the argument that the leprosaria were expressions of lay piety does not necessarily tell us about the engagement of people with leprosy with this form of charity. The rules for the houses and charters marking donations to them, central to this argument, were almost always expressive of the intentions of donors and of authorities outside the communities.[8] Sermons and hagiographic literature likewise came from the perspective of people who did not have the disease. We can learn that religious thinkers like Jacques de Vitry imagined people with leprosy in the late twelfth century as martyrs suffering 'purgatory in this life' ('purgatorium in hac vita'), but we do not know if people with leprosy saw the matter thus.[9] Similarly, the legend of Saint Pérégrin, a *leprosus* rewarded with a divine cure for

---

[4]   Luke Demaitre, *Leprosy in Premodern Medicine: A Malady of the Whole Body* (Baltimore: Johns Hopkins University Press, 2007), pp. 138–41; Rawcliffe, pp. 190–95; Touati, *Maladie et société*, pp. 149–51, 281–94; François-Olivier Touati, 'Contagion and Leprosy: Myth, Ideas, and Evolution in Medieval Minds and Society', in Lawrence I. Conrad and Dominik Wujastyk (eds), *Contagion: Perspective from Pre-Modern Societies* (Aldershot: Ashgate, 2000), pp. 79–201 (pp. 193–8).

[5]   Rawcliffe, pp. 104–30; Touati, *Maladie et société*, pp. 380–428.

[6]   Demaitre, p. 41; Rawcliffe, pp. 28–9.

[7]   Touati, *Maladie et société*, p. 126; Bourgeois, pp. 34–5.

[8]   Joseph Avril, 'Le IIIe concile du Latran et les communautés des lépreux', *Révue Mabillon*, 60 (1981), 21–76 (pp. 55–76).

[9]   See Touati, *Maladie et société*, p. 199.

his eagerness to attend the consecration of the basilica of Saint Denis, suggests that some medieval people entertained the idea that the pious *leprosus* or *leprosa* was especially beloved of Christ, but we do not know if people with leprosy themselves entertained this idea.[10]

Narrative sources, however, even when generated by authors who did not have leprosy, are not without value for an understanding of what might have been the position of people with the disease. Hagiography and chronicles, after all, do offer stories that describe the behaviour of people with leprosy, and, even if we assume that the stories are essentially fictional, it can also be assumed that they are meant to represent behaviour that was at least plausible. Rawcliffe, for instance, sees in the legend of Saint Pérégrin evidence for ideas about mercy toward the pious *leprosus*. But the story also describes a *leprosus* who took certain actions. Anticipating that he would not be allowed to watch the consecration of the basilica, he hid in the chapel on the eve of the event. When Christ appeared to him and asked him to bear witness to miracles that he had seen in the night, Saint Pérégrin declined because he did not want to call attention to his presence.[11] These kinds of detail suggest the agency, the range of possible action, that was available for people with leprosy, in this case the possibility that people with leprosy developed strategies to meet their own spiritual needs and that they were likewise strategic about being seen.

It is, of course, ill-advised to generalise from a single narrative, so, for this chapter, I have aggregated narrative sources from the diocese of Liège in order to search for patterns in the representation of the actions of people with leprosy. I used two bibliographic resources, Sylvain Balau's *Les sources de l'histoire de Liège au Moyen-Âge; étude critique* and the *Narrative Sources of the Medieval Low Countries* database, to generate a list of 255 texts with a connection to the medieval diocese of Liège either because they were written by someone who lived there or by someone, such as Thomas of Cantimpré, who had spent significant time in Liège and wrote about events in the diocese.[12] Because I wanted to know when leprosy and its sufferers began to be the subjects of story-telling, I searched for texts from the eighth century through 1350, the later date reflecting a rough estimation of a point at which we might say that the leprosarium movement, having begun in the mid-twelfth century, had arrived at a kind of maturity. The sources include saints' lives, chronicles and annals and letters that the editors of *Narrative Sources* selected for their narrative content. In this group, I found 33 sources with references to people with leprosy, 26 of them from the eleventh through thirteenth centuries, the period prior to and during the rise of the leprosaria.

I have focused on the diocese of Liège because it was a veritable hotbed of Christian lay piety and charitable endeavour, many of its lay pious movements giving birth to groups or institutions that had vulnerable members of society

---

[10]   Rawcliffe, pp. 112–14.

[11]   Rawcliffe, pp. 112–13.

[12]   Sylvain Balau, *Les Sources de l'histoire de Liège au Moyen-Âge; étude critique* (Brussels: H. Lamertin, 1903); Deploige (ed.), *Narrative Sources* (see n. 2, above).

as constituents or members. The episcopate was host to the earliest and most impressive formation of a movement of religious women, the beguines, and in the 1160s and 70s, at the same time that people with leprosy created communities outside the cities of Liège and Huy, Lambert Le Bègue, a Liégeois priest, led a movement of lay Christians, particularly the poor, to whom he gave vernacular translations of scripture. By the turn of the thirteenth century, lay persons in Liège had founded four hospitals and an extensive urban almonry.[13] Second, one of the most important leprosaria of the region, Mont Cornillon, located just outside the City of Liège, was alleged to be the site of a significant uprising of the residents of the house against a saint. In 1242 and again in 1247, they violently expelled their prioress, Juliana of Mont Cornillon, when she attempted to impose stricter monastic conventions on them.[14] In other words, Mont Cornillon was a leprosarium where it seems that the intentions of the residents, some combination of people with leprosy and their caregivers, were in conflict with standards for piety that were expected of them, and these residents, sick and well, acted on their own behalf. The following seeks to understand better what the intentions of the residents, at least of the people with leprosy, might have been.

The Dominant Narrative: Penitence and Gratitude

Before looking at the actions and attitudes attributed to people with leprosy, it is important to establish that nearly all the narrative sources represent leprosy as a disease under the control of God and his earthly agents, saints and holy people. The idea of the saintly or divine control of individual cases of leprosy emerges in eleventh-century Liège in a series of hagiographical works beginning with the anonymous second book of the *Miracula* of Saint Remaclus, the patron of the monastery of Stavelot.[15] The author complained of a monk of Stavelot who, 'aggravated by the pleasures of the flesh, grew to abominable faults and

---

[13]   Walter Simons, *Cities of Ladies: Beguine Communities in the Medieval Low Countries, 1200–1565* (Philadelphia: University of Pennsylvania Press, 2001), pp. 24–34; R.I. Moore, *The Birth of Popular Heresy* (1975; repr. Toronto: University of Toronto Press/Medieval Academy of America, 1995), pp. 101–11; Pierre de Spiegeler, *Les Hôpitaux et l'assistance à Liège: Xe–XVe siècles: aspects institutionnels et sociaux* (Paris: Les Belles Lettres, 1987), pp. 57–81; Paul Bertrand, *Commerce avec Dame Pauvreté: structures et fonctions des couvents mendiants à Liège, XIIIe–XIVe siècles* (Geneva: Droz, 2004), pp. 471–9.

[14]   *De B. Iuliana Virgine, Priorissa, Montis-Cornelii apud Leodium, Promotrice Festi Corpus Christi*, in Godefrid Henschen and Daniel von Papenbroek (eds), *Acta Sanctorum Aprilis*, 3 vols (Antwerp: Michael Cnobarus, 1675), I, 443–77 (pp. 466–9). The *Acta Sanctorum* in its entirety is now available online in a subscriber-only database <http://acta.chadwyck.com>.

[15]   Balau, pp. 65–6, 68–9.

uncleanness in addition to the defence of dangerous errors'.[16] Even after Remaclus appeared to the monk to threaten the punishment of an incurable disease, the monk could not achieve a heartfelt remorse, so Remaclus gave him leprosy. It is difficult to tell from the *vita* what the monk's response was to having the disease except that, when his brothers placed him in a hut and abandoned him to solitude, even leaving his meals on a bench outside his door, the narrative leaves no hint that the rebellious monk objected to this treatment. We are left to believe that he had fallen into a compliant silence at last.

A similarly ambiguous story of saintly manipulation of leprosy occurs in the *vita* of Saint Hiltrudis composed by a monk of Waulsort Abbey sometime in the latter half of the eleventh century.[17] Here, a woman named Ermentrudis entrusts her infant, Haduidis, into the care of girl named Roberga.[18] In the night, Roberga begins to hear the voices of angels coming from the church devoted to Hiltrudis, but the girl must listen to the voices over the infant's incessant crying. In the morning, Hiltrudis appears and points out to Roberga that she had not been able to hear perfectly the voices of the celestial choir, and she gives Haduidis leprosy. Hiltrudis, however, explains to Roberga that the point of this act is not so much punitive as purely directed toward an expression of power. She tells Roberga that she intends to heal the infant after a short time and that she is acting 'in the interest of testimony and of the confirmation of the divine praise that you heard. For the restored health of the infant in this very spot will back up your declarations about the praises of the angels that you heard'.[19] Hiltrudis, in other words, is producing a visible, public miracle so that those who are allowed private audience with the divine will be believed. A *vita* from the same period, that of Saint Guldila, replicates the moral logic of Hiltrudis's act.[20] A woman with leprosy named Eremfreda approaches Guldila who then falls to her knees in prayer, saying to God:

> either you wish this woman to be ground down with the most unclean leprosy because of her sins, so that she, corrected, will repent and, clearing her crimes, may be cleansed by a miracle; or, in such conditions, you wish her to be healthy

---

[16]   *Miracula prima, secunda et tertia Remacli Stabulensis*, in Johannes Pinius and others (eds), *Acta Sanctorum Septembris*, 8 vols (Antwerp: Bernardus Albertus Vander Plassche, 1746), I, 696–721 (p. 709): 'aggravatus carnis voluptate, vitiis abominabilibus atque immunditiæ insuper ad patrocinium erroris periculosius accreverat.'

[17]   Balau, p. 252.

[18]   *Vita sancti Hiltrudis*, in Johannes Stiltingus and others (eds), *Acta Sanctorum Septembris*, 8 vols (Antwerp: Bernardus Albertus Vander Plassche, 1760), VII, 461–501 (p. 498).

[19]   *Vita sancti Hiltrudis*, p. 498: 'ob testimonium et confirmationem, quam audisti, laudis divinæ. Nam asseveranti tibi de laudibus angelicis, quas audisti, sanitas infantulæ illico restituta testimonium perhibebit.'

[20]   Balau, p. 248.

so that by means of the omen of her cure your magnificence may be made plain
so that you may be praised for your works.[21]

Guldila brings about the cure, having laid out the whole purpose of leprosy as a mechanism for the production of repentance and gratitude not just from the *leprosa* in question but from all those who might witness her cure.

It is in these eleventh-century narratives that we also see the first representation of repentance coerced by the deployment of the message that leprosy is a punishment for disobedience. In Sigebert of Gembloux's *vita* of Saint Maclovis, written between 1071 and 1092, Sigebert imagined a response from those stricken with the disease.[22] Maclovis, evangelising in Brittany, responds to the truculence of the local people by cursing them with leprosy, among other afflictions. Thus, the Bretons, 'not being able to withstand the affliction of curses and worse, decided together in a shared council humbly to implore the holy man for pardon'.[23] Maclovis grants their wish and restores them and their lands to health. The Bretons pledge to comply with the saint's wishes and eventually beg Maclovis to remain with them in their territories. Though this narrative itself is fantastic, it includes a representation of the actions of people with leprosy in response to their disease. Sigebert did not mark this response as strange or unusual, so the story suggests that, under the right pressure, people with leprosy normally took up penance.

The framework of penance and gratitude persists into the twelfth century where it appears in the *Poeme de Trudone* by Rodulfus Trudonensis, a brief work, written between 1108 and 1136, the substance of which was incorporated into the fourteenth-century continuation of the *Gesta abbatum Trudonensium*.[24] It tells the story of how Trudo had cured 'a certain nobleman' ('quidam nobilium') of leprosy, and of how this nobleman responded with appropriate thanks: 'He was not ungrateful; indeed, for such a service, he himself took care to consign the town of Seny to the saint.'[25]

---

[21]   *Vita Guldilae*, in *Acta Sanctorum* (1 January 1643), pp. 513–23 (p. 517): 'Siue ergo voluisti hanc mulierē immundissima atteri lepra propter eius peccata, vt pænituisset correcta, eius delendo crimina, eam mirabiliter munda; siue idcirco vt eius curationis omine tua claresceret magnificentia, eam mirabiliter sana, vt a tua magnificeris facture.'

[22]   Balau, p. 209; NaSo ID S069.

[23]   Sigebert de Gembloux, *Vita Maclovi Alectensis*, in Jacques-Paul Migne (ed.), *Patrologia Latina* CLX (Paris, 1854), pp. 729–46 (p. 745): 'nec valentes ultra sufferre maledictionis et ultionis molestiam, communicato consilio deliberaverunt a sancto viro humiliter implorare veniam.' See also the *Patrologia Latina Database* <www.pld.chadwyck.com> available to subscribers.

[24]   Rodulfus Trudonensis, *Poeme de Trudone*, in J. Brassine (ed.), *Mélanges Godefroid Kurth*, 2 vols (Liège: Impr. Vaillant-Carmanne; Paris: H. Champion, 1908), II, 113–19 (pp. 118–19); NaSo ID R120; R. Köpke (ed.), *Gesta abbatum Trudonensium (continuatio tertia)*, in *MGH*, Scriptores 10 (Hannover, 1852), pp. 364–81, 387–443 (p. 366); NaSo ID G058.

[25]   *Poeme de Trudone*, p. 119: 'Nec fuit ingratus, sed quidem pro munere tanto | Curavit villam Senni contradere sancto.'

There are three major characteristics of these mostly eleventh-century narratives that are important for what will follow. First, most of the stories bind leprosy to sin. It is a punishment from God or his saintly intermediaries for specific acts. Second, there is generally no question of care or charity of goods or labour toward the *leprosi* or *leprosae*; relief for the pain of the disease comes only, if at all, in the form of miracle cure. Indeed, where charity was concerned, it flowed in the other direction; the noble *leprosus* gave Seny to the poor of God, the monks of Saint Trond. Third, people with leprosy appear in these narratives for the most part individually. Except for the collectively punished Bretons, we see people with leprosy seeking their cures or enduring their disease alone.

Resistance and Care

There are four major shifts that occur in narratives about people with leprosy beginning in the twelfth century. First, the idea of the miracle cure is all but banished and in its stead appears the idea of care. Well-wishers offer material assistance and labour to people with leprosy who are, in turn, rarely imagined as the source of charity for clerics. Second, authors continue to imagine leprosy as a punishment for sin, but they are far more interested in the penitence of those who care for people with leprosy than that of the people with leprosy themselves. Third, people with leprosy appear in numbers either in leprosaria or in other groupings. Finally, people with leprosy in these stories no longer merely endure whatever fate the saints assign to them. Beginning in the twelfth century, stories about *leprosi* and *leprosae* involve self-assertion and resistance.

A narrative from early in the twelfth century brings together three of these themes. The first *Gesta abbatum Trudonensium*, written between 1114 and 1137, describes the controversial rise of Lupon to the abbacy of Saint Trond. The Liégeois Bishop Otbert, who had achieved his office in 1091 by the imperial appointment of Henry IV, that is, without election by *clerus et populus*, commenced his reign by summarily replacing the abbots of three monasteries. One of his appointments was Lupon.[26] Amidst the ensuing turmoil, the chronicler reported, Lupon 'was seen to commit himself to the washing away of his sins by great alms and by supporting poor people and travellers and also sometimes by washing people with leprosy, wiping down those to be cleaned with his own hands'.[27] It is difficult to imagine exactly how Lupon's repentant gesture took place. Where did he find

---

[26]   R. Köpke (ed.), *Gesta abbatum Trudonensium*, in *MGH*, Scriptores 10 (Hannover, 1852), pp. 227–72, 281–91 (pp. 250–51); NaSo ID R113; Jean-Louis Kupper, *Liège et l'église impériale, XIe–XIIe siècles* (Paris: Société d'Édition 'Les Belles Lettres', 1981), pp. 140, 391.

[27]   *Gesta abbatum Trudonensium*, p. 251: 'accingere se videbatur ad diluenda peccata sua per multas elemosinas et per suscipiendos pauperes et peregrinos et etiam interdum leprosos levandos, tergendos manibusque propriis ungendos.'

these people with leprosy ready to be cleaned? The description seems to be of people who needed to be washed and who needed assistance in the task, and who are assembled at some place, bringing to mind the fact that bathing was a regular part of the regime of care in some leprosaria.[28] The description of Lupon's gesture suggests that people with leprosy had gathered in the diocese as early as the first quarter of the twelfth century.

Hugh of Floreffe's *c.* 1229 *vita* of Yvette of Huy, an anchoress at Grands Malades leprosarium, demonstrates that the figure of the menacing saint had not entirely disappeared from representations of people with leprosy, but it encourages a different understanding of the fate of the punished sinners. The *vita* tells of a woman from the town whom Yvette 'knew for her secret excesses'.[29] She contracted leprosy because she did not reform herself after Yvette saw her in a dream in which, before a council of saints, 'fire seemed to flame out of her most secret place and devastate the upper parts of her body'.[30] Like the wicked monk of Stavelot, the excessive woman disappears from the narrative after she contracts the disease. Nevertheless, it must be remembered that her meetings with Yvette take place on the grounds of a leprosarium where people with leprosy have community and, we are told early in the narrative, access to care. Yvette, before becoming a recluse, worked among the residents of Grands Malades. She washed linens, poured water, set the table, helped people with leprosy in and out of their beds, and she bathed the hands and feet of those who were not able to wash themselves.[31]

Indeed, in the later narratives, people with leprosy whose needs went unmet were likely to rebel. The *c.* 1241–51 *Vita Odiliae* attests to such in a story about the Liégeois priest John, the son of the *vita*'s titular subject.[32] John, whom the text refers to as the 'man of God' (*vir Dei*), adopts a young boy named Helias in order to tutor him in religious texts, and Helias, after entering John's home, falls ill with leprosy.[33] John, moved by compassion, prays to good effect for a cure. But when Helias feels strong enough to ask his patron if he might move to Paris to continue his studies there, John adamantly refuses, 'upbraiding him and recounting the

---

[28]   Rawcliffe, pp. 228–9.

[29]   Hugh of Floreffe, *De B. Ivetta, sive Ivtta, Vidua Reclusa, Hui in Belgo*, in *Acta Sanctorum* (Antwerp: Ioannes Meursius, 1643), pp. 863–87 (p. 879): 'notam sibi, pro quibusdam occultis excessibus.' For the translated quotations, I consulted Jo Ann McNamara (trans.), *The Life of Yvette, Anchoresse of Huy*, in Anneke B. Mulder-Bakker (ed.), *Living Saints of the Thirteenth Century: The Lives of Yvette, Anchoress of Huy; Juliana of Cornillon, Author of the Corpus Christi Feast; and Margaret the Lame, Anchoress of Magdeburg* (Turnhout: Brepols, 2011), pp. 70–141 (pp. 120–21).

[30]   Hugh of Floreffe, *De B. Ivetta*, p. 879: 'videbatur ignis egredi a secretiori loco artuum eius, et quasi superiores corporis partes reliquas deuastare penitus.'

[31]   Hugh of Floreffe, *De B. Ivetta*, p. 870.

[32]   Andrea Neten, 'Étude critique de la *Vita Odiliae, c.* 1241–1251' (unpublished thesis, Université de Liège, 1993), pp. 6–19, 31–4; Balau, pp. 444–5.

[33]   C. De Smedt and others (eds), *Vita B. Odiliae Viduae Leodiensis. Libri duo priores*, *Analecta Bollandiana*, 13 (1894), pp. 190–287 (p. 235).

misery of his former state of disease'.[34] To prevent any disobedience, John attacks the boy through prayer, giving him grave respiratory symptoms. Eventually, he cures Helias again, but not completely; Helias, fearing death, asks to return to his parents. John again objects, threatening, 'Indeed, if you were to go anywhere, leaving me behind, before the tenth day, without any doubt you will die'.[35] Though Helias does, in fact, make his way to his parents' home, John follows him and retrieves the dying boy, who, in his final days, embraces repentance and bequeaths his inheritance to John: 'Therefore, all things having been done correctly, the boy, having joined in taking an oath, at once promised to give his revenues, if it was permissible, to the servant of God'.[36]

Though Helias eventually falls into compliance, he does so after a prolonged period of resistance to a 'servant of God' who had control over his health. Helias has complex personal needs, familial and even vocational, that the pious caretaker refuses to honour, so Helias acts on his own behalf. Though the narrative has things go badly for Helias in the end, it is significant that this kind of assertion was, at least to one thirteenth-century writer, imaginable. In Helias's second bout of illness, the self-assertion that led to it continues even in its midst.

This kind of psychological complexity and resistance appears in the early fourteenth-century *Gesta sanctorum Villariensium*.[37] The anonymous writer recorded that a *conversus* of Villers, like the monk of Stavelot, endured segregation from his community because he had leprosy. Here, however, the narrative includes the separated *leprosus*'s response to this turn of events: 'he was tired, as much by the tedium of solitude as by the rottenness of dying.'[38] Depressed, the *conversus* decides to commit suicide by throwing himself into a river and then changes his mind after the Virgin Mary consoles him: 'the sick man truly from that day and from then on, most patiently tolerated the whip of the Lord'.[39] This conclusion does not erase the totality of the experience and the behaviour that the anonymous author represented. For this author, it was plausible to think that a person with leprosy might vacillate in his patient acceptance of punishment and that he might rebel from it. Moreover, Mary, attended by saints, offers physical comfort. Finding the *conversus* helplessly lying on his floor, unable to right himself on his injured feet, Mary returned him to his bed.[40] The story also suggests the importance of

---

[34]   *Vita B. Odiliae Viduae Leodiensis*, p. 235: 'ipsum increpans et aegritudinis pristinae palam revolvens miseriam.'

[35]   *Vita B. Odiliae Viduae Leodiensis*, p. 235: 'Si enim vadas alicubi, me relicto, ante diem decimum procul omni dubio morieris.'

[36]   *Vita B. Odiliae Viduae Leodiensis*, p. 236: 'Omnibus igitur rite peractis, coniuratus puer suum quantocius, si liceret, reditum Dei famulo repromisit.'

[37]   NaSo ID G078.

[38]   E. Martène and U. Durand (eds), *Gesta sanctorum Villariensium* (Paris, 1717), pp. 1309–74 (p. 1368): 'fatigatus esset, tum taedio solitudinis, tum foeditate morbi.'

[39]   *Gesta sanctorum Villariensium*, p. 1369: 'Infirmus vero ab illo die et deinceps, patientissime flagellum Domini toleravit.'

[40]   *Gesta sanctorum Villariensium*, p. 1369.

community not only with the rest of the religious of Villers, but specifically with fellow sufferers. Better cared for than the monk of Stavelot, the *conversus*'s attendant visits him later in the night and asks after his needs. What he wishes for, the *conversus* says, is a visit from a certain Brother Johannes, who, like himself, could not join the brothers and *conversi* at Villers because gout confined him to his room.[41]

Thus it is not surprising also to find in this later period representations of people with leprosy in groups and making their needs known. In Gilles of Orval's *Gesta pontificum Tungrensium, Traiectensium et Leodiensium* people with leprosy manage to turn the tables on a holy person by confronting him in numbers.[42] In Gilles account, Saint Servatius of Tongeren had to remove all the relics from that city because of an imminent attack. The move to transport the relics to Maastricht met with 'the objections of the sick and of the people with leprosy'.[43] Evidently dependent on the relics for the maintenance of their health and the possibility of a cure, the gathered people with leprosy and other illnesses prevailed in their confrontation with the saint: Servatius immediately cured them. For Gilles of Orval, it was plausible that people with leprosy could exert collective pressure to have their needs met.

Causality

It is difficult to untangle these narrative threads involving assertiveness, care and collectivity to find the relationship between them and thus to propose an explanation for the shift in storytelling about people with leprosy. If we take the chronology of the narratives as the most important indication, then we have to believe that it was collectivity that came first. We have, after all, the early-twelfth-century episode of Lupon finding some group of *leprosi* and *leprosae* to bathe. Moreover, documentary evidence allows us to know of the certain existence of leprosaria in Liège beginning sometime prior to 1176. By 1250 there were at least nine of them.[44]

Thus, we get the following chain of events. People with leprosy throughout the eleventh century received the continual message that their disease presented them with the task of repentance. By the twelfth century, certain well-wishers, activated by the ideal of the *vita apostolica* joined them in penitential piety, which the latter group expressed through care. We see indications of such motivations in the activities of Lupon. A little later, Hugh of Floreffe attributed similar concerns

---

41   *Gesta sanctorum Villariensium*, p. 1369.

42   Gilles of Orval, *Gesta pontificum*, p. 28.

43   Gilles of Orval, *Gesta pontificum*, p. 28: 'obiectio infirmorum et leprosorum.'

44   Ernest Persoons, Walter de Keyzer, Marleen Forrier and Michel van der Eycken, *La Lèpre dans les Pays-Bas (XIIe–XVIIIe siècles)* (Brussels: Archives Générales du Royaume, 2000), pp. 51–63.

to Yvette of Huy, who joined the community at Grands Malades as a caregiver so that she could perfect her humility and, she hoped, contract the disease.[45] Juliana of Mont Cornillon was a virtuosa of penance. Her *vita* records her as having told a priest that she was guilty of all sins insofar as she felt insufficient anxiety about the offence to God of the sins of all people.[46] These two groups, then – pious, redemption-seeking *leprosi* and *leprosae* and pious, redemption-seeking well-wishers – formed the leprosaria in order to live a semi-monastic life conducive to their spiritual ambitions. Sometime later, perhaps energised by the solidarity provided by the leprosarium movement, people with leprosy developed a kind of self-assertion that in fact rejected isolation, indifferent care, coercion and even the task of penance itself.

Nevertheless, it is possible to see things otherwise. Most of the eleventh-century narratives allow almost no expression to the people with leprosy whom they represent. Some of them are silent after they contract the disease. Others are allowed merely to voice their wish for a cure and their gratitude upon its receipt. There are, however, two early narratives which afford an expanded sense of the lives of people with leprosy. Stephen of Saint Trond's *Miracula Sancti Trudonis* lists the healing miracles associated with Trudo in the years 1050–51, including a single *leprosus* who approaches the well at the Abbey of Saint Trond seeking a cure.[47] After he bathes with the well water, the *leprosus*, who is, uniquely in the medieval narratives from Liège, called 'rusticus', returns to his home 'with his neighbours'.[48] This is a striking detail because the man had come to Saint Trond from Wavre, a journey of some 80 kilometres. Stephen thus recorded, alongside the miracle cure, an incident of significant, bodily aid offered to a *leprosus*. First, people had managed to get word to him about the healing well. Then, he found some number of people from Wavre to support him on a long journey to the Abbey. Though the *leprosus* in the story does not speak, we get the image of someone with an ongoing social existence.

At about the same time, an anonymous author wrote about an isolated *leprosus* dependent on less than exemplary care. In the *Vita Sancti Berlendis*, written between 1049 and 1051, Saint Berlendis's father, stricken with leprosy, lives with his daughter and servants, having been abandoned by other members of

---

[45]   Hugh of Floreffe, *De B. Ivetta*, p. 870.

[46]   *De B. Iuliana*, p. 447. For translations I consulted Barbara Newman (trans.), *The Life of Juliana of Cornillon*, in Mulder-Bakker (ed.), *Living Saints of the Thirteenth Century*, pp. 184–302.

[47]   Stephen of Saint Trond, *Liber Secundus Miraculorum Sancti Trudonis*, in Giuseppi Bettinelli and others (eds), *Acta Sanctorum Ordinis Sancti Benedicti*, 9 vols (Venice: Sebastian Coleti and Josephum Bettinelli, 1738), VI, 83–104 (p. 97); J. Brassine, 'Une source du livre II des "miracula sancti Trudonis"', *Bulletin de la Société d'art et d'histoire du diocèse de Liège*, 26 (1935), 29–52 (pp. 30–31).

[48]   Stephen, *Miraculorum Sancti Trudonis*, p. 97: 'con convicaneis suis.'

his household.[49] One day, the narrative tells us, he noticed that Berlendis, after offering him a drink, carefully washed the cup before drinking from it herself. Berlendis's father silently 'endured extraordinary indignation', and then set off for Nivelles where he handed over all his property to the Abbey of Saint Gertrude and 'deprived the daughter of all right of inheritance from her father and her mother'.[50] While the *vita* frames the story providentially in terms of the development of Berlendis's piety and that of the physical plant of the Abbey of Saint Gertrude (whose dead hand actually protrudes from her crypt to receive the *leprosus*'s charter), there is no mention in the story of sin or a miracle cure. Rather, the story focuses on the necessity of dignified care. A miracle cure was among the other cultural materials available to the writer of this *vita* that he could have used to slip the record of a charitable donation into the text and to explain Berlendis's poverty. The narrative, however, turns in the direction of imagining the felt experience and indignation of the *leprosus*. This example makes it possible that the story of the nobleman who gave the town of Seny to the Abbey of Saint Trond enclosed a similar note of indignation. As mentioned above, this story appeared in the *Poeme de Trudone*, composed by Rodulfus, a brother of the Abbey. In addition to noting the nobleman's gratitude to Saint Trudo, the narrative records that the nobleman's younger brother challenged the gift suggesting that this brother perceived himself as having been disinherited. Though Rodulfus represented the nobleman's aims as entirely spiritual, just like Berlendis's wealthy father, the *leprosus* in the *Poeme* disinherited one of his relatives in favour of a monastery.

Can we take these stories as suggestions that the leprosaria started not to express piety but to express the need for the kind of community enjoyed by the *rusticus* of Wavre and the kind of care withheld from Berlendis's father? It is perhaps best to think of this phenomenon as a reflection of the complex lives of medieval people with leprosy. The case of Gilles of Duras, who was the count of a region near the abbey of Saint Trond of which he was the sub-advocate, demonstrates this complexity. Gilles's history appears in Gilbert of Mons's 1205 *Chronicle of Hainaut*, which reports that Gilles contracted leprosy sometime prior to 1184 and gave up nearly all of his lands and titles to his two brothers, Cono and Pierre.[51] Gilles's condition is further attested in the second continuation of the *Gesta Abbatum Trudonense*, which covers the years 1138–80 and which confirms Cono's possession of the title of sub-advocate of Saint Trond as well as the reason for that: Gilles had been 'scourged meanwhile with the Lord's whip of severe

---

[49]   NaSo ID H053.

[50]   *Vita Berlendis*, in *Acta Sanctorum Februarius*, 3 vols (Antwerp: Iacobus Meursius, 1658), I, 378–81 (p. 379): 'mirabili indignatione tulit ... filiam omni paternæ maternæque hæreditatis iure priuauit.'

[51]   Gilbert of Mons, *Chronicon Hanoniense*, in Léon Vanderkindere (ed.), *La Chronique de Gislebert de Mons* (Brussels: Hayez, 1904), pp. 1–332 (pp. 237–9). For translations of this text, I consulted Gilbert of Mons, *The Chronicle of Hainaut*, (trans.) Laura Napran (Woodbridge: Boydell, 2005), p. 130.

leprosy'.[52] Additionally an 1183 letter of Guibert of Gembloux affirms that Gilles was 'by the judgement of God, sprinkled with the stains of deadly leprosy'.[53]

Gilles himself used the language of divine purpose and personal repentance in a charter of 1173, which was the first in which he referred to himself as the 'former count of Duras' ('quondam comes') and to his brother Cono as the count.[54] The charter declared Gilles's intention to turn over his familial chapel of Saint Medard and its holdings to the Hospitallers of Saint John, and it begins with a statement of the ideas about leprosy that clerical writers had circulated for more than a century:

> [I]f I can return adequate gratitude to him who deigned to view my blindness with absolute compassion, I, Gilles, formerly Count of Duras, am not ashamed, tardily it is granted, to ignite the long sleeping sparks of faith in me lest, having been imprisoned by the shadow of worldly happiness, withdrawing willingly from the inexhaustible light of the true sun, I should lay out my couch in the gloom. Indeed, the truth says: I do not want the death of a sinner, rather that he be converted and live.[55]

In the first document in which it is clear that Gilles had given up his titles, he prefaced his act of donation to a religious order with a description of a spiritual conversion. Since other sources confirm that he gave up his titles because he had leprosy, it is clear that Gilles here described his personal sense of the meaning of the disease. He wrote that it was light to the blind, a cause for gratitude and the beginning of redemption from sin. He expressed his conversion by giving to religious, whom he described in another charter as 'the poor' ('pauperibus').[56]

Gilles seems to have embraced the penitential ideal, and yet further documents suggest that Gilles's conversion did not prevent him from a certain righteous obstreperousness. Gilles was eager to settle the Hospitallers at Saint Medard, and along these lines he transferred to them, among other things, eight bonniers of land

---

[52]   R. Köpke (ed.), *Gesta abbatum Trudonensium (continuatio secunda)*, in *MGH*, Scriptores 10 (Hannover, 1852), pp. 333–661 (p. 359): 'lepra mulctatum severiatis suae flagella interim castigibat'; NaSo ID G057.

[53]   Guibert of Gembloux, 'Epistola de Martino ad Philippum archiepiscopum Coloniensem', in Albert Derolez (ed.), *Guiberti Gemblacensis Epistolae*, 2 vols (Turnhout, Brepols, 1988), I, 170–78 (p. 170): 'Dei iudico morbo leper respersum.'

[54]   Mathias Joseph Wolters, *Notice historique sur l'ancien comté de Duras en Hesbaie* (Gand: Gyselinck, 1855), p. 88.

[55]   Wolters, p. 88: 'notum sit omnibus tam futuris quam presentibus, quod ego Gilius quondam comes Durachiensis, dignas si possim grates ei referre, qui cœcitatem meam elementer miserari dignatus est, ne mundane felicitis umbra captus, et a veri solis inexhausto lumine sponte recedens, in tenebris sternam lectutum meam, fidei scintillulas in me diu sopitas accendere, licit sero, non erubesco. Dicit enim veritas: nolo mortem peccatoris, sed magis ut convertatur et vivat'; R. Hanon de Louvet, *Histoire de la ville de Jodoigne*, 2 vols (Gembloux: Imprimerie J. Ducolot, 1941), II, 357–8.

[56]   Wolters, p. 86.

and the tithes of nearby Molembais.[57] The interesting problem with Gilles's plan is that his mother, Julienne, had already given the eight bonniers and the tithes to the Premonstratensian Abbey of Heylissem in 1164.[58] Gilles's challenge to this gift, which ecclesiastical mediators dismissed in 1179, was particularly aggressive because his brother Pierre had just finished unsuccessfully contesting the same gift to Heylissem, and the Abbey had just received a third confirmation of its rights.[59] Gilles adamantly defended his interests, which may have been spiritual. After all, Gilles's specifications for the foundation at Saint Medard are extraordinarily specific and filled with angelic and Biblical symbolism. His motives could also have been political. Other local lords had shunned Heylissem, which owed its origins and funding to outsiders to the region. Indeed, Heylissem did not attract significant endowments until Henry I of Brabant, having installed himself as Heylissem's advocate, managed to inspire local vassals to enhanced generosity. Gilles's move to distance himself from this implantation aligned him more closely with his noble allies whose sons joined other chapters when they sought the religious life.[60] Gilles's response to having leprosy appears in both narrative and documentary sources to have been complex, vacillating between (or perhaps holding simultaneously) the condition of a penitent turning away from the world and one of being willing to struggle and manoeuvre in the world to express his own spiritual needs and/or to maintain political alliances. It might also be added that Gilles's agenda for Saint Medard could well have been aimed at ensuring that he received adequate physical care as his disease progressed. The Hospitallers, after all, maintained service to the sick as a central aspect of their mission.[61]

A peculiar episode concerning Gilles in the *Chronicle of Hainaut* further suggests that Gilles had not entirely made a break with the shadow of worldly happiness. Gilles seems to have chosen as the site of his retirement the town of Jodoigne, which he held as an allod. After he had relinquished his other titles, Gilles began calling himself the Count of Jodoigne.[62] Jodoigne, however, lay in the defunct county of Brugeron, which the Dukes of Brabant had coveted for almost a century.[63] In 1182 Godefroid III of Brabant attacked Jodoigne and

---

[57] Wolters, p. 87.

[58] E.H.J. Reussens, *Documents relatifs à l'abbaye norbertine d'Heylissem*, in *Analectes pour servir à l'histoire ecclésiastique de la Belgique*, ser. 2, vol. 8 (1893), pp. 205–6.

[59] Wolters, p. 88; Reussens, pp. 218–24.

[60] Georges Despy, 'Le Temporal de l'abbaye d'Hélécine au XIIe siècle: Un piège pour les Norbertins', *Revue du Nord*, 72 (1990), 427–41 (pp. 431–6).

[61] Jonathan Riley Smith, *The Knights Hospitaller in the Levant, c. 1070–1309* (New York: Palgrave Macmillan, 2012), pp. 69–70.

[62] Reussens, p. 234.

[63] Georges Despy, 'Franchises urbains et rurales: les ducs de Brabant et l'ancien comté de Brugeron aux XIIe et XIIIe siècles', in Jean-Marie Duvosquel and Erik Thoen (eds), *Peasants and Townsmen in Medieval Europe: Studia in Honorem Adriaan Verhulst* (Gent: Snoek-Ducaju & Zoon, 1995), pp. 631–49 (pp. 631, 641).

took Gilles hostage. After a period of peace negotiated by Philippe of Heinsberg, the Archbishop of Cologne, Godefroid's son Henry attacked again in 1183 and definitively brought Jodoigne under Brabançon hegemony.[64]

It was at this point, so wrote Gilbert of Mons, that Gilles, perhaps having dispensed with all gestures of renunciation, armed himself and took revenge on Henry and his accomplice, Count Philippe of Flanders: 'remaining for a while at Duras and for a while at Clermont, he harassed the Duke of Louvain and the Count most often, and capturing their merchants, he took away from them wine, scarlet cloth and silver, and he forced the imprisoned men to pay a heavy redemption'.[65] According to Gilbert, Gilles eventually wound up in the entourage of Henry of Namur, a group regarded by Gilbert as 'treacherous toadies' devoted to criminal enterprise in that principality.[66] Gilbert reported that his patron, Baldwin V of Hainaut, arrested Gilles sometime around 1187 or 1188 and held him in the Castle of Ath. No other documents or narratives support any of this. In fact, for the period in question, Gilles's behaviour seems to have followed along the lines suggested by the 1173 charter for the Hospitallers. Gilles's charters for the year 1188, while milder in their religious sentiment, are still aimed toward giving properties to religious institutions, in this case the Cistercians of Signy whom he invited to settle in Clermont.[67] Yet, it must be marked that a *leprosus* aggressively defending his interests did not prompt incredulity in Gilbert.

The idea of this complexity, so clearly evident in the case of Gilles, might explain why the communities that people with leprosy and their caregivers formed were often less observant than penitent figures like Juliana would have hoped. The monastic aspects of the leprosaria (holding goods in common, the adoption of habits, and so on) support a conception of the houses as religious communities. But many aspects of the leprosaria were not traditionally monastic. They were mixed houses (and in fact took in whole families); members were rarely cloistered; people with leprosy were not always required to maintain the liturgical hours or even to attend mass.[68] The unusually early regulations for Mont Cornillon require attendance at chapter meetings, the sharing of goods and a novitiate, but they say nothing about sexual segregation in the house, ritual observance, or limitations on mobility.[69] Elsewhere, rules often came into being through episcopal initiative

---

[64]   Hanon de Louvet, II, 72–3.

[65]   Gilbert of Mons, *Chronicon Hanoniense*, p. 238: 'quandoque apud Clarum Montem, ducem Lovaniensem et comitem sepius infestabat, et eorum mercatores capiens, eis vina et scarlatas et alios pannos et argentum auferebat, et illos incarceratos ad gravem redemptionem cogebat.'

[66]   Gilbert of Mons, *Chronicon Hanoniense*, pp. 221–3.

[67]   Wolters, pp. 99–100.

[68]   Touati, *Maladie et société*, pp. 405–28, 447–55; Rawcliffe, pp. 128–31, 263–6; Avril, pp. 48–52.

[69]   AEL, Hôpital de Cornillon, MS 76, fols 1r–2r; for editions of these documents, see Émile Denis (ed.), *Sainte Julienne et Cornillon: étude historique* (Liège: Printing Co. Société Anonyme, 1927), pp. 148–51.

decades after the communities had appeared in order to restrict diverse local customs that had developed in the houses.[70] Some of the local practices, suggested by the emphases of the rules, indicate communities that were far from conventual. At Chateaudun and Grand Beaulieu in Chartres people with leprosy had to be threatened with punishment for failure to attend religious services.[71] At Lille, a 1239 rule from Walter, the bishop of Tournai, corrected residents for allowing meals shared between men and women, permitting marriage after entry into the house, dicing, visits to the nearby village, wandering on the main highway outside the house, absence from mass, disobedience and an 'irreligious and conspicuous demeanour'.[72] These houses seem to have supported needs other than that of penitence.

It is suggestive that the narrative sources from Liège occasionally show the abandonment or shunning of relatively elite people with leprosy, and, apart from later representations of organised charity, only the *leprosus rusticus* has the support of his neighbours. These sources suggest that people with leprosy, particularly elites, experienced rejection. While neighbours accompanied the *rusticus* of Wavre for 160 kilometres so that he could receive a cure at the Abbey of Saint Trond, Berlendis's father suffered the indignity of his daughter's unwillingness to drink from his cup. He was abandoned by all other members of his household as was the nobleman of Seny. Religious *leprosi* found themselves completely ostracised from their communities. The leprosaria could have seemed for some to be a good setting for the assumption of a life of penitential piety, but they might also have addressed the problems of shame, abandonment and isolation that people with leprosy confronted in elite milieux. Indeed, by the twelfth century, the eleemosynary behaviour of elites with leprosy did not focus merely on the poor of Christ. It focused on the leprosaria. Gilles of Duras was one of the earliest donors to Mont Cornillon, giving members rights to cut wood in his forest at Clermont.[73] Touati's analysis of the records of 33 admissions of people with leprosy to Grand Beaulieu in Chartres, reveals the participation and donations of seven nobles, two members of wealthy bourgeois families, a priest and a monk.[74] Membership records are very sparse for the leprosaria of Liège, but it is clear that at least one elite family, that

---

[70]   Avril, pp. 44–6, 48–52, 55–76.

[71]   Touati, *Maladie et société*, pp. 635–8, 647–9.

[72]   Léon le Grand, *Statuts d'hôtels-dieu et de léproseries: recueil de textes du XIIe au XIVe siècle* (Paris, 1901), p. 191: 'habitum corporis nimis irreligiosum et notabilem gerat.'

[73]   AEL, Hôpital de Cornillon, MS 76, fol. 5r; MS 78, fol. 21v; see also Denis (ed.), *Sainte Julienne et Cornillon*, pp. 153–4. Denis additionally saw a copy of this document in AEL, Hôpital de Cornillon, MS 77, fol. 20v. I have examined this register and, though archivists have made efforts to restore it, the writing on the pages is no longer visible to the naked eye.

[74]   Touati, *Maladie et société*, pp. 318–19.

of Herman, a vassal of the Count of Loos, joined Mont Cornillon in 1185, with the Count approving the transfer of this Herman's entire fief to the leprosarium.[75]

In 1202 the poet Jean Bodel wrote 540 lines that remain one of the few medieval expressions of the experience of leprosy from the point of view of a person with the disease.[76] In his *Congés*, Bodel takes his leave from friends and associates as he prepares to enter a leprosarium, and it is Bodel's invocation of his strong and numerous ties to his community that gives the poem its poignancy. Bodel does not want to leave. He bids farewell to his friend Jean Boschet with grief: 'Crying, I remember morning and night | the goodness that I have found in you.'[77] Bodel's reasons for departure are unclear. He mentions no legal requirement that he leave his home city of Arras, and regulations for the expulsion of people with leprosy from the confines of Arras do not appear in urban statutes of 1194 and 1211, statutes which otherwise address the conditions for entry into the city and various kinds of infractions to public peace.[78] The poem suggests the possibility that Bodel's illness inspired in him a spiritual renewal and compelled him to retreat from the world: 'And since reason commands me | to live a penitent life | And things are taking a bad turn for me, | Let God who offered himself | Allow me to endure so much | That for me the sun will rise in these shadows.'[79] Bodel's words recall those of Gilles of Duras, hoping not to lay out his couch in the gloom. They also express ambivalence that mirrors Gilles's vacillation. For if the special poignancy of Bodel's *Congés* derives from the poet's melancholic farewells to friends, who include a local castellan and the aldermen of Arras, its special bite comes from a tension between expressions of piety and the implication that Bodel has taken up this piety because he has worn out his welcome among these friends. Bodel concludes a stanza devoted to one of his associates, Wibert de la Sale, whose skin 'has no tumours or blisters' by noting that he himself 'can no longer sit at table | among healthy folk'.[80] Bodel tells another friend that 'shame

[75]   AEL, MS Hôpital de Cornillon, MS 76, fols 19r–19v.

[76]   Jean Bodel, *Congés*, in Pierre Ruelle (ed.), *Les Congés d'Arras: Jean Bodel, Baude Fastoul, Adam de la Halle* (Brussels: Presses Universitaires de Bruxelles, 1965), pp. 59–67, 149; Annette Brasseur, 'La poésie des adieux: Les *Congés* de Jean Bodel, essaie de mise en français moderne', in Jean-Claude Faucon, Alain Labbé and Danielle Quéruel (eds), *Miscellanea Mediaevalia: Mélanges offerts à Philippe Ménar*, 2 vols (Paris: H. Champion, 1998), ii, 195–213 (p. 196). All translations unless otherwise noted are my own. For translations of the *Congés*, I have consulted Brasseur's modern French edition of the poem.

[77]   Bodel, *Congés*, p. 85, ll. 17–18: 'Plorant recor et soir et main | les bien que j'ai trouvez en toi.'

[78]   Arras (France) and Adolphe Henri Guesnon, *Cartulaire de la commune d'Arras: recueil de documents tiré des archives de la Mairie* (Arras, 1863), pp. 3–6, 8–14.

[79]   Bodel, *Congés*, pp. 91–2, ll. 187–92: 'Et puis que raisons me commande | A estre en vie peneande | Et mes affaires me bestorne, | Cil Diex qui de lui fist offrande | Le me laist endurer si grande | Que en ces tenebres m'ajourne.'

[80]   Bodel, *Congés*, p. 88, ll. 95–6: 'n'a ne sor os ne gale'; ibid., p. 88, l. 93: 'ne puis mais nape tenir | Entre sains.'

and torment are driving him mad' and warns him that he may no longer see his friends because 'They have endured enough discomfort'.[81] These expressions put Bodel in company with Berlendis's father. But Bodel either had no means or no will for vengeance, and he chose the *vie peneande*. Nonetheless, Bodel's piety was complicated and ambivalent, driven as much by shame as by penitence.

Narrative sources in Liège tell us that for two centuries, people with leprosy, particularly elites, had met with disgust and moral judgement. Instead of receiving bodily care, people with leprosy were encouraged by holy persons, who meted out the disease as a punishment, to think only of miracles. The legend of the saintly miracle cure was very old. Five hundred years before Gilles of Orval described the scene outside the Church of Saint Lambert in Würzburg, another clerical author wrote how Lambert's relics, freshly installed at his new jewel-encrusted basilica in Liège, cured blindness, impairments of the feet and legs and leprosy.[82] Slowly, however, stories began to include images of other kinds of help for people with leprosy, help that addressed everyday bodily and psychological needs: to be assisted getting in and out of bed, to be washed, to be accompanied. Eventually, these sufferers participated in a movement of community formation, the leprosarium movement, which brought them together to receive this kind of help. If the leprosaria expressed a kind of quasi-monasticism and could support the penitential life, they also, like the lives of people with leprosy themselves – Jean Bodel, Gilles of Duras – expressed complex and sometimes conflicting aims. These included the hope for community itself. They also included the wish, found in narratives that predate them, for the ordinary work of care instead of the miraculous intervention of cure.

---

[81]   Bodel, *Congés*, p. 95, ll. 280, 285: 'hontes et ennuis m'enyvre … Assez en ont soufert la cuivre.'

[82]   B. Krusch (ed.), *Vita Landiberti episcopi Traiectensis vetussima (Vita prima Lamberti Leodiensis)*, in *MGH*, Scriptores rerum Merovingicarum 6 (Hannover-Leipzig, 1913), pp. 353–84 (p. 383).

Chapter 4

More Blessed to Give *and* Receive: Charitable Giving in Thirteenth- and Early Fourteenth-Century *Exempla*

Spencer E. Young

Contemporary research suggests a variety of motives for charitable giving. These range from the altruistic satisfaction derived from meeting the needs of others to the selfish enjoyment of social prestige accrued from a well-publicised bequest. Other potential motives for giving may include gratitude for one's blessings in life, empathy for the hardships of others, a desire to avail oneself of particular tax incentives or even a belief in limiting the financial inheritance of one's heirs.[1] Examining which motives are privileged or encouraged at different times, as well as the ways solicitations for donations are made, enriches our perspective on the interrelationship of prosperity and poverty. This chapter contributes to a better understanding of these issues by focusing on how charitable obligations were constructed and conveyed in the Latin west (especially France) during the thirteenth and early fourteenth centuries, a time of significant social, intellectual and economic changes. The chapter begins with a general sketch of the late medieval landscape of charitable giving. It then surveys stories about almsgiving found in contemporary *exempla* collections, one of the more fruitful sources for uncovering how people thought (and were taught to think) about this practice. By considering the role of almsgiving in these *exempla*, this chapter explores how the experiences and attitudes associated with charitable giving reflected and responded to broader changes within the social and religious dynamic during this period.

The Landscape of Charitable Giving

The prospective donor in thirteenth-century Europe navigated a varied social terrain, a 'bewildering context' of innovation and tradition.[2] Several of this

---

[1]   See, for instance, Paul G. Schervish, 'Why the Wealthy Give: Factors which Mobilize Philanthropy among High Net-Worth Individuals', in Adrian Sargeant and Walter Wymer (eds), *The Routledge Companion to Nonprofit Marketing* (London and New York: Routledge, 2008), pp. 165–81.

[2]   James Davis, *Medieval Market Morality: Life, Law and Ethics in the English Marketplace, 1200–1500* (Cambridge: Cambridge University Press, 2012), p. 30.

terrain's contours stand out most prominently. First and foremost, the rapid urbanisation and monetisation over the preceding century and a half meant that the demographic profile of the donor himself (or, albeit in restricted ways, herself) had diversified.[3] New social stratifications were both increasingly visible in more densely populated towns and increasingly acute as the economic gains of widespread commercial growth had benefited some constituencies more than others. One consequence of this transformation was that the quantity of mercantile gifts to the poor began to rival that of aristocratic gifts.[4] These donations could take the form of personal almsgiving but were also manifested through larger-scale initiatives such as endowments for institutions like hospitals or colleges, where the disadvantaged might find increased access to shelter, care (both spiritual and physical) or education. Yet the expansion of lay charitable giving was not solely attributable to the actions of the *nouveau riche*. Through community endeavours like charity ales and other efforts at mutual assistance, such as free home repairs, people at all socio-economic levels were able to participate actively in helping meet the needs of the poor.[5] In some cases, those initiatives organised by the poor themselves may have been the most successful at helping meet the challenges of poverty.[6] The expansion of both formal means to provide assistance (such as through charitable bequests and allocations in wills), and informal (such as *ad hoc* giving in response to a pauper's entreaties), was further stimulated by the increased circulation of money, along with similar mechanisms like tokens.[7]

---

[3]   Several theologians discussed the rights of women (especially wives) to give alms, though they rarely granted this privilege independent of the husband's consent. Thomas of Chobham, active in the late twelfth and early thirteenth centuries, had affirmed this right. Theologians of the later thirteenth and early fourteenth centuries, however, were much more restrictive. See Sharon Farmer, 'Persuasive Voices: Clerical Images of Medieval Wives', *Speculum*, 61 (1986), 517–43 (esp. 534–8); and Ian P. Wei, *Intellectual Culture in Medieval Paris: Theologians and the University c. 1100–1330* (Cambridge: Cambridge University Press, 2012), pp. 282–7.

[4]   Michel Mollat, *The Poor in the Middle Ages*, pp. 153–6.

[5]   On the so-called 'charity ales', see the discussion in Judith M. Bennett, 'Conviviality and Charity in Medieval and Early Modern England', *Past & Present*, 134 (1992), 19–41. Various types of non-monetary assistance, such as clothing, house repair or legal aid, were encouraged by the churchman Jacques de Vitry in his *ad status* sermons. See Jessalynn Bird, 'Medicine for Body and Soul: Jacques de Vitry's Sermons to Hospitallers and their Charges', in Peter Biller and Joseph Ziegler (eds), *Religion and Medicine in the Middle Ages* (Woodbridge: York Medieval Press/Boydell, 2001), pp. 91–108 (pp. 93–4).

[6]   See, with special reference to thirteenth-century Parisian women, Sharon Farmer, *Surviving Poverty*, p. 164.

[7]   Tokens provided the poor with greater opportunities to determine for themselves what they needed as they no longer needed to rely on 'in kind' donations determined by the donors. See William J. Courtenay, 'Token Coinage and the Administration of Poor Relief during the Late Middle Ages', *Journal of Interdisciplinary History*, 3 (1972), 275–95. A less benign interpretation of tokens is found in Bronisław Geremek, *Poverty: A History*, (trans.) Agnieszka Kolakowska (Oxford: Blackwell, 1994), p. 38.

This development also meant that greater numbers of people had at least some liquid means for making charitable contributions. For medieval Christians, means entailed moral obligation. Yet the suspect origins of some personal income streams prompted painstaking reflection upon the rights of certain less worthy social types – prostitutes and usurers in particular – to offer assistance in ways that might also redound to their spiritual credit. The solution to this particular conundrum arose from more sophisticated ways of looking at money, its acquisition and its circulation.[8] As the century wore on, rigorous engagement with Aristotle's work on exchange in the *Nichomachean Ethics,* and a growing concern for mathematical precision, combined with frequent experience using money to inspire even more innovative and perceptive insights into the complex workings of the economy.[9]

The increased circulation of money, of course, eased social mobility in both directions.[10] This factor was sufficiently disruptive on its own. The actual upward mobility of some spawned even more imitators who found money a congenial instrument in their attempts to realise their social ambitions. It also facilitated the ruinous downward mobility of many of their peers. As theologians' anxieties over the usurer's alms suggest, however, several observers worried that economic expansion was coming at a heavy moral cost. Moralists like Jacques de Vitry openly lamented its effects as nothing less than a catastrophe, charging that the disease of avarice seemed to afflict almost everyone and that its effects were bringing about the ruin of people from all social classes.[11] Jacques de Vitry was hardly the only churchman to fulminate against the seeming pervasiveness of money, commerce and the vice of avarice. A similar horror appeared throughout several literary and artistic genres with increasing frequency, leading the historian Lester Little to argue for its displacement of pride as the chief vice in the popular framework

---

[8]   Early thirteenth-century concern with this particular problem is treated in greater detail within the context of theologians' discussions of almsgiving in Spencer E. Young, *Scholarly Community at the Early University of Paris: Theologians, Education and Society, 1215–1248* (Cambridge: Cambridge University Press, 2014), pp. 133–69. For the later thirteenth- and early fourteenth-century discussions, see Wei, pp. 348–53.

[9]   Joel Kaye, *Economy and Nature in the Fourteenth Century: Money, Market Exchange, and the Emergence of Scientific Thought* (Cambridge: Cambridge University Press, 1998); and Idem, *A History of Balance, 1250-1375: The Emergence of a New Model of Equilibrium and its Impact on Thought* (Cambridge: Cambridge University Press, 2014), esp. pp. 20-127. On this issue, see also Alexander Murray, *Reason and Society in the Middle Ages* (Oxford: Oxford University Press, 1978), esp. pp. 25–58, 141–210. On general developments in medieval economic thought, see Odd Langholm, *Economics in the Medieval Schools: Wealth, Exchange, Value, Money and Usury According to the Paris Theological Tradition, 1200–1350* (Leiden: Brill, 1992).

[10]   Murray (pp. 81–109) notes money's importance for increased social mobility starting in the eleventh century, though argues that it was much less decisive than influential patronage networks.

[11]   Jacques de Vitry, *Historia occidentalis*, (ed.) John Frederick Hinnebusch (Fribourg: Fribourg University Press, 1972), cap. 2, p. 78.

of the seven capital vices.[12] Money's insidiousness therefore provoked a strong counter-reaction, manifested in such well-known phenomena as the emergence of the mendicant friars, though they were only the most enduring legacy of the rush to emphasise the spiritual benefits of renouncing rather than seeking monetary wealth. Yet, as both medieval and modern critics have argued, the influence of the mendicant movement was not an unambiguous benefit for the poor. At times, they even siphoned away donations from those who were involuntarily bound to a life of poverty.[13]

Greater social mobility posed another awkward challenge to those who were concerned with the fulfilment of charitable responsibilities. For even some very perceptive reformers of this period maintained rather traditional views about the divine origin of social stratification and the obligations it entailed. This belief was expressed most succinctly in the longstanding idea about the symbiotic relationship between the wealthy and the poor manifested through charitable giving. People of means were supposed to offer relief to those without, while their poor recipients were expected to offer in exchange prayers for the sake of their donors' souls.[14] Moralists stressed both sides of the transaction. The theologian Thomas of

---

[12]   Lester Little, 'Pride Goes before Avarice: Social Change and the Vices in Latin Christendom', *American Historical Review*, 76 (1971), 16–49. As Murray (pp. 77–80) points out, there is an important distinction between the vice's prevalence and its psychological primacy, with avarice attaining the former more surely than the latter. However, the early fourteenth-century *exempla* collection of the Dominican Jean Gobi offers one example of avarice attaining even psychological primacy among the capital vices: 'quod hujus causa erat avaricia que est causa omnium viciorum, superbie, invidie, et cetera.' See Jean Gobi, *Scala coeli*, (ed.) Marie-Anne Polo de Beaulieu (Paris: Centre National de la Recherche Scientifique, 1991), p. 208. Moreover, the discourse and emphasis on avarice in the high and later Middle Ages was not without precedent. See Richard Newhauser, *The Early History of Greed: The Sin of Avarice in Early Medieval Thought and Literature* (Cambridge: Cambridge University Press, 2000).

[13]   For a medieval critique, see Andrew G. Traver, 'William of Saint-Amour's Two Disputed Questions *De quantitate eleemosynae* and *De valido mendicante*', *Archives d'histoire doctrinale et littéraire du moyen-âge*, 62 (1995), 295–342. For a modern critique, see Kenneth Baxter Wolf, *The Poverty of Riches: St. Francis of Assisi Reconsidered* (Oxford; New York: Oxford University Press, 2003).

[14]   See James William Brodman, *Charity and Religion*, pp. 36–8; Diana Wood, *Medieval Economic Thought* (Cambridge: Cambridge University Press, 2002), pp. 63–7. However, thirteenth-century theologians offered a more sophisticated and nuanced explanation of precisely how almsgiving transforms the soul of the donor. See, for instance, my treatment in Young, pp. 157–64. This view was not restricted to medieval Christians. Mark R. Cohen (*Poverty and Charity in the Jewish Community of Medieval Egypt* (Princeton, NJ: Princeton University Press, 2005), p. 189) has observed a similar reciprocity in medieval Egypt, which he attributes to the 'vocabulary of patronage ... of Middle Eastern society'. Although this was a common practice in medieval Islam, one Muslim scholar, Abū Ṭālib al-Makkī (d. 996), claimed that the recipient and the donor should both pray for each other since the donor should not receive a prayer merely for fulfilling his obligation. See Adam

Chobham had even argued that it was a mortal sin for recipients not to pray for the souls of their almsgivers.[15] Poor relief was thus strongly connected to the pursuit of salvation, an idea buttressed by scriptural warrant through oft-cited maxims like those from Ecclesiasticus ('water quencheth a flaming fire and alms resisteth sins') and the Gospel of Luke ('give alms; and behold all things are clean unto you').[16] Yet such giving was not typically promoted for the sake of eradicating poverty. Instead, hearkening back to the classic formulation found in the life of the seventh-century St Eligius, many moralists also believed that God had arranged society with both rich and poor for the express purpose that both might be saved through pursuing a reciprocal relationship based upon the mutual exchange of almsgiving and prayers.[17] Alexander of Stainsby, the university-educated bishop of Coventry and Lichfield from 1224 to 1238, succinctly made the point in a treatise he wrote on the seven deadly sins.[18] An active proponent of the pastoral agenda articulated within the late twelfth-century Parisian school of Peter the Chanter, Alexander included this treatise among the statutes he prepared during the latter half of his episcopate for regular dissemination among all the parishioners of his diocese. In the section warning against avarice, Alexander counselled that 'everyone ought to be content whether God gives them a little or a lot, because God gives poverty to a man so that through enduring it he might have eternal life and he gives riches to a man so that he might obtain the same [i.e. eternal life] through generosity in almsgiving.'[19]

These features of conventional high medieval thinking about poverty and poor relief, in particular the emphasis upon the rewards of the donor over the permanent alleviation of the recipient, have provoked an important interpretive disagreement about the nature of charitable giving during this period. Michel Mollat has criticised the ostentatious, prideful and condescending nature of such

---

Sabra, *Poverty and Charity in Medieval Islam: Mamluk Egypt, 1250–1517* (Cambridge: Cambridge University Press, 2000), p. 35.

[15]   See Farmer, *Surviving Poverty*, p. 61, n. 58.

[16]   Ecclesiasticus 3. 33 and Luke 11. 41. On the former, see Miri Rubin, *Charity and Community*, p. 64, n. 62; Mollat, p. 71. Another important proof-text was Daniel 4. 27.

[17]   Cited in Mollat, p. 44; and Geremek, p. 20. Similar views were echoed throughout the twelfth and thirteenth centuries.

[18]   See F.M. Powicke and C.R. Cheney (eds), *Councils and Synods, with Other Documents Relating to the English Church, ii: A.D. 1205–1313*, 2 vols (Oxford: Oxford University Press, 1964), I, 209–26. The treatise on the sins is found at I, 214–20. On Alexander see Nicholas Vincent, 'Master Alexander of Stainsby, Bishop of Coventry and Lichfield, 1224–1238', *Journal of Ecclesiastical History*, 46 (1995), 615–40. Alexander had theological training (perhaps at Paris) and had apparently taught St Dominic in continental schools.

[19]   *Councils and Synods*, I, 218: 'Sive enim modicum sive magnum dat deus, contentus debet esse quilibet, quia paupertatem dat homini ut per patientiam habeat vitam eternam, divitias ut per elemosinarum largitionem similiter illam optineat.'

alms, where the poor recipients 'served more as means than ends'.[20] Based upon evidence from thirteenth- and early fourteenth-century wills revealing more discriminating charitable distribution (and made by only a minority of the laity in any case), Teofilo Ruiz has made a similar assessment regarding Castilian society, thus extending the prevalence of an apparently selfish and secular *mentalité* to Iberia. Ruiz argues that this period experienced a transition in emphasis 'from heaven to earth', with more ostensibly secular interests replacing religious and charitable ones.[21] This historiographical tendency to compartmentalise religious and secular motives behind charitable giving has been challenged most recently by James William Brodman, who contends that religious motives and practical considerations are not so easily separable during this period. Instead, Brodman advocates a more expansive notion of religiosity to make sense of the various possible motives involved in charitable giving during the high and later Middle Ages. At this time, he claims, charitable motives were 'between two worlds', the commingling of charity and salvation-seeking part of a complex variety of religious acts involving clerical and lay, ecclesiastical and secular, and public and private elements.[22]

The complicated question of how to assess the religious nature of charitable giving during this period reflects the tension experienced by those who lived among and observed medieval donors. As some contemporary reports implied, the boundaries of spiritually meritorious giving could not be determined by scripture alone. Jacques de Vitry again serves as a valuable witness. Condemning as false a spate of preachers he claimed were sent by the devil, Jacques accused this group of deceiving the humble faithful and seeking their own glory and prosperity by appealing directly to the basest instincts of the worst elements of society. He further reproached these pseudo-preachers of 'making usurers, and other men who are deceived because of filthy lucre … feel safe in their sins by perversely reciting that passage in the gospel, "Give alms; and behold all things are clean unto you", by calling good evil and evil good, and by putting darkness for light and light for darkness'.[23] In stressing the 'perverse' citation by these preachers of a scripture that was otherwise an important part of medieval views on giving, Jacques illustrated

---

[20] Mollat, p. 71. Mollat also credits the mendicant friars with bestowing a new dignity upon the poor (pp. 119–34), a thesis contrary to the view in Wolf, pp. 110–11, n. 10.

[21] Teofilo F. Ruiz, *From Heaven to Earth: The Reordering of Castilian Society, 1150–1350* (Princeton, NJ: Princeton University Press, 2004), esp. pp. 1–36, 110–32.

[22] Brodman, pp. 35–44, 267–85.

[23] Jacques de Vitry, *Historia occidentalis*, p. 104: 'Feneratoribus autem et aliis deceptis hominibus "turpis lucri gratia" adulantes, ipsos in peccatis suis reddebant securos, peruerse illud euangelicum recitantes: "Date elemosinam et omnia munda sunt uobis", dicentes bonum malum et malum bonum, ponentes tenebras lucem et lucem tenebras.' The issue of a preacher's right to remuneration was vigorously discussed by Peter the Chanter and his colleagues. See John W. Baldwin, *Masters, Princes and Merchants: The Social Views of Peter the Chanter and His Circle*, 2 vols (Princeton, NJ: Princeton University Press, 1970), I, 108–9.

how the desire to pay alms in order to receive a forgiveness of sins could find itself on either side of the line separating virtue from vice, depending upon who was making the promise. In this case, he was most offended by the appeal to usurers, a wealthy but utterly avaricious social element chosen not because they deserved forgiveness of their sins but because of their potential to reward these alleged false preachers with money and honour.

In addition to orthodox reservations about dubious invocations of Luke 11. 41, evidence also exists for grassroots resistance to the conventional model, as seen in doubts about the absolute power of alms to cleanse one's sins. Most germane to the issue of the religious nature of almsgiving at this time is the fact that such doubts tended to surface in individuals who aroused suspicion of deeper heterodoxy. Thus in the early fourteenth century we encounter in the south of France some intriguing gossip about a certain Bor of Tignac who supposedly expressed to a neighbour his doubts about the salvific value of alms as part of a larger scepticism about the immortality of the soul. According to the second-hand testimony of Guillaume de Corneillan the younger, Bor had reportedly ridiculed belief in the power of alms to remit sins, allegedly telling Guillaume's father-in-law that 'the priests talk nonsense when they tell us to give alms for the salvation of souls. All that is rubbish!'[24] Whether or not Bor ever, in fact, made such statements, disbelief in the efficacy of alms was one of several positions that an inquisitor might have expected to find in connection with other heterodox views. That such doubts were relayed to an inquisitor as a means of casting suspicion upon a neighbour reinforces thereby the normative, mainstream character of belief in the redemptive potential of alms.

Thirteenth- and early fourteenth-century charitable donors attuned to the moral climate of their age thus had to negotiate a complicated landscape of obligations and opportunities. Anyone who had some money was expected to make a contribution to relieving the burdens of the poor. But the acquisition of means that might be used to pay alms was an activity fraught with the danger of avarice, an apparently ubiquitous vice so spiritually poisonous that it was often equated with dropsy.[25] The patristic notion that charitable giving had redemptive value was widely known; the idea was sufficiently familiar to inspire meaningful and potentially threatening doubts about its legitimacy. The same proviso extends to ideas about

---

[24] Emmanuel Le Roy Ladurie, *Montaillou: The Promised Land of Error*, (trans.) Barbara Bray (New York: Vintage Books, 1979), p. 338. Guillaume further testified that his father-in-law told him, in connection with Bor's scepticism about the value to the soul of almsgiving, that Bor had also said 'When a man dies, the soul dies too. It is just the same as with animals. The soul is only blood'.

[25] For relevant imagery see the examples in Richard Newhauser, 'The Love of Money as Deadly Sin and Deadly Disease', in Jörg O. Fichte, Karl Heinz Göller and Bernhard Schimmelpfennig (eds), *Zusammenhänge, Einflüsse, Wirkungen. Kongressakten zum ersten Symposium des Mediävistenverbandes in Tübingen, 1984* (Berlin: de Gruyter, 1986), pp. 315–26; rept. in his *Sin: Essays on the Moral Tradition in the Western Middle Ages* (Aldershot: Ashgate/ Variorum, 2007), VII.

the social order that belief in spiritually efficacious almsgiving inhabited. An emphasis upon divine providence as the source of such social hierarchies existed alongside the experience of changes to those hierarchies. Contemporaries further observed that such upheavals were not always or necessarily the product of divine intervention but rather the consequence of commercial acumen. Amidst such complexity, a variety of reasons for charitable giving might be encouraged or privileged. The balance of this chapter will focus on several different pitches that were made available to preachers for encouraging prospective donors to fulfil their obligations to pay alms, exploring how contemporary religious concerns affected the experience of charitable giving in the thirteenth and early fourteenth centuries.

Promoting Charity: Almsgiving in Thirteenth- and Early Fourteenth-Century *Exempla*

The payment of alms to the poor was encouraged through a variety of channels in the high and later Middle Ages. Perhaps the most personal means came while in the confessional, where, along with prayer and fasting, confessors frequently imposed almsgiving as a work of penitential satisfaction. Yet the most stirring admonitions about the moral responsibility of charitable giving occurred in sermons. Indeed, a great deal of Jacques de Vitry's aforementioned anxiety about the pseudo-preachers' campaigns for alms stemmed from their allegedly perverse appropriation of what divinely-inspired preachers were also doing.[26] As the frequent invocations of biblically based promises of sin-remission suggest, pithy scriptural maxims were an important part of the preacher's repertoire of persuasions to induce desired behaviours. Even more effective, however, were the short tales (*exempla*) designed for insertion in sermons for the purposes of moral instruction.[27] As the thirteenth-century author of one of the most important collections of *exempla* argued in his prologue, these stories were the most effective device for transforming human behaviour for the better, provoking both the learned and the simple to reject evil and to perform good works.[28] Constructed

[26] See also Bird, pp. 101, 107–8. A similar concern motivated some critics of indulgences and indulgence sellers. See R.N. Swanson, *Indulgences in Late Medieval England: Passports to Paradise?* (Cambridge: Cambridge University Press, 2007), esp. pp. 223, 278–9.

[27] See the succinct definition in Claude Brémond, Jacques Le Goff and Jean-Claude Schmitt, *L''Exemplum'* (Turnhout: Brepols, 1982), pp. 37–8: 'un récit bref donné comme véridique et destiné à être inséré dans un discours (en général dans un sermon) pour convaincre un auditoire par une leçon salutaire.'

[28] Stephen of Bourbon, *Tractatus de diversis materiis praedicabilibus, i: Prologus, prima pars. De dono timoris*, (eds) Jacques Berlioz and Jean-Luc Eichenlaub (Turnhout: Brepols, 2002). This idea was not new to Stephen, however; it echoes remarks found in Gregory the Great, *Homilia 39 in Evangelia*, in Jacques-Paul Migne (ed.), *Patrologia Latina* (Paris, 1854), 76.1300B.

and disseminated because of their presumed ability to move people to action, then, the many *exempla* dealing with almsgiving provide an invaluable window onto the motives that preachers tried both to cultivate and to manage in their efforts to persuade charitable giving.

Exempla dealing with almsgiving are not, of course, straightforward guides to how people (whether preachers or their audience) thought about charitable giving. The complicated nature of their production, transmission and reception raises many questions, several of which are likely unanswerable, about how faithfully they represent the attitudes of late medieval Christians. Accordingly, *exempla* texts must be mined for insight with caution. Yet the demands of responsible interpretive restraint should not overshadow their remarkable usefulness for uncovering how people thought about charitable obligations. *Exempla* (along with other genres of this period) were intended not only to reflect social realities but were also active in shaping those realities.[29] Attention to how moralists employed *exempla* both to condition and reflect the experience of charity can tell us a great deal about why particular motives were foregrounded in the work of religious exhortation. Moreover, *exempla* narratives are also especially revealing because their very existence depended on their capacity to appeal to widespread sensibilities, whether to the various preachers who included a specific *exemplum* in a sermon or to audiences who might hear the story and act upon the feelings it inspired. Those who collected and disseminated the *exempla* were themselves, in most cases, experienced preachers and administrators of pastoral care. These authors were often well positioned to judge which stories might be most effective. Nor were they merely passive transmitters of *exempla*; when stories and images show up in multiple collections, this is likely because they met the needs of preachers and their audiences. And the most successful *exempla* were determined as such precisely because they moved their hearers to actions that were (at least minimally) consistent with the aims preachers had for their audiences.[30]

The subject of almsgiving arises frequently in *exempla* collections and towards a variety of ends. Narratives on this topic that appear in thirteenth- and early fourteenth-century collections are a mixture of tales that derive from patristic-era texts like Gregory the Great's *Dialogues* or the *Vitae patrum*, and stories of more recent vintage (including some that are presented as the personal experience of the collector himself). The most influential collections for this task are the many *exempla* culled from the sermons of Jacques de Vitry, those found in the Cistercian monk Caesarius of Heisterbach's *Dialogus miraculorum* and the available

---

[29] See Gabrielle M. Spiegel, 'History, Historicism, and the Social Logic of the Text in the Middle Ages', *Speculum*, 65 (1990), 59–86 (p. 77).

[30] Admittedly, *exempla* collections contained more stories than would have been preached. See Peter von Moos, 'L'*Exemplum* et les *Exempla* des Prêcheurs', in Jacques Berlioz and Marie Anne Polo de Beaulieu (eds), *Les 'Exempla' médiévaux: Nouvelles perspectives* (Paris: H. Champion, 1998), pp. 67–81. However, the repetition of certain stories in multiple collections certainly suggests their widespread usage.

fragments of his *Libri viii miraculorum*, the *Tractatus de diversis materiis praedicabilibus* compiled by the Dominican friar Stephen of Bourbon and the *Scala coeli* of the Dominican Jean Gobi. Other useful resources include (but are not limited to) the *Liber exemplorum ad usum praedicantium* by an anonymous Irish Franciscan and the Dominican Thomas of Cantimpré's *Bonum universale de apibus*.[31] Several key themes emerge from these *exempla*, highlighting some of the more prominent motivations for charitable giving that likely resonated with prospective thirteenth- and early fourteenth-century donors.

As might be expected, the promise of salvation through almsgiving arises frequently in *exempla* on the subject. Perhaps reflecting the expansion of potential donors, the promise of salvation through almsgiving (with the corollary expectation of giving) is even extended to paupers themselves. For instance, Caesarius of Heisterbach's *Libri viii miraculorum* includes the story of one migrant labourer who relied upon alms to supplement the income he received from his occasional employment. Because of his great love for the Virgin Mary, Caesarius tells us, this man generously passed on much of the alms he received to other paupers. Consequently, at the moment of his death, he was successfully able to petition Mary for assistance, with all those who were nearby having heard her voice promising that he would enjoy paradisiacal rest.[32] This particular story also circulated in other venues, with a truncated version appearing in the *exempla* collection of the anonymous Irish Franciscan. Attesting to the story's evident popularity, this friar reports having found the tale in the book of another nameless Franciscan who claimed to have heard it from the Dominican Simon of Hinton, prior of his order's English province from 1254 to 1261.[33]

Such was the strength of the relationship perceived between alms and salvation that it also drove some more startling narratives. One that appeared in several collections from this period is an older *exemplum* from the life of the seventh-century saint John the Almoner. This story concerns a certain wealthy toll collector named Peter, renowned for never giving alms until, exasperated at a particularly importunate beggar, he threw a loaf of bread at the pauper because he did not have a stone at hand (not all versions include this last detail). When Peter later grew ill to the point of death, he experienced a vision wherein he was brought to judgement. Despite his many wicked works, he was saved only on account

---

[31]   Frederic C. Tubach, *Index Exemplorum: A Handbook of Medieval Religious Tales* (Helsinki: Suomalainen Tiedeakatemia, 1969). Although Tubach's *Index* is merely preliminary, it is an invaluable resource for locating many of the *exempla* on this subject.

[32]   Aloys Meister (ed.), *Die Fragmente der Libri VIII miraculorum des Caesarius von Heisterbach* (Rome: Spithöver, 1901), 3.1, p. 185.

[33]   A.G. Little (ed.), *Liber exemplorum ad usum praedicantium, saeculo xiii compositus a quodam fratre minore anglico de provincio Hiberniae* (Aberdeen: Aberdeen University Press, 1908), 1.53, p. 32. On Simon of Hinton, see Simon Tugwell, 'Hinton, Simon of (fl. *c.* 1248–1262)', *Oxford Dictionary of National Biography* (Oxford: Oxford University Press, 2004), online edition at <http://www.oxforddnb.com>.

of having (admittedly ungraciously) made that painful offering. Promising to mend his ways, Peter arose with renewed health and subsequently offered alms cheerfully and frequently.[34] There is little reason, of course, to point to such stories as evidence for a medieval audience's rather naive credulity and assume that they took every element of these narratives as reflecting a literal truth.[35] While some may have believed in the overwhelming efficacy of a single act of charity, others would surely have recognised it as a mere device. This latter perspective was certainly the intention. Indeed, the version recorded by the anonymous Irish Franciscan concludes with a lengthy disquisition explaining that no one should believe that Peter's single act was sufficient to counteract his many wicked deeds. Instead, he explains, the Lord was showing to Peter that by leading a life of charitable giving he would eventually accumulate enough good works to outweigh his evil ones (as, the friar further points out, the hagiographical narrative makes self-evident). The story's narrative traction and its evident popularity therefore derived from a conviction that it conveyed a more general truth: alms were useful for salvation. Without the context of salvation seeking as a motive for charitable giving, the story could hardly have resonated in a way that led to its extensive distribution.

The salvific value of almsgiving was not restricted to the donor's own soul. Charitable giving was, in fact, one of many suffrages offered for the souls of one's dead relatives and friends. Caesarius of Heisterbach's *Dialogus miraculorum* provides an account of a man who was visited by a recently deceased friend. When he asked his friend whether prayers or alms would be more useful for his soul, the reply came back 'Alms, alms, for prayers are tepid'.[36] As in the case with Peter the toll-collector, post-mortem alms could also benefit those who had lived rather less pious lives. The Dominican Jean Gobi includes a tale that he attributes to Jacques de Vitry about an avaricious bishop who had spent his life enriching the powerful nobles of his diocese at the expense of the poor. Appearing to a priest after his death, he recounted that he would remain in purgatorial torments until sufficient alms had been paid on his behalf. The priest conveyed the request to the late bishop's parents and managed to gather just enough in alms to secure his release.[37] In cases like this, alms seem to have been given more with the soul of one's family or friends in mind than the material improvement of the paupers who might benefit from

---

[34]   For references to several versions of this *exemplum*, see Tubach, *Index exemplorum*, #181.

[35]   See Susan Reynolds, 'Social Mentalities and the Cases of Medieval Scepticism', *Transactions of the Royal Historical Society*, 6th ser., 1 (1991), 21–41 (p. 30).

[36]   Caesarius of Heisterbach, *Dialogus miraculorum*, (ed.) J. Strange, 2 vols (Cologne: J.M. Heberle, 1851), 12.32, ii, 342. The narrator of the *Dialogus* does go on to claim, however, that masses are a superior suffrage to both.

[37]   Jean Gobi, *Scala coeli*, no. 487, p. 367. As Polo de Beaulieu's editorial apparatus indicates, this *exemplum* is among a group whose attribution to Jacques de Vitry is dubious. On these so-called *exempla extravagantia*, see Thomas Frederick Crane (ed.), *The Exempla, or Illustrative Stories from the Sermones vulgares of Jacques de Vitry* (London: Folklore Society, 1890), pp. l–li.

their receipt. Yet a strict dichotomy between the two motives did not necessarily prevail. Certainly, some Christians gave alms half-heartedly, as is implied by the late twelfth-century theologian Peter the Chanter's complaint that many of his contemporaries gave alms only grudgingly and would rather fast for three days instead.[38] But underlying Peter's remarks is the acknowledgement of a range of multiple suffrages that were available. The Dominican Thomas of Cantimpré, for instance, listed seven effective suffrages in his *Bonum universale de apibus*: tears, prayers, fasting, vigils and corporal affliction, almsgiving, restitution of debts and masses.[39] Others could add to Thomas's list the acts of pilgrimage, crusade, and even mere devotion to the faith.[40] Although alms were generally perceived as one of the more powerful suffrages, Christians of the thirteenth and fourteenth century nevertheless had a range of options to choose from. The decision to give alms often involved a deliberate decision to prefer poor relief to other kinds of suffrages. In any case, alms given without charity were generally viewed as worthless, as Caesarius of Heisterbach's haunting tale of a deceased Bavarian ministerial's visit to his wife articulates. Because he had given alms vaingloriously, the man had been consigned to eternal and inexpressible torment.[41]

Several other important features of medieval views on almsgiving also appear in *exempla* disseminated in this period, such as the importance of discriminate giving and the identification of the poor with Christ.[42] Jean Gobi, for example, incorporated both concepts in a story derived from Gregory the Great about a devout provost who shows several kindnesses to a pauper covered in filth. In the course of washing the man before bringing him to a meal, the provost notices that the pauper's feet and hands bear the wounds of the cross. When the provost attempts to gather his friends, however, the divine redeemer vanishes, leaving behind only a written note warning about the great curse that comes upon those who serve the vanities of the world by giving their food and money to actors rather than the poor.[43] Stories focused on these aspects of giving extended the promise

---

[38]   Peter the Chanter, *Summa de sacramentis et animae consiliis*, (ed.) Jean-Albert Dugauquier, 5 vols (Louvain: Nauwelaerts, 1954), 3.19.257, IV, 263.

[39]   Thomas of Cantimpré, *Bonum universale de apibus* (Douai: B. Belleri, 1627), 2.53.15, p. 500.

[40]   See the list of twelve suffrages in Stephen of Bourbon, *Tractatus de diversis materiis praedicabilibus*, 1.5.7, p. 167.

[41]   Caesarius of Heisterbach, *Dialogus miraculorum*, 12.19, II, 329. It is notable that he is not among the souls in Purgatory as that is the only group for whom suffrages had value.

[42]   On discriminate giving, see Brian Tierney, 'The Decretists and the "Deserving Poor"', *Comparative Studies in Society and History*, 1 (1958–59), 360–73; Brian Tierney, *Medieval Poor Law: A Sketch of Canonical Theory and Its Application in England* (Berkeley: University of California Press, 1959), pp. 47–9, 53–62; and Wood, pp. 60–63. On the identification of the poor with Christ, with special reference to the well-known story about St Martin, see Mollat, pp. 23–4.

[43]   Jean Gobi, *Scala coeli*, no. 483, p. 366. The written note is not included in the recounting of this tale found in Gregory's homily. See Gregory the Great, *XL Homiliarum*

of an experience of charity that accorded the poor dignity while also expressing dissatisfaction with contemporary tendencies to allot one's charitable resources to social elements that medieval moralists found disreputable.

Religious motives for charitable giving, even if not always centred solely on the welfare of the poor themselves, were therefore a critical ingredient in the kinds of messages that preachers had at their disposal. Whether encouraging almsgiving as a responsibility that could also benefit one's own soul, or the souls of one's family and friends, thirteenth- and early fourteenth-century donors were encouraged to consider their responsibilities towards the poor from a perspective that also included otherworldly interests. Moreover, cheerfulness and kindness were the normative emotions pleasing to God that many of these moral tales urged upon audiences of prospective donors, supported by scriptural proof-texts declaring that 'God loveth a cheerful giver' (ii Corinthians 9. 7) and that givers should 'in every gift shew a cheerful countenance, and sanctify [their] tithes with joy'.[44] Yet these more conspicuously religious concerns are not the only reasons for giving alms found in these collections. Other motives were also a characteristic element of moralising about almsgiving during this period, including those that might appear at first glance to be more in line with avarice than religious charity.

According to the account in Matthew, after Jesus admonished a wealthy young man to sell his possessions, give to the poor and follow him, the apostle Peter inquired of Jesus what the apostles would receive for having abandoned everything. Jesus responded that 'everyone that hath left house, or brethren, or sisters, or father, or mother, or wife, or children, or lands for my name's sake, shall receive an hundredfold and possess everlasting life' (Matthew 19. 29).[45] The gospel account's lack of precision about the exact nature of this 'hundredfold' remuneration gave rise to multiple opinions over the centuries, with different views expressed on whether this referred to a literal repayment (with substantial interest!) of material goods or simply to spiritual benefits (whether in this life or the next).[46] Thirteenth- and early fourteenth-century *exempla* drew upon both the spiritual and temporal interpretations of the hundredfold promise. Among the more popular tales inspired by this passage is one that concerns a rich man who gives money to a bishop after hearing him invoke the promise in a sermon. Several varieties of this particular story exist (including one where the man is a Muslim convert to Christianity). Yet they all attest that after his death the man arranges for

---

in evangelia libri duo, 2.23, in Migne (ed.), *Patrologia Latina*, 76.1183.

[44] See, for instance, the many scriptural and patristic references gathered by the thirteenth-century Dominican William Peraldus in the section on 'how alms ought to be given' located in his *Summa de virtutibus et vitiis* (Venice: Paganinus de Paganinis, 1497), 1.8.7, fol. 327, col. a.

[45] Other biblical passages also discuss rewards in exchange for giving up material things, such as Malachi 3. 6–12 regarding the payment of tithes.

[46] I am currently preparing a more detailed study on the interpretive tradition of the hundredfold reward.

the bishop to learn that he has received eternal life and the hundredfold reward (in some cases this comes in response to a protest lodged by the late man's sons that the promised hundredfold was never received).[47] While most versions of this *exemplum* state that he received his payment in the next life, it is not altogether clear if it came in the form of temporal gain.

Other *exempla* discussed more clearly the possibility of temporal rewards. The Dominican Stephen of Bourbon provided prospective preachers perusing his treatise with two such cases. In the first, which Stephen claims to have heard in a sermon given by a theological master while he was a student at the University of Paris, a man offers a cow to his priest in response to hearing the hundredfold promise. But after considerable time elapses, and with no reward in sight, the man decides to murder the priest for having made such a seemingly worthless guarantee. In a shocking twist, the man receives his reward when he discovers a store of gold while on his way to exact his revenge upon the priest.[48] Stephen's second *exemplum* (which is a retelling of the jongleur Jean Bodel's fabliau *Brunain, la vache au prestre*[49]) relates the experience of a pauper who also made a bovine offering to a wealthy priest promising the hundredfold reward. That very night, the cow led all of the priest's own cows, along with enough other cows to number one hundred, back to the pauper's home. When the pauper was brought before the episcopal court to face accusations of theft, he successfully defended himself with the claim that this was merely the fulfilment of the priest's divinely inspired promise.[50] Evidently, the preaching of the hundredfold promise was an ordinary enough occurrence to serve as a plausible context for each of these narratives. Moreover, both *exempla* indicate that the specifically temporal interpretation of the hundredfold promise was not only deemed fit for public dissemination but that expectation of future temporal abundance was presented as a legitimate motive for giving alms.

Despite contemporary anxieties about avarice and proclamations of the praiseworthiness of voluntary poverty, then, the gospel of prosperity also found a hearing.[51] In fact, among the nine 'perfections' that Jean Gobi declared almsgiving

---

[47]   For more on the various versions of this story and its late antique origins, see Francis R. Swietek, 'The Alms Repaid a Hundredfold: A New Latin Version of a Popular *Exemplum*', *Fabula*, 17 (1976), 169–81.

[48]   A. Lecoy de La Marche (ed.), *Anecdotes historiques* (Paris: Librairie Renouard, H. Loones, 1876), 2.7.142, p. 121.

[49]   Pierre Nardin (ed.), *Jean Bodel, Fabliaux*, 2nd edn (Paris: Nizet, 1965), p. 97.

[50]   Lecoy de La Marche, 2.7.143, p. 122.

[51]   On some modern incarnations of this view of divine providence, see Milmon F. Harrison, *Righteous Riches: The Word of Faith Movements in Contemporary African-American Religion* (Oxford: Oxford University Press, 2005), esp. pp. 70–74, 95–101; Kate Bowler, *Blessed: A History of the American Prosperity Gospel* (Oxford, New York: Oxford University Press, 2013).

induces in us, an increase of temporal goods is listed first.[52] To this effect, Jean included several stories about divinely orchestrated compensation for alms given, including a version of the tale noted above about the deceased wealthy man's communication to his bishop of having received his hundredfold reward. The most entertaining of these is his retelling of a popular tale about a young Bordelais merchant and his would-be bride, a Sultan's daughter abducted from Alexandria by pirates and sold into slavery.[53] The story begins with details about the young man's mother. As he was her only son, she desired nothing more than for him to be wealthy. To help him towards that end, she arranged an apprenticeship with his merchant uncle. But while he was away visiting another city on business, he overheard in a sermon that the best path to wealth was not commerce but almsgiving (thereby rhetorically setting the two approaches in opposition). Instead of completing his business, the young man contributed his money as alms for the reconstruction of a local church dedicated to St Nicholas. On a later trip, he used his money to purchase the beautiful Alexandrian slave girl, to the horror and shame of his parents who believed that he had done this solely for immoral purposes. Instead, the girl was baptised and even stimulated him to greater piety. Although poor, they hoped to get married. Blessed with an unparalleled skill for crafting jewellery (*iocalia*), she devised a plan for them to obtain enough money to afford marriage. After multiple voyages to Alexandria and encounters with her father (who recognised that she alone could produce such wares), the young man was eventually caught, tortured and forced to give up her location, whereupon she was seized and brought back to her father while he was sent back to Bordeaux. Undeterred, he sought a return to Alexandria to reclaim his bride. Without any means of travel, he petitioned St Nicholas, who provided a ship because of the alms the youth had given previously for rebuilding his church. Once there, the young man managed to find the girl and they made off with considerable treasure back to Bordeaux. Upon their arrival, the ship disappeared and they were able to get married with the store of riches they had accumulated.

Perhaps more than any other, this *exemplum* is useful for highlighting the way that some medieval moralists positioned almsgiving as an alternative to commerce as a means for acquiring wealth. As James Davis has reported in his extensive survey of late medieval market morality, the didactic literature on this subject is virtually unanimous in its denunciation of moneymaking.[54] One of the most revealing details of this story, then, is the miraculous appearance and disappearance of the ship provided by the aid of St Nicholas, just one of many elements of similarly supernatural assistance that abound in these tales of enrichment. Whether through the behaviour of cows or through the mysterious

---

[52]   Jean Gobi, *Scala coeli*, no. 469, p. 360: 'Elemosina multas perfectiones inducit in nobis. Primo est bonorum temporalium multiplicativa.'

[53]   Jean Gobi, *Scala coeli*, no. 474, pp. 362–3.

[54]   Davis, pp. 34–136, but esp. pp. 52, 134. However, Davis does not consider anywhere the material regarding the hundredfold promise.

disappearance of alms beneficiaries and/or almsgivers' benefactors, supernatural elements are conspicuous in several *exempla* that include material rewards for alms or emphasise the temporal interpretation of the hundredfold promise.[55] By drawing attention to the miraculous, these narrative features highlight the contrast between the avaricious wealth acquisition by those dependent upon their own efforts and the worthy enrichment of the pious who receive their increase through divine means. This repeated deployment of a 'hyper-providential' view of the economy, where legitimate wealth remains subject to divine will and orchestration, paralleled and reacted to the increasingly naturalistic explanations of the causes of economic growth.[56] In fact, it is no surprise that several authors of these collections, including the Dominicans Stephen of Bourbon and Jean Gobi, spent much of their careers as pastoral specialists in the south of France where doubts about the virtue of almsgiving like those attributed to Bor of Tignac were feared to be common. Rather than merely trying to channel pervasive greed towards more laudable purposes, preachers who repeatedly promised temporal rewards for almsgiving were also engaging in a larger struggle against the broader social shifts they felt were undermining more traditional religious views about a grander design behind the existence and purpose of wealth and poverty.

Although they are not the only useful source on the subject, *exempla* help illuminate several important aspects of the experience of charitable giving during the thirteenth and early fourteenth centuries. Moralists tasked with encouraging this practice possessed a multifaceted repertoire designed to stress the religious responsibility to pay alms. They emphasised how the expansion of monetary means conferred upon even more people the responsibility to pay alms as a part of obtaining salvation, and highlighted the power of alms as a suffrage for those tormented in the increasingly well-defined Purgatory.[57] They promoted the identification of the poor with Christ and traded upon anxieties about the consequences of avarice by offering a morally licit way to achieve economic stability. In each of these cases, almsgiving was intimately tied to one's relationship with the divine. This was especially important in light of the way that social, economic and educational changes had provoked less providential ideas about the causes and consequences of poverty and wealth. For those who had ears to hear the moralists' messages, charitable giving was one way of remaining in, and reaping the rewards of, a world reassuringly regulated by divine design.

---

[55]   In addition to those listed already, see also Jean Gobi, *Scala coeli*, nos. 469, 471–2, pp. 360–61.

[56]   A similar interpretation regarding different hyper-providentialist reactions in England during the same period, and from where I have also borrowed this term, is in Carl Watkins, 'Providence, Experience and Doubt in Medieval England', in Yola Bataski, Subha Mukherji and Jan-Melissa Schramm (eds), *Fictions of Knowledge: Fact, Evidence, Doubt* (Houndmills: Palgrave Macmillan, 2012), pp. 40–60.

[57]   Jacques Le Goff, *The Birth of Purgatory*, (trans.) Arthur Goldhammer (Chicago: University of Chicago Press, 1984); Wei, pp. 185–220.

Chapter 5

A Market for Charitable Performances? Bequests to the Poor and their Recipients in Fifteenth-Century Norwich Wills

Philippa Maddern

Among the means by which charity was disbursed in late medieval England the wills of the wealthier sectors of the population are generally acknowledged to be important.[1] Though as J.A.F. Thomson pointed out as long ago as 1965, it is impossible to calculate exactly the value of charitable bequests (due to the testators' habits of leaving gifts in kind rather than cash, making imprecise provisions for the residue of their estates, and leaving flat-rate bequests to an unspecified number of poor people), the scale of giving is often assessed as generous.[2] Furthermore, testamentary charity is often taken to be identical to practical help for the poor. Heath goes so far as to state that in late medieval Hull, '[I]f we measure the priorities of our testators by the consistency of certain bequests, then the poor must have stood very near the top of the list'.[3] Miri Rubin identifies funerals as 'the times when the poor were treated with greatest liberality and honour' (as determined by the will of the deceased).[4] Cullum and Goldberg found that approximately a quarter of 2,286 lay York wills of the fourteenth and fifteenth centuries included specifically charitable bequests.[5] Thomson found a smaller, but still solid, proportion of London testators supporting their local hospitals – 23.4 per cent of wills in the period 1401–49, and 17.8 per cent in the period 1479–86, and noted that 'Bequests in general terms to the poor are extremely common.'[6] Wills often specified that any residue after all debts and bequests were settled should

---

[1]   See, for example, Miri Rubin, *Charity and Community*.

[2]   J.A.F. Thomson, 'Piety and Charity in Late Medieval London', *Journal of Ecclesiastical History*, 16.2 (1965), 178–95 (p. 180).

[3]   Peter Heath, 'Urban Piety in the Later Middle Ages: The Evidence of Hull Wills', in R.B. Dobson (ed.), *The Church, Politics and Patronage in the Fifteenth Century* (Gloucester: Sutton, 1984), p. 224.

[4]   Rubin, p. 260.

[5]   P.H. Cullum and P.J.P. Goldberg, 'Charitable Provision in Late Medieval York: "To the Praise of God and the Use of the Poor"', *Northern History*, 29 (1993), 24–39 (p. 24).

[6]   Thomson, pp. 183, 187.

be expended in works of charity and piety for the good of the testator's soul,[7] and Clive Burgess's research on late medieval Bristol suggests that these bequests were no mere matter of form; a widow might dispense charity from her husband's estate for years after his death.[8] Though Anne Warren expresses doubts about the scale of charitable giving, hers is perhaps a minority view.[9] Tanner concludes that 'charitable bequests were a prominent and regular feature of wills in Norwich ... from as early as wills survive in large numbers'.[10]

The impression that large sums of money were transferred from the wealthier classes to the poor via wills is strengthened by frequent reference to undeniably lavish donations. William Setman (1429) and John Terry (1524), both wealthy merchants of Norwich, are cases in point. Setman bequeathed the rents from two houses, plus approximately £90 from a total of £350 money bequests to various charitable uses, including a distribution of £20 immediately after his death to 'the most needy poor people' in Norwich and the surrounding villages, and a further £40 to be given to 'the poor, and especially the lame, blind or seriously ill' living continuously in Norwich for the three years after his death. John Terry, even more exceptionally, left over half the total of his cash legacies – about £868 plus money from the sale of houses, tenements and lands, out of a total of £1,300 – in charitable bequests.[11]

This scale of charity seems even more impressive in view of the fact that it may have been exceeded by *in vivo* donations. Testators were frequently urged to give alms while still living, on the grounds that the benefits of gifts made in life far outweighed belated testamentary attempts to atone for a lifetime's niggardliness. The author of the late fourteenth-century *Book of Vices and Virtues*, for example, sarcastically assessed deathbed bequests as about as useful to the donor's soul as a lamp carried behind, rather than before, a traveller on a dark road.[12] In the dialogue *Dives and Pauper*, Dives naively suggests that 'alle men myztyn ben holpyn with her rychesse aftir hyr death', to which Pauper bluntly replies 'It is nout so, but only [th]ey schul ben holpyn with her goodis aftyr her deth [th]at deseruedyn be her

---

[7]   Norman P. Tanner, *The Church in Late Medieval Norwich 1370–1532* (Toronto: Pontifical Institute of Mediaeval Studies, 1984), p. 135.

[8]   Clive Burgess, 'Late Medieval Wills and Pious Convention: Testamentary Evidence Reconsidered', in Michael A. Hicks (ed.), *Profit, Piety and the Professions in Later Medieval England* (Stroud: Sutton, 1990), pp. 20–21; and Clive Burgess, '"By Quick and by Dead": Wills and Pious Provision in Late Medieval Bristol', *English Historical Review*, 102 (1987), 837–58 (esp. pp. 841–5).

[9]   Anne K. Warren, *Anchorites and their Patrons in Medieval England* (Berkeley: University of California Press, 1985), pp. 207–8, 228, quoted in Anne M. Scott, *'Piers Plowman' and the Poor* (Dublin: Four Courts Press, 2004), pp. 130–31.

[10]   Tanner, p. 135.

[11]   Tanner, pp. 241, 243, 245–6.

[12]   W.N. Francis (ed.), *The Book of Vices and Virtues: A Fourteenth-Century English Translation of the Somme le Roi of Lorens d'Orleans*, EETS o.s. 217 (Oxford: Oxford University Press, 1942), p. 215.

lyue ... as [th]ey [th]at don elmesse aftir her stat'.[13] The solid proportion of testators who did leave charitable bequests may, then, have regarded testamentary charity as the culmination of a lifetime of giving those 'almes' which, according to other devotional writings were 'a princepal thyng / [Th]at plecyt ihesu heuene kyng.'[14]

It is, of course, generally accepted that testamentary charity combined self-interest with benevolence in what Burgess neatly terms 'self-interested altruism'.[15] Thomson confidently asserts that 'Behind all giving in the Middle Ages lay one basic motive, the good of the donor's soul'.[16] Yet the comment of the York clerk John de Roucliff, in his will of 1384, that his bequest to 50 poor people was made 'to the praise of God and the use of the poor', suggests that saving one's soul and helping the poor seemed less easily distinguishable to late medieval testators than it might to us.[17] The prayers of the poor, beloved of God, were particularly efficacious at speeding souls through Purgatory; no doubt those will-makers who urged their executors to distribute the residue of their goods in 'dedys of pyte and mercy to the moost pleasur of god and profite of my sowle and of the sowles of our frendys and all Cristen sowles' knew it.[18] Alms cancelled sin as effectively 'as water quenchyt fyr', wrote the late fourteenth-century author of a poem on the works of mercy.[19] The whole transaction could thus be represented even by religious,

---

[13]   Priscilla Heath Barnum (ed.), *Dives and Pauper*, EETS o.s. 275, 280, 2 parts (Oxford, 1976 and 1980), part 2, p. 265; cf. Cullum and Goldberg, p. 25: 'deathbed charity was considered to be of little value'.

[14]   From a late fourteenth-century didactic poem on the works of mercy. See W.L. Braekman, 'A Middle English Didactic Poem on the Works of Mercy', *Neuphilologische Mitteilungen: Bulletin of the Modern Language Society of Helsinki*, 79 (1978), 145–51 (p. 148).

[15]   Clive Burgess, '"An Afterlife in Memory": Commemoration and its Effects in a Late-Medieval Parish', in Peter Clarke and Tony Claydon (eds), *The Church, The Afterlife and The Fate of the Soul* (Woodbridge: Boydell/Ecclesiastical History Society, 2009), p. 203.

[16]   Thomson, p. 194.

[17]   Quoted in Cullum and Goldberg, p. 24: 'ad laudem dei et utilitatem pauperum'; see also Heath, p. 225: John Osay of Hull, whose will of 1429 specified that his gifts of £30 to the prisoners, poor, blind and lame were 'for my soul and the souls of all my benefactors'; and Scott, *'Piers Plowman'*, p. 128.

[18]   TNA, PROB 11/8/147, Will of Alice Cooke of Norwich (24 August 1487). The phrase translates the standard Latin 'melius deo complacere & animae mee prodesse'; see, for example, NRO, NCC Surflete, fol. 32r, will of John att Hagh (made 1428). See also Scott, *'Piers Plowman'*, pp. 45, 126; Christopher Dyer, *Standards of Living in the Later Middle Ages: Social Change in England c. 1200–1520* (Cambridge: Cambridge University Press, 1989), pp. 235–6; Carole Rawcliffe, *Medicine for the Soul: The Life, Death and Resurrection of an English Medieval Hospital: St. Giles's, Norwich, c. 1249–1550* (Stroud: Sutton, 1999), pp. 4–6. As Rawcliffe points out, the notion had a long history: Herbert de Losinga, first bishop of Norwich (d. 1119), preached that 'the Church's poor are themselves among the saints ... make them your friends'.

[19]   Braekman, p. 147.

with no apparent sense of incongruity, as prosaically fiscal. Cardinal Beaufort, the highest-ranking cleric in England when he made his will in 1446–47, expressed his charitable and pious bequests as a kind of spiritual currency exchange, acting 'to commute my worldly goods into heavenly ones'.[20] To testators, therefore, the outcome of testamentary charity was a win all round – the poor were relieved and the wealthy saved in one transaction.

But was deathbed charity actually intended to provide poor relief? And did it succeed in doing so? Who among the poor (if any) did it benefit and how?

The first indication that charity and poor relief were not co-terminous in the minds of testators comes from the fact that the language of fifteenth-century wills, and the patterns of bequests in them, strongly suggest that 'pious uses' and 'deeds of alms' were so closely connected as to be almost a single category, or at least highly interchangeable. Burgess found that among Bristol testators, contributing to the liturgical furnishing, decoration or repair of one's parish church, or establishing temporary or permanent chantries, rendered the donor a charitable 'benefactor' (literally a 'good doer') of the church, for whose soul prayers were owed.[21] One could, therefore, exercise charity without necessarily giving anything to the poor; though typically the generous donor would give both to their parish church and neighbouring religious houses, and to selected groups of poor people. Ann Warren found that will-makers who were generous to anchorites also tended to give more largely to other groups of poor people. Voluntary poverty – for instance, that of anchorites or mendicant friars – was viewed by testators as just as deserving an object of charity as involuntary need, if not more so.[22] The 1429 will of Thomas Cok of St Stephen's parish Norwich illustrates the point. Cok left donations to the high altar of St Stephen's and the upkeep of its fabric; to its parish priests and clerk; to the four orders of friars in Norwich; to seven priests to celebrate for his soul for a year; to the sisters of Norman's hospital; and to prisoners and the sick in the various city leper-houses.[23] His charitable giving thus comprised a great range of beneficiaries, both lay and religious, poor and relatively prosperous. Bequests to the poor, then, must be seen as only a part of charitable provisions of wills, and often not the main part. For Norwich, Tanner's study of late medieval wills shows that more testators gave to parish churches than to anything else, generally in money to the high altar and church upkeep. He calculates that 85 per cent of the clergy and 95 per cent of the laity left bequests to their church, as opposed to just less than 40 per cent of testators who left money to at least some of the five sick-houses at the city gates.[24] The proportion of testators leaving bequests to the sick

---

[20]   G.L. Harriss, *Cardinal Beaufort: A Study in Lancastrian Ascendancy and Decline* (Oxford: Clarendon Press, 1988), pp. 378–80 (quote from p. 378, n. 8): 'bona terrestria mea in celestia commutare.'

[21]   Burgess, '"An Afterlife in Memory"', pp. 203–29.

[22]   Scott, *'Piers Plowman'*, pp. 130–31, citing Warren.

[23]   NRO, NCC Surflete, fols 42v–43r, (proved 20 July 1429).

[24]   Tanner, pp. 126, 133–4.

poor was also outstripped by those patronising local houses of friars – 'Each of the four friaries in Norwich received bequests from between 44 and 47 per cent of both lay and clerical testators between 1370 and 1532.' Amounts of money given to the sick and/or poor were often less than those donated to religious institutions or individuals. Tanner found that the four Norwich friaries each usually received between 3s. 4d. and £1 in bequests 'though a fair number of testators left several pounds'; whereas bequests to the leper houses usually ranged only between 6d. and 1s. 8d. per house, or 1d. to 4d. per inmate.[25] The differential pertained within individual wills. The value of Thomas Cok's testamentary bequests to hospital sisters, the sick and the imprisoned amounted to only 13.3 per cent of the value of his total charitable bequests (including those to his parish church and religious institutions).[26]

Furthermore, closer scrutiny of bequests apparently directed towards the involuntarily needy rather than to religious institutions suggests that even in these cases, the possible aim – and certain function – of charity was less to provide adequate relief to the genuinely poor, than to construct a series of ostentatiously charitable performances on the parts of both donors and recipients.

How can we deduce this? Admittedly the chances of discovering actual testimony from the beneficiaries as to their experience of testamentary doles are vanishingly small. But a finegrain analysis of a sample of bequests to the poor allows us to uncover, in more detail, who were the 'poor' who commonly received deathbed charity, and who was excluded; what patterns of behaviour potential beneficiaries had to adopt; and by how much individual paupers could benefit. The plentiful wills recorded for probate in the Norwich Consistory Court from 1377 comprise an excellent source, allowing us to track, roughly if not with pinpoint accuracy, broad trends of testamentary alms to the poor by Norwich donors. Furthermore, the various institutions for the care of the poor in late medieval Norwich have been well-studied, so that we have some contextual knowledge of the bequests made. So numerous are the wills that for this paper I have taken only a sample; those wills whose authors lived in Norwich, which included specific bequests to the poor, and which were *proved* (not merely made) in the years 1417–19 and 1427–29 and, for later comparison, 1487–89 and 1497–99. In all, this sample comprises 75 wills and 222 individual bequests.

The range of poor people who could have been the objects of these testators' charity was extremely large. Even if we exclude the well-understood contemporary

---

[25]   Tanner, pp. 119, 133. Bequests to leper houses in Norwich wills in the twelve years I have studied range between 2d. and 6s. 8d. per house.

[26]   NRO, NCC Surflete, fols 42v–43r; cf. also NRO, NCC Hyrning, fols 49v–50r, the will of Joan Eton (proved 1419), in which bequests to the sick, poor and prisoners comprised only 14.9 per cent of all charitable donations, including those to her parish, Norwich cathedral and the four Norwich friaries.

category of the undeserving poor (those too idle to work for their living),[27] the numbers must have been great. McIntosh stresses the predominance of what she acutely terms 'life-cycle poverty'; the phenomenon whereby, in a society in which large numbers of people depended on daily labour to earn a living, yet which had few formal safety nets against illness, incapacity or natural disaster, those too young, old, ill, injured or generally incapacitated to undertake constant heavy work could easily fall, either temporarily or in the long-term, into indigence. At worst these unfortunates died from the combined effects of homelessness, illness and starvation.[28] The plight of John Osbarn, 'old and decrepit' and epileptic, who died in a ditch on the road from Barnet to St Albans as he was 'going begging' in 1415 may not have been uncommon.[29] Unsurprisingly, sufferers from this type of poverty were often explicitly targeted for charity; the ordinances of one late medieval Essex almshouse specified the 'lame, crooked, blind and bed-ridden' as their primary clients.[30] Yet some particular circumstances conducing to life-cycle poverty seem to have gone almost unremarked, by either contemporaries or historians. McIntosh, for instance, notes the problems of widows and young orphans, but ignores the difficulties of young women who bore children outside matrimony. Yet single mothers from poor families 1350–1500 were apparently expected to live and support their children on maintenance payments averaging a near-starvation rate of no more than 3d. a week.[31]

McIntosh, too, is inclined to believe that between at least 1350 and 1465 in England, 'poverty was relatively mild'. Those able to work were unlikely to face real need, because prevailing economic and demographic conditions produced (comparatively) high wages, low prices and plentiful employment. The labouring classes were thus more able both to support themselves, and to help those of their number suffering episodes of life-cycle poverty. In her view, it was not until the later sixteenth century that people willing to work were commonly 'unable to find employment' or could not earn enough to support their families.[32] This, however, may not be entirely true. Granted, in post-Black Death England the

---

[27]   See, for example, Marjorie K. McIntosh, *Poor Relief in England*, p. 41; Margaret Aston, '"Caim's Castles": Poverty, Politics and Disendowment', in Dobson (ed.), *The Church, Politics and Patronage*, pp. 45–67.

[28]   Marjorie K. McIntosh, 'Local Responses to the Poor in Late Medieval and Tudor England', *Continuity and Change*, 3 (1988), 209–45 (pp. 210–11); cf. her *Poor Relief in England*, pp. 5, 71–2.

[29]   TNA, JUST2/101, fol. 1r, Coroners' Inquisition, 24 July 1415 on Osbarn's body. The jury swore that Osbarn was 'senex & decrepidus transiens mendicando' when he suffered an epileptic fit and drowned in the roadside ditch.

[30]   Dyer, *Standards of Living*, p. 243 (almshouse of Saffron Walden).

[31]   Philippa Maddern, '"Oppressed by Utter Poverty": Survival Strategies for Single Mothers and their Children in Late Medieval England', in Scott (ed.), *Experiences of Poverty*, pp. 41–62 (esp. pp. 53–6).

[32]   McIntosh, *Poor Relief in England*, pp. 6, 15; and McIntosh, 'Local Responses', pp. 210–11, 213–14 (quote from p. 211).

wages of skilled urban workmen such as building craftsmen generally improved. In the two decades 1481–1500, for instance, a thatcher could earn up to 6d per day, and a thatcher's mate, 3.25d. to 3.5d. The buying power of wages also increased in this period.[33] But not all plebeians could count on such comfortable earnings. Relatively well-paid work, such as harvesting, was seasonal.[34] Lawrence Poos found the daily wage labour market in late medieval Essex to be 'highly episodic and discontinuous'; at some periods 1376–1450 some manors hired unskilled labourers, on average, for as little as 3.8 days *a year*.[35] Rural labourers were often perforce mobile, ranging over distances of up to twenty miles to find day-work.[36] Some desperate wage-seekers surely ventured into towns; indeed, the arrival in urban centres of itinerant job-seekers was apparently a well-known phenomenon in the late fourteenth and early fifteenth centuries, as London references to suspect 'travelling' men suggest.[37] Women and young boys were always paid less than men,[38] and since not all higher-paid jobs were available to women, by the late Middle Ages many undertook low-paid intermittent employment such as ale-selling, huckstering, or laundry work. I suspect, therefore, that from 1350 onwards there was always a group of individuals and families in England who, however willing and able to work, could not count on sufficient earnings to sustain them through periods of un- or under-employment.

Besides these categories, contemporaries undoubtedly (though perhaps incorrectly) distinguished a different group of poor people; those able, but unwilling to work. As early as the late fourteenth century the reprehensible figure of the 'sturdy beggar' emerged in lay English writings. Unsurprisingly, orthodox opinion held that these figures deserved no charity. Following the flurry of legislation designed to keep labourers labouring after the first outbreak of the Black Death, the Cambridge parliament of 1388 specifically ordered that able-

---

[33] Dyer, *Standards of Living*, pp. 214–17.

[34] Cf. TNA, C1/214/66, the case of John Matthew of Winchelsea, a 'maryner' who, in the 1490s, apparently regularly travelled to Great Yarmouth, staying for five weeks 'in the tyme of fisshyng vpon that coost'.

[35] L.R. Poos, *A Rural Society after the Black Death: Essex 1350–1525* (Cambridge: Cambridge University Press, 1991), p. 212 and table p. 212, n. 15. The highest average number of labourer-days hired a year was 39.8.

[36] Poos, *A Rural Society*, pp. 215–16.

[37] A.H. Thomas (ed.), *Calendar of Select Pleas and Memoranda of the City of London, A.D. 1381–1412* (Cambridge: University Press, 1932), pp. 78–9: a 1384 order to innkeepers to receive no wayfarers without surety of their good conduct; and A.H. Thomas (ed.), *Calendar of Pleas and Memoranda Rolls Preserved among the Archives of the Corporation of the City of London, A.D. 1413–1437* (Cambridge: University Press, 1933), p. 33: return on indictment of John Spence of Little Torrington, Devon (1415).

[38] Sandy Bardsley, 'Women's Work Reconsidered: Gender and Wage Differentiation in Late Medieval England', *Past & Present*, 165 (1999), 3–29; John Hatcher, 'Women's Work Reconsidered: Gender and Wage Differentiation in Late Medieval England', *Past & Present*, 173 (2001), 191–8.

bodied beggars were to be kept in their place of work and forbidden any alms. Only the impotent were to be relieved, and even they should be prevented from wandering about asking for charity.[39]

Which, therefore, of the groups of the 'poor' were Norwich testators willing to support? Those suffering from life-cycle or family-circumstance poverty? Those fallen into comparative poverty from a position of relative wealth? Those battling to make an uncertain wage cover ordinary expenditure on food, clothes or fuel?

The first glaringly obvious feature of the Norwich wills is that to attract charity, it was rarely enough just to be struggling to make unreliable wages cover unrelenting living expenses. Especially later in the century, testators did leave money and resources – sometimes on a generous scale – simply to 'the poor' or to sub-groups of them, such as those in the testator's parish, without further specification or strings attached. Robert Brythtled made his will in December 1486 leaving 10 marks (£6 13s. 4d.) 'to the poor'.[40] William Setman's generous donations have already been described.[41] Sometimes equal largesse was distributed in bread rather than money. In 1499 William Smyth, pinner, specified his wishes exactly:

> Item I wull that euery pore hushold in thys paryche [St John Berstrete] and the
> paryche of all seyntis that wull take almes at my beryeng day or whan I am kept
> for haue a penyworth of Bred and euery household that wull tak almes in the
> por parysshes next adyoynyng haue a ferthyn bred or an halpeny bred by the
> dyscrecon of myn executoris vn to xx schyllyngworthe bred be so expendyd.[42]

It is worth noting that if this dole were shared equally between the two named parishes and their adjoining districts, it might have reached up to 120 households in St John's Berstrete and All Saints alone; and (in the form of farthing bread) up to 480 households in the neighbouring parishes. Its range was thus potentially very wide, though each household would receive only one comparatively small allowance. Similarly, Bishop James Goldwell, presumably mindful of the particular duty of bishops to give alms, was one of the most generous of such donors, leaving a hundred quarters of wheat to be baked into bread 'to be distributed to the poor'.[43]

---

[39] Aston, p. 57; McIntosh, *Poor Relief in England*, pp. 5–6, 41; though as she rightly points out (p. 43), there is little sign in the statutory evidence that these anxieties persisted at the same levels throughout the fifteenth century.

[40] NRO, NCC A. Caston, fol. 304r, leaving ten marks or £6 13s. 4d. to the poor ('pauperibus'); cf. NRO, NCC Multon, fol. 72, will of Edward Howse, of St Mary, Coslany (made 21 May 1497, probate 11 January 1498), leaving 3s. 4d. to be distributed 'pro anima mea' to the 'pauperibus' of that parish.

[41] See above, n. 11.

[42] NRO, NCC Wight, fols 22v–23r, written 16 Oct 1499, proved 11 November 1499.

[43] TNA, PROB 11/11/750: 'ad distribuend. pauperibus'; on bishops' alms generally, see Dyer, *Standards of Living*, p. 241.

But these types of bequest were exceedingly rare. Norwich donors strongly preferred other types of charity to other sorts of 'poor' people, as the following table shows:

Table 5.1   Proportions of bequests to varying groups of 'the poor' in Norwich, 1417–19, 1427–29, 1487–89 and 1497–99, in order of preference.

Type of bequest	Percentage of total bequests (Number = 222)
To St Giles or Norman's hospitals, or to the brothers/sisters of the hospitals	33.3%
To leper houses/'sick houses' or to individual lepers/sick people	28.4%
To prisoners in the Castle or Gildhall	14.0%
Specifically to inmates lying sick in hospital	8.1%
To 'the poor', with no further specification or obligation	7.7%
To 'the poor' specifically enjoined to attend funeral and/or pray for the soul of the testator	3.2%
To sick/disabled people not in hospitals	3.2%
Other bequests (e.g. to individuals)	2.3%

* Note: Figures have been rounded to one decimal place, resulting in a slight discrepancy in the total

Of 222 individual legacies, only seventeen – 7.7 per cent – specified poverty alone as the qualification for the bequest, and demanded no compensatory action on the part of the recipients. These donations were not evenly spread throughout the century. There were no such gifts in the period 1417–19, and only four in the years 1427–29. It follows that from the viewpoint of possible recipients, at best these doles comprised as Tanner remarks, 'small and occasional wind-falls' rather than substantial relief.[44] In some years, even later in the century, no one benefited. Sometimes the donation would be restricted to a single district. The only such bequest in 1427, from the will of Elizabeth Wylbey, directed that 20s should be distributed among a fortunate minority – 'the poor' of Conesford, Berstrete and their neighbouring districts.[45]

---

[44]   Tanner, p. 110.

[45]   NRO, NCC Hyrnyng, fol. 153, (made 1 February 1427, proved 13 March 1427). It should be noted that testators tended to favour their own parish or immediate neighbourhood in relation to all sorts of bequests. Tanner (pp. 123, 127) found that only 13 per cent of the laity and 17 per cent of the clergy gave to religious houses outside Norwich, and that,

Although the amounts given were sometimes impressive, the need was so great that these doles were often either spread extremely thinly among the possible recipients, or restricted to a lucky few. Bishop Goldwell's bequest of wheat to make bread for the poor is instructive. Goldwell directed that exactly 26 loaves should be made from each quarter of wheat, presumably one loaf for each person. Since the whole quantity was to be distributed over four dates, starting with the day of his burial, in lots of 20 and 30 quarters, the number of recipients was potentially extremely large – up to 780 on any one day. Clearly Goldwell was confident that his executors would easily find nearly 800 poor people at a time in late medieval Norwich; but equally worrying is the reflection that no recipient would benefit by more than one day's fairly scanty meals, though the quality of bread they received would almost certainly be far better than they could normally purchase.[46] A similar estimate of the number in need in Norwich at the end of the fifteenth century derives from the will of Roger Banestyr, who left a penny each to 'the prysoners blynde lame & bedrede in [th]e seid Cyte ... as fer as iiij marc wull stretche' – that is to at least 640 recipients.[47] In some cases, the benefit was even less than a penny in money or bread. The 'ferthyn bred' (farthing loaf) distributed to the poor of adjoining parishes at William Smith's funeral in 1499 probably constituted hardly more than a token snack.[48] The practice of giving a small amount to a large number of the poor may well have been common throughout late medieval England; Burgess notes that at obits (anniversary memorial services) in All Saints, Bristol, as much as half the total expenditure on the service might be spent on penny doles or loaves to a crowd of paupers.[49]

In contrast William Setman's carefully thought-out provision of 3d. a week to the most needy poor over three years would at least, in years of low bread prices, have enabled the recipients to buy sufficient bread to sustain life.[50] But £40 at the rate of 3d. per week would stretch to only twenty people over the three years. These beneficiaries cannot have represented so much as a tithe of the indigent population, even if conditions in 1429 were much better than those in 1499. Hence the competition for alms – either to be included among the recipients of each

---

though bequests were made to parish churches apart from the testator's own, the home church was almost always favoured.

[46]   See James Davis, 'Baking for the Common Good: A Reassessment of the Assize of Bread in Medieval England', *Economic History Review*, 57 (2004), 465–502 (esp. p. 471), on the various types of bread baked in late medieval England. It is likely that the poor used only the cheapest three sorts of bread – 'treyt', which was made of low-quality whole grain, not only wheat; 'all common corn' which 'probably used mixed grain, such as oats, barley and rye'; and 'horsebread', made from peas and beans.

[47]   NRO, NCC Multon, fols 109v–110r, Roger Banestyr (made 11 November 1497, proved 24 January 1499).

[48]   NRO, NCC Wight, fols 22v–23r; see above, n. 42.

[49]   Burgess, '"An Afterlife in Memory"', pp. 212–13.

[50]   See my calculations of what 3d. per week might purchase in food in Maddern, p. 56.

dole, or to receive more than one dole in the shortest possible time – must have been intense.

What proportion of the population even such large bequests as Bishop Goldwell's could benefit is almost impossible to establish. Norwich, in common with most large English manufacturing towns, may have weathered the recurrent epidemics of the fourteenth and fifteenth centuries better than the surrounding countryside; but the demographic effects of the Black Death were nevertheless severe. In the early fourteenth century, the best calculations suggest that Norwich had a population of between 15,000 and 25,000. By the 1370s, the Poll Tax – supposed to record all men and women over the age of fourteen except for the very poor and those in religious orders – listed only 3,952 names. It is generally accepted that the total population throughout the late fourteenth and fifteenth centuries could not have exceeded 8,000 at most; but this estimate depends on unprovable assumptions about the number of people who were under the age of fourteen, regular clergy, or very poor.[51] Hence what proportion of the population were poor, elderly, or chronically ill at any one time is unknown. At best, we might hazard a guess that Bishop Goldwell's bequest might have benefited about 10 per cent of the whole city; William Setman's, only 0.25 per cent.

How were the beneficiaries actually selected? By whom? And how were the doles distributed? On these questions, contemporary Norwich texts are almost mute. Certainly testators expected their executors to oversee their *post-mortem* charity, and sometimes to distribute it in person. In 1419 Joan Eton particularly specified that her bequests to St Giles and Norman's hospitals, the mendicant friars, the prisoners and the leper houses were to be distributed by her executors 'as in my will'. In 1429, William Setman culminated his already generous almsgiving with the stipulation that the residue of his goods should be sold, and the profits distributed among 'the poor, that is, the blind, lame, paralytic, bedridden, decrepit, lepers, widows, orphans and other poor people having most need, *according to the discretion of my executors*' (emphasis mine); while in 1498, Katherine Kerre bequeathed 2d. to 'iche lepere' present in the sick houses 'what tyme my executoris come there to vysyte them'. Since she also directed her executors to 'yeve in almes to the most nedy people' of the parishes of St John Maddermarket, Holy Cross and St Giles, Kerre clearly expected them to have discriminating knowledge of the degrees of poverty in their localities.[52] Executors and other officers of the testator's family may therefore have had a hand in choosing those fortunate poor

---

[51] Carole Rawcliffe and Richard Wilson (eds), *Medieval Norwich* (London: Hambledon and London, 2004), pp. 20, 29, 158, 214 and 318. Earlier figures are largely based on calculations of numbers of parishes and (presumed) average congregations. See also D.M. Palliser (ed.), *The Cambridge Urban History of Britain, vol. 1, 600–1540* (Cambridge: Cambridge University Press, 2000), pp. 758, 761.

[52] NRO, NCC Hyrnyng, fols 49v–50r, (1419); Tanner, pp. 242–4: 'pauperibus, videlicet cecis claudis paraliticis, languentibus in lectis decrepitis leprosis viduis, orphanis et aliis egenis maiorem necessitatem habentibus secundum discrecionem executorum

who would receive doles at funerals, obits and in the performance of the will, even though no Norwich executors' accounts survive to prove the point. Yet truly discriminating distribution can surely only have taken place when the numbers of recipients were limited. Evidence of the practical process of distributing doles is completely lacking; but it is hard to see how the most zealous executor could ensure that among the hundreds of recipients of Bishop Goldwell's bread dole all were truly worthy and none managed to secure more than one loaf for themselves or their families.

It is also possible that particularly later in the century, and in bequests limited to certain parishes, the churchwardens of the parish took a hand both in choosing worthy recipients and distributing doles. McIntosh's close study of churchwarden's accounts pre-1546 found that in approximately 24 per cent of parishes, churchwardens were involved in intervening in some way on behalf of the poor of their parish (ranging from distributing charity on feast days to placing poor children as apprentices); they might therefore be expected to know who deserved aid.[53] By 1518, for instance, the Lambeth parish assembly granted the churchwardens the 'awthoryte' to put 'feble people' 'In to the almus howsse'.[54] Obviously it was part of the churchwardens' job to identify those sufficiently needy and incapacitated to require institutionalisation. But McIntosh found almost no direct early evidence of churchwardens' involvement in distributing testamentary charity, and believes that 'churchwardens were rarely asked to administer such bequests prior to 1547'.[55] Yet some late medieval London churchwardens did record receiving payments for pious and charitable bequests directly from executors – 'Item of Thomas Rivelles byquest by the handes of his executurs, *Summa* 54s 4d' wrote the churchwardens of St Mary at Hill, London for 1496–97. They also regularly (though not invariably) accounted for money paid to the poor at obits.[56] John Bedham's will of 1472, from the same London parish, specifically required the 'wardeyns' to 'pay to iij poure people most nedefull ... dwellyng in the said parissh of seynt Mary atte hill, euery Sonday wekely euery yere for euermore [4d each]'. Thereafter the churchwardens faithfully complied, often recording both payments and the names of the three fortunate recipients, who must have been well known to them. One, William Paris, was clearly a favoured beneficiary; his alms were often supplemented over at least

meorum'; NRO, NCC Multon, fols 89v–91r: Kerre made the same stipulation regarding her bequests to prisoners in the Castle and Gildhall gaols.

[53]   McIntosh, *Poor Relief in England*, pp. 101–5 and Appendix F.

[54]   Quoted in Beat A. Kümin, *The Shaping of a Community: The Rise and Reformation of the English Parish, c. 1400–1560* (Brookfield, VT: Scolar Press, 1996), p. 48.

[55]   McIntosh, *Poor Relief in England*, p. 103.

[56]   Henry Littlehales (ed.), *The Medieval Records of a London City Church (St Mary at Hill) A.D. 1420–1559*, EETS o.s. 125 (London: Kegan Paul, Trencham Trübner & Co, 1904; Millwood: Kraus Reprint, 1972), p. 221. For specific accounts, see ibid., pp. 97 (1479–81), 140 (1487–88), 154–5 (1489–90), 167–8 (1490–91), 179–80 (1491–92), 191 (1492–93), 202–3 (1493–94), 211 (1494–95).

17 years by payments for small jobs done around the parish, such as 'mendyng of a wyndowe' (2d.), 'kepynge & wachyng of the cherche the space of x wekes' (8s.) and, with Reynold Bull, another almsman, 'watchynge of the [Easter] sepulture' (6d.).[57] Unfortunately, no churchwardens' accounts survive for medieval Norwich; possibly if they did, they would show similar involvement of churchwardens in the distribution of charity and the choice of its recipients. It may even be that the tendency for Norwich testators to leave money specifically to the poor of their own, or neighbouring, parishes was governed by their desire to ensure that their charity would reach recipients known to them, their executors or their churchwardens, and hence proved to be both needy and deserving.

How then could the poor maximise their chances of receiving the comparatively rare and small benefits available to them from wills? Table 5.1 shows again that the apparently most obvious strategy – that of offering prayers directly for the soul of the benefactor, either at the funeral or in a series of remembrances shortly afterward – cannot have benefited many Norwich paupers. True, some testators painstakingly elaborated arrangements for the involvement of the poor at their funerals and obits; Thomas Snellyng, an early sixteenth-century Norwich butcher, specified that his hearse should be attended by eighteen poor men holding lights, each of whom was to receive a penny and dinner; that all his neighbours and fellow-parishioners, rich and poor, were to be invited to the post-funeral repast; and that every other poor man, woman and child attending after his funeral mass was to receive a halfpenny loaf.[58] But he was in the minority. Despite the commonly-known late medieval practice of distributing mourning gowns among the poor for attendance at the funeral, only seven of the 222 bequests in my sample explicitly left money for this purpose (though other testators may have assumed that their executors would do so, paying for it as part of the funeral expenses they were enjoined to meet).[59]

From the point of view of possible recipients, the problems of adventitious generosity also plagued charity specifically in return for prayers. There could be good money to be earned – but only rarely, and often only by a few. Bishop

---

[57]   Littlehales (ed.), *Medieval Records of a London City Church*: for Bedham's will, pp. 16–17 (quote from p. 17); for records of the payments (1477–94), pp. 89, 110, 141, 154, 204; for William Paris's odd paid jobs around the church, pp. 134 (1487–88), 173 (1491–92), 185 (1492–93), 197 (1493–94); cf. also ibid., pp. 154, 174, 186 (three jobs in 1492–93 for a total payment of 8d.), 198. The most Paris can be shown to have earned in any one accounting period, counting his weekly dole of 4d., was £1 6s. 4d. in 1491–92, or an average of just over 6d. per week.

[58]   Tanner, p. 99.

[59]   Sheila Sweetinburgh, 'Clothing the Naked in Late Medieval East Kent', in Catherine Richardson (ed.), *Clothing Culture, 1350–1650* (Aldershot: Ashgate, 2004), pp. 109–22 (esp. pp. 114–15), Table 7.1. Sweetinburgh finds, in comparison, that in East Kent 1400–1540, 6 per cent of male and 9 per cent of female testators left clothing alms in their wills, much lower proportions than for food alms (bequeathed by 25 per cent of male and 32 per cent of female testators). See also, for specific bequests of mourning robes, ibid., p. 119.

Goldwell's will is again a good example. He ordered his executors to distribute 6s. 8d. every Sunday for the three years following his death to 'twenty poor men', who would thus receive 4d. a week each for three years. If the same twenty men benefited every week, the sum would certainly provide a useful safety net – but if the recipients differed every week, everyone received less. Also, if the offer tacitly included the gift of a funeral gown the benefit to the recipients might have been enhanced; but in general Norwich wills are silent on the issue of clothing given to the poor attending funerals or obits, and whether they were permitted to keep it after the ceremony. In any case, few donors could afford to be as generous as Bishop Goldwell. In 1497 Robert Bulle, priest of St Gregory's Norwich, charged his executors to keep a trental (the performance of 30 dirges and masses) in the month after his decease, each dirge and mass to be attended by 'iiij pore men to pray for my sowle', and each pauper to have, for every attendance, 1d. Four exceptionally fortunate men from one parish, in this one year, thus had the opportunity to earn the welcome sum of 2s. 6d. But even for them the amount did not add up to more than a poverty-line existence for a month. Bulle also stipulated that 'euery howshold in Seint Gregoris parysshe in Norwiche tht wyll take Almes shall haue vj d to pray for my sowle'; a bequest which extended the range of recipients at least throughout the parish, but limited the amount each family would receive.[60] Some testators merely offered an indefinite number of the poor attending the funeral 1d for that one day.[61] One, at least, demanded the prayers of the poor in return for what we might consider not a charitable donation but a belated payment of dues. In 1498, Katherine Kerre, an otherwise generous provider of 10 separate charitable bequests, also directed 'tht eny poor person tht I haue wronged & can be proved be recompensed & desyred to pray for myn sowle'.[62]

It is true that the vague injunction to 'pray for my soul' may not have entailed long labour on the alms-receiver in return for a welcome few pence. But some well-thought-out rituals took significant amounts of time. Bishop Goldwell's 20 poor bedesmen, for instance, were to receive their money when the bell was rung for high mass, and were then to 'proceed to my tomb and there pray for my soul, and wait until the end of high mass'.[63] For a working man or woman, even to attend an entire funeral on a day other than a Sunday might entail losing the money they would have earned during that time (though presumably even a penny comprised a higher rate of pay per hour than many labouring jobs). But however we calculate it, the fact of the matter was that the prayers of the poor, however highly valued in theory, were cheaply bought in practice. Testators were certainly willing to pay much more for the prayers of professionals – chantry priests, monastics, or houses

60   NRO, NCC Multon, fols 52v–53r.
61   See, for example, NRO, NCC Hyrnyng, fols 32r–33r, will of John Danyell (1418); and NRO, NCC Multon, fols 81v–83r, will of John Bishop (made 1497, proved 1498).
62   NRO, NCC Multon, fols 89v–91r.
63   TNA, PROB 11/11/750: 'postea vadant ad tumbam meam & ibidem orent pro anima mea & expectent vsque finem altam missam.'

of friars – than they were for the prayers of the poor, either because they thought them more effective or because the genuinely needy, who could not afford to refuse even the lowest payment for intercessory alms, simply had less bargaining power. In 1419 Joan Eton left 20s. to the nuns of Carrow for prayers for her soul, and another 20s. plus eight marks per year (£3 4s.) for life to her chaplain, William Toly to pray for her soul. These sums comprised over four times the amount she gave to charitable causes, such as to hospitals, leper houses and prisoners. In 1487 William Hemmyng similarly left eight marks for an honest chaplain to celebrate for a year for the souls of him and his parents; but only 2d. each to the sisters of Norman's hospital.[64] Ordinary lay poor people, however many prayers they were prepared to offer, could expect only minimal returns. Furthermore, bequests to the poor, as opposed to those to parish churches, friaries and mass priests, often formed only a small minority of charitable legacies. The wills of Thomas Cok, Emma Clerk and Joan Eton show that they devoted respectively only 13.3 per cent, 13.6 per cent and 14.9 per cent of the value of their charitable bequests actually to the poor, or to brothers and sisters of hospitals nominally devoted to caring for the poor.[65]

In fact, Table 5.1 shows that Norwich testators overwhelmingly preferred to direct their charity to different groups of poor people – those institutionalised either in hospitals or prison. Nearly 70 per cent of bequests went either to the institutions that provided shelter to the elderly, indigent and ill, or directly to their inmates, while a further 14 per cent were directed to the 'poor prisoners' in the two city gaols. How far did these charities constitute effective poor relief?

First, it must be noted that even the inmates of all the five leper/sick houses at the gates of Norwich, plus the two main hospitals (originally intended to accommodate the sick and elderly poor) cannot have comprised more than a small proportion of those struggling to survive in Norwich in the late Middle Ages. The new chancel, nave and infirmary hall at St Giles, the largest hospital in Norwich and one popular with testators, was finished in 1396 and could have provided beds for up to sixty patients. But by the late fifteenth century, a detached *domus Dei* or *domus pauperum* housed an unknown, but probably much smaller, number of the sick and poor. In 1451, the hospital was said to be home to seven impoverished scholars, while two nurses cared for eight 'debilitated paupers'. The hospital also maintained its founder's commitment to feed 13 paupers at the gates every day.

---

[64]   NRO, NCC Hyrnyng, fols 49v–50r; NRO, NCC A. Caston, fols 294v–295r; Tanner (p. 100) assesses the usual rates of pay as eight marks for a priest to celebrate for a year, and about five marks for an annual of masses.

[65]   NRO, NCC Surflete, fols 42v–43r, 44r; NRO, NCC Hyrnyng, fols 49v–50r. It is impossible to calculate accurately the proportion of bequests to the poor as compared to all legacies in these wills, due to the fact that the exact value of many bequests remained unstated (e.g. bequests of land, clothes, devotional objects, or of unstated amounts of uncollected debt, or in cases where fixed sums were bequeathed to an unstated number of recipients).

In the years 1479–1503, only 13 named bedridden patients occur in the records, though the hospital still admitted 'a few deserving cases in search of overnight shelter', and housed an unknown number of aged priests, no longer able to work and hence possibly in poverty.[66]

Similarly, Norman's or St Paul's hospital, originally founded in the twelfth century to support 'the sick, infirm and child-bearing poor', by the fifteenth century had become primarily an almshouse for respectable women, though it also maintained a subsidiary almshouse for the sick poor.[67] There were, apparently, 24 sisters in the mid-fifteenth century, but only about twelve by the early sixteenth, caring for an unknown, but probably small, number of poor patients.[68] These were apparently almost the only institutions functioning as almshouses in late medieval Norwich. Only one new eleemosynary foundation appeared in the fifteenth century – the almshouse probably founded by the brothers John and Walter Daniel just before 1418, and referred to in their wills of 1418 and 1424 respectively. Since it was never mentioned again, it was probably shortlived.[69]

The numbers of inmates in the leper houses (which, as their function became less specialised came to be called 'seke houses' by the late fifteenth century) is unrecorded; but it appears none of the five Norwich houses that received nearly 30 per cent of all charitable donations in this sample was large or populous.[70] The habit of testators later in the century of leaving either 1d. to each leper/sick person or 12d. to each house, or leaving multiples of 12d. to be 'euenly … deuyded' among the inmates of each house, may suggest that they expected about a dozen regular inmates in any house at any one time.[71] It is therefore unlikely that the

---

[66]   Rawcliffe, *Medicine for the Soul*, pp. 166–7.

[67]   Carole Rawcliffe, 'Sickness and Health', in Rawcliffe and Wilson (eds), *Medieval Norwich*, pp. 301–26 (p. 325); Tanner, pp. 133–4.

[68]   Tanner, pp. 133–4.

[69]   Tanner, p. 133; cf. NRO, NCC Hyrning, fols 32r–33r, will of John Danyell.

[70]   Carol Rawcliffe, *Leprosy*, pp. 332–3.

[71]   For bequests of one penny per person, see, for example, NRO, NCC A. Caston, fol. 302v, will of Edward Dilham (1487); NRO, NCC A. Caston, fol. 311, will of Henry Thurton (1487); NRO, NCC Wolman, fol. 18v, will of Margaret Skipwith (1488); NRO, NCC Multon, fols 52v–53r, will of Robert Bulle (1497); NRO, NCC Multon, fol. 86, will of Alice Gylber (1498); NRO, NCC Multon, fols 92r–93r, will of Nicholas Noble (1498); NRO, NCC Multon, fols 110r–111r, will of William ffak (1499). For bequests of 12d. per institution, see, for example, TNA, PROB 11/8/63, will of John Cooke of Norwich (1487); NRO, NCC Typpes, fol. 119, will of Elizabeth Jenny (1497); NRO, NCC Multon, fol. 48, will of Richard Fox (1497); NRO, NCC Multon, fol. 72, will of Edward Howse (1498); NRO, NCC Multon, fol. 73r, will of Adam ffrances (1498); NRO, NCC Multon, fols 81v–83r, will of John Bishop (1498); NRO, NCC Multon, fols 109v–110r, will of Roger Banestyr (1499). Note that Banestyr makes it clear that the money is not to be devoted to general institutional upkeep, but was to be given directly 'to [th]e seke folkys'. For bequests to be divided among the residents, see NRO, NCC Wight, fols 4v–5r, will of John Neell (1499), 12d. to each house to be 'inter leprosis ibidem equaliter diuidend'; and NRO, NCC

combined population of institutionalised elderly and sick poor in all the hospitals in Norwich in the fifteenth century ever exceeded two hundred (2.5 per cent of the possible total population), and at many times it must have been much smaller. Compared to the several hundreds of poor households or individuals identified as the recipients of bread or penny doles,[72] this figure is not large.

Furthermore, all hospital inmates were not necessarily paupers. St Giles's took in ex-servants of the hospital, perhaps more on the basis of connection than outright need.[73] Though early in the century the sisters of Norman's hospital were termed 'poor sisters' in some wills,[74] by 1492 the residents ('full sisters') were purchasing their membership of this quasi-monastic community at the rate of at least 10 marks (£6 13s. 4d.), a sum exceeding the annual income even of a master craftsman in regular work. In return the hospital was supposed to pay the eight sisters then resident a dole of 8d. a week, though the episcopal visitation of the hospital found that the stipend was 'often in arrears, sometimes by eight weeks, sometimes by ten'.[75] In better times, however, the fairly frequent bequests of between 1d. and 12d. each for the resident sisters of Norman's hospital must rather have added to their comfort than relieved outright poverty.[76] Even the in-patients of the leper hospitals, or 'seke houses', were not necessarily paupers. Henry and Richard Wellys, possibly from the one family, were both styled lepers, and both lived in St Leonard's hospital, just outside Norwich. Yet Henry died in 1448, leaving cash bequests of 11 shillings, and ordering his executors to discharge his debts, pay for his funeral and perform charitable works for his own soul; while Richard, even

---

Wight, fol. 18v, will of William Fenne (1499), two shillings to each house 'euenly to be deuyded a mong theme'.

[72]   See nn. 42, 46, 47 above.

[73]   Rawcliffe, *Medicine for the Soul*, p. 166. William Hogepound, formerly the hospital brewer, moved to the almshouse in 1500.

[74]   NRO, NCC Hyrning, fols 49v–50r, will of Joan Eton ('pauperibus sororibus') (1419).

[75]   A. Jessopp (ed.), *Visitations of the Diocese of Norwich A.D. 1492–1532* (London: Camden Society, 1888; New York: Johnson Reprint Corporation, 1965), p. 14: 'Item quod stipendia sunt multotiens a retro non soluta aliquando per viij septimanas aliquando per decem.' There were also seven 'half sisters' listed, who took some vows, but may not have been residents in the house. The number of sick or elderly paupers cared for (if any) is not mentioned.

[76]   See, for example, NRO, DCN 67/1a, fol. 4r, will of John Midelton (proved 1417), leaving 6s. 8d. to the whole and half sisters (over 3d. each, if there were then 24 sisters); NRO, NCC Surflete, fol. 41v, will of John Olyuer, chaplain (proved 1429), leaving to each whole and half sister 6d.; NRO, NCC Surflete, fols 42v–43r, will of Thomas Cok (proved 1429), leaving to the sisters 13s. 4d. to be divided between them (over 6d. even if there were then 24 sisters); NRO, NCC A. Caston, fol. 304r, will of Robert Bryghtled, yeoman (proved 1487), leaving 12d. to each sister; NRO, NCC Wolman, fol. 18v, will of Margaret Skipwith (proved 1488), leaving 4d. to every whole and half sister.

more prosperous, was able in 1466 to distribute about £10 in money, plus other resources in the form of uncollected debts and moveable possessions.[77]

Nevertheless, these hospitals did cater for some lay people, who, either permanently or temporarily, through old age or illness, had come to want. Why then were testators so much more often willing to give to them, rather than simply to the labouring poor (or even the sick and elderly) of their neighbouring parish? What did they require of these recipients of charity?

I suggest that two main factors encouraged testators to give preference to these institutions. Firstly, the fear that charity might be wrongly distributed to the undeserving may have led will-makers to treat the hospitals as guarantors both of the genuine need and the good moral character of their inmates. Secondly, and more subtly, giving to institutions (including prisoners in the city gaols) allowed testators to perform, in one act, all the Seven Corporal Works of Mercy – feeding the hungry, giving drink to the thirsty, clothing the naked, providing shelter to the homeless, visiting the sick and the imprisoned and burying the dead. Donors could thus identify themselves as ideal Christian almsgivers. According to the Bible, those who offered the Seven Corporal Works effectively offered them to Christ; in consequence, at the Last Judgement He would invite them, 'Come ... inherit the kingdom prepared for you from the foundation of the world'.[78]

Late medieval English people were apparently extraordinarily fearful that otherwise capable labourers might feign, or even produce, illness or disability specifically to deceive charitable donors. As Anne Scott notes, the *Jacob's Well* text warns against those who 'getyn mete and monye of pyteous folk wyth wyles, as to makyn hem seme crokyd, blynde, syke, or mysellys [lepers], and are nozt so'. Langland himself inveighed against mendicants whose feigned illnesses produced 'scepticism and confusion in would-be donors'.[79] Tales of beggars who deliberately stole and mutilated children to maximise their eleemosynary profits circulated both in France and England. Capgrave in his *Abbreuiacion of Cronicles* for the year 1417 related how beggars had stolen three children from the author's home town of Lynn, blinded one, 'broke [the] bak' of another and amputated the hands and feet of the third '[th]at men schul of pité gyue hem good'.[80] In 1469, a

---

[77]   Rawcliffe, *Leprosy*, pp. 263, 364.

[78]   From the sermon on the Last Judgement, Matthew 25. 31–46, quote from v. 34.

[79]   Scott, *'Piers Plowman'*, pp. 78–9 (quote from p. 79); cf., however Mark Amsler ('Poverty as a Mobile Signifier: Waldensians, Lollards, *Dives and Pauper*', in Scott (ed.), *Experiences of Poverty*, pp. 227–51 (esp. pp. 240–41, 245–6, 248)), who argues that 'poverty' and 'the poor' had many meanings in late medieval English texts. Amsler also notes that the 'good' poor were identified as hard-working, humble, undemanding, yet properly grateful for any help they received.

[80]   *John Capgrave's Abbreuiacion of Cronicles*, (ed.) Peter J. Lucas, EETS o.s. 285 (Oxford: Oxford University Press, 1983), p. 249. Capgrave had recycled the story from the works of Thomas Walsingham. For examples from France, see Scott, *'Piers Plowman'*, p. 78, quoting Bronisław Geremek, *The Margins of Society in Late Medieval Paris*, (trans.) Jean Birrell (Cambridge: Cambridge University Press, 1987), pp. 202–4.

Wisbech man was cited to his local ecclesiastical court for having 'mutilated' his wife apparently so that she would more effectively 'beg from door to door'.[81]

In turn, this discourse spawned general suspicion of the practice of consistent begging. Late fourteenth-century Wycliffites, in the course of attempting to prove that mendicant friars could not legitimately demand alms, produced a moral taxonomy of mendicancy. '*Declamatoria*' ('clamorous begging' or openly asking for charity) was justified only by extreme necessity, or if a 'strong man' temporarily could not find labour. '*Insinuativa*' implied asking for alms, but was legitimate if truly needy people begged solely to relieve their need. Best of all was '*innuativa*' in which the genuinely poor relied solely on the mute showing of their condition to rouse the goodwill of the merciful.[82] But distrust of habitual begging was clearly not limited to Lollard sympathisers. John Cambridge, ex-mayor of Norwich, in his will proved 1442 expansively provided bedding and clothing to at least sixty 'right pore folk that han many childeren'; but specifically excluded 'common beggeris' from this bequest.[83]

Any poor person hoping for relief from testamentary charity therefore faced a severe quandary. The appearance of good health was suspect, suggesting unwillingness, rather than inability, to find work. But the appearance of disease or disability might be equally doubtful, implying attempted fraud on the alms-giving public. To ask for charity invited suspicious questioning as to whether the request represented habitual begging, or a genuine but temporary subsistence crisis. In effect, in order to receive charity the poor were implicitly required to provide proof both of their genuine need and/or disability and of their good faith in requesting alms.

Some of the poverty-stricken might find such guarantees through personal acquaintance with donors. John Groos in 1488 had no doubt that his servant Alice who had 'lost hir sight and is blynd', deserved to 'haue hir fundyng in mete and drynk aslong as she leuyth'.[84] But for those with no such connections, hospitals provided an identity of moral poverty and consequently a licence to beg alms, either personally or vicariously. All hospitals and leper houses examined possible candidates for entry. Donors could thus feel reassured that the residents were genuinely in need (bed-ridden, disabled, elderly) and hence legitimate objects of charity. Even temporary hospital patients were routinely required to make full confession before entry to the hospital, ensuring that the state of their souls was

---

[81] Lawrence Poos (ed.), *Lower Ecclesiastical Jurisdiction in Late-Medieval England: The Courts of the Dean and Chapter of Lincoln, 1336–1349, and the Deanery of Wisbech, 1458–1484* (Oxford: British Academy/Oxford University Press, 2001), p. 276: 'mutilavit eam in membris'; 'hostiatim mendicare'. The culprit admitted that he had a wife who habitually begged ('habet uxorem continue mendicantem'), but did not confess to the mutilation charge.

[82] Aston, pp. 57–8.

[83] Rawcliffe, 'Sickness and Health', p. 315.

[84] NRO, NCC Wolman, fol. 8, John Groos (1488).

healthy, whatever their physical condition. Long-term residents of leper/sick houses might be asked either to make a full monastic profession, or at least, as *conversi*, to swear oaths of poverty, chastity and obedience. They could also be expelled for misconduct.[85] Hence their good behaviour could be safely assumed.

Not surprisingly, inmates in the leper/sick houses, once granted asylum, could legitimately beg alms from travellers passing through the city gates near which their houses were almost invariably situated, either in person, or through healthy 'proctors' acting on their behalf.[86] As Rawcliffe remarks, 'Once decently and protectively clad in the livery of a hospital, they became deserving objects of Christian compassion, whose search for alms was legitimised by membership of a religious community.'[87] As a bonus to donors, the occupants of such quasi-monastic communities necessarily took part in the masses and prayers for the donors' souls, thus maximising the salvation benefit of charity.

In terms of improved possibility of receiving alms if one were ill or disabled, the advantages of entering a hospital were thus clear. One-third of all bequests went to support the hospitals or their staff, and a further 8.1 per cent of bequests were directed specifically to the sick and needy in the hospitals; whereas only seven bequests (3.2 per cent of the total) went to the sick or disabled living in the community, rather than in an institution. Yet to become a justified object of charity in this way could entail onerous performances on the poor. The places available could not have sufficed to provide for all the sick poor of Norwich, and some classes of the poor were ineligible for all institutions. St Giles's hospital took only male patients, and was reluctant to house those suffering from long-term contagious diseases, such as lepers.[88] Women and sufferers from these kinds of diseases had to compete for places in the leper houses.[89] Even eligible patients had to leave their families (temporarily or permanently), join a rule-dominated institutional community, accept patiently the burden of sickness or disability and continue to demonstrate, ostentatiously, their gratitude. For some, residence entailed captive participation in an endless round of masses, prayers, confession and supplications for the souls of donors to the house.[90] Finally, the disparity between numbers of bequests to the institutions and their monastic staff as compared to the patients within the hospital shows that even the poverty-stricken who managed to gain a

---

[85]   Rawcliffe, *Medicine for the Soul*, p. 105: Rawcliffe, *Leprosy*, pp. 263, 335.

[86]   Rawcliffe, *Leprosy*, pp. 199, 288–9, 308. An English pontifical of *c*. 1425 is illustrated by the picture of a leper (already missing some extremities, and with an aggressively blotched face) sitting by the wayside, with the words 'Sum good my gentyll mayster for god sake' issuing from his mouth.

[87]   Rawcliffe, *Leprosy*, p. 266.

[88]   Rawcliffe, *Medicine for the Soul*, p. 163.

[89]   Occasional bequests to sick women and children in these institutions show that women were admitted. See, for example, NRO, NCC Multon, fol. 86, will of Alice Gylbert (1498), leaving a penny 'to iche sekeman at the gatys and woman'; Rawcliffe, *Medicine for the Soul*, p. 203.

[90]   Rawcliffe, *Medicine for the Soul*, pp. 7, 105–6.

hospital place and maintain their role as legitimate recipients of alms were less favoured as objects of charity than were the institutions and staff.

What then can have been the motives of donors in giving such small sums to such a selective group of the needy? Possibly each testator reckoned on a large proportion of their peers likewise donating to the poor (some perhaps even more generously than themselves), so that the whole sum would be considerable. Those who gave money to the leper houses, for instance, lacking historians' hindsight, were not to know that they were among a minority of testators (just less than 40 per cent); or that the bequests were 'always modest sums' (between 6d. and 1s. 8d. to each house, or 1d. to 4d. per inmate).[91]

Alternatively, donors might calculate that *in vivo* charity, and the support of peers and families, also helped poor people, relieving them of the responsibility for doing so.[92] Certainly, among the better-off neighbourly charity might be expected. Most Norwich guild ordinances enjoined charity to needy brothers or sisters of the guild. Members of the prestigious Guild of St George, for instance, were ordered that 'what brother or sister of this fraternite falle in pouert, euery brother and sister shal payen, in the woke, to the kepers of this fraternite, a ferthyng; of whiche siluer the pouer brother or sister shal haue, in the woke, viij. d.'[93] But this generosity was in some ways of a different type than charity to the chronically needy. Except, perhaps for the 'Poor Men's Guild' (said specifically to be founded by 'pouere men' from the 'pouere parish chirche' of St Augustine), membership of the guilds was limited to relatively prosperous merchants and artisans. Those requiring assistance were not expected to be lifetime paupers or poor labourers, but to have fallen into temporary poverty 'by auenture of the werld' or 'be godis sendyng'.[94] Immediately such phrasing led to the assumptions, firstly that the assistance would be short-term ('lestende his myschefe', as the Peltyers' Guild ordinances put it), and secondly that no help would be forthcoming for those whose distress might be thought to result from their own fault. '[I]f it be his foly, he schal nout han of the elmes' severely remarked the Peltyer's guildsmen, to which exclusion the Carpenters' Guild added those who had come to want through 'ryotous lyuyng'.[95] Thus like recipients of testamentary bequests, these objects of charity were subject to a 'worthiness check' before potential donors would part with their money; but unlike gifts to the plebeian poor, charity to these more elite unfortunates assumed

---

[91]   Tanner, pp. 133–4.

[92]   See above, nn. 12–14.

[93]   Lucy Toulmin Smith (ed.), *English Gilds; The Original Ordinances of More than One Hundred Early English Guilds*, EETS o.s. 40 (London: Oxford University Press, 1870; repr. 1963), p. 18; cf. similar ordinances, for the Guilds of St Botulph (p. 16), St Katherine (p. 20), St Christopher (p. 24), Holy Trinity (p. 26), the Peltyers' Guild (p. 31), the Tailors' Guild (p. 35), the Carpenters' Guild (p. 38) and the Poor Men's Guild (pp. 40–41).

[94]   Smith (ed.), *English Gilds*, pp. 20, 24, 31, 35, 38, 40.

[95]   Smith (ed.), *English Gilds*, pp. 31, 38. The Tailors' Guild specifically excepted any 'theffe proued' (ibid., p. 35).

a different – and markedly more generous – living standard among the recipients. Holy Trinity Guild allowed the unfortunate up to 12d. a week, and the Peltyer's Guild, 14d. – both well above the average bequests to the 'poor' in wills.[96] It seems doubtful, therefore, that testators could view guild charity as an addition to, or substitute for, donations to the labouring or long-term poor.

Of one thing we can be sure; as Dyer rightly says, 'No one expected a remedy for poverty'.[97] Charity, it was assumed, could not – indeed should not – remove the poor finally and altogether from misery; poor people, by Biblical assurance, were a constant feature of society.[98] I suspect, therefore, that the apparently token nature of testamentary charity signals its symbolic, rather than economic, function in testators' minds.

Ideal recipients of charity were, I suggest, supposed to embrace the role of the grateful objects of the Seven Corporal Works of Mercy so vividly portrayed in the fifteenth-century windows of All Saints, North Street, York.[99] That donors were heavily influenced in their choices of testamentary charity by their belief that performing the Seven Works would both serve God and ensure their salvation is hardly a novel insight.[100] Because hospital inmates required food, drink, clothing and housing, and were often ill or disabled, and since hospitals and leper houses also arranged burials of deceased members, donating to these institutions fulfilled at one stroke six of the seven Works of Mercy.[101] The remaining one – visiting and providing for prisoners – could be met by leaving doles to the prisoners in the Norwich Castle gaol and the city's Gildhall prison, a strategy adopted in a small, but not insignificant proportion of bequests – 14 per cent of the total (see Table 5.1).

The poor were thus supposed to present themselves as visibly hungry, thirsty, scantily clad, homeless, disabled, ill, or imprisoned – and humbly grateful. In the York Works of Mercy window, the thirsty (one of whom is also disabled and

---

[96]   Smith (ed.), *English Gilds*, pp. 26, 31. By contrast, the Poor Men's Guild could manage only 3d. per week (ibid., pp. 40–41).

[97]   Dyer, *Standards of Living*, p. 235.

[98]   Matthew 26. 11. The context is Jesus's rebuke to his disciples for suggesting that the woman who poured precious ointment over his feet should rather have given its value to the poor: 'For ye have the poor always with you; but me ye have not always'. Cf. Mark 14. 7; John 12. 8.

[99]   Images available through Sarah Stanbury and Virginia Raguin's 'Mapping Margery Kempe' website, at the 'Works of Mercy (Corporal Works of Mercy)' page <http://college. holycross.edu/projects/kempe/parish/mercy.htm≥ [accessed 16 February 2014].

[100]   See, for example, Rawcliffe, *Medicine for the Soul*, p. 67; and Cullum and Goldberg, pp. 28–30. On popular knowledge of the Seven Corporal Works, note that Richard Whitford, in his popular treatise *A Werke for Housholders or for Them Yt Haue the Gydynge or Gouernaunce of Any Company* (London: Wynkyn de Worde, 1530) urged household heads to 'teche your folkes' 'the vij werkes of mercy whiche you shuld (after your power) set such in werke as you teche them in voice' (n.p.).

[101]   On the burials of hospital inmates, see Rawcliffe, *Medicine for the Soul*, p. 6.

thus doubly deserving) crouch before their comfortably-clad donor; the naked –
decorously clad in underpants but little else – raise their hands in wonder, gratitude,
or possibly prayer; the sick man is apparently already safely institutionalised,
since a veiled nurse stands by his bed; the imprisoned, immured in the stocks,
cannot raise their hands or alter their posture, but they gaze devotedly at their well-
heeled visitor. Certainly testamentary bequests were sometimes intended to entail
the re-performance of such charitable rituals, the executors standing in for the
deceased donor. Thus, only the lepers in the five leper-houses who were 'ther ...
whan my Ex[ecutors] come there to visite them' were to have the penny promised
to them in John Brystemer's will of 1498.[102] It is not too much to imagine, on
these occasions, the executors re-enacting the part of the charitable testator and
performer of the Seven Works of Mercy, while the recipients were mustered to
register their gratitude and (no doubt) their obligation to pray for the donor.[103]

Furthermore, for the whole charitable system of the exchange of alms for
salvation to subsist, the indigent and imprisoned had to remain in that condition,
or at least be replaced by a constant further supply of properly poverty-stricken
recipients of the Seven Corporal Works. The form and levels of testamentary charity
certainly tended to reinforce, rather than to remove, the relative social status of the
elderly, sick and indigent. The prayers of the poor, as we have seen, were less
well-rewarded than those of professional clerics and monastics. More and greater
bequests were made to those staffing the hospitals in which the poor were nursed,
than to the poor themselves. As Sweetinburgh observes of charitable clothing
bequests in Kent, clothing marked 'social and economic distinctions between the
rich and the poor', while 'connecting them in an interdependent relationship'.
'The rich', she argues, 'used clothing as a badge of worthiness to pin on the poor,
visually demarcating the "good" poor from the idle beggar by giving gifts only to
the former'.[104] Many bequests to prisoners, in particular, seemed designed to keep
them incarcerated, rather than help them emerge. Since imprisonment was not a
legal punishment in the English medieval justice system, prisoners in the Gildhall
and Castle were almost certainly there for one of two reasons; either they could not
provide sufficient surety to appear in court, or they had been imprisoned for debt.
Could it have been to ensure that they could not use charitable donations to pay
these dues and get out of gaol, that over 50 per cent of bequests to prisoners (16 out
of 31 cases) were for food alone, rather than in money?[105] Even William Gyllern's

---

[102]   NRO, NCC Multon, fols 70v–71r; cf. NRO, NCC Wight, fols 3r–4r, will of Robert
Cooke (1499) and NRO, NCC Multon, fols 89v–91r, will of Katherine Kerre (1498),
directing her executors to deliver directly her bequests both to prisoners and to the inmates
of the leper houses.

[103]   Or as Rawcliffe (*Leprosy*, p. 321) puts it, 'Such occasions no doubt served for the
ritual commemoration of the deceased'.

[104]   Sweetinburgh, p. 109.

[105]   See, for example, NRO, NCC A. Caston, fols 300v–301r, will of Ralph Est (1487):
'brede and vitall' to the value of 12d.; NRO, NCC A. Caston, fols 324r–325r, John Carleton

generous provision in 1499 of 2s. 6d. worth of meat, bread and 'ale of the beeste' could only briefly ameliorate the prisoners' lives, not procure their release.[106]

How, then, was charity constituted and experienced through testamentary disposition in fifteenth-century Norwich? To testators, charitable donations, especially either to religious institutions (such as their parish church or local friary) or to hospitals, resulted in both material enhancement of religious services and genuine (if temporary) relief of suffering, plus an early release of the soul from Purgatory. Some of the donors were generous. William Setman's bequest of £40 to the lame, blind and sick of Norwich alone represented the annual income of a knight. Other bequests were probably a continuation of long-term *in vivo* alms-giving. '[P]oore Margaret', to whom Robert Machon left 4d. in 1499 was presumably known to him beforehand as a charity-recipient; while 'old Roger', bequeathed 12d. in Thomas Sustede's 1428 will was living 'in my household'.[107]

To the institutions who received so large a proportion (33 per cent) of testators' charity, the bequests no doubt constituted a small addition to their yearly income – but no more than that. The amounts were very moderate, and fluctuated wildly, providing an unreliable source of funds. In the period 1417–19 *all* hospitals received a total of £2 in bequests; in 1427–29, £1 1s. 6d.; in 1487–89, 17s. 8d.; in 1497–99, £4 13s. 8d. Exactly how these amounts compared to institutional income from other sources is difficult to say, since financial accounts of all late medieval Norwich hospitals and leper-houses are not available; but a comparison of these figures with the income of St Giles hospital from its endowed lands, leases and appropriated church livings, suggests that hospitals – especially the older, more-established ones – relied overwhelmingly on land and rents, not charity, for their upkeep. Even in 1429, when yields and profits from landed estates were declining, St Giles received £15 per year from the farm of estates at Calthorpe and Erpingham and the Calthorpe church living at Calthorpe. These estates themselves were only a tiny proportion of the 41 manors, rents and livings held by St Giles in Norfolk. Thus their share of the £1 1s. 6d. given to *all* hospitals 1427–29 must have been a miniscule item in their annual income.[108]

(1487): 'bred and ale' to the value of 2s.; NRO, NCC Multon, fol. 55r, Peter Petyrson (1497): 'in brede and in vitall' to the sum of 3s. 4d.; and NRO, NCC Wight, fol. 1v, John Snyterton (1499): 'xij d in vetell'. Note that by contrast, only 3.7 per cent of bequests to other charitable objects were in kind rather than in cash.

[106]   NRO, NCC Sayve, fols 23r–24r, (1499).

[107]   NRO, NCC Multon, fols 113r–115r; NRO, NCC Surflete, fols 25r–26v: 'antiquo Rogero in hospicio meo'.

[108]   Rawcliffe, *Medicine for the Soul*, pp. 70–76; Jessopp (ed.), *Visitations*, p. 14. The brief comment by the Visitation team at Norman's Hospital, in 1492, that the sisters' stipends were sometimes in arrears because the *redditus* (rents, dues) of the house were often also paid late suggests that they too were reliant primarily on endowments, rather than charity, for their running expenses; Tanner (p. 134) notes that Norman's Hospital had 'a fairly substantial income from endowments'.

For the poor, finally, testamentary charity provided only unsatisfactory relief. A healthy worker struggling to live on low-paid, unpredictable and intermittent employment at best received only rare, unpredictable and scanty relief from bequests. If one were lucky (and presumably approved of in one's local parish) one might be chosen to receive a bread dole on the day of burial, or even a funeral gown and money for attending the obsequies and praying for the soul of the dead. But such support provided no dependable income-supplement and was particularly ill-paid. Anyone in poverty who had been forced to travel from their hometown to seek work would be at a disadvantage – simultaneously unknown to the donor or their executors, and suspect as a possible common beggar. Single mothers, though often in dire poverty, apparently could expect no help from will-bequests. The only way to access reasonably frequent and reliable (though small) charitable bequests was through residence in a hospital or leper-house; but this in turn demanded difficult qualifications – a certified and serious illness or disability, a willingness to leave home and family and join, sometimes by oath, a quasi-monastic community. Once in the institution, the constant performance of ritual confession and prayers for the dead was entailed on the inmate, often, again, for scanty charitable support. Finally, despite any price-inflation, the amount of alms did not rise markedly throughout the century from their initial low levels.[109]

Thus in late medieval Norwich wills, charity and poor relief were never synonymous. Even the overlap between them was in some regards slight. Comparatively few of the poor were objects of charity; conversely, many higher-value charitable donations went to well-off organisations and individuals. However, both wealthy donors and poor recipients joined in the experience of charity; the fulfilment of the donor's will commonly instantiated a series of performances in which both donors (vicariously) and recipients had specific roles to play and identities to establish. Testators were posthumously presented as ideal performers of the Seven Works of Mercy; the poor were expected to enact the role of the grateful recipients, the friends of Christ whose prayers would procure the donor's early release from Purgatory. Yet the payments for these performances were very often slight. In this performance market the scales were heavily loaded in favour of (elite) donors and against (working) recipients.

---

[109] McIntosh ('Local Responses', p. 233) notes that well into Elizabethan times a weekly dole of 6d. per week was still considered standard poor relief.

Chapter 6

The Forms and Functions of Monastic Poor Relief in Late Medieval and Early Sixteenth-Century England

Neil S. Rushton

The largest amount of institutional charity in England throughout the Middle Ages was administered by the religious houses. But there have been only limited attempts to quantify and qualify the amounts of income redistributed from the monastic endowments to the poorest members of society in the form of charity. This is partly due to a restriction of the source material as very few monastic houses have good series of surviving internal accounts. However, there are various sources that do allow for analyses of monastic charitable provision at a national and localised scale from the twelfth century onwards. In terms of quantitative analysis the administrative records of Westminster Abbey and Norwich Cathedral Priory provide sufficient data to allow reasonable measurements of monastic poor relief at these two Benedictine houses from the late thirteenth century to the Dissolution. Although these monasteries were somewhat atypical in terms of wealth and prestige, the surviving records do provide an opportunity to assess the administration of institutional poor relief that is not available elsewhere during the Middle Ages in England.[1]

Measuring the amount of monastic charitable provision at a national scale is enabled by the existence of a government tax assessment known as the *Valor Ecclesiasticus* compiled in 1535. Amounts of charity expended by the religious houses and hospitals over the accounting year 1534–35 are recorded in some detail, allowing both quantitative and qualitative analyses of the data. These analyses suggest that the amount of provision at this date was considerably higher than previously allowed by historians. Both the internal records of Westminster Abbey and Norwich Cathedral Priory and also those of the *Valor Ecclesiasticus* suggest that throughout the late Middle Ages the social welfare role of monasteries was well developed in that they carried out a diverse range of charitable activities.

---

[1] Only Durham Cathedral Priory, Worcester Cathedral Priory and Canterbury Cathedral Priory have surviving series of internal accounts that allow similar analysis, and none of these contains coverage as consistent as Westminster and Norwich.

Monastic Poor Relief in Medieval England

Monastic charitable provision operated within paradigms formed by the changing social perceptions of the poor and appropriate forms of relief over the course of the later Middle Ages. From a general 'Patristic' view of the poor as representatives of Christ on Earth prevalent during the early Middle Ages, the poor became increasingly sub-divided into deserving and undeserving from the mid-thirteenth century onwards.[2] Attitudes were particularly affected by the socio-economic dislocations caused by the Black Death in the mid-fourteenth century, when the sudden lack of labourers provoked a fierce reaction by the landowning class against those poor receiving charity who were able to work for a living.[3] It only took a year after the first outbreak of plague in England for Edward III's government to pass legislation to enable control of the problem. The 1349 Ordinance of Labourers stated that:

> Because that many valiant Beggars, as long as they may live of begging, do refuse to labour, giving themselves to idleness and vice, and sometimes to theft and other abominations; none, upon the said pain of imprisonment, shall, under the colour of pity or alms, give anything to such, who may labour, or presume to favour them in their sloth, so that thereby they may be compelled to labour for their necessary living.[4]

---

[2]	Maria A. Moisa, 'Fourteenth-Century Preachers' Views of the Poor: Class or Status Group?', in Raphael Samuel and Gareth Stedman Jones (eds), *Culture, Ideology and Politics: Essays for Eric Hobsbawm* (London: Routledge & Kegan Paul, 1982), pp. 160–75; J.D. Dawson, 'Richard FitzRalph and the Fourteenth-Century Poverty Controversies', *Journal of Ecclesiastical History*, 34 (1983), 315–44; Michel Mollat, *The Poor in the Middle Ages*; Wendy Scase, *'Piers Plowman' and the New Anti-Clericalism* (Cambridge: Cambridge University Press, 1989), pp. 47–83; David Paul Rudd, 'The Involuntary Poor in English Religious Writings from the Late Middle Ages to 1600' (unpublished doctoral thesis, Lancaster University, 1992), pp. 38–41; Larry Catá Backer, 'Medieval Poor Law in Twentieth Century America: Looking Back Towards a General Theory of American Poor Relief', *Case Western Reserve Law Review*, 44 (1995), 871–1041; Christopher Dyer, 'Work Ethics in the Fourteenth Century', in James Bothwell, P.J.P. Goldberg and W.M. Ormrod (eds), *The Problem of Labour in Fourteenth-Century England* (Woodbridge: York Medieval Press/Boydell, 2000), pp. 21–41; Neil S. Rushton, 'Monastic Charitable Provision in Late Medieval England, c. 1260–1540' (unpublished doctoral thesis, University of Cambridge, 2002), chap. 1; Neil S. Rushton, 'Charity', in W.C. Jordan (ed.), *Dictionary of the Middle Ages Supplement* (New York: Thomson/Gale, 2004), pp. 97–107; Marjorie K. McIntosh, *Poor Relief in England*; Christopher Dyer, 'Poverty and its Relief', 41–78.

[3]	John Hatcher, 'England in the Aftermath of the Black Death', *Past & Present*, 144 (1994), 3–35.

[4]	23 Edward III, c. 7, see *Statutes of the Realm*, 9 vols (London, 1810–28), I: 1101–1301, (ed.) W.E. Taunton, 308: 'Et quia multi validi mendicantes, qaumdiu possent ex mendicatis elemosinis vivere, laborare renuunt, vacando ociis et peccatis et quandoque latroniciis et aliis flagiciis, nullus sub pena imprisonmenti predicta, talibus qui coimode

By the sixteenth century there was an ingrained concept of the able-bodied poor as miscreants, characterised in the 'Rogue and Vagabond' literature and implemented in further repressive government legislation against beggars.[5]

Monasteries had to implement their strategies of poor relief within these perceptual paradigms. Despite a continued adherence to the doctrine of the poor being Christ's representatives and the entrenched concept of the spiritual efficacy of almsgiving to all who might ask, the religious houses were implementing procedural guidelines regarding charitable provision from an early date. By the early sixteenth century, monastic houses were operating systems of welfare provision that were directed mostly at targeted sections of the poor at the expense of general indiscriminate almsgiving. However, the religious houses were not acting as a centralised institution supplying standardised quantities and types of poor relief. They had each to rely on their own endowment for funds – endowments that usually came loaded with the benefactors' conditions – and they were free to interpret the ideal promulgated in the Rule of the sixth-century founder of Benedictine monasticism:

> In the reception of the poor and travellers, special attention should be shown, because it is in them that Christ is more truly welcomed.[6]

This was, of course, a hazy concept, which could be manipulated by religious houses to suit their own environment and time. Chapter four of the Rule also advised monks that they were to relieve the poor, not forsake charity, visit the sick and clothe the naked.[7] The brevity of the Rule's mandates on the logistics of monastic charitable provision suggests that the eleemosynary aspect of monasticism was originally considered only a small part of its proper function.[8] However, by the twelfth century the monastic obedientiary system was well developed in most

---

laborare poterunt, sub colore pietatis vel elemosine quicquam dare seu eos in sua desidia confovere presumat, ut sic compellanter pro vite necessare laborare.'

[5]   Thomas J. Kelly, *Thorns on the Tudor Rose: Monks, Rogues, Vagabonds and Sturdy Beggars* (Jackson: University Press of Mississippi, 1977), pp. 55–80; Rab Houston, 'Vagrants and Society in Early Modern England', *Cambridge Anthropology*, 6 (1980), 18–32; A.L. Beier, *The Problem of the Poor in Tudor and Early Stuart England* (London: Routledge, 1983), pp. 13–19; A.L. Beier, *Masterless Men*, pp. 123–6; Paul Slack, *Poverty and Policy in Tudor and Stuart England* (London and New York: Longman, 1988), pp. 104–6; Arthur F. Kinney (ed.), *Rogues, Vagabonds and Sturdy Beggars: A New Gallery of Tudor and Early Stuart Rogue Literature Exposing the Lives, Times, and Cozening Tricks of the Elizabethan Underworld* (Amherst: University of Massachusetts Press, 1990), pp. 11–62.

[6]   *The Rule of St Benedict*, (ed. and trans.) Justin McCann (London, 1951), chap. 53: 'Pauperum et peregrinorum maxime susceptioni cura sollicite exhibeatur, quia in ipsis magis Christus suscipitur.'

[7]   *The Rule of St Benedict*, chap. 4.

[8]   Chapter 4 of the rule allows prohibitions on 'murmuring' and 'drowsiness' as much prominence as charity.

medium to large Benedictine houses, and amongst the most important of the conventual officials was the almoner.[9] The eleventh-century *Decreta Lanfranci* stipulated that the almoner was regularly to visit the locality of the house in order to discover 'who is living there and requiring sustenance'.[10] But it is only from the monastic customaries of individual houses that the welfare responsibilities of the almoner and his household are delineated in any detail.

Most customaries date from the twelfth and thirteenth centuries, and amongst the mass of material relating to the liturgical requirements of the year there are often instructions for the duties and obligations of the monastic officials, including the almoner. In 1219 at one of the oldest Benedictine houses, Abingdon Abbey in Berkshire, the almoner was restricted to five household servants who were to collect the leftover food of both the refectory and all other households 'inside the small gate' ('infra parvam portam') in order to distribute to the poor of the town. One servant was also to be attached to the almoner to 'go through the vill and diligently and faithfully search out the destitute, the feeble and such as are truly indigent', much as had been ordained by Lanfranc over a century earlier.[11] In effect these instructions were part of what were periodic reforms of irregularities, which had presumably crept into the established practice of monastic almsgiving from the remains of refectory meals – the abbot 'strictly forbids other obedientiaries remunerating their servants in food or stipend from the almonry'.[12] The same priorities are repeated in the thirteenth-century customary of Eynsham Abbey in Oxfordshire (Benedictine), where food was collected from the refectory and all autonomous households within the precinct by the almoner or his household servants in order to distribute to the poor on a daily basis.[13]

A rare surviving Augustinian customary, from Barnwell Priory in Cambridgeshire, gives quite a detailed breakdown of the way in which the almonry was to be administered.[14] The almoner was advised to be discreet and

---

[9]   David Knowles, *The Monastic Orders in England* (Cambridge: Cambridge University Press, 1949), pp. 431–9.

[10]   David Knowles (ed.), *Decreta Lanfranci Monachis Cantuariensibus Transmissa* (Siegburg: Thomas Nelson and Sons, 1967), p. 74: 'Qui non habent unde se sustentare valeant.'

[11]   C.F. Slade and Gabrielle Lambrick (eds), *Two Cartularies of Abingdon Abbey*, 2 vols (Oxford: Oxford Historical Society, 1990–91), I (1990), 107. Document L167 is part of a customary inserted into the cartulary.

[12]   Slade and Lambrick (eds), *Two Cartularies*, I, 107. For the charitable provision provided from refectory food see, Barbara Harvey, *Living and Dying in England 1100–1540: The Monastic Experience* (Oxford: Oxford University Press, 1993), pp. 10–16. For external injunctions against abuses, see below.

[13]   Antonia Gransden (ed.), *The Customary of the Benedictine Abbey of Eynsham in Oxfordshire* (Siegburg: F. Schmitt, 1963), pp. 189–92.

[14]   John Willis Clark (ed.), *The Observances in Use at the Augustinian Priory of St Giles and St Andrew at Barnwell, Cambridgeshire* (Cambridge: Macmillan and Bowes, 1897), pp. 172–9.

careful sharing out alms (*particionibus*), but the subsequent instructions allowed for quite a wide remit. Priority was to be given to 'travellers, the destitute, poor chaplains, mendicants, and lepers', in the regular distributions which took place two or three times a week; while 'whenever possible the elderly and infirm are to be looked after at any time they come to the almonry or precinct'.[15] It is also clear that the almonry was serving the purpose of a hospital for the sick poor ('infirmis pauperibus'). They were to receive not only regular material relief, but were also to be 'admonished' ('commonere') concerning the welfare of their souls – the material was to be inseparable from the spiritual.[16]

At the Benedictine abbeys of St Mary's, York, and Bury St Edmunds in Suffolk responsibility for charity (as at Barnwell) was to be shared by the almoner with other obedientiaries.[17] At Bury the cellarer and the sacrist both had welfare duties written into the thirteenth-century customary, including the provision of cloth to make cloaks for 26 paupers at Christmas and Easter.[18] The wording and layout of the York customary, however, signals a warning in using these customaries as anything but the most general guides for the actual practice of monastic charitable provision. These customs were evidently heavily influenced by a standardised usage that had been developed on the continent and applied (in theory) in all large religious houses in western Europe.[19] This is not to say that the application of the regulations for charity were not adhered to by the houses in question, but only that they were probably an ideal which, by the thirteenth century, was in need of formalising and clarifying.

Despite the concern of these customaries with the need to collect refectory leftovers for distribution to the poor, the main corpus of welfare relief administered by monasteries derived from their ordinary income – sourced from the endowment of lands and rents by benefactors – which usually came burdened with provisos as to how relief to the poor (if any) should be administered from such funds. In 1256 at Westminster Abbey, Abbot Richard de Crokesley assigned lands to the value of almost £50 to the infirmary of the abbey, with the clause that 4,000 poor were to

---

[15]   Clark (ed.), *Observances in Use*, p. 172: 'peregrinos, palmarios, capellanos, mendicantes, et leprosos … senes autem et decrepitos, claudos, et cecos, in lectis decubantes, in annona competenti debet frequenter visitare.'

[16]   Clark (ed.), *Observances in Use*, pp. 174–5, 178–9. The customary also allowed for a stock of socks and linen to be kept lest Christ should turn up at the almonry 'in forma pauperis' (p. 178).

[17]   Abbess of Stanbrook and J.B.L. Tolhurst (eds), *The Ordinal and Customary of the Abbey of Saint Mary York*, 2 vols (London: Henry Bradshaw Society, 1936–37), II (1937), 274–9; Antonia Gransden (ed.), *The Customary of the Benedictine Abbey of Bury St Edmunds in Suffolk* (London: Henry Bradshaw Society, 1973), pp. 7, 53–5, 64–5, 83.

[18]   Gransden (ed.), *Customary of the Benedictine Abbey*, p. 55.

[19]   See Willibrord Witters, 'Pauvres et pauvreté dans les coutumes monastiques du Moyen Âge', in Michel Mollat (ed.), *Études sur l'histoire de la pauvreté*, 2 vols (Paris: Publications de la Sorbonne, 1974), I, 177–215 (pp. 198–204).

be given 1d. each on the day of his anniversary and the week following.[20] Such an elaborate scheme of poor relief was usually reserved for high status abbeys, but it does illustrate in dramatic fashion how eleemosynary benefactions to monasteries could legally oblige that monastery to conduct its charitable provision in accordance with the donor's wishes – whether or not this was how the house wished to conduct its welfare to the poor. It is a point nicely made in the fifteenth-century *Doctrinal of Sapience*:

> Somme may demaunde as doon the relygyous, whiche haue not wherof to doo
> almesses, for they haue nothyng propre to them self. The relygyous of the cloystre
> sayen trouthe, for they may nothynge gyue wythout licence of hys souerayn.[21]

Most monastic cartularies include a number of chartered grants, which outline the wishes of the benefactor in regard to the logistics of the charitable provision encompassed in the conferral. These could include anniversary distributions, such as Richard de Crokesley's at Westminster, which ensured that the donor would be remembered as a beneficent Christian at least once a year. More importantly, the donor's *soul* would be remembered once a year when those receiving relief would be encouraged to pray for his or her speedy passage through Purgatory. The 'gostly gyftes of holy preyere' from the *Pauperes Christi* were what the deep pocketed grantors were after in return for their generosity, and so they evidently felt able to stipulate the conditions which would allow for this into their charters.[22]

At a small priory such as the Augustinian Stoke by Clare in Suffolk, gifts *ad opus pauperum* were likely to be small scale, but would still come with attached conditions that limited the ways in which the canons could distribute the charity. In the first half of the thirteenth century there were a number of charters which included provision for the poor as a condition of the grant.[23] When Gila, widow of Simon assigned a tenement in Childerditch to the priory in *c*. 1228–29 she

---

[20]   WAM, 5400, 5405; Barbara Harvey, *Westminster Abbey and its Estates in the Middle Ages* (Oxford: Clarendon Press, 1977), p. 391.

[21]   Joseph Gallagher (ed.), *The Doctrinal of Sapience* (1489; Heidelberg: Winter, 1993), p. 85.

[22]   For this see, Joel T. Rosenthal, *The Purchase of Paradise: Gift Giving and the Aristocracy, 1307–1485* (London: Routledge & Kegan Paul, 1972), pp. 11–30; Clive Burgess, 'A Service for the Dead: The Form and Function of the Anniversary in Late Medieval Bristol', *Transactions of the Bristol and Gloucestershire Archaeological Society*, 105 (1987), 183–211; Clive Burgess, '"A Fond Thing Vainly Invented": An Essay on Purgatory and Pious Motive in Later Medieval England', in S.J. Wright (ed.), *Parish, Church and People: Local Studies in Lay Religion 1350–1750* (London: Hutchinson, 1988), pp. 56–84. The quote is from Priscilla Heath Barnum (ed.), *Dives and Pauper*, EETS o.s. 275, 280, 2 parts (Oxford, 1976 and 1980), part 1, p. 65.

[23]   Christopher Harper-Bill and Richard Mortimer (eds), *Stoke by Clare Cartulary*, 3 vols (Woodbridge: Boydell & Brewer, 1982–84), II (1983), nos 573, 574, 579, 580, 594, 602, 606, 608, 612, 615, 617, 628, 631.

ensured that the charitable provision was going to help her as much as it did the recipients – she gave: 'two shillings on my obit day for the good of the poor.'[24] Likewise, her son Richard stipulated in grants of a tenement in Haveringland and rents in Toppesfield that 2s. from each was to be distributed by the almoner on his own and on his mother's anniversaries.[25] These grants placed restrictions on the way in which the canons distributed relief to the poor.

The monastic charitable provision recorded in the *Valor Ecclesiasticus* tax assessment of 1535, demonstrates that many religious houses and hospitals were still, in the very last years of their existence, obliged to carry out the wishes of testators in regard to charity, by distributing annual provision on the days of their anniversaries.[26] Thus, the Benedictine house of Dover Priory (Kent) accounted for its entire recorded annual charitable provision of nearly £14 by way of twenty-nine anniversary distributions.[27] The same restrictions were in place at the smaller Augustinian Huntingdon Priory (Hunts.) where all £9 5s. 4d. was stipulated to be distributed on eleven anniversaries through the year.[28] While at the Benedictine nunnery of Godstow Abbey (Oxon.) most (just under £17) of the total annual provision of a little over £19 was being distributed in its proprietary manors on the anniversaries of various benefactors.[29]

However, charity distributed as anniversary doles is a minority feature in the *Valor Ecclesiasticus*. By the sixteenth century, religious houses and hospitals seem mainly to have imposed their own criteria on the way provision was administered by carrying out daily or weekly programmes of relief. Indeed, it is also quite probable that many of the anniversary distributions recorded in the *Valor Ecclesiasticus* were, for the sake of administrative convenience, the result of the government tax commissioners taking charter grants as written evidence of actual practice, when in fact the sums were being used in more useful ways.

Very illuminating, in relation to this, are the references to almsgiving at religious houses and hospitals in surviving episcopal visitation records and self-regulating chapter ordinances.[30] These were overwhelmingly concerned with

---

[24]   Harper-Bill and Mortimer (eds), *Stoke by Clare Cartulary*, no. 579: 'duos solidos in die anniversarii mei ad opus pauperum.'

[25]   Harper-Bill and Mortimer (eds), *Stoke by Clare Cartulary*, nos 573 and 574.

[26]   *Valor Ecclesiasticus*, I (1810), 53–5. See below for a full discussion of the evidence from the *Valor Ecclesiasticus*.

[27]   There was also a small distribution on Maundy Thursday, which was nonetheless included as part of another anniversary.

[28]   *Valor Ecclesiasticus*, IV (1821), 253–5.

[29]   *Valor Ecclesiasticus*, II (1814), 191–6.

[30]   See, A.H. Thompson (ed.), *Visitations of Religious Houses in the Diocese of Lincoln*, 3 vols (Lincoln: Lincoln Record Society, 1914–23); W.A. Pantin (ed.), *Documents Illustrating the Activities of the General and Provincial Chapters of the English Black Monks 1215–1540*, 3 vols (London: Camden Society, 1931–37); J.A. Evans (ed.), 'Ely Chapter Ordinances and Visitation Records 1214–1515', in *Camden Miscellany*, 17 (1940), pp. 1–74. The main introduction to A.H. Thompson's three volume work is especially useful.

ensuring that almoners took steps not to allow misappropriation of refectory food meant for the poor.[31] For example, at Ely Cathedral Priory in 1403, after some evident tomfoolery, Archbishop Thomas Arundel passed injunctions that:

> No monk is to confer the residual of his food, namely the bread and beer with his dish, to any secular as a wage for them to eat within the monastery: all the remains from tables throughout the monastery are to be given in alms through the almoner, to those truly in need without any diminution. And the brethren, when they receive new clothing, are to give their old clothing to the almoner or the chamberlain, who will, at the discretion of the prior, distribute them to the poor.[32]

The first thing to notice is that this type of charitable provision, while evidently liable to abuse if not regulated, was clearly carrying on at many religious houses and hospitals throughout the later Middle Ages, and yet it finds no place in any quantitative records.[33] It is indeed impossible to quantify it in any realistic terms, but it must at least be considered when any attempt to enumerate monastic charity is made.

Secondly, is the fact that the visitation *detecta/* injunctions and chapter ordinances very rarely notice abuses of charity from ordinary income. The *detecta*, *comperta* and subsequent injunctions from the episcopal visitation at the Augustinian Laund Priory in Leicestershire in 1440 treated the misappropriation of obit-alms to servants instead of the local poor, but it is an exception to the rule.[34] The imposed legal obligations of a grant demanding some form of charitable provision from the newly created ordinary income were rarely contravened by religious houses – something encouraged by the second statute of Westminster of 1285, which gave the donor the right to sue for recovery of land should their attached stipulations not be adhered to.[35]

Customs and grants made before 1300 were subject to the prevailing traditional patristic ideology concerning the poor and their relief. When eligibility discrimination became a major issue after the Black Death, monasteries were not receiving the amount of land endowments they had in previous centuries and they

---

[31] For example, Thompson (ed.), *Visitations of Religious Houses*, I (1914), 2, 19, 23, 37, 41, 89, 105, 121; II (1918), 14, 39, 67, 169, 181, 208; III (1923), 223, 234, 249, 252, 255, 261, 289, 304, 307, 309, 313, 372–80; Pantin (ed.), *Chapters of the English Black Monks*, I (1931), 10–11, 36–9, 79–80, 95, 235–6, 257, 269; II (1933), 10–11, 47, 87, 204–5; III (1937), 42, 128–9, 281, 304; Evans (ed.), 'Ely Chapter Ordinances', pp. 9, 17, 34, 37–9, 55–6, 66.

[32] Evans (ed.), 'Ely Chapter Ordinances', pp. 55–6.

[33] David Knowles, *Religious Orders*, 3 vols (Cambridge: Cambridge University Press, 1979), III, 265; Harvey, *Living and Dying*, pp. 10–16.

[34] Thompson (ed.), *Visitations of Religious Houses*, II, 179–81.

[35] 13 Edward I, c. 41, see *Statutes of the Realm*, I, 92; Margaret Aston, '"Caim's Castles"', pp. 45–81 (pp. 63–4).

were not producing customaries to suit the new socio-economic climate.[36] So were monastic institutions still the most effective instruments for the redistribution of their donors' wealth to the poor? And how did they fit into the newly developed ideological paradigm of charitable provision in the later Middle Ages?[37]

Monastic Poor Relief at Westminster Abbey and Norwich Cathedral Priory *c.* 1275–1540

From its foundation in the tenth century Westminster Abbey was the wealthiest monastic house in England for most of the Middle Ages. It enjoyed consistent royal funding that helped to maintain a net income of £1,641 in *c.* 1300 and £2,827 in 1535.[38] It was thus in a stronger position to supply larger amounts of charitable provision than most religious houses in the country. However, in many ways, the poor relief strategies of the Westminster monks do seem to have been similar to those elsewhere, as discussed below, in terms of both type and proportional quantity. From the 1290s the obedientiary accounts allow for analysis of this poor relief at the abbey.[39]

The pre-Black Death obedientiary account rolls do not survive in consistent series and so there is only a limited amount of statistical analysis that can be carried out. However, from the turn of the fourteenth century it is clear that there were large amounts of charity being supplied to the poor in the almonry outside the west gate of the abbey, but that most of these funds were being supplied from outside of the almoners' department, partly from the small amounts handed over by various obedientiaries but most especially from the warden of the estate of Edward I's consort Queen Eleanor of Castile. Figure 1 shows that this royally funded department was supplying *c.* 58 per cent of all money known to be spent on poor relief at Westminster in the first half of the fourteenth century for the anniversary distribution.

This averaged a little over £102 per annum from the total income from the estate of Queen Eleanor, which was worth *c.* £146 in 1303 and *c.* £151 in 1342.[40]

---

[36]   Primarily because customaries were produced principally for liturgical purposes, which were not particularly affected by socio-economic change.

[37]   For the idea that even a 'symbolic level' of monastic poor relief remobilised wealth in a way that ceased at the Reformation, see Ilana F. Silber, 'Monasticism and the Protestant Ethic: Asceticism, Rationality and Wealth in the Medieval West', *Journal of British Sociology*, 44 (1993), 103–22 (p. 113); and also for a theory of redistribution, Ilana F. Silber, 'Gift-Giving in the Great Traditions: The Case of Donations to Monasteries in the Medieval West', *Archives Européenes de Sociologie*, 36 (1995), 209–43.

[38]   Harvey, *Westminster Abbey and its Estates*, p. 63.

[39]   I have made an in-depth analysis of poor relief at Westminster and Norwich, in Neil S. Rushton, 'Poor Relief Provision at Westminster Abbey and Norwich Cathedral Priory in the Later Middle Ages, *c.* 1275–1540' (forthcoming).

[40]   WAM, 23635 (1302–03); WAM, 23683 (1341–42).

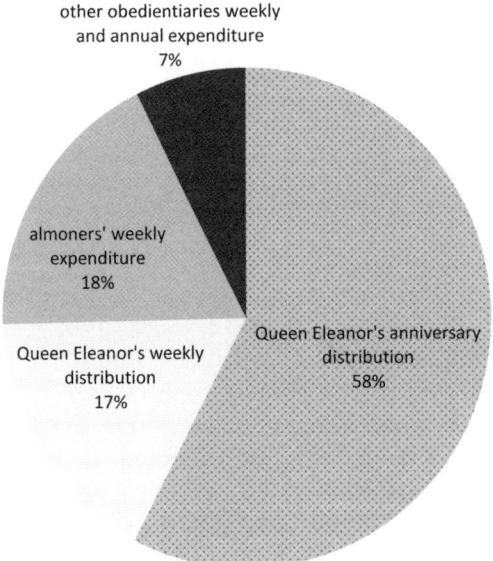

other obedientiaries weekly
and annual expenditure
7%

almoners' weekly
expenditure
18%

Queen Eleanor's weekly
distribution
17%

Queen Eleanor's anniversary
distribution
58%

Figure 6.1   Proportional funding of poor relief at Westminster Abbey in the
               pre-Black Death period

This provision was to be administered to the poor on the eve and on the day of
Queen Eleanor's anniversary (29 November), and there must have been thousands
of applicants for the penny doles. During the Great Famine year of 1315 charitable
expenditure for this anniversary was increased to the very large sum of £150 –
presenting the possibility of 36,000 penny doles given out over the course of two
days. Barbara Harvey has described the kind of chaotic situation this could involve
and the inevitably indiscriminate nature of the provision if this sort of money was
being given out in the course of two days.[41] If there were these large numbers of
claimants turning up at the almonry for the distribution at the end of November
each year, the only method of gaining any sort of control over the situation would
have been to allow a congregation in the open areas of the almonry courtyard
while the pennies were given out.[42] The tokens of lead dispensed by the Royal
Almoner in order to organise doles at the palace of Westminster as early as 1240
may well have been imitated by the monastic almoner – indeed it is difficult to see
how such a general distribution of cash could have been organised without some
form of ticket system.[43]

---

[41]   WAM, 23643; Harvey, *Living and Dying*, pp. 28–30.
[42]   For the almonry at Westminster see, Neil S. Rushton, 'Spatial Aspects of the
Almonry Site and the Changing Priorities of Poor Relief at Westminster Abbey *c.*
1290–1540', *Architectural History*, 45 (2002), 66–91.
[43]   W.J. Courtenay, 'Token Coinage', 275–95; Harvey, *Living and Dying*, p. 28.

Unfortunately, we do not know who were being given this financial assistance. The numbers of poor estimated for the fifteenth and sixteenth centuries were likely to have been of an entirely different magnitude in the early fourteenth century when population pressure was most severe. Indeed the scale of almsgiving at Westminster in the pre-Black Death period, as well as other urban monasteries where records exist, suggests that the numbers of people reliant at least partly on charity was very large – certainly much larger than after 1350. But in many ways the prevailing social attitudes of the period allowed for this type of charitable provision. General distributions demonstrative of genuine Christian charity were condoned – the very wording of Eleanor of Castile's charter ordering the distributions was that charity should be disbursed to 'all who should come' – the monks were not to make any means-tested assessments as to the worthiness of the recipients.[44]

These large-scale distributions of charity were accompanied by weekly distributions and also the maintenance of varying numbers of poor and sick within a building in the almonry known as the *hospicia*. Just over £30 of the weekly distributions were supplied by the additional funds of Queen Eleanor's estate, specified for the purpose. Most of the remainder came from the income of the almoner, which went mostly to maintain the *hospicia* and to keep an unspecified number of charity boys in the almonry school. However, it was only after the Black Death that the large anniversary distributions began to decline in importance and to be replaced to some extent by a larger number of smaller weekly distributions and increased amounts of money spent on the maintenance of the poor within the almonry.

Between 1350 and 1540 the annual amount of poor relief provision at Westminster Abbey rose from under £100 to almost £400 (Figure 6.2). This was achieved mostly through the beneficence of royal foundations such as those of Richard II and Anne of Bohemia, Henry V, Henry VII, and Margaret Beaufort.[45] However, the anniversary distributions declined during this period, so that by the sixteenth century they accounted for only 26 per cent of all poor relief at the abbey. Throughout the post-Black Death period the emphasis was increasingly on providing charity on a weekly basis to those coming to the almonry and to providing funds for the inmates living in the almonry and the charity boys in the almonry school. Indeed, the almoners' provision to the almonry inmates and the schoolboys doubled over this period, while the weekly sums provided by royal endowments increased the overall amounts of poor relief available from the 1390s.

As population levels in Westminster increased during the late fifteenth century there was perhaps more need for charity as poor immigrants settled in the town, or

---

[44]   R.D. Trimmer and C.G. Crump (eds), *Calendar of Charter Rolls, vol. 2: Henry III, Edward I, 1257–1300* (London: H.S.M.O, 1906), pp. 411, 424–6. For an extended discussion on the prevailing 'Patristic' attitude to the poor and poor relief in the central Middle Ages, see Rushton, 'Monastic Charitable Provision', chap. 1; and Rushton, 'Charity'.

[45]   Harvey, *Living and Dying*, pp. 24–7.

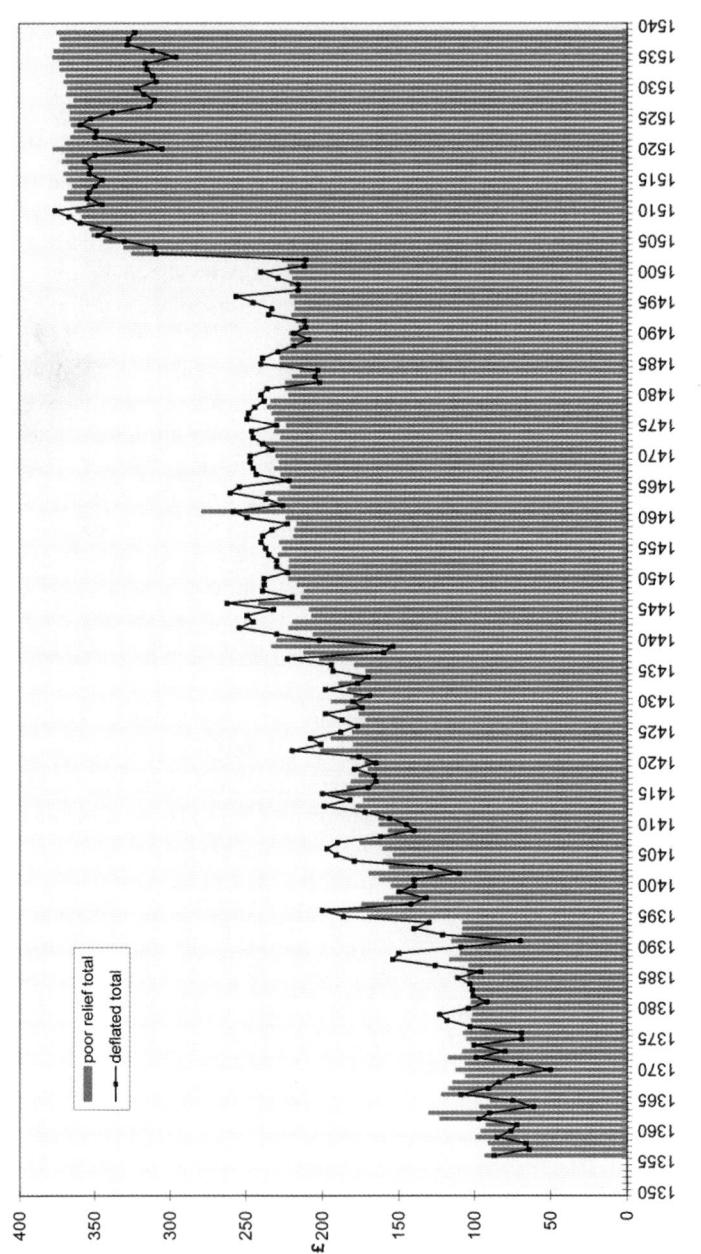

Figure 6.2   Total poor relief at Westminster Abbey 1350–1540

came to the abbey from London to receive poor relief. Unfortunately, no recipient of alms from the abbey is ever named, and so it is not possible for us to evaluate the types or the numbers of people receiving relief. There were almost certainly lists of recipients of the weekly distributions drawn up, as there were in the post-Dissolution period in the New Foundation, when there were 39 named people from Westminster receiving between 3d. and 4d. each per week.[46]

The only recipients of alms that we do know about are those fortunate enough to be granted a place in the almshouse of Henry VII that was built next to the almonry site in 1503 at a cost of over £500. Twelve men and three women occupied a two-storey building with private rooms and garderobes. The men were usually royal or abbey servants and were indulged with an annual average of £62 for their overall maintenance during the sixteenth century, 17 per cent of all charity provided by the abbey. The almshouse and its occupants are representative of the general social ethos towards the poor and their relief that had become prevalent by the end of the Middle Ages. This was an ethos that directed charity to the deserving poor – the sick, the disabled and the elderly – at the expense of general distributions to those able to make it to a distribution site such as the almonry at Westminster.[47]

The monks of Westminster continued to operate various strategies of poor relief throughout the later Middle Ages. Anniversary distributions in the almonry were never completely phased out and the almoner remained responsible for the school, the *hospicia* and numbers of almsmen housed within the almonry. The average mean proportion of poor relief to income at Westminster Abbey over the period 1300 to 1540 was 9.18 per cent. As will be shown, this not inconsiderable amount was mirrored elsewhere in the country.

At Norwich Cathedral Priory there were two major differences in the levels and types of charitable provision: the constraints imposed upon the priory by falling income throughout the fifteenth and sixteenth centuries in contrast to the better funded royal abbey, and the prevalence of supplying charity in the form of victuals and clothes at the priory rather than cash, as was mostly the case at Westminster.

Norwich Cathedral Priory had nothing like the same resources available to it as Westminster Abbey, and was indeed operating in debt for large proportions of the fourteenth, fifteenth and sixteenth centuries. For evidence of income and expenditure at the priory we are not reliant only upon the *Valor Ecclesiasticus* and the chance annual survival of a complete set of obedientiary account rolls, because there are preserved a set of documents known as the *Status Obedientiarum*.[48] These documents survive for eleven years from 1363 to 1534, and delineate the total receipts and expenditure of every obedientiary at the priory as well as the master of its dependent St Paul's hospital and the sub-priors of the priory cells in Norfolk, allowing for as accurate a picture as possible of the state of the priory's

---

[46]   WAM, 37462–37547. The names are contained in lists for the period 1551–55, and show a turnover of recipients of the order of approximately 15 per cent each week.

[47]   Similar conclusions are reached by Maddern, Chapter 5 in this volume (Ed.).

[48]   NRO, Archives of Norwich Cathedral Priory, DCN 1/13/1–6.

finances during this period. The *Status Obedientiarum* demonstrates that the priory was recorded as being in debt for every recorded date outside the 1470s. In itself this was not fatal to the financial administration of the priory; providing the aggregate of debts did not exceed a single year's income then the institution was able to operate at a functional level.[49] However, the difference in income to Westminster Abbey, and the subsequent ability to fund poor relief, was substantial. At the beginning of the fifteenth century Norwich was perhaps 75 per cent the size of Westminster in terms of income, but by the last decade of both houses' existence it had become *c.* 31 per cent.[50]

This curtailed the priory's ability to provide poor relief for Norwich throughout the post-Black Death period. Although the priory managed to sustain a relatively steady average proportion of poor relief to income during this time – between 9.45 per cent and 10.1 per cent – the real amounts of poor relief dropped from over £170 to under £100. This probably represents a more common picture of what was happening to the poor relief efforts of English religious houses after the Black Death than that of Westminster Abbey. But Norwich Cathedral Priory was also supplying the majority of its charity in the form of food or clothing rather than in cash as at Westminster.

In the pre-Black Death period the amounts of grain being milled and baked into bread for the poor within the almonry were considerable. Between 1283 and 1346 an annual average of almost 384 quarters of various grains and pulses were milled. For instance, in 1282–83 436 quarters of unspecified grain was set aside for the poor at a cost to the almoner of £109 13s.[51] This huge amount was baked into bread at a cost of £5 and distributed between 3 March and 1 August. This level of provision may have provided as many as 90,000 loaves of bread depending on the grain used.[52] However, it was a provision that was being distributed to the poor only at certain times of the year. Through the 1280s the provision was always made from either February or March until July or August over a period of five months of the year. No further explanation is forthcoming for this policy of poor relief, but it is most likely that the second half of the year after the harvest was a time of increased necessity for the poor of the town and its hinterland and

---

[49]   E. Stone, 'Profit-and-Loss Accountancy at Norwich Cathedral Priory', *Transactions of the Royal Historical Society*, 12 (1962), 25–48. However, the sums recorded for income always included certain amounts of bad debt, which was more of a notional assessment of cash received rather than a realistic cash income. These bad debts could deflate the figures for income given in the *Status Obedientiarum* by as much as 20 per cent.

[50]   *Valor Ecclesiasticus*, III (1817), 289. These figures relate to the net income of Westminster Abbey against the net income of Norwich Cathedral Priory derived from the gross income recorded in the *Status Obedientiarum* in 1410 and the figure given in 1535 of almost £875.

[51]   NRO, DCN 1/6/5.

[52]   These calculations are based on B.M.S. Campbell, J.A. Galloway, D. Keene and M. Murphy, *A Medieval Capital and its Grain Supply: Agrarian Production and Distribution in the London Region c. 1300* (London: Institute of British Geographers, 1993), pp. 191–2.

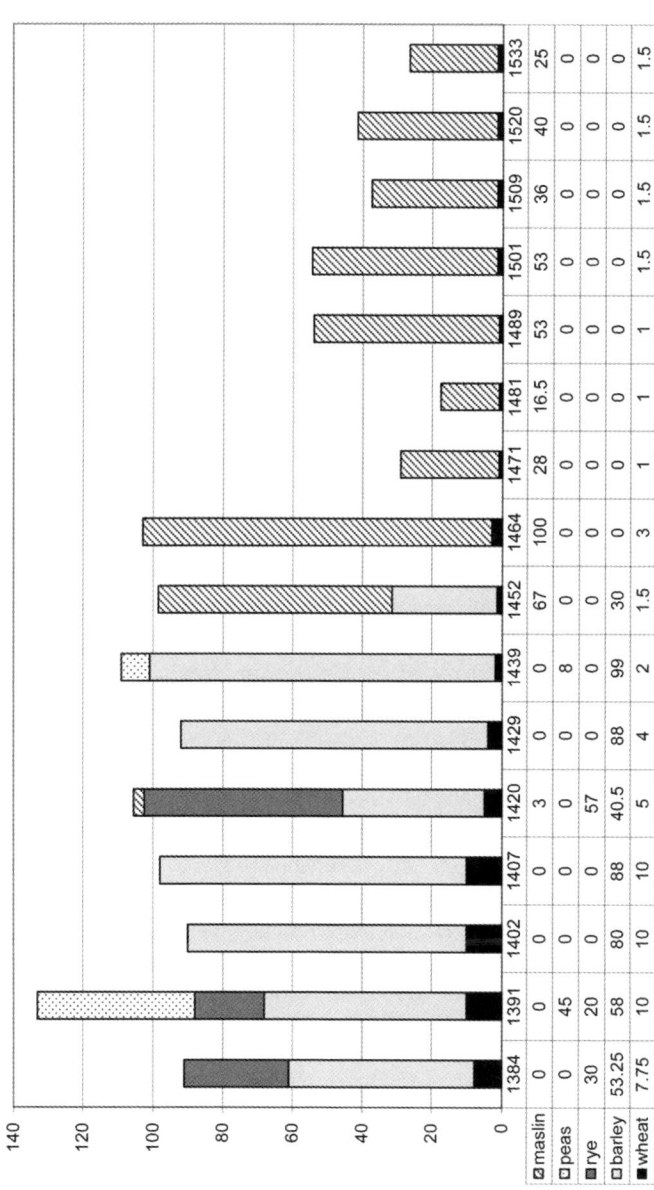

	1384	1391	1402	1407	1420	1429	1439	1452	1464	1471	1481	1489	1501	1509	1520	1533
maslin	0	0	0	0	3	0	0	67	100	28	16.5	53	53	36	40	25
peas	0	45	0	0	0	0	8	0	0	0	0	0	0	0	0	0
rye	30	20	0	0	57	0	0	0	0	0	0	0	0	0	0	0
barley	53.25	58	80	88	40.5	88	99	30	0	0	0	1	0	0	0	0
wheat	7.75	10	10	10	5	4	2	1.5	3	1	1	1	1.5	1.5	1.5	1.5

decadal years

Figure 6.3   Totals of grain milled by the almoner to make into bread for poor relief at Norwich Cathedral Priory 1380s–1530s. Decade years are dependent on surviving documents.

so provision was made up until harvest time of the year in question. This would, however, have denied the poor any provision of relief during much of the winter. But the survival of an early series of priors' account rolls demonstrates that it was not only the almoner who was responsible for providing grain for milling, baking and distribution to the poor as bread. In the late thirteenth century, apart from the amounts of grain set aside for the Maundy week distributions amounting to between five and ten quarters, the office of the prior distributed an average of six quarters directly to the almoner for distribution at 'diverse times'.

The office also accounted for a standard amount of two quarters four bushels to 'recluses' in the town (presumably hermits), varying totals of between 7 and 29 quarters for prisoners in Norwich Castle and a further large amount of unspecified grain averaging *c.* 65 quarters which was usually described as *liberaciones.*[53] This terminology would suggest it was the provision for the prior's household, but on a single occasion in 1279–80 the wording makes it clear that the 65.5 quarters provision was categorised as poor relief with the wording 'liberaciones ad opus pauperibus et tenentibus'.[54] This suggests that this annual amount may have partly constituted the provision made for the daily feeding of 12 poor men in the conventual refectory, which in 1535 was described as an 'ancient observation'.[55] If correct, the priory evidently catered for a steady number of poor through the post-harvest period each year, until February or March when extra amounts were provided by the almoner for what may have been large numbers of people for whom the supplementary charity of several loaves of bread each week may have been an essential concomitant to their survival.

The post-Black Death account rolls of the almoner at Norwich only survive in series from 1378. By this time the amounts of grains being milled specifically for the use of the poor had been severely reduced from their pre-1350 levels. Figure 6.3 shows that until the 1460s decadal figures for the amounts of grain averaged about 100 quarters per annum, and after 1470 the figure never rose above 60 quarters. The cheaper maslin was also the common grain type used after 1450, demonstrating a desire to economise on poor relief spending.[56]

In the late fifteenth century and into the sixteenth century the amounts of grain for poor relief averaged *c.* 40 quarters per annum, and by the last recorded account year only 25 quarters of maslin and one and a half quarters of wheat were processed for poor relief.[57] This was close to the 25 quarters recorded in

---

[53]   The thirteenth-century priors' account rolls are NRO, DCN 1/1/1–14. The first nine rolls have been damaged by damp, but are still largely legible apart from along their right hand sides where they have been mostly destroyed.

[54]   NRO, DCN 1/6/5.

[55]   *Valor Ecclesiasticus*, III (1817), 287.

[56]   For different types of bread, especially that given to the poor, see Maddern, Chapter 5 in this volume, p. 88, n. 46.

[57]   NRO, DCN 1/6/137.

the *Valor Ecclesiasticus* two years later.[58] This kind of provision would still allow for something like 6,000 loaves of bread, but it was only a shadow of the amounts that had been distributed in the pre-Black Death period, and less than half of the average provision made in the first half of the fifteenth century. Unlike Westminster Abbey, Norwich Cathedral Priory did not receive any significant endowments with which to fund an increased amount of charity in the fifteenth and sixteenth centuries. Dwindling revenues and an almost constant residual debt forced economies in every aspect of monastic life, and the poor who had been able to rely on the priory's charity when they needed it were among those who suffered.

It is not known whether the monks of Norwich Cathedral Priory provided poor relief mostly in kind rather than in cash because of tradition or silver money shortage. Either way it is difficult to make direct comparisons with Westminster Abbey of amounts spent on poor relief over long periods of time because it is not always clear how much grain was purchased and how much came from the priory's manors as demesne production or tithe. By 1535 the *Valor Ecclesiasticus* records the total amount of poor relief as £89,[59] still a considerable sum of charity for the poor of Norwich but much reduced from the annual sum of *c.* £170 supplied before 1350. This can partly be explained by the demographic disaster of the Black Death and its effect on the number of poor in the city after 1350, but the dwindling resources of the priory estates from this time forced the monks to reduce all expenditure, including poor relief. The *Valor Ecclesiasticus* allows us to make an assessment of the state of poor relief at the majority of other religious houses in England in the early sixteenth century.

Monastic Poor Relief in Early Sixteenth-Century England

The survey now known as the *Valor Ecclesiasticus* was compiled in 1535 as the result of a fiscal bill passed through Parliament in 1534 that secured for the Crown 10 per cent of all ecclesiastical income.[60] The survey was an assessment of the income from all ecclesiastical lands and rents for the year 1534–35. The reason the *Valor Ecclesiasticus* allows for an evaluation of monastic charitable provision is because the county commissioners were under instructions to deduct from the gross income of each house – apart from legally indentured rents, stipends and pensions – any alms which the religious were obliged to give to the poor by either charitable bequests of benefactors or through custom.[61] The resultant net

---

[58]   *Valor Ecclesiasticus*, III (1817), 287.

[59]   To which should be added the £9 in alms provided by the priory's cell of Lynn.

[60]   26 Henry VIII, c. 3, see *Statutes of the Realm*, III: 1509/10–1545, (ed.) W.E. Taunton, 493–9.

[61]   The *Valor Ecclesiasticus* is held in TNA under the classmark E 344/26. The instructions to the commissioners are at TNA, E 344/1, fol. 1.

income was the sum upon which the religious were taxed.[62] As such it is the only pre-Dissolution source that allows for the collection of a large enough dataset to compile a viable quantitative analysis of monastic charitable provision at a national scale.

Such an analysis was attempted as part of Alexander Savine's 1909 study of monastic financial management in the *Valor Ecclesiasticus*.[63] However, Savine's methodology in quantifying the evidence for monastic charity was fundamentally flawed. First, he simply excluded 47 houses (including – inexplicably – the largest distributor of charity: Bury St Edmunds Abbey). Second, he counted very few hospitals in his analysis (whether dependent on a monastery or not). Third, Savine accepted without question the criteria of the Henrician commissions, respecting what should be allowed to count as poor relief. Fourth, he assumed that those houses recorded as supplying no charity by the commissioners *were* in reality supplying nothing. Subsequently, Savine arrived at the low figure of *c.* two and a half per cent as the proportion of alms to gross income being distributed in charity by the religious houses of England on the eve of the Dissolution.[64]

The historical perpetuation of Savine's figure has had a very long half-life. Three generations of historians have repeated it and thus fashioned it into an orthodoxy that has usually been used to castigate the charitable efforts of the monasteries. Between 1926 and 1998 12 extremely influential historians in 14 different works invoked the low estimate as a realistic assessment of the inadequacy of monastic welfare.[65] According to W.K. Jordan, 'Savine's careful analysis of the *Valor*

---

[62]   All calculations of alms as a percentage of income in the *Valor Ecclesiasticus* first take off from gross income the rents, stipends and pensions allowed as exemptions by the commissioners. Then, before subtracting the alms, the percentage is obtained. This method allows for a percentage outlay on poor relief from the (at least potentially) real income of the monasteries and hospitals, rather than the crude gross income as calculated by Savine (for which see below).

[63]   Alexander Savine, *English Monasteries*, pp. 227–42.

[64]   Savine, p. 239.

[65]   They are: R.H. Snape, *English Monastic Finances in the Later Middle Ages* (Cambridge: Cambridge University Press, 1926) p. 115 (with incorrect page reference to Savine); Sydney Webb and Beatrice Webb, *English Poor Law History: The Old Poor Law* (London: Longmans, Green, 1927; Camden, CN: Archon, 1963), p. 17; Geoffrey Baskerville, *English Monks and the Suppression of the Monasteries* (London: Cape, 1937), p. 31; A.G. Dickens, 'An Elizabethan Defender of the Monasteries', *Church Quarterly Review*, 130 (1940), 236–62 (pp. 253–4); *The Book of William Morton, Almoner of Peterborough Monastery 1448–1467*, (eds) W.T. Mellows and P.I. King (Oxford: Oxford University Press, 1954), p. xxvii; Wilbur K. Jordan, *Philanthropy in England 1480–1660* (London: Routledge, 1959), p. 59; A.G. Dickens, *The English Reformation* (London: Batsford, 1964), p. 56; G.W.O. Woodward, *The Dissolution of the Monasteries* (London: Pitkin, 1966), pp. 21–3; Christopher Haigh, *The Last Days of the Lancashire Monasteries and the Pilgrimage of Grace* (Manchester: Manchester University Press for the Chetham Society, 1969), pp. 53–4; W.R.D. Jones, *The Tudor Commonwealth 1529–1559* (London:

Ecclesiasticus lends full support to the inferences which may be drawn from the extensive contemporary literature … that the quality of monastic alms was even less impressive than the quantity'.[66]

Savine's analysis, and the general historiographical acceptance of the lack of useful monastic poor relief by the sixteenth century, has recently been revised.[67] By adding the religious houses and hospitals missed by Savine and recalculating the values of poor relief recorded by the government commissioners in the *Valor Ecclesiasticus* these new studies demonstrate that in fact the proportion of monastic poor relief to income was closer to 5 per cent.[68]

Even this figure, however, underestimates the real level of poor relief being provided by the monasteries and hospitals of England in the 1530s. The two most vital determinants of underestimation from the data in the *Valor Ecclesiasticus* are the missing values for 277 houses and the impact of commissioner bias in the recording of poor relief. The latter is difficult to measure, but it seems certain that there was extensive underassessment in certain parts of the country by commissioners working for the Crown and attempting to maximise the levels of taxation taken from religious houses. For example, the *Valor Ecclesiasticus* seems to indicate that certain parts of Lincolnshire, in contrast to others, were entirely devoid of monastic charity. Closer inspection, however, reveals that the areas in question correspond to the deaneries that served as administrative units for certain members of the commission – Yarborough, Grimsby, Walshcroft and Wraggoe. Hence, their apparent lack of charity is more than likely an artifact of under-recording by the six commissioners (out of a total of 31 appointed for the county) designated to survey these deaneries.[69] Thornton Abbey, one of the wealthiest of them, enjoyed a net income of £594 17s. 2¾d., though, according to the *Valor Ecclesiasticus*, it had no charitable obligations.[70]

So, any assessment of the quantity of monastic charity derived from the *Valor Ecclesiasticus* must first control, as much as possible, for the characteristics of the commissions that made the evaluations. This caveat does not necessarily imply negative control in every instance. The commissioners who belonged to the families who founded monasteries, and often still had relatives within them, were

Athlone, 1970), p. 118; Christopher Haigh, *Reformation and Resistance in Tudor Lancashire* (Cambridge: Cambridge University Press, 1975), p. 120; Carlo M. Cipolla, *Before the Industrial Revolution: European Society and Economy, 1000–1700* (London: Methuen, 1981), p. 22; Joyce Youings, *Sixteenth-Century England* (Harmondsworth: Penguin, 1984), p. 256; Christopher Dyer, *Standards of Living*, pp. 240–41.

[66] Jordan, p. 59.

[67] Neil S. Rushton, 'Monastic Charitable Provision in Tudor England: Quantifying and Qualifying Poor Relief in the Early Sixteenth Century', *Continuity and Change*, 16 (2001), 9–44; Neil S. Rushton and Wendy Sigle-Rushton, 'Monastic Poor Relief in Sixteenth-Century England', *Journal of Interdisciplinary History*, 32 (2001), 193–216.

[68] Rushton and Sigle-Rushton, pp. 201–3.

[69] The Lincolnshire entries are at *Valor Ecclesiasticus*, IV (1821), 1–143.

[70] *Valor Ecclesiasticus*, IV (1821), 73–4.

hardly likely to have been hostile to them. In the northern counties, the Pilgrimage of Grace, the only popular rebellion at least partly inspired by the Dissolution of the lesser houses, was instigated with the collusion of several members of the conservative gentry. Ultimately, however, the political environment of 1535 did not make for a commission sympathetic to the fair taxation of the religious houses.[71]

Using an Ordinary Least Square (OLS) regression, the variables that would be most likely to affect the recording of charitable provision in the *Valor Ecclesiasticus* have been used in order to create a model whereby we can estimate the 'real' level of monastic charitable provision if the 'bias' included in the source is negated, or 'set to zero'.[72] The inclusion in the regression model of the variables of religious order, geographical location of house (highland/lowland) and environment of house (urban/rural) control for any differences these determinants may have had. The regression analysis tends to confirm that bias on the part of the commissioners influenced the recorded levels of charity. Setting the probability of zero charity to zero produces a more realistic value of charity.

The overall results of the regression are presented in Table 6.1, where the full sample represents all houses recorded in the *Valor Ecclesiasticus* and the restricted sample represents all houses with a net income over £50 recorded in the *Valor Ecclesiasticus*, so as to allow for the probability that most houses with an income under £50 (*n* = 125) could perhaps afford little or no charity. The estimates suggest that actual charitable provision on the eve of the Dissolution amounted to just over 7 per cent of monastic income – a figure almost three times higher than the one calculated by Savine and subsequently perpetuated in the historiography of the twentieth century. Using these models, the total estimated national sum of monastic charitable provision from the *Valor Ecclesiasticus* falls between £10,630 and £13,265.[73]

---

[71] Knowles, *Religious Orders*, III, 320–35; Haigh, *Last Days of the Lancashire Monasteries*, pp. 61–85; C.S.L. Davies, 'Popular Religion and the Pilgrimage of Grace', in Anthony Fletcher and John Stevenson (eds), *Order and Disorder in Early Modern England* (Cambridge: Cambridge University Press, 1985), pp. 58–91; Anthony W. Shaw, 'The Involvement of the Religious Orders in the Northern Risings of 1536/7: Compulsion or Desire', *Downside Review*, 407 (1999), 89–114.

[72] The full statistical results of this estimation model can be found in Rushton and Sigle-Rushton.

[73] These sums are derived from the calculation: 7.18 per cent to 8.96 per cent of [(total net monastic/hospital income) £142,834 + (recorded poor relief) £5,218] £148,052. Alternatively, multiply £19.13 or £15.32 by 694, the total number of all monasteries and hospitals included in the *Valor Ecclesiasticus* (inclusive of all houses for which incomplete records exist). The *actual* total of monastic provision would be higher if allowance were made for the houses that do not appear in the *Valor Ecclesiasticus* at all. However, these were mostly small houses and hospitals (worth under £50) and the friaries (more likely to receive than give alms) and so would not raise the figure significantly.

Table 6.1   Predicted poor relief of religious houses recorded in the *Valor Ecclesiasticus*, from OLS estimation model.

	Average predicted poor relief per house for the full sample	Average predicted poor relief per house for restricted sample
Predicted average poor relief from OLS regression	£19 13s.	£15 32s.
Predicted poor relief as a percentage of monastic income	8.96%	7.18%

	Total predicted poor relief for the full sample of houses	Total predicted poor relief for the restricted sample of houses
Predicted total poor relief from OLS regression	£13,265	£10,630

Despite the evidence of inaccuracy in the *Valor Ecclesiasticus* data, there are still reasons to interpret the results of the regression with caution. First, the model specification assumes that a record of zero provision provides an adequate measure of bias and that the variables selected pertain to recorded but not actual charity. If the regressors in the bias function are somehow capturing county- or house-level characteristics that are associated with actual charitable provision, the model is eliminating too much bias. The choice of zero-recorded charity as an indicator of bias implies that houses with a higher probability of no provision were also subject to a higher level of under recording. This underlying relationship cannot be verified with the data at hand. Given that the quality of some of the data has been brought into question, other data in the *Valor Ecclesiasticus* may be similarly flawed. The religious houses assessed in the *Valor Ecclesiasticus* were probably as eager to undervalue their incomes as the assessors were to undervalue their exemptions against taxation. Since this study attempts to correct for the undervaluation of almsgiving and not the undervaluation of income, the estimated charity as a percentage of income may be too high. It should be remembered, though, that income recorded in the *Valor Ecclesiasticus* was a *notional* value derived from expectations of rents and other dues, and that in reality much of this income would have been in arrears and thus not available to the monastic house when providing charitable provision.[74] This would tend to negate any argument that suggests monastic income recorded in the *Valor Ecclesiasticus* should be revised upwards and thus charity as a proportion of that income downwards. Both contextual and empirical evidence support the hypothesis of a systematic

---

[74]   See John Hatcher, 'The Great Slump of the Mid-Fifteenth Century', in Richard Britnell and John Hatcher (eds), *Progress and Problems in Medieval England* (Cambridge: Cambridge University Press, 1996), pp. 237–72 (pp. 256–7).

measurement error in the *Valor Ecclesiasticus* data that tends to underestimate monastic charitable provision.

Conclusions

Monastic poor relief changed in conjunction with social attitudes to the poor and charity over the course of the Middle Ages. The evidence from Westminster Abbey and Norwich Cathedral Priory demonstrates that the religious were adapting their relief strategies to the socio-economic dislocations brought about by the Black Death in the mid-fourteenth century, and attempting to impose more discriminatory methods of social welfare. This was achieved by the investment of more resources into housing the known poor and weekly distributions of cash or food rather than the large anniversary doles that predominated in the pre-Black Death period.

However, monastic charity never became a commodified system of poor relief. By either donation or sale, proportions of the wealth of the very richest in the land – primarily the top 5 per cent – was divested, in the shape of land or tenements, to the biggest corporations in the land: monasteries. Part of the function of these corporations was to convert this wealth into cash by way of rents, and then to distribute it, either directly in cash or in provisions bought with the cash, to the poorest, say 20 per cent, of society. By the time of the compilation of the *Valor Ecclesiasticus* in 1535 this sum may have ranged from approximately seven to nine per cent of the total monastic income, potentially as much as £13,000 per annum being directed to the poor in various forms of charity. Monasteries were thus the administrative instruments of the largest form of wealth redistribution in English medieval society. In some respects whether monastic charitable provision became more efficient and useful to the poor over the course of the later Middle Ages is irrelevant. Deserving or not, it was principally the poorest 20 per cent of society who were receiving this welfare provision and it was they who were always the least able to escape from the cycle of poverty in which their society trapped them. Transferring the income from tied-capital from the wealthiest sectors of society – the landed aristocracy, gentry and merchant classes – and converting it into ready cash for those who would be forced to spend it almost immediately could only help fuel the commercialisation of the English economy and increase market opportunities for the poorest sectors of urban and, to a lesser extent, rural communities. Despite being instruments of feudal society, English religious houses, in the name of Christian charity, were the largest providers of social welfare to the poorest members of the populace. Despite fundamental changes in the logistics of charity during the later Middle Ages, monastic charity remained mostly decommodified – social redistribution was more important than a rigid, work-ethic based welfare system.

Unfortunately for the poor, the Reformation which dissolved the monastic corporations did not immediately replace this infrastructure of redistribution. Instead, national and local government went about the commodification of labour with the introduction of varying degrees of discriminatory poor laws and regulations which insisted only those deemed as the 'deserving' poor should receive relief. The poverty problem was most acute in the generation between the Dissolution of the monasteries and the introduction of compulsory poor rates at local and national levels in the 1560s and 1570s. Rapid population growth, spiralling inflation, and an inconsistent replacement strategy for the suppressed institutions which had supplied as much as £13,000 per annum in charitable provision caused a social crisis described by both contemporaries and by early modern historians.[75] This social crisis was most acute in the urban centres. Despite income from urban rents, the estates, and therefore the wealth, of the religious houses were predominantly based in the countryside. In terms of charitable provision a disproportionate amount of this rural income was diverted to funding schemes in urban areas because that is where most of the large monasteries were based by the end of the Middle Ages. Therefore the effect of the monastic system of wealth redistribution was that not only did it transfer income from the tied-capital of landed estates to the propertyless poor, but that it also helped to redistribute the wealth of the countryside into urban areas.

The failure, in the first generation after the Dissolution, adequately to replace the funds for charitable provision supplied by urban monasteries, caused a serious escalation of the poverty problem in the towns of mid-sixteenth century England. However, most English religious houses in the sixteenth century had, since the late fourteenth century, been faced with a declining or static income, the value of which was also diminishing in real terms from at least the 1520s because of inflation. Even if the Dissolution had never happened, the monasteries would still have eventually needed help from secular authorities to deal with the growing problem of social poverty, because it had begun to take on a new dimension and required the kind of administrative infrastructure to control it which only government could provide. The systems of poor relief and wealth redistribution operated by the religious houses for centuries would have required the reform and restructuring of these institutions for them to have continued to provide a genuinely efficient welfare programme for the poorest members of urban and rural society. Unfortunately for them, and for the poor, the religious houses of England were not given the opportunity of reform but were instead suppressed, dissolved, and taken out of the socio-economic equation.

---

[75]   Slack, p. 13.

Chapter 7

Changing the Practice of Charity in Sixteenth-Century Norwich: 'the verie nedefull and urgent reformacion'[1]

Lesley Silvester

This study documents the provision of and motivation for poor relief in sixteenth-century Norwich. Much of the scholarship concerning the religious reform of the sixteenth century has debated the impact of the Reformation and related the religious doctrine of the Reformation to political concerns: the idea of 'godly rule'.[2] This question of religious and moral infiltration into the political sphere lies behind the decisions made by the civic authorities that shaped the way in which charity was administered in Norwich during the sixteenth century. Matthew Reynolds has described Norwich as a 'hotbed of puritanism and radical dissent from the 1560s to the end of James I's reign'.[3] I will investigate whether this influenced the authorities' decision making, in relation to the background of the economic and religious environment of the city.

Historians have debated the extent to which Protestant leanings contributed to tighter social control. Margaret Spufford has argued that social control and a 'stricter moral code of behaviour' were not related to Protestantism and not new to the late sixteenth century.[4] She suggests that reforming elements can be seen as early as the thirteenth century, when the country experienced a time of similar population pressure and inflation to the sixteenth century.[5] Keith Wrightson on the other hand, shows that a slow but fundamental process of social change

---

[1]   *Records*, ii, 344.

[2]   Robert Tittler, 'Reformation, Resources and Authority in English Towns: An Overview', in Patrick Collinson and John Craig (eds), *The Reformation in English Towns 1500–1640* (New York: St Martin's Press, 1998), p. 190.

[3]   Matthew Reynolds, *Godly Reformers and their Opponents in Early Modern England: Religion in Norwich c. 1560–1643* (Woodbridge: Boydell, 2005), p. 19.

[4]   Margaret Spufford, 'Puritanism and Social Control?', in Anthony Fletcher and John Stevenson (eds), *Order and Disorder in Early Modern England* (Cambridge: Cambridge University Press, 1985), p. 41.

[5]   Spufford, p. 48.

occurred in the late sixteenth and early seventeenth centuries, which owed much to religious reform.[6]

Prior to the Dissolution, the religious houses of Norwich played a large role in administering charity in the form of food and clothing for the poor and in running hospitals and leper houses.[7] In the churches of medieval and early sixteenth-century Norwich, charity was also seen in offerings to the poor that were either made in church or set out as bequests in wills which were then doled out in formal relief as alms. In these forms, charity was an unconditional practice of the giving of food and shelter to the poor, but by the early sixteenth century it increasingly became the giving of money, usually through the medium of an almoner and was administered through the monasteries, the guilds and the fraternities. Charity then became a different exercise, turning into the more conditional practice of poor relief, whereby only deserving applicants might receive it. After the Dissolution, when the religious houses ceased to exist, there was pressure on the civic authorities to look after the poor as this could no longer be left to the Church, although civic authority continued administering relief through the church system.

The Reformation was partly responsible for this change, which caused a notable alteration in the way in which poor relief was executed.[8] Initially Thomas Cromwell's statute of 1536 directed the collection and administration of poor relief to local parishes and over the sixteenth century other bills gradually developed the administration of poor relief into the beginnings of the civil parish.[9] Assistance to the poor was collected within the parish by laypersons elected by the parish authorities and then distributed each week to those deemed needy of relief. This practice in itself created a change in how the poor were perceived. The historian Felicity Heal has remarked that this giving of money at third hand causes the giver and the recipient to be distanced from each other and creates an 'otherness' of the poor.[10] This 'otherness' and distance makes it easy to give the poor derogatory labels, and set them into divisive social categories.

Authorities in all parts of England were becoming concerned and various laws and statutes were enacted to combat this perceived problem. In Norwich, efforts to improve poor relief were present even prior to the Reformation. Neil Rushton shows elsewhere in this volume that by the early sixteenth century, religious

---

[6]   Keith Wrightson, *English Society 1580–1680* (London: Routledge, 2003), esp. pp. 201–21.

[7]   See Rushton, Chapter 6 in this volume, pp. 109–21.

[8]   Marjorie K. McIntosh, 'Poverty, Charity and Coercion in Elizabethan England', *Journal of Interdisciplinary History*, 35 (2005), 457–79 (p. 460); Neil S. Rushton 'Monastic Charitable Provision', 9–44.

[9]   Paul Slack, *The English Poor Law 1531–1782* (Basingstoke: Macmillan, 1990), p. 18; Marjorie K. McIntosh, 'Local Responses', 209–45 (pp. 229–30).

[10]   Felicity Heal, *Hospitality in Early Modern England* (New York: Oxford University Press, 1990), pp. 16–17; Anthony Fletcher and John Stevenson, 'Introduction', in Fletcher and Stevenson (eds), *Order and Disorder*, p. 14.

houses had begun to impose more discriminatory methods of social welfare.[11] At the same time, the authorities in the city were frequently taking measures to deal with the poor.[12] The town employed a Master Beggar and in 1531 began granting licences to beggars. After the statute of 27 Henry VIII c. 25, in 1536, the municipal authority began administering poor relief.[13] As early as 1520 soaring corn prices due to a bad harvest caused the Aldermen to provide a grain stock, an expedient that was continued in various ways throughout the sixteenth century.[14] In 1554 the stock was made permanent by a bequest from William Castleton, the first Dean of Norwich.[15] An entry from the Norwich Assembly begins with a statement that the poor for many years have been relying on spinning as their only means of survival. Butchers were to be compelled to bring their fleeces to market with the meat from slaughtered sheep and to sell the fleeces 'openly in the market to poore women until the hour of xij'.[16] It seems the fleeces were being sold 'in gret and gorre sommes' to the trades that used them, which left the poorest skins in which there was no profit for the poor to buy.[17] This shows that, as early as 1532, the Norwich authorities were putting into place orders to assist the poor, and that charity was not just the domain of the religious houses.

A marked prejudice against the poor was seen in literature, images and in the language used to mark the poor as being responsible for their own misfortune.[18] Robert Jütte has shown that the use of pejorative terms in describing the poor increased during the sixteenth century, widening the distinction between the deserving and the undeserving poor.[19] According to Craig Muldrew, 'the difference between wealth or sustenance and poverty was often a judgment of individual moral worth defined in terms of credit or the failure thereof. Poverty was often thought of as a condition of competitive moral failure.'[20] Sickness and disease were thought to be caused from association with sin and disorder, they were not just 'a physical

---

[11] Rushton Chapter 6 in this volume, pp. 106, 126.

[12] The ways in which the corporate authorities of Norwich carried out measures of poor relief is discussed in detail and compared with York, Bristol and Exeter in N.D. Brodie, 'Beggary, Vagabondage and Poor Relief: English Statutes in the Urban Context, 1495–1572' (unpublished doctoral thesis, University of Tasmania, 2010).

[13] *Records*, ii, xcviii.

[14] *Records*, ii, xcvii.

[15] *Records*, ii, xcviii.

[16] *Records*, ii, 119.

[17] *Records*, ii, 119.

[18] For literature see discussion by Patrick Collinson, 'Puritanism and the Poor', in Rosemary Horrocks and Sarah Rees Jones (eds), *Pragmatic Utopias: Ideals and Communities, 1200–1630* (Cambridge: Cambridge University Press, 2001), pp. 242–58; for paintings, see Virginia G. Tuttle, 'Bosch's Image of Poverty', *Art Bulletin*, 63 (1981), 88–95; for both image and language, see Robert Jütte, *Poverty and Deviance*, chap. 2.

[19] Jütte, pp. 8–14.

[20] Craig Muldrew, *The Economy of Obligation: The Culture of Credit and Social Relations in Early Modern England* (New York: St Martin's Press, 1998), p. 311.

process but also a moral one'.[21] Philippa Maddern has discussed medieval body politics whereby 'Dissolute behaviour constituted a direct and rebellious attack on Christ's physical body, which, in true Augustinian fashion was instantly refracted in a violent breakdown of public and social order'.[22] These Catholic notions of bodily health displaying moral values appear to have become Protestant values by the late sixteenth century. A vagrant class was being manufactured; labelling them as such created paupers and delinquents. As well, the numbers of so-called 'masterless men', the able-bodied sturdy vagabonds, gave rise to fears of uprising and disorder, not entirely without justification as seen in several towns in Europe during the sixteenth century.[23]

These changes in the perception of the poor then resulted in attitudinal changes in the provision of charity. In contrast to the humanist view of the poor as not being responsible for their condition, the view of Reformists such as Martin Bucer that charity should not be indiscriminate gained currency.[24] Although Bucer is not as well known as some Protestant reformers such as Luther, more recently his doctrine is being seen as an important contribution to the sixteenth-century Reformation.[25] In particular, he emphasised the role of proper discipline in the Church, a role that included obedience to the Church and the 'oversight of morality in the parish'.[26] The Archbishop of Canterbury, Thomas Cranmer, invited Bucer to England and from 1549 until he died in England in 1551, he was Regius Professor of Divinity at Cambridge.[27] In that time he became close to Matthew Parker who was later to become Archbishop of Canterbury and was co-executor

---

[21]   Paul Slack, *The Impact of Plague in Tudor and Stuart England* (London: Routledge & Kegan Paul, 1985), p. 29.

[22]   Philippa Maddern, 'Order and Disorder', in Carole Rawcliffe and Richard Wilson (eds), *Medieval Norwich* (London: Continuum, 2004), pp. 189–212 (p. 211).

[23]   Jütte, pp. 185–90; Henry Kamen, *Early Modern European Society* (London and New York: Routledge, 2000), p. 182. See also Farmer, Chapter 2, pp. 40–41, and Elliott, Chapter 8, pp. 159–60, in this volume.

[24]   Martin Bucer, *A Treatise, how by the Worde of God, Christian mens almose ought to be distributed* (s.l., 1551). See also, discussion in Steve Hindle, *On the Parish?*, pp. 99–104; Jütte, p. 12; Kamen, pp. 182–3.

[25]   Diarmaid MacCulloch suggests that he influenced John Calvin. See his *Reformation: Europe's House Divided 1490–1700* (London: Allen Lane, 2003), pp. 180–82, 197; see also *Martin Bucer: Reforming Church and Community*, (ed.) D.F. Wright (Cambridge: Cambridge University Press, 1994); J. William Black, 'From Martin Bucer to Richard Baxter: "Discipline" and Reformation in Sixteenth- and Seventeenth-century England', *Church History*, 70 (2001), 644–73; Mark E. VanderSchaaf, 'Archbishop Parker's Efforts Toward a Bucerian Discipline in the Church of England', *Sixteenth Century Journal*, 8 (1977), 85–103; Hastings Ellis, 'The Contributions of Martin Bucer to the Reformation', *Harvard Theological Review*, 24 (1931), 29–42.

[26]   Black, pp. 647–8; MacCulloch, p. 181; VanderSchaaf, p. 85.

[27]   VanderSchaaf, p. 85.

of Bucer's will as well as delivering the sermon at his funeral.[28] Parker was later responsible for introducing disciplinary canons within the Church of England for both clergy and laity that corresponded with the discipline suggested in Bucer's *De Regno Christi* and *Censura*.[29] It is likely that the consequence of Parker's affinity to Bucerian principles affected the religious environment of Norwich. He was a native of Norwich and parishioner of St Clement's church which Reynolds has described as 'an early well-spring of reformed teaching'.[30]

There is evidence that the administrative environment of Norwich was significantly influenced by the religious reforms of the sixteenth century. Muriel McClendon has shown that as early as 1539, religious reform was causing disruption of traditional authority, both secular and religious, and suggested, 'religion permeated virtually all aspects of early modern society'.[31] There were numerous incidents in which churches were ransacked, church services disrupted and clergy assaulted during the 1540s from both Protestant and Catholic sympathisers.[32] However, the Norwich authorities rarely took action against those activists, seemingly preferring to tolerate 'religious differences, so long as they did not erupt into open and uncontrollable conflict'.[33] In McClendon's view, this toleration enabled Norwich to achieve a 'quiet reformation', which was further aided by the influence of a Protestant-dominated aldermanry.[34] She has identified a change in the religious orientation of the aldermanic council that took place around 1558/9 after a severe influenza epidemic.[35] At this time, 10 of the 24 aldermen died, an unprecedented incident, and by examining their wills, McClendon has suggested that at least seven of those who died were probably Catholic.[36] The religious views of the remaining aldermen and the 10 new aldermen are not as easily discerned but there is evidence of Protestant reformism creeping into the magistracy over the following decade and this was particularly noticeable in the administration of poor relief. This reformist culture not only stemmed from their beliefs but was reinforced by close ties between a number of the aldermen and some radical Protestant clergy.

However, Matthew Reynolds, while also providing evidence of Protestantism influencing the Norwich authorities, disagrees strongly with McClendon's notion

---

[28]   VanderSchaaf, p. 92.

[29]   VanderSchaaf, p. 98.

[30]   Reynolds, p. 45.

[31]   Muriel C. McClendon, '"Against God's Word": Government, Religion and the Crisis of Authority in Early Reformation Norwich', *Sixteenth Century Journal*, 25 (1994), 353–69 (p. 369).

[32]   McClendon, '"Against God's Word"', p. 362.

[33]   McClendon, '"Against God's Word"', p. 362.

[34]   Muriel C. McClendon, *The Quiet Reformation* (Stanford: Stanford University Press, 1999), pp. 197–9.

[35]   McClendon, *Quiet Reformation*, pp. 195–9.

[36]   McClendon, *Quiet Reformation*, pp. 195–6. On p. 198 she has noted that wills are 'notoriously inexact sources'.

of a 'quiet reformation'. He argues that the changeover to Protestantism was not without religious conflict, particularly conflict between the city clergy.[37] He further suggests that the Norwich authorities, with the support of reforming clergy, created a religious contest that began in the early years of the reign of Elizabeth I.[38] He describes the 1570s as 'a watershed in Norwich corporation's transformation into a godly magistracy'.[39] Reynolds's thesis is radically opposed to earlier studies of Norwich's journey through the Reformation. Yet, whether the Reformation in Norwich was quiet or noisy, the evidence suggests that the authorities did have a strong early Protestant persuasion, which articulated the direction of their treatment of the poor in sixteenth-century Norwich.

So, who were the Norwich authorities? Each year all the freemen of Norwich elected 60 men from among themselves to serve on the Common Council. This council was required to meet four times a year but usually was convened more often 'to deliberate on municipal affairs'.[40] The actual magistracy of Norwich comprised the sheriffs, aldermen and mayor, 26 men who formed the governing body of the city.[41] The two sheriffs were elected annually but the 24 aldermen were elected for life and each year the mayor was chosen by and from these 24 men.[42] So, in principle, any man who was a freeman of the city of Norwich could aspire to become a common councillor, and further, to be elected into other civic offices, culminating with the office of mayor. However, in practice only a small number of freemen ever ended up as anything more than a common councillor. The men that did aspire to and reach higher office in Norwich were part of what has been termed 'the provincial urban middle class'.[43] Taking a closer look at these aldermen between the time of the Reformation and the introduction of the Elizabethan Poor Law toward the end of the sixteenth century suggests that the council's administration of poor relief became influenced by Protestant reform. Examining the genealogies of the aldermen alongside their wills, the Norwich parish registers, and the records of freemen and apprentices, reveals how these families were closely intertwined with each other, as well as with other merchants and landowners in Norfolk, Suffolk and London.

One of these aldermen, John Aldrich, merits a detailed biography, as the Aldrich family played a prominent part in the politics of Norwich throughout the sixteenth

---

[37]   Reynolds, p. 42.

[38]   See review by Martha C. Skeeters, *Anglican and Episcopal History*, 76 (2007), 249–51.

[39]   Reynolds, p. 40.

[40]   For a detailed explanation of the Norwich electoral system, see John Thadewald Evans, 'The Political Elite of Norwich, 1620–1690: Patterns of Recruitment and the Impact of National Affairs' (unpublished doctoral thesis, Stanford University, 1971), pp. 9–46.

[41]   Evans, p. 23.

[42]   Evans, pp. 26–32.

[43]   Peter S. Bearman and Glenn Deane, 'The Structure of Opportunity: Middle-Class Mobility in England, 1548–1689', *American Journal of Sociology*, 98 (1992), 30–66 (p. 32).

century. John's father was Thomas Aldrich, a draper, who had been active in the corporate life of Norwich and served the city twice as mayor.[44] Thomas died in 1529 and his son John followed in the footsteps of his father to be part of the merchant elite of Norwich.[45] John had been an apprentice to his father and became a freeman grocer in 1541/42 and an alderman in 1545.[46] By 1551 he became a sheriff of Norwich and was later burgess in Parliament for Norwich in 1555, 1558 and 1572.[47] He achieved his first mayoralty in 1558 and was again mayor in 1570.[48] It was in this year that the aldermen, led by Aldrich, ordered a Census of the Poor to be taken, which was a significant step in establishing poor law reform in Norwich.

The Aldrich family was among a number of wealthy Norwich families who had benefited by having the means with which to acquire the religious buildings and lands that came available after the dissolution of the monasteries. A number of Norwich churches and friaries were torn down which resulted in many changes of ownership, to the benefit of both the large landholders of Norfolk and the Norwich civic authorities.[49] During the sixteenth century the family had also augmented and strengthened their wealth by making judicious marriages and business ventures. John Aldrich had married into another Norwich dynasty, the Sothertons. This family, similar to that of Aldrich, had been active in the politics of Norwich since the early sixteenth century, and had provided the city with a number of aldermen, officeholders and two mayors.[50] The register of the church of St Clement's in Norwich shows a number of these families tied strongly to this parish, with the entries of any event connected to the city elite written much larger than others on the same page. As mentioned above, this parish church was the home parish of Matthew Parker, a reformer who would later become Archbishop of Canterbury.[51]

There were two influences on John Aldrich that contributed to his attitudes and then decision-making regarding the poor. His brother Thomas, a substantial landowner, had been a bit player in the Kett uprising of 1549, being forced by Kett to be present at negotiations with the rebels, along with the then mayor Thomas Codde.[52] This rebellion was followed a few years later in 1553 by a petition

---

[44]   Francis Blomefield, *An Essay Towards a Topographical History of the County of Norfolk*, 11 vols (London: William Miller, 1805–10), III (1806), 218.

[45]   TNA, PROB 11/23, 1529, pp. 69–70.

[46]   John L'Estrange, *Calendar of the Freemen of Norwich from 1317 to 1603*, (ed.) Walter Rye (London: Elliot Stock, 1888), p. 2; Timothy Hawes, *Index to Norwich City Officers 1453–1835* (Norwich: Norfolk Record Society, 1989), p. 2.

[47]   Blomefield, *Topographical History*, III, 277, 359.

[48]   Hawes, p. 2.

[49]   Christopher Barringer, 'The Changing Face of Norwich', in Carole Rawcliffe and Richard Wilson, with Christine Clark (eds), *Norwich Since 1550* (London and New York: Hambledon and London, 2004), pp. 1–34 (p. 2).

[50]   Hawes, p. 142.

[51]   Reynolds, pp. 45–6.

[52]   Blomefield, *Topographical History*, III, 227.

sent to the Queen that has been described by R.W. Hoyle as an example of 'a continuing tradition of agrarian agitation after the failure of Kett's revolt'.[53] The role of the poor in the Kett uprising had caused subsequent Norwich authorities to be aware of managing the needs of the poor to prevent dissatisfaction and recurrent agitation such as the petition of 1553.[54] A second influence on Aldrich at this time was his alignment with other members of the Norwich elite who were strong adherents to Protestant reform in the mid-sixteenth century. Reynolds has discussed this in detail, showing the domination of this elite not just within the business and political structure of Norwich but in the offices of the Church as well.[55] My own research into the family histories of other aldermen at the time of the census in 1570 supports Reynolds's argument. The inventory of Robert Suckling who became mayor in 1572 lists a number of reformist books among his belongings, including a Geneva Bible, Foxe's *Book of Martyrs* and Calvin's *Institutions*.[56] Suckling had a large house adjacent to St Andrew's church where John More was minister. His son Edmund became Dean of Norwich Cathedral, two of his grandchildren married into the Aldrich family and later family papers suggest his eldest son was out of favour due to becoming a Romanist.[57]

Aldrich was elected to his second mayoralty of Norwich at a time of shifting social and economic change. His mayoralty actually began just a few weeks prior to a 1570 uprising in Norwich. The uprising had been led by local gentry and was nominally aimed at encouraging the citizens of Norwich to 'expulse the Strangers from the city and realm'.[58] The Strangers were Dutch and Walloon families, some of whom had been invited to Norwich in 1565 to stimulate its flagging textile economy.[59] The number of immigrants was meant to be limited to 300, but increased markedly in a very short time due to an increase of Protestant refugees arriving in England from the Low Countries fleeing from persecution. The substantial population increases of the immigrant communities were not confined to Norwich alone and this was beginning to cause a degree of unease. However, Reynolds has produced a convincing argument that the 1570 rebellion was led by Catholic sympathisers aligned with the 1569 Northern rebellion that

[53]   R.W. Hoyle, 'Agrarian Agitation in Mid-Sixteenth-Century Norfolk: A Petition of 1553', *Historical Journal*, 44 (2001), 223–38 (p. 223).

[54]   Hoyle (p. 233) suggests this petition was a later attempt to quantify the grievances that led to Kett's rebellion: 'hatred of landlords which the commons exhibited makes Norfolk a place apart.'

[55]   See in particular for Aldrich, Reynolds, pp. 44–50.

[56]   F.R. Beecheno, 'The Sucklings' House at Norwich', *Norfolk and Norwich Archaeological Society*, 20 (1921), 158–78 (p. 176).

[57]   Beecheno, p. 163; see also Joseph James Muskett (ed.), *Suffolk Manorial Families: Being the County Visitations and Other Pedigrees* (Exeter: William Pollard, 1894–1908). This son, also called Robert, lived in Campania for many years.

[58]   Blomefield, *Topographical History*, IV (1806), 284.

[59]   John Pound, 'Government to 1660', in Rawcliffe, Wilson, with Clark (eds), *Norwich Since 1550*, pp. 35–61 (p. 40).

was aimed at replacing the Queen with the Duke of Norfolk.[60] The rebels were encouraged to incite the city's people to remove the Protestant Strangers by the unease that had sprung up around the country against the immigrants. However, they may have been unaware that the unease was less apparent in Norwich and that the aldermanic council was less sympathetic to the Catholic cause. Aldrich and his fellow aldermen passed a number of acts to prevent trouble during the time of the uprising. One of these prohibited trading on the Sabbath day and also prevented congregation of the 'mean and base sorts' on Sundays, which, as Reynolds aptly points out, was 'the one day of the week when they would have had time on their hands to make trouble'.[61] However, these acts also followed the Bucerian model of church ministry being entwined with secular magistry, where Bucer wanted to disallow the operation of markets and 'profane activities' on Sundays.[62] Aldrich was subsequently appointed to try the rebels in July.[63] It has been suggested that this rebellion was the main catalyst that contributed to the setting up of the 1570 Norwich census of the poor, the document that underpinned the administration of poor relief in Norwich from that date forward.[64] However, it was also a chance for the Norwich authorities to put reforming practice into the town.

In itself, the Norwich census was not a new procedure. An earlier census had been taken in the city in 1545, however there is no trace of it in the records and according to Hudson and Tingey it was taken for a slightly different purpose. There were many empty houses in the city at this time, rents were low, and city authorities were concerned that in order to obtain rents, house owners were letting houses and rooms to anyone.[65] This document was ordered specifically to count the numbers of itinerants, where they were living and for how long they had been in the city.[66] It appears to have been used 'to draw up some regulations for the landlords of the beggars' but there is no evidence that this was carried out.[67] As well, there are surviving documents for some other towns that used similar methods to classify their poor but not on the same scale as the Norwich census: Worcester in 1557, Warwick in 1587, Ipswich in 1597, Huddersfield in 1622 and Salisbury in 1635.[68] There was also an earlier precedent in Paris in 1535 whereby

---

[60] Reynolds, pp. 54–7; McClendon, *Quiet Reformation*, pp. 224–5.

[61] Reynolds, p. 56.

[62] Patrick Collinson, 'The Reformer and the Archbishop: Martin Bucer and an English Bucerian', *Journal of Religious History*, 6 (1971), 305–30 (p. 324); VanderSchaaf, p. 90.

[63] See Reynolds, p. 57; and John Pound, 'An Elizabethan Census of the Poor: The Treatment of Vagrancy in Norwich, 1570–1580', *University of Birmingham Historical Journal*, 7 (1962), 135–61 (pp. 144–5).

[64] John F. Pound (ed.), *The Norwich Census of the Poor 1570* (Norwich: Norfolk Record Society, 1971), pp. 8–9.

[65] *Records*, II, cii.

[66] *Records*, II, cii.

[67] *Records*, II, cii.

[68] See discussion and comparison of these in Paul Slack, *Poverty and Policy*, pp. 73–80; McClendon, *Quiet Reformation*, p. 230.

the Parlement commissioned lists of inhabitants to determine the extent of poverty in the city, at the same time outlawing both begging and giving of alms.[69] Even prior to that, a similar system in Ypres may have been a model for that in Paris.[70] The close business ties of many of the Norwich elite with the Low Countries may also have had some bearing on the implementation of the census. Aldrich, along with several other aldermen and merchants, belonged to the Norwich Merchant Adventurers Company. The Norwich merchants had been in constant contact with European merchants for many years and it is likely they were aware of any social changes, especially in those towns that had been home to the Strangers.

Few theories have been advanced to explain the implementation of the census. Was the rebellion of 1570 really the catalyst, as Pound has suggested? Did the authorities fear it would become another such uprising as that of the Kett rebellion in 1549? This earlier revolt had caused Norwich to be the first provincial city to legislate for compulsory contributions to be exacted from citizens to be used for poor relief, as many of the poor had been eager to participate in the unrest.[71] The mid-sixteenth century saw similar uprisings, including the 1549 Prayer Book rebellion in Cornwall and the Wyatt rebellion of 1553, which caused authorities around the country to be concerned at the level of unrest.[72] Therefore poor relief was a way of looking after the poor in times of hardship to prevent them from becoming rebellious. Whether the perception that the poor were easily pushed to rise against authority was a valid perception is not clear. The city's concerns about the poor continued from that time especially during the famine years of the 1550s when the aldermen and Commons raised funds to ensure a permanent grain stock to be established for times of scarcity.[73] There was even an attempt to license beggars when it was realised that the unemployed poor could not be compelled to work unless there was work to be found for them.[74] This was not confined to Norwich; the whole of England had experienced increasing levels of poverty from the early sixteenth century, and by mid-century, central government had responded by enacting a number of poor relief statutes.[75] Some of these measures taken by the city authorities at this time appear to be altruistic, yet the overall impression gained

---

[69]   See also Farmer, Chapter 2, pp. 5, 27–8, and Broomhall, Chapter 9, pp. 179, 184, 185, in this volume.

[70]   H.C.M. Michielse and Robert van Krieken, 'Policing the Poor: J.L. Vives and the Sixteenth-Century Origins of Modern Social Administration', *Social Service Review*, 64 (1990), 1–21.

[71]   Pound (ed.), *Norwich Census*, p. 8.

[72]   McIntosh, 'Poverty, Charity and Coercion', p. 461; Tim Harris, *The Politics of the Excluded, c. 1500–1850* (Basingstoke: Palgrave, 2001), p. 3; Slack (*Poverty and Policy*, p. 54) discusses the threat of poverty to the 'common weal'.

[73]   William Castleton, last prior and first Dean of Norwich, initially established this in his will of 1554. See *Records*, ii, ci–cii.

[74]   *Records*, ii, cii.

[75]   Paul A. Fideler, '*Societas, Civitas* and Early Elizabethan Poor Relief', in Charles Carlton with Robert L. Woods, Mary L. Robertson and Joseph S. Block (eds), *State,*

in the two decades leading up to the census is one of a city oligarchy eager to do what was necessary to rid their city of an annoying problem. In January of 1557 the Norwich assembly agreed to 'see suche poore folkes as be able to work ... shall be sett a worke frome hensforthe from tyme to tyme' which could be construed as a good thing to be able to provide work for those who needed it.[76] However, just a few months later in April of the same year, the same Assembly was enacting that no tenements were to be let to poor persons not earning a living or those persons who had not lived in the city for three years, legislation that must have increased the number of vagrant poor.[77] That the Norwich authorities considered the poor to be a serious problem can be seen in the way in which Norwich managed to administer and to continue to implement compulsory taxation to be used for poor relief. Although Royal injunctions, backed by a statute of 1547, had ordered a collection of charitable alms for the poor to be made each Sunday and holy day,[78] Norwich was the first provincial town to enforce this regulation in 1549.[79]

McClendon has discussed the concern of the authorities in Norwich regarding increasing social disorder during the decades between the Reformation and the census. We have seen that her argument suggests that there was a changing of the guard, whereby the city officials became predominantly Protestant, which influenced an increasing force for moral discipline in the city.[80] The figures produced by McClendon for the offences punished by the Mayor's court support this theory. Prosecutions for two of the 'moral' offences, those of evil rule and sexual misconduct, show that over a thirty-year period from 1540 to 1570, evil rule increased ten-fold and the frequency of sexual misconduct prosecutions doubled.[81]

The incidence of other offences also increased during this time, and the punishment for offences became more severe. Instances of vagrancy punished in the Mayor's court between 1550–51 and 1559–60 totalled just five cases.[82] In the following 10 years from 1560–61 to 1569–70, which led up to the census, these numbers increased to 114 cases.[83] Was this because the general incidence of crime and disorder was increasing or was it due to the increased diligence of the authorities in prosecution of misdemeanours? McClendon has pointed out that categories of offences were 'inexact and overlapping'.[84] For instance, 'evil rule'

Sovereigns and Society in Early Modern England: Essays in Honour of A.J. Slavin (New York: St Martin's Press, 1998), p. 62.

[76]   *Records*, II, 132.

[77]   *Records*, II, 132.

[78]   Marjorie McIntosh, *Poor Relief in England*, pp. 128–9.

[79]   Pound, 'An Elizabethan Census', p. 136; see also Steve Hindle, *The State and Social Change in Early Modern England, c. 1550–1640* (Basingstoke: Macmillan, 2000), p. 147.

[80]   McClendon, *Quiet Reformation*, p. 209.

[81]   McClendon, *Quiet Reformation*, Appendix 6.

[82]   McClendon, *Quiet Reformation*, Appendix 6.

[83]   McClendon, *Quiet Reformation*, Appendix 6.

[84]   McClendon, *Quiet Reformation*, p. 216.

could mean crime of a sexual nature, but could also refer to other misbehaviour. The increase in this category of crime could be simply a change in definition.

When examining the process of how and why the census came to be, some anomalies become apparent. Most of the discourse in what is known as the *Mayor's Book of the Poore* appears to be written soon after the census yet the characterisation of the behaviour and habits of the poor seem to be at odds with the people described in the census. For instance, after the census, the mayor compiled a book of *Orders for the Poor*, which listed numerous regulations and instructions to be brought into effect, and spelt out in detail why they were necessary:

> Fyrste, for that dyverse of the cittizens felte themselves agreed that the cittie was so replenysshed wt great nombres. poore people bothe men, women and chyldren, to the nombre of ijM and ccc parsons whoe for the most parte wente dayely abroade from dore to dore counterfeattinge a kinde of worke but indeede dyd verie lyttle or none at all.[85]

These comments do not seem to have any relevance to the people of the census. The census enumerated almost a quarter of the population of Norwich at that time but very few of them fitted the descriptions in the *Orders*.[86] They were the settled poor; all were living in houses or tenements, apart from a few families and individuals that were living in the towers and gatehouses of the city.[87] Very few were expelled from the city after the census, and the majority had lived in Norwich for at least 10 years.[88] As well, the preamble to *Orders* unequivocally states that the poor 'moste shamefullie abused ther bodies and brought forth basterdes in such quantitie'.[89] From this statement, it might be expected that there were large numbers of children born out of wedlock in Norwich, but there are only three instances in the census where children were described as illegitimate.

This exemplifies the way in which sixteenth-century society 'confused moral status with economic status' that resulted in prejudicial judgments.[90] The *Orders* contained not only scathing indictments of the behaviour of the poor, but sharp criticism of those who gave charity to the poor, stating that they were giving so much that it was more profitable for people to beg than work. This latter criticism reflects the Protestant ideal that charity should not be indiscriminate but targeted

---

[85]   *Records*, ii, 345.

[86]   Margaret Pelling, *The Common Lot: Sickness, Medical Occupations and the Urban Poor in Early Modern England* (London and New York: Longman, 1998), p. 77.

[87]   Pound (ed.), *Norwich Census*, p. 13.

[88]   Lesley Silvester, '"hav dwelt here ever. No alms. Veri pore": Life Experiences of the Poor in Sixteenth-Century Norwich – A Longitudinal Study' (unpublished doctoral thesis, The University of Western Australia, 2013). The origins of those in the census are discussed in detail in chap. 4.

[89]   *Records*, ii, 344.

[90]   Slack, *Policy and Poverty*, p. 4.

Plate 1   Pose de la Première pierre de la Chapelle

Source: Cracow, Czartoryski Museum and Library, MS 3092 II, Nicolas Houel, 'Le Manuscrit de la Maison de la Charité chrétienne', 1582, fol. 81.

Reproduced by kind permission of the Princes Czartoryski Foundation, Cracow.

Plate 2   Exercices Spirituels
Source: Cracow, Czartoryski Museum and Library, MS 3092 II, Nicolas Houel, 'Le Manuscrit de la Maison de la Charité chrétienne', 1582, fol. 101.
Reproduced by kind permission of the Princes Czartoryski Foundation, Cracow.

Plate 3   Le Bureau des Bienfaiteurs
Source: Cracow, Czartoryski Museum and Library, MS 3092 II, Nicolas Houel, 'Le Manuscrit de la Maison de la Charité chrétienne', 1582, fol. 45.
Reproduced by kind permission of the Princes Czartoryski Foundation, Cracow.

Plate 4   La Charité ouvre les portes du Ciel
Source: Cracow, Czartoryski Museum and Library, MS 3092 II, Nicolas Houel, 'Le Manuscrit de la Maison de la Charité chrétienne', 1582, fol. 61.
Reproduced by kind permission of the Princes Czartoryski Foundation, Cracow.

Plate 5   Festin du Bon Riche

Source: Cracow, Czartoryski Museum and Library, MS 3092 II, Nicolas Houel, 'Le Manuscrit de la Maison de la Charité chrétienne', 1582, fol. 889.

Reproduced by kind permission of the Princes Czartoryski Foundation, Cracow.

Plate 6   L'Apothicairerie

Source: Cracow, Czartoryski Museum and Library, MS 3092 II, Nicolas Houel, 'Le Manuscrit de la Maison de la Charité chrétienne', 1582, fol. 69.

Reproduced by kind permission of the Princes Czartoryski Foundation, Cracow.

Plate 7   A beggar and a wealthy man
Source: Collégiale Saint-Martin, Champeaux, France. Photograph by Joe Scott, used with permission.

Plate 8   Saint Sulpice le Pieux ministering to sick, maimed and
               lame petitioners.
Source: Parish Church of Saint-Sulpice-de-Favières, Favières, Essonne, France. Photograph by the editor, Anne M. Scott.

Plate 9   St Martin shares his cloak with a beggar.
Source: University of Leeds, Special Collections, Brotherton MS 4, fol. 158r. Reproduced with Permission.

Plate 10   HM 1088, fols 225v–226. Christ carrying his cross assisted by the poor.
Source: The Huntington Library, San Marino, CA. Reproduced with Permission.

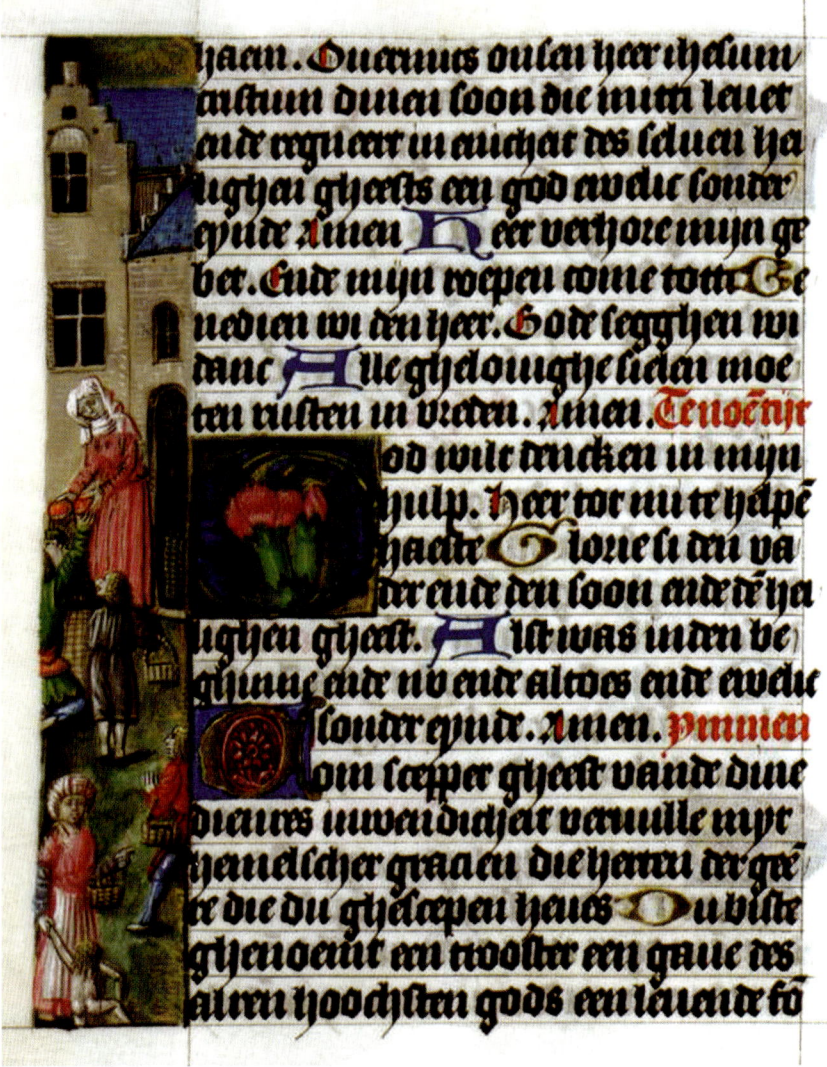

Plate 11   Brotherton MS7 fol. 52v. The Works of Mercy: Feeding
          the Hungry.
Source: University of Leeds, Special Collections. Reproduced with Permission.

Plate 12   Brotherton MS7 fol. 46v. The Works of Mercy: Clothing the Naked.

Source: University of Leeds, Special Collections. Reproduced with Permission.

ye And noble prince excellent
my lord the prince my lord gracious
I humble seruamt And obedient
Vnto yowr estate hye And glorious
Of whiche I am full tendr and full ielous
me recomamde vnto yowr worthynesse
with hert entier And spirite of mekenesse

Plate 13   BL Royal MS 17 D VI fol. 40r. The author, Hoccleve, presents his
book to King Henry V.
Source: © The British Library Board, Royal 17 D. VI, f.40. Reproduced with Permission.

toward those who were deserving of assistance. The book listed a number of orders and reforms in great detail, for example, no one was to beg in pain of six stripes with a whip; no one was to feed beggars at their doors or they would be fined; various work places were to be set up and persons compelled to work there. This included setting out work hours and conditions such as '... they shall not eate but as they can earne'; select women were to be appointed to look after and teach groups of children.[91] There is nothing specifically Protestant in these reforms but there is evidence of reforming influence. Concern about both physical and moral corruption of the poor and indigent can be seen in the Mayor's preamble to the *Orders* after the census. The mayor notes that the poor 'so corrupteth one another that the charge to heale them is verie greate' and 'defiled ther bodies with filthiness' and 'their ffleshe was eaton wt vermyne'. These statements are then linked to the disorder they brought to the city, '(by their disorder) the maiestrates of the cittie are so trowbled with searchinge and correctinge them that the cheife cawses of comon wealthe is fayne to give place eyther to be talked of or reformed'.[92]

Did the Protestant values of Aldrich and his fellow aldermen have a direct bearing on the implementation of the census? He initially appointed three commissioners to oversee the census, his brother-in-law John Sotherton, his business partner Simon Bowde and Thomas Beamond, a close friend of Protestant reformer Robert Watson.[93] Reynolds convincingly argues that Aldrich was a Protestant reformer and his commission was stacked with like-minded relatives and business colleagues. He states, 'the mayor began a programme to quell the menace from the 'great multitude of mean and base sort" that had been deemed susceptible to the wiles of Catholic plotters.[94] The census was a major attempt to find the scope of the problem and remedy the situation to prevent further unrest from occurring. The remedies and proceedings resulting from the census were tabled in 'a booke for reformacion preferred unto the Maior to declare to the whole asembly, who presented the same and uppon the verie nedefull and urgent reformacion the same booke was granted, retified, and confirmed'.[95] The evidence certainly points to the reformist leanings of the mayor and aldermen having influenced the reasoning and decision to carry out the 1570 Norwich census of the poor.

After the census, poor relief was centred even more directly on the parish, and compulsory contributions were collected from the parish rich to be given as needed to the parish poor. However the rules and regulations governing the collection and distribution of alms were firmly led by the council of Mayor and Aldermen. Each ward of the city was allotted two deacons whose purpose was to oversee the poor. The deacons' orders show that they were expected to be responsible for a number of tasks; once a month they were to search their ward and remove any persons

---

[91] *Records*, II, 344.
[92] *Records*, II, 345–7.
[93] Reynolds, p. 57.
[94] Reynolds, p. 57.
[95] *Records*, II, 344.

that had not 'remayned three yeris in the citie' and to have 'a contynuall eye' that no other persons should settle unless they were able to 'lyve of themselves'; they were to notify the authorities of those in need that 'awlmes can not suffise' so that they could be provided for; those that were unemployed and able were to be set to work to 'se they ronne not abowght'; those that would not work were to be sent to the select women or the Bridewell; they were to certify the number of disordered persons to be punished weekly; the number of, and age of, children not able to be looked after by their parents were to be listed; 'bygge wenshes or boys' not able to be kept by their parents were to be put into service; vagabonds and loiterers, drunkards and disordered persons were to be noted and punished; all money and goods given for the relief of the poor was to be recorded and the deacons were to dole out money as they saw fit.[96] For carrying out their duties, the deacons were to be paid 3s. 4d. and if they refused to carry out their duty they were fined 40 shillings.[97] These orders for the deacons were carefully thought out and there is no doubt that the authorities wanted to keep a serious check on the city poor. One of the two deacons was to keep his office for two years, in order to instruct the newer deacon, presumably because the longer-serving one would know the inhabitants of his ward, and therefore know if there were any vagrant newcomers.[98]

The content of the census document indicates that the authorities had a pressing need to establish concrete information on not just the extent of poverty within the town, but also the level of poverty within this census cohort. The detailed information in the census entries suggests that the enumerators were charged with finding specific information. Almost every entry describes the names, ages, sex, family size, occupation, origins and the length of time a family had been living in Norwich. As well, a subjective assessment of a person's capacity to work and state of health was noted. This allowed the authorities then to direct charity to the needy in an orderly fashion, and to keep control over the numbers of poor. The census document was a template, situated within the same book as the *Orders for the Poor*, which the Norwich authorities then used to fashion their poor relief scheme.

As mentioned earlier, Norwich had been one of the first provincial towns to enact compulsory contributions for poor relief in 1549 and, along with the rest of the country at that time, dealt with its poor by aiding those deemed deserving and punishing the undeserving. After the census, it continued this way but introduced measures to facilitate its control over the poor population of the city. The first undertaking was to remove any obvious beggars and families or individuals who had been in Norwich for fewer than three years. Another measure was to ban indiscriminate almsgiving as it was thought that overgenerous almsgivers contributed to an increased number of beggars. An order of major importance was to set up schemes for the provision of work, training and learning 'so as no

---

[96]   *Records*, II, 354–5.
[97]   *Records*, II, 353–4.
[98]   *Records*, II, 355.

parson shoulde have neede to goe abegginge'.[99] This was done in a comprehensive manner, by turning the Normans' poorhouse into a Bridewell, and part of St Giles hospital was to be used for bringing up children. Children and young women in each ward were also to be put to work with select women from their ward.

The Bridewell was modelled on an earlier one that had been established in 1553 when Edward VI gave one of his houses, Bridewell, to the City of London to be used as a workhouse for the poor.[100] This was the forerunner to the establishment of houses of correction for the poor in other parts of the country and was a move that implied that the poor needed correction as opposed to charity. In 1571 the Norwich Bridewell was set up at what was known as the Norman Spital.[101] This hospital in the parish of St Paul had been used for the relief and lodging of the poor since the twelfth century. It had survived the dissolution by covenant and was to be used for the 'relief of poor Strangers, vagrants, sick and impotent persons'.[102] After the census, those occupying rooms and houses there were turned out, and the *Mayor's Book of the Poore* states 'all such as have lying at Normans above two nights commanded to go away'.[103] There appears to be no concern about where these folk were to go. Gregory Acres, who was noted as lying sick in the Normans in the census, was 'commanded to look him another house'.[104] The Bridewell was to become a prison for both men and women who were able to work but not willing, where those committed would be made to serve 'twentie and one dayes at the leaste, and longer yf cawse serve, and they shall not eate but as they can earne (excepte som frende wyll be bownde for them)'.[105] It was thought important enough that the mayor was to be the governor although the daily charge was under a bailiff with his wife and family.

The criteria used to select which twelve children were to be brought up at the St Giles hospital is not spelled out. However, the ward deacons were charged to note children who were too young to work and that their parents were unable to sustain, so it is probable that these children became inmates of St Giles.[106] The children were to be under the charge of a bailiff and his wife to be taught 'in letters and other excersises (as their capacities shall be hable to attayne)' and brought to sermons on Holy Days 'as they maye learne to encrease in vertwe'.[107]

---

[99]   *Records*, II, 344.

[100]   John Stow, *A Survey of London, written in the year 1598*, (ed.) William J. Thoms (London: Whittaker, 1842), p. 154.

[101]   *Records*, II, ciii–civ.

[102]   Blomefield, *Topographical History*, IV, 433. After the census in 1570 its function was changed when the city corporation broke the lease and turned it into a Bridewell. The Spital changed from a place of poor relief to a place of punishment for being poor.

[103]   NRO, NCR Mayor's Book of the Poore, Case 20c, 1571, unpaginated.

[104]   Pound (ed.), *Norwich Census*, p. 26; and NRO, NCR Mayor's Book of the Poore, Case 20c, 1571, unpaginated.

[105]   *Records*, II, 348.

[106]   *Records*, II, 354.

[107]   *Records*, II, 352.

Committees from each ward were to appoint 'so manye selecte women as shal suffyse to receyve of persons within that warde'.[108] These women were to take in each day up to twelve children, women and maids as ordered by the deacons of the ward. The children were to be taught 'letters' and should be from the poorest families that were unable to pay for their learning. This order implies that the women chosen as select women were required to be literate in order to teach children. As some select women were chosen from the census poor, it is an indication that they once had the resources to become literate which suggests they had not always been among the very poor.

The women and maids sent to the select women were to be made to work 'tyll their handes be browght into such use and their bodies to such paynes as labore and learninge shall be easier to them than idleness'.[109] They were expected to 'fynde the stuffes and the woorking tooles' and if they did so would receive the profits of their work. If they could not provide their own tools then the select women could provide them but would only pay them for work done and keep profits themselves. The select women were to receive 20 shillings a year in payment. This may seem a goodly sum of money for the time but these women had to work long hours in supervising the women sent to them by the deacons. They were expected to ensure work was carried out by threat of punishment and were given leave to 'give punnishment, six stripes with a rodde' if necessary. The hours they had to supervise were from before eight in the morning until eleven, then a break for dinner and to work again from one until past four in the afternoon. In the summer months it was from six in the morning until seven in the evening with a similar dinner break. Penalties for disobedience to the select women were harsh. The parents of disobedient children could be punished by losing their weekly relief. Recalcitrant youths were to be sent to Bridewell to receive punishment and a collar of iron. Those women appointed to be select women had little say in the matter. If they refused, they should 'suffer inprisonemente by the space of twentie dayes at the leaste'.[110] In effect, this meant that the select women were as much shackled to the power of the authorities as their charges.

Although treatment of the poor using these measures is harsh by today's standards, throughout the records are cases that show the authorities were attempting to alleviate the circumstances of the deserving poor. Those receiving relief included older women who did not appear to have any extended family support, the sick and disabled, the elderly unable to work and those families with a large number of dependent children. Extra payments were given in times of sickness or special needs. All of this created a whole new level of administration to carry out the orders for the poor. The Norwich authorities' provision for the poor after the census extended beyond the payment of alms to other forms of assistance. Special payments for medical treatment, for firewood in winter and shoes, clothes

---

[108] *Records*, II, 352.
[109] *Records*, II, 352–3.
[110] *Records*, II, 353.

and burials are noted in the poor relief accounts.[111] John Bell the mason was given a special payment when his house was burnt down after the 1579 plague outbreak; others were paid to keep orphaned children.[112] These measures were one part of a strategy taken by the authorities to discourage and eliminate itinerant begging and vagrancy within the city, which was in turn to influence the national treatment of the poor in England.[113]

The select women scheme, the Bridewell and the use of St Giles in the education of poor children were among a number of social welfare implementations by the Norwich authorities that were centred on Protestant reformism. Bucer's pamphlet of 1551 on the distribution of alms stated the ways 'that this godlie provision for the Poore and needie be restored'.[114] Paul Fideler has suggested that Bucer's pamphlet made 'compelling justification' containing directions such as 'congregation centred poor relief; giving the deacons in each parish responsibility to distinguish needy from undeserving and supervise, distribute and account for poor relief funds; bring up youth virtuously trained in good arts'.[115] This reads like a prototype of the Norwich poor relief expedients. All of these measures were listed in the *Orders* and carried out by the Norwich authorities. Aldrich and his fellow aldermen made Norwich a veritable blueprint of Calvinist philosophy, as followed by Martin Bucer, which was further cemented by the appointment of ministers such as John More and Thomas Robartes.[116] Both men were prominent reformers who had been at Cambridge. Robartes's college had been Corpus Christi, which earned him the ministry at St Clement's, the home parish of Archbishop Matthew Parker who had also attended Corpus Christi. More attended Christ's college and was given the ministry at St Andrew's where his 'rigid Calvinism' and preaching earned him the title of 'Apostle of Norwich'.[117]

It could be argued that a number of the Norwich reforms were not specifically Protestant as they were similar to reforms seen in other European towns of Catholic persuasion. In Paris at the end of the fifteenth century, the Hôtel-Dieu was placed under municipal authority at the request of its canons and in 1519 there was a push to reform other Parisian hospitals.[118] Throughout the sixteenth century, parallels can be found between the development of poor relief in both Norwich and Paris. Both cities had changed from ecclesiastically charitable institutions having responsibility for the poor, to civic administrations governing

---

[111] NRO, NCR Mayor's Book of the Poore, Case 20c, 1571–79, unpaginated.

[112] NRO, NCR Mayor's Book of the Poore, Case 20c, 1571–72, unpaginated.

[113] Pound, 'An Elizabethan Census', p. 149.

[114] Bucer, *A Treatise.*

[115] Paul Fideler, *Social Welfare in Pre-Industrial England* (Basingstoke and New York: Palgrave Macmillan, 2006), p. 79.

[116] Fideler, *Social Welfare*, p. 93; Reynolds, p. 64.

[117] Reynolds, pp. 64–5; Fideler, *Social Welfare*, p. 93.

[118] See Farmer, Chapter 2, pp. 22–4, in this volume, and Broomhall, 'The Politics of Charitable Men', pp. 137–43.

the charitable endeavours of the city. As Peter Brown has remarked, 'For both Catholic and Protestants, the "reform" of errant groups was a dominant concern.'[119] There was, however, a difference in the implementation of poor relief as between sixteenth-century Paris and Norwich. In Paris, it was influenced greatly by the efforts of particular men and it could be argued that they had a personal interest in gaining spiritual and temporal reward. For instance, Lisa Keane Elliott has shown that Nicolas Houel's vision for his *Maison de la Charité chrétienne* was firmly ingrained in a Catholic conviction that charity was an obligation that would provide heavenly rewards.[120] Houel and others, such as Jean Martin, were also able to gain social credit from their charitable endeavours by using professional connections and even royal patronage.[121] In Norwich, John Aldrich and his aldermen were at the forefront of development of poor relief in the 1570s but their motives appear less personal and more controlling. There is no evidence that they used any of their personal wealth to better the situation of the poor, apart from paying the legislated poor rates or leaving small bequests in their wills.

The evidence strongly points to the Norwich mayors and aldermen of the last half of the sixteenth century as having been influenced by a reforming Protestantism. Although Reynolds argued that religious dispute was a hallmark of reforming Norwich, and McClendon claims that it was marked by tolerance, both have shown that Protestantism was the agency behind the Norwich authorities. Society had been changing since the Reformation, and with different regents came different faiths. There was pressure on civic authorities to look after the poor as this no longer could be left to the Church. However, civic authority was administering relief through the church system, but it was the attitudes of the civic authorities that were shaping the way in which poor relief was administered in Norwich. Two deacons were appointed to each city ward and were to be responsible for the oversight of the poor in their ward. The duties for these deacons in the *Orders* mirror the *Treatise* by Bucer on the distribution of alms. The way in which the authorities attempted to regulate the behaviour of the poor displayed a sixteenth-century form of social engineering. They were organising society within a framework of both church and municipality into a disciplined conformity. Their insistence on both labour and learning reinforced their view that poverty resulted from moral corruption, as was prevalent in the contemporary literature of the time.[122]

---

[119]   Peter Brown, 'Remembering the Poor and the Aesthetic of Society', *Journal of Interdisciplinary History*, 35 (2005), 513–22 (p. 516).

[120]   Elliott, Chapter 8 in this volume.

[121]   Broomhall, 'The Politics of Charitable Men' p. 149.

[122]   Paul Slack, 'Social Policy and the Constraints of Government 1547–58', in Jennifer Loach and Robert Tittler (eds), *The Mid-Tudor Polity c. 1540–1560* (London: Macmillan, 1980), p. 115; R.H. Tawney and Eileen Power (eds), *Tudor Economic Documents, Being Select Documents Illustrating the Economic and Social History of Tudor England*, 3 vols (London: Longmans Green, 1924), III, 407–58.

The Norwich authorities were then, it seems, foremost in using the findings from the 1570 census to enact wide-reaching changes in the charitable endeavour, centred on poor relief administration. What was motivating the authorities is not clear, as their management was, contrastingly, both punitive and altruistic. At the same time as denigrating the behaviour of the poor and sending them for punishment to Bridewell, they were providing health assistance to those in need, another practice that had been put forward by reformers.[123] They also openly practised methods of social engineering to organise the poor inhabitants to conform to their own ideal of 'proper' behaviour. The poor relief books after the census show that the authorities were intent on checking up on the poor and carefully accounting for all monies spent and received in each parish. I believe one of the reasons for the census was that of noting, not only the needy poor, but also those who might slip into the poverty net at any time, or those on the brink. The civic leaders could class it as good practice and forward thinking, in that the information gained from the census could allow for better planning in the future. Their poor relief practice appears very much aligned with that described in the *Beutelordnung* of 1521, which Lindberg has ascribed to Luther's authorship.[124] It states that stewards of the poor were required to 'visit the poor householders personally to inquire diligently into their need and deprivation, not to wait until they are penniless and in extreme poverty'.[125]

From the mid-sixteenth century, the Norwich hierarchy seem to have moulded the city in a way that conforms to many of the characteristics described by Robert Tittler as paving 'the way for the onset of "godly rule" in post-reformation towns'.[126] They were able to benefit economically by the dissolution of the monasteries, both by acquiring resources for the town and for themselves. As Norwich was a county itself, the authorities were able to hold legal authority over their resources and this authority 'accelerated the tendency to urban oligarchy'.[127] However, in the words of Paul Slack, much of the social reform 'depended on individual personalities'.[128] In Norwich that personality was John Aldrich and the civic reforms in poor relief that he and his fellow aldermen oversaw allowed Norwich to be held up as an example of good governance and order for many years.[129]

---

[123]   Pelling, *The Common Lot*, esp. 'Healing the Sick Poor: Social Policy and Disability in Norwich, 1550–1640', pp. 79–102.

[124]   Carter Lindberg, '"There Should Be No Beggars"', 313–34 (pp. 324–7).

[125]   See discussion on this in Lindberg, pp. 324–7. There are differing views on who wrote the *Beutelordnung*, Luther or Karlstadt, and Lindberg conforms to the Luther camp.

[126]   Tittler, p. 192.

[127]   Tittler, p. 192.

[128]   Paul Slack, *From Reformation to Improvement* (Oxford: Clarendon Press, 1999), p. 44.

[129]   Slack, *Reformation to Improvement*, p. 45; John Pound, *Tudor and Stuart Norwich* (Chichester: Phillimore, 1988), p. 67. See also Reynolds, pp. 44–7.

Chapter 8

In Pursuit of Charity: Nicolas Houel and his *Maison de la Charité chrétienne* in Late Sixteenth-Century Paris

Lisa Keane Elliott

Late sixteenth-century Paris was a hotbed of religious and political divide, particularly from the outbreak of civil war in 1562 between the French Catholics and Protestants, those converts to the new 'heretic' religion of Jean Calvin. The outbreaks of civil war until the peace settlement of Henri IV with his Edict of Nantes in April 1598, were temporarily halted by uneasy truces, however violence and unrest remained in Paris, as in other French towns and cities. Following the Peace of Saint-Germain in 1570, in which one of the conditions ordered the destruction of Catholic monuments to victories over the Protestants, citizens of Paris converged upon the cemetery of the Holy Innocents where guards had been ordered by the king to remove the Cross of Gastines. The guards were attacked and forced to hide their weapons in an attempt to divert attention from themselves as the crowds descended upon the cemetery. The crowd also 'smashed the windows and workshops of ... Huguenots' in the area, whilst others 'took a few small things from the Huguenots' houses'.[1] Violent skirmishes between the two groups and attacks by the majority Catholics against the minority Protestant population were a daily occurrence in Paris. Exacerbating the religious and political unrest were regular outbreaks of plague causing great devastation upon the city's populace. In the final four decades of the sixteenth century, Paris was hit by plague from 1560–62, 1566–68, 1577 and a devastatingly long outbreak from 1580–86, which resulted in the death of around 30,000 Parisians. This was followed, according to the historian Pierre Chaunu, by 'the terrible years' of 1595–97.[2] In his journals, Parisian Pierre de L'Estoile wrote of an outbreak of another disease, *la coqueluche*, that swept through Paris in mid-1580, killing 10,000 people in six days. He described the

---

[1] Jean de la Fosse, *Journal d'un curé ligueur de Paris sous les trois derniers Valois*, entry for 1570–71, quoted in Barbara B. Diefendorf, *The Saint Bartholomew's Day Massacre: A Brief History with Documents* (Boston: Bedford/St Martin's Press, 2009), pp. 80–81.

[2] Jean-Noël Biraben, *Les hommes et la peste en France et dans les pays européens et méditerranéens*, 2 vols (Paris-La Haye: Mouton, 1976), II, 111; Pierre Chaunu, *La Mort à Paris, XVIe, XVIIe et XVIIIe siècles* (Paris: Fayard, 1978), p. 184.

disease as 'characterised by headache, stomach ache, intestinal trouble and much pain in all parts of the body'.[3] Added to this were climate anomalies and disasters, floods, droughts and frosts that caused havoc on harvests and threatened the livelihoods of many Parisians, particularly the poorer classes. In the early 1570s, weather caused continual damage to the annual harvests, leaving Parisians short of basic provisions and sending the cost of grains, for example, sky rocketing beyond the reach of the capital's poorer citizens.[4]

Amid the violence, chaos and turbulence of civil war, religious division, disease and economic desolation, were individuals who sought to ease the troubles of the time through charitable endeavours directed toward Paris's poor and 'malheureux', and encouraging their fellow citizens into adopting the same benevolent 'Christian' attitude as a more peaceful way of combating heresy. In 1573, the duke and duchess of Nevers established a charitable foundation in which dowries were awarded annually to legitimately born girls within their provinces deemed 'the most destitute of resources and needs' *and* proven to live according to the 'Catholic Apostolic and Roman religion'.[5] In the foundation's mission document, the duke and duchess decried the 'little charity' demonstrated by those entrusted to administer their 'good and holy' foundation in its early years, which was 'to the prejudice of the poor girls' and a threat to their 'perfection of Christian charity', which they had established in 'these times so turbulent and full of heresies, divisions and impiety'.[6] Jean Martin, a governor of Paris's Grand Bureau des Pauvres published a treatise in 1580 extolling the virtues of the charitable citizen wielding his 'true and holy' benevolence 'like a strong lance against our enemy'.[7] Pierre de L'Estoile wrote a glowing tribute to the Duchess of Savoy (the daughter of François I) on her death in September 1574, extolling her many 'perfections', which included 'such marvellous charity'. 'In short', he wrote, 'she

---

[3]   Pierre de L'Estoile, *The Paris of Henry of Navarre as seen by Pierre de l'Estoile: Selections from his Mémoires-Journaux*, (trans. and ed.) Nancy Lyman Roelker (Cambridge, MA: Harvard University Press, 1958), p. 74, entry for June 1580; Robert Weston, 'Whooping Cough: A Brief History to the 19th Century', *Canadian Society for the History of Medicine*, 29 (2012), 329–49.

[4]   Micheline Baulant and Jean Meuvret, *Prix des céréales extraits de la Mercuriale de Paris (1520–1698)*, 2 vols (Paris: S.E.V.P.E.N., 1960–62), I (1960), 30–71, 88–97; Andrew A. Appleby, 'Grain Prices and Subsistence Crises in England and France, 1590–1740', *Journal of Economic History*, 39 (1979), 870–82.

[5]   AP-HP, Hôtel-Dieu, liasse 1397–1411, côté 6349, *La Fondation faicte par Messeigneur et Dame, les Duc, et Duchesse de Nivernois et de Rethelois: Princes de Manthoue, &c., Pairs de France. Pour marier d'orsenavant par chacun an à perpetuité, en leurs terres et Seigneuries, jusques au nombre de soixante pauvres filles, destituées de toutes facultez et moyen. Bien heureux est celui qui entend au pauvre et indigent: car Dieu le delivrera en la perilleuse journée. Psaume 40. L'An MDCV*, pp. xix, xxii.

[6]   *La Fondation faicte par Mes-seigneur et Dame*, pp. x, xv, xix.

[7]   Jean Martin, *La police et reiglement*, p. 47.

was a *true Christian*.[8] In a world of chaos there existed some people with the means and motivation to undertake charitable works and encourage others to do likewise. In the wake of the civil wars and religious division, the Catholic doctrine of 'good works' was pitched as not only a means through which to fulfil one's Christian obligations to God's 'poor members', but also as a peaceful means of combating the Protestant 'heresy'.

One such philanthropist was Parisian apothecary Nicolas Houel who, in 1576, approached King Henri III of France, seeking permission to establish a charitable institution in Paris for poor orphaned children.[9] No one is sure where Houel found the inspiration for his *Maison de la Charité chrétienne* and despite a number of treatises by the man himself, he has left few firm clues about the origins of his plan or why he decided upon such a path. What he has bequeathed historians are detailed plans of what he envisaged his maison to be, his compassionate benevolence toward the poor orphaned boys in his care, his Christian sense of duty towards God's 'poor members' and his hope that his fellow Christians, particularly the country's most influential and wealthy citizens, would aid his foundation with their patronage and beneficence. In his treatises, Houel extolled Christian, read 'Catholic', charity as the best means of demonstrating one's own Christian faith, drawing on tropes utilised by some of his contemporaries to counter the aggression and violence of the civil wars, promoting charity as a weapon with which to defend the true faith of France.

This chapter will explore through his extant treatises the ways in which Nicolas Houel sought to acquire the continued patronage and financial assistance of Paris's wealthy citizens toward his *Maison de la Charité chrétienne*. It will examine the ways in which Houel expressed his intent for his charitable endeavour and the language and rhetoric he employed in doing so, to determine whether there was a tone of secular governing rhetoric or more personal, religious language. The chapter will also examine who Houel identified as potential benefactors and how he attempted to inspire their charitable intent towards his maison. And finally, it will examine how Houel represented poverty and 'God's poor members' in his treatises, particularly the poor orphaned boys whose welfare was at the heart of his *Maison de la Charité chrétienne*.

Who was Nicolas Houel?

In one of his studies on Houel, the art historian Jules Guiffrey laments the 'injustice' history has served upon 'this obscure practitioner who played a significant role

---

[8]   de L'Estoile, *The Paris of Henry of Navarre*, p. 36, entry for September 1574 (emphasis added).

[9]   Alexandre de Laborde, *Un philanthrope au XVIe siècle: Nicolas Houel, fondateur de la Maison de la Charité chrétienne* (Paris: La Société des bibliophiles françois, 1937), p. 31.

in his lifetime, left abundant evidence of the extent and variety of his scientific knowledge, his passions for the arts and letters, and created an institution' that formed the basis for modern innovations.[10] Fortunately, since Guiffrey penned his lament, other historians have sought to discover more about the elusive Houel and within archives in Paris and Cracow are conserved manuscripts by the man himself, which this study will draw upon. A biography, *Notes sur Nicolas Houel et sa famille*, by Léon Mirot, archivist at Paris's Archives Nationales, was published in 1926, and gathers clues from various sources on the life of Houel and his family.[11] What is known about Houel, in brief, is that he was a Parisian apothecary who, in 1548, was given permission to establish his own pharmacy near the place de Grève, a prime location in the heart of Paris near the Hôtel de Ville, the city's town council building, and the Palais de Justice, the home of the Parlement of Paris.[12] In 1556, he was appointed an alderman of Paris, which indicates he had become an established figure on the governing scene of Paris; this was a position which, Barbara Diefendorf writes, also came with 'the broadest responsibility for local charities'. As far as his personal life is concerned, Houel was married three times and had at least two sons to his first wife, but at this point, we know nothing of the fates of young Jhérosme and Guilbert.[13]

The extant evidence does, however, demonstrate the reasons why Houel was renowned amongst his contemporaries. In addition to his professional and civic responsibilities, Houel was an accomplished artistic designer, man of letters and philanthropist, who has left behind a remarkable legacy of his myriad talents and interests. Within Paris's Bibliothèque Nationale are, among his many treatises, two pharmaceutical treatises from 1573, as well as his 1580 treatise *Advertissement et déclaration*, concerning the *Maison de la Charité chrétienne*, and *La Procession de la Reine Louise de Lorraine au chrétienne de Maison de charité de Nicolas Houel*.[14] Of particular interest is Houel's treatise *Le Manuscrit de la Maison de la Charité chrétienne*, the original of which is preserved in the collections of Cracow's Czartoryski Museum and Library and forms the basis of Alexandre de Laborde's 1923 study. In this manuscript, Houel illustrated life

---

[10]   Jules Guiffrey, *Nicolas Houel, apothicaire parisien fondateur de la Maison de la Charité chrétienne et Premier Auteur de la Tenture d'Artémise* (Paris: H. Champion, 1898), p. 179.

[11]   Léon Mirot, *Notes sur Nicolas Houel et sa famille* (Paris, 1926). Unfortunately this source could not be accessed in time for the completion of this essay.

[12]   Guiffrey, p. 181; Christian Warolin, 'Nicolas Houel et Michel Dusseau, apothicaires à Paris au XVIe siècle', *Revue d'histoire de la pharmacie*, 88 (2000), 319–36 (p. 320).

[13]   Barbara B. Diefendorf, *Paris City Councillors in the Sixteenth Century: The Politics of Patrimony* (Princeton, NJ: Princeton University Press, 1983), pp. 71–2, 86; Warolin, 'Nicolas Houel et Michel Dusseau', pp. 320–21, 323.

[14]   Nicolas Houel, *Advertissement et déclaration de l'institution de la maison de la Charité chrestienne establie ès faux-bourgs Sainct Marcel, par l'authorité du roy et sa court de parlement, 1578* (Paris: P. Chevillot, 1580); Nicolas Houel, *La Procession de la Reine Louise de Lorraine au chretienne de Maison de charité de Nicolas Houel* (Paris, 1580).

within his maison and his endeavours to expand its function and facilities for the consideration of potential benefactors. It is his 1562 treatise, *Histoire de la Royen Arthemise Contenant quater livres, recueillie de plusieurs Autheurs*, with engravings by France's official court painter Antoine Caron,[15] and preserved in Paris's Bibliothèque Nationale, that seems to have inspired Houel's foray into a literary and artistic world, and is likely to have demonstrated to him the financial and social potential of such creative endeavours.[16] The work was commissioned by France's queen regent Catherine de Médicis, her choice of Houel indicating the high regard in which he was held by his contemporaries for his skills beyond that of his profession. It is in this manuscript that we see some of the religious tropes and themes that Houel would later employ in his treatises relating to his *Maison de la Charité chrétienne*, particularly that of 'Christian' charity.

Nicolas Houel and the *Maison de la Charité chrétienne*

On 18 December 1576, Nicolas Houel presented directly to the king, Henri III, his proposal for a charitable institution in which he would house and educate legitimate orphaned children of Paris in the science of the apothecary. Financial restraints prevented the king from approving Houel's request as presented; however, Houel was given space within the orphanage of the Enfants Rouges to establish an apothecary training school and a pharmacy for the honest poor of Paris. (The Enfants Rouges had been established in 1536 by François I at the instigation of his sister, Marguerite de Navarre, to house and educate the poor orphaned children whose parent/s had died in Paris's Hôtel-Dieu, joining the orphanages of the Hôpital de la Trinité, established in 1201, and the Hôpital le Saint-Esprit established in 1363.)[17] Henri III ordered the funding for Houel's training school and pharmacy to come from the monies collected during recent investigations into the administrative and financial corruption within French hospitals:[18]

---

[15]   Sheila ffolliott, 'The Ideal Queenly Patron of the Renaissance: Catherine de' Medici Defining Herself or Defined By Others?', in Cynthia Miller Lawrence (ed.), *Women and Art in Early Modern Europe: Patrons, Collectors, and Connoisseurs* (University Park: Pennsylvania State University Press, 1997), pp. 99–110, (p. 109).

[16]   Nicolas Houel, *Histoire de la Royen Arthemise Contenant quater livres, recueillie de plusieurs Autheurs. En laquelle sont contenues plusieurs singularitez dignes de remarque touchant l'antiquité. Ensemble un petit discours de l'excellence de la plate painture* (Paris, 1562).

[17]   AP-HP, Hôtel-Dieu, liasse 876, côtés 4213 & 4214, 'Hôpital des Enfants à Dieu titre Rouges. Établi pour recevoir les Enfants male non malades, orphelins et delaiss de leurs pères et mères malades en étrangers et morts à l'Hôtel-Dieu'; Jacques Depauw, 'L'Assistance a Paris á la fin du XVIe siècle', *Bulletin Société Française d'Histoire des Hôpitaux*, 59 (1989), 10–24 (p. 15); Jean Imbert, *Histoire des hôpitaux en France* (Toulouse: Privat, 1982), pp. 155–7.

[18]   'Déclaration pour la reddition des comptes des maladeries et hôpitaux, Blois, 30 janvier 1577', in Isambert, Decrusy, Taillandier (eds), *Recueil général des anciennes lois*

Letters patent of the king Henri III approving the foundation by Nicolas Houel, apothecary in Paris, of a charitable institution in the Enfants Rouges hospital, where a certain number of orphan children are to be educated and trained in the work of the apothecary and where medicine is to be prepared for the shamefaced poor of Paris. The king endows this new foundation with the sums of money arising from court actions relating to the accounts of the church hospitals, leper hospitals, sick houses and confraternities of this kingdom and from the embezzlements made by the governors and administrators therein.[19]

Houel did not stay long at the Enfants Rouges for the old hospital of Lourcine located in the *faubourg* of Saint-Marcel just outside the city walls became available in early 1578. The Lourcine had been founded in 1292 by Marguerite de Provence, the widow of Louis IX, and used for various charitable purposes over the centuries.[20] The historian Michel Félibién writes that, by the 1570s, the hospital was 'deserted and abandoned by bad conduct, everything ruined, the poor not [being] lodged and the divine service not said nor celebrated'.[21] An *arrêt* of the Parlement of Paris in January 1578 transferred the Lourcine to Houel to realise his dream of a *Maison de la Charité chrétienne*.[22] By the time of the floods in April 1579 that caused great devastation to the fledgling hospital, Houel already had 21 'pauvres couchez' (poor recumbents) in his care, showing that he wasted no time in getting his charitable endeavour up and running.[23]

---

françaises depuis l'an 420 jusqu'a la révolution de 1789, 29 vols (Paris: Belin-Leprieur/ Verdière, 1822–33), xiv (1829), Part II, p. 318.

[19]   Letters patent of Henri III, 18 December 1576, quoted in Michel Möring (ed.), *Inventaire Sommaire des archives hospitalières antérieures à 1790, vol. 1: Hôtel-Dieu* (Paris: Grandremy et Henon, 1882), p. 332: 'Lettres patentes du roi Henri III approuvant la fondation faite dans l'hôpital des Enfants-Rouges, par Nicolas Houel, apothicaire à Paris, d'une maison de charité où seront instruits un certain nombre d'orphelins ausquels on apprendra l'état d'apothicaire et où seront préparés des medicaments pour les pauvres honteux de Paris. Le Roi assigne à cette nouvelle fondation les deniers provenant de la recherché des comptes des hostels-dieu, leproseries, maladeries et confrairies de ce royaume et des malversations commises par les gouverneurs et administrateurs.'

[20]   AP-HP, Hôtel-Dieu, liasse 878, côté 4222, 'Arrêt du Parlement de Paris ordonnant que les vénériens seront recus et soignés à l'Hôtel-Dieu de Lourcines', 'l'hôpital de l'Hostel-Dieu de Lourcines ... étants ès fauxbourgs Saint-Marceau', 25 September 1560; Jean-Pierre Babelon, *Nouvelle Histoire de Paris: Paris au XVIe siècle* (Paris: Hachette, 1986), p. 172; Émile Gilbert, *La Pharmacie à travers les siècles: antiquité, moyen âge, temps modernes* (Toulouse: Vialelle et Cie, 1886), p. 253; M.G. Planchon, 'Les Jardins des apothicaires de Paris', *Journal de pharmacie et de chimie*, 25 (1893), pp. 292–3.

[21]   Michel D. Félibién, *Histoire de la ville de Paris* (1795), quoted in Guiffrey, p. 248; see also Babelon, pp. 172–3; Planchon, p. 293.

[22]   Planchon, pp. 294–5; de Laborde, p. 32, n. 5.

[23]   Nicolas Houel, *Ample discours de ce qui est nouvellement survenu ès faulxbourgs S. Marcel lez Paris, ensemble les miracles advenus en la maison de la Charité chrestienne naguères establie esdits faulxbourgs* (Paris, 1579), fol. xii.

What exactly was Houel's inspiration behind and intention for his *Maison de la Charité chrétienne*? Why did he choose to direct his charitable efforts toward Paris's poor orphaned boys? A will he made while bedridden with an unspecified illness in 1551 reveals his long-held charitable convictions. In addition to bequests to various charitable institutions, Houel singled out the Parisian orphanages of the Enfants Rouges and Trinité. Guiffrey wrote that Houel's concern for poor orphans was due to his not having any children of his own, but the 1551 will mentioned a two-year-old son, Jhérosme, and Warolin notes that another son, Guilbert, was born soon after the will was written.[24] Given that the fate of Houel's sons is unclear, it is possible that their early demise inspired his future charitable endeavours for the young orphaned boys of Paris. Houel's treatises do not indicate if this hypothesis is correct, but they do very clearly demonstrate his personal religious sensibilities. In his *Advertissement*, Houel stated his first intention as the establishment of a chapel in which divine service would be conducted for the health and prosperity of the maison's royal and noble patrons, whom he named.[25] The establishment of the chapel within the hospital was in keeping with the traditional Catholic attitude and approach to charitable institutions at this time. It would demonstrate the religious nature of Houel's charitable endeavour and assure potential benefactors that their charity would be rewarded in the traditional Christian way. Recipients of Christian charity were obligated to show gratitude to their benefactors by attending masses celebrated in their honour and saying prayers for their spiritual welfare.[26] In addition, during this period of violent religious division, the charitable act became a way in which benefactors could publicly, and peacefully, demonstrate their allegiance to the Catholic faith. The Council of Trent had recently reaffirmed the Catholic doctrine and the practice of salvation through charity:

> Abound in every good Work, knowing that your labour is not in vain in the Lord. For God is not unrighteous to forget your Work and Love, which ye have shewed toward his name. ... And therefore Life Eternal is set before them that do good, and hope in God to the end, and Grace is mercifully promised to the sons of God through Christ Jesus; and is faithfully to be given them as a reward for their good Works and merits.[27]

Houel drew upon this concept in his pursuit of patronage and benefactors. The essence of this doctrine can be detected throughout Houel's treatise and my recent papers on the Nevers Foundation and Jean Martin's treatise on Paris's

---

[24] Guiffrey, p. 184; Christian Warolin, 'Un testament authentique de Nicolas Houel (5 septembre 1551)', *Revue d'histoire de la pharmacie*, 82 (1994), 331–41 (p. 334).

[25] Houel, *Advertissement*, sig. Bv.

[26] Michel Mollat, *The Poor in the Middle Ages*, pp. 42–5, 264; Brian Pullan, 'Foreword', in Bronisław Geremek, *Poverty: A History*, p. viii.

[27] *The Canons and Decrees of the Council of Trent Celebrated under Paul III, Julius III, Pius IV, Bishops of Rome* (London, 1687).

Grand Bureau des Pauvres indicate that this traditional form of charity was being promoted as the preferred demonstration of one's religious allegiance during the contentious period of religious division in late sixteenth-century Paris.[28] As well as assuring potential benefactors that their charity would result in their due spiritual rewards, Houel and his like-minded contemporaries offered opportunities for their fellow citizens to associate themselves publicly with a 'very Christian', read very Catholic, enterprise.

More importantly for Houel, naming his illustrious and 'very charitable' patrons advertised that his maison had the support of the greatest people in the kingdom and was therefore a worthy institution to which Christian charity could be safely directed. The illustration from *Le Manuscrit de la Maison de la Charité chrétienne* (Plate 1) depicts the queen, Louise de Lorraine, wife of Henri III, attending the ceremony of laying the foundation stone by Houel for the maison's new chapel. The event is quite an occasion with the maison's young orphans, religious elders and other notable persons in attendance. The queen is depicted surrounded by her fellow patrons, the king and his mother, Catherine de Médicis, and notable men and women whose likenesses were no doubt familiar to their contemporaries. The image not only illustrates Houel's intention to provide religious instruction for his charges, but also seeks to legitimise his charitable endeavour and encourage others to follow the Christian example of those patrons depicted (Plate 1).

Houel's second intention was focused on the beneficiaries of his charity, the poor orphaned boys, 'born in loyal marriage', who would be lodged, fed and 'educat[ed] in the fear of God, … [in] good letters and knowledge of pharmacy'.[29] Houel's intended beneficiaries were legitimate orphaned boys for whom *necessity* was the determining factor of their acceptance at the maison, in addition, one assumes, to their Catholicism. In an illustration from his 1580 treatise, *La Procession de la Reine Louise de Lorraine*, one can see children, accompanied by an adult, being led to and accepted into the maison.[30] This suggests that the children were not necessarily bereft of familial support, but that the means to provide for their education was a burden their kin were unable to bear. Indeed, in a recent paper, Warolin presents three contracts between Houel and the guardians of three boys admitted to the maison. Six-year-old Nicolas Charton, 'orphaned of father', was apprenticed to the maison, possibly by his mother, for six years. He would receive bed, board and clothes, and be taught 'piety and good letters', as

---

[28]   Lisa Keane Elliott, 'Jean Martin', pp. 65–83; Lisa Keane Elliott, 'Charitable "Intent"', pp. 159–82.

[29]   Houel, *Advertissement*, sig. Br: 'II. Le second membre comprend l'institution d'un certain nombre de *pauvres* orphelins, nes en loyal mariage, lesquels, en premier lieu, sont instruits en la crainte de Dieu, etc … puis es bonnes lettres, pharmacie et cognoissance des simples.'

[30]   'L'Apothicairerie de la Maison de la Charité Chrétienne', in Guiffrey, plate III. The new entrants to the hospital can be seen in the top left of the image being led into the hospital by their guardians.

would six-year-old Jacques Bocquet admitted to the maison by his guardian on 30 April 1586. Houel also seemed to provide assistance to orphaned boys who were not intended for a future as an apothecary. On 21 April 1586, the widowed mother of thirteen-year-old Gabriel Tanneur signed her son over to Houel's care. Houel promised to find Gabriel an apprenticeship of his choice in return for fulfilling his obligations to attend mass and perform other spiritual functions for the profit of the maison's chapel.[31] These examples reveal that Houel's intention for his maison was not only to provide spiritual and pharmaceutical training for orphaned boys, but also to act as, in effect, an employment agent. While his primary objective during the early years of the maison, was to train poor orphans in the sciences of the apothecary, equipping them with a trade and offering them some protection against an impoverished future into which they might otherwise have been condemned, as the contracts above indicate, his scope for the orphans' 'training' extended beyond pharmacy and religious knowledge. In two panels of *La Procession de la Reine Louise de Lorraine*, boys can be seen undertaking music lessons within an 'École de Musique' and mathematics in a school of arithmetic.[32] The *Procession* sketches visualised Houel's long-term goals for his *Maison de la Charité chrétienne* – to provide an all-round education to those poor orphaned boys admitted to his maison. Given the extent of his plans, support for Houel's maison was no doubt strong among Paris's governing authorities as the capacity and resources of the city's other orphanages were being overburdened by the great need of the city's poorer citizens, thus forcing limits upon admittance.[33] Houel's intent was in keeping with the practice of the city's other orphan hospitals, all of which offered their charges training and spiritual guidance for their future.[34]

Spiritual education was considered an important part of a child's preparation for future life and all Parisian hospitals offered a spiritual element to their services, therefore it was important for Houel to advertise his intention to follow this established tradition and legitimise his charitable endeavour within a religious context. It is significant that Houel placed the establishment of the chapel as his first intention and that the spiritual education of the poor orphaned boys was placed above their secular education, clearly establishing for potential benefactors that his charitable endeavour was a *holy* endeavour. An illustration in Houel's *Le Manuscrit* titled 'Exercices Spirituels' depicts the maison's children being guided in their spiritual devotions by priests and supported by their benefactors, who were

---

[31]   Christian Warolin, 'Trois contrats passés avec Nicolas Houel, intendant et gouverneur de la Maison de la Charité chrétienne en 1586', *Revue d'histoire de la pharmacie*, 86 (1998), 63–6 (pp. 63–4).

[32]   See the procession panels, plates 9 and 10 in Francis A. Yates, *Astraea: The Imperial Theme in the Sixteenth Century* (London: Routledge and Kegan Paul, 1975). The original panels are held at the BnF, Département des Estampes, rés. Pd 30.

[33]   Depauw, pp. 15–16, 22.

[34]   Kristin Elizabeth Gager, *Blood Ties and Fictive Ties: Adoption and Family Life in Early Modern France* (Princeton, NJ: Princeton University Press, 1996).

no doubt also in attendance to receive the spiritual rewards that the prayers of the grateful children would bring (Plate 2). We see a similar practice described in Dolly MacKinnon's chapter in this volume, with her orphaned children devoting their life to learning and performing musical prayers on behalf of their benefactors.

In his 1578 treatise, *L'Ordre et Police gardez en l'institution de l'Appothiquairerie*, Houel stated that his poor orphans would be dressed in purple uniforms as purple was a 'celestial' colour and that they would perform an annual procession to:

> publicly demonstrate to the people the great works of this Christian House, and how the alms and benefactions are employed and distributed, and in order to maintain his goodwill and willingness to continue his holy charity towards that house, once a year, on the Monday of the first week in Lent, there shall be a procession of all the children, both those who are at the chapel and other children who serve in the apothecaries. They will be accompanied by the burgesses and former governors, the four chaplains and other clergy. [35]

In each of his treatises, in words and illustrations, Houel was proclaiming the godly nature of his endeavour, establishing it as a legitimate Christian charity to which patrons and benefactors could direct their charity safe in the knowledge it was being used in aid of the deserving poor. Indeed, on the frontispiece to his *La Procession* drawings, in a 'Prière à Dieu' ('Prayer to God'), Houel stated that through his written and artistic endeavours he sought to inspire in his audience 'the ardour of charity'.[36] Houel sought continuously to invoke and inspire the religious sensibilities of potential donors toward his charitable endeavour.

Houel's third intention for his *Maison de la Charité chrétienne* was to establish 'a well-organised dispensary, stocked with all kinds of medicines for the relief and treatment of the aforementioned *pauvres honteux*, and especially to minister to the needs of those who are charged with the care of women and children ruined and impoverished by the long wars and the ravages of the times'.[37] Here,

---

[35]   Nicolas Houel, *L'Ordre et Police gardez en l'institution de l'Appothiquairerie maladie* (Paris, 1578–80), quoted in Valérie Auclair, 'Un logis pour l'âme des rois. Nicolas Houel (ça. 1520–ça. 1587) et les dessins de procession à la maison de la Charité chrétienne pour la famille royale', in Isabelle de Conihout, Jean-François Maillard and Guy Poirier (eds), *Henri III mécène des arts, des sciences et des lettres* (Paris: Presses de l'Université Paris-Sorbonne, 2006), pp. 39–54 (p. 42): 'pour monstrer publiquement au peuple les grandes charges de ceste Maison Chrestienne, et comment les aumônes et bienfaits sont employez et distribuez, et pour tousjours lui donner bon vouloir de continuer sa saincte Charité envers ladicte Maison. Se fera une fois l'an, le lundi de la premiere semaine de Karesme, une procession de tous les Enfants, tant de ceux qui seront à la Chappelle que des autres enfants qui servent à l'Appoticairerie, Accompagnez des bourgeois anciens gouverneurs, des quatre Chappellains et autres gens d'Église.'

[36]   Houel, quoted in Auclair, p. 43; p. 41, figure 1.

[37]   Houel, *Advertissement*, fol. Bv: 'l'établissement d'une apothicairerie ordonnée par un bon ordre, garnie de toutes sortes de médicamens pour le secours et traitement desdits

Houel placed his maison within the context of the religious wars. It was intended that the maison's orphan trainees and their learned teachers would also provide physical solace and medical relief to those *pauvres honteux* (shamefaced poor) for whom circumstances of life – unemployment, illness, war, famine – had led to impoverishment. Jean-Pierre Gutton describes these shamefaced poor as those of status who had lived on income from property and had no need to resort to manual labour. Their impoverishment was shameful hence the adjectival use of *honteux*, and they preferred to seek discreet modes of poor relief rather than the public shame of begging. Olwen Hufton describes the shamefaced poor as 'victims of circumstance'.[38] By expressing his intention of providing poor relief for the city's *pauvres honteux*, Houel assured potential benefactors that their Christian charity would be directed toward the deserving poor and not utilised indiscriminately. The maison's young charges, once qualified, would ' [go] to treat and medicate the infirmities and maladies of the *pauvres honteux* of the city … [so they would not have to] leave their homes to go to the Hôtel-Dieu'.[39] The discreet offer of assistance in their home enabled the *pauvres honteux* to save face by avoiding public forms of relief, and the public proclamation of the maison's benefactors meant they knew to whom to direct their gratitude and prayers.

In his statement regarding his fourth and fifth intentions for his *Maison de la Charité chrétienne*, Houel expressed his desire to build a hospital in which the 'pauvres honteux passants' (passers-by) could find a night's shelter, spiritual solace and physical succour. Again, there was an assurance to his audience that their donations would be directed toward the honest and deserving poor. In his discussion of his plans for the establishment of a 'herb garden, which … is filled with many beautiful fruit trees and fragrant plants, rare and necessary, and various species', Houel expressed his desire that the medicines produced from this garden would be utilised by the servants of the maison 'for the relief of the sick, rich and poor alike'. Houel's *Jardin des Simples* was to be a source of healing for all Paris's ailing citizens, which he wrote must be seen as 'a great benefit and great ornament for the city of Paris'.[40] Houel was presenting his maison and all its facilities as the city's all-purpose charitable facility from which the city's honest, deserving Christians could receive medicinal aid, the city's orphaned boys learn a profession, the *pauvres honteux* find relief from their sufferings, the wealthy citizens direct their Christian generosity, and the spirit of Christianity and the Catholic faith shine as a beacon of hope, faith and healing for the glory of God and the city of Paris.

---

pauvres honteux, et spécialement pour subvenir à la nécessité de ceux qui sont charges de femmes et enfants, ruines et appauvris par la longueur des guerres et injures du temps.'

[38]   Jean-Pierre Gutton, *La Société*, p. 9; see also Geremek, pp. 139, 180; Olwen Hufton, *The Poor of Eighteenth-Century France, 1750–1789* (Oxford: Clarendon Press, 1974), p. 215; Mollat, p. 268; Paul Slack, *Poverty and Policy*, pp. 27–8, 106.

[39]   Houel, *Advertissement*, fol. Br.

[40]   Houel, *Advertissement*, fols Biiv–Biir.

Anxiety about Paris's poor was a ceaseless concern for the governing authorities of Paris throughout the sixteenth century, as the city's governing elite struggled to find the resources to cater for the ever-increasing pauper population. From 1516, the Paris town council adopted and doggedly followed a policy of employment or expulsion upon Paris's vagabonds and *gens sans aveu* (masterless men). If they did not volunteer to serve on the work programmes, they could be forced to join the chain gangs where, under watch of a guard, the poor would be chained 'two by two', to work on city projects such as digging ditches or repairing the boundary walls in return for 2 *sous* a day and lodgings in which they were locked and guarded each night.[41] Concerns over the welfare of the city's orphaned children also increased as the lack of resources and places in the existing hospitals of Trinité and Saint-Esprit were overwhelmed by demand. Houel's contribution to these problems was no doubt well received by the Parisian authorities as another much-needed resource in an extremely over-stretched welfare system, as well as the potential for providing another source of medical aid for the city's ailing populace, 'rich and poor alike'.

Inspiring 'the ardour of charity': Houel's Promotion of his Charitable Christian Endeavour

Nicolas Houel established his *Maison de la Charité chrétienne* during a period of violent religious upheaval. Since March 1562, France had been embroiled in religious wars that had resulted in violent acts of reprisals against those of the new Protestant religion that shocked many moderate Catholics. In the aftermath of the horrors witnessed by Parisians during the Saint Bartholomew's Day Massacre on 24 August 1572, moderate Catholics like Nicolas Houel sought to promote the Catholic faith through more peaceful means.[42] In his treatise on Paris's Grand Bureau des Pauvres, Jean Martin lamented 'the dark world' Paris had become where 'Charity sleeps' and its citizens were 'embroiled in peril' and 'avarice'. 'Simple, miserable people', Martin implored, 'change your hearts, become charitable'. He believed that those who lived charitable lives 'never lose battles, because charity holds like a strong lance against our enemy'.[43] The duchess and duke of Nevers

---

[41] 'Ordonnance faite par messieurs de la Ville sur le gouvernement desdite vaccbons après qu'ils seront livres à la ville, 26 fevrier 1516', in *Registres des délibérations*, I: 1499–1526, (ed.) François Bonnardot, p. 228.

[42] Étienne Pasquier, quoted in Mack P. Holt, *The French Wars of Religion, 1562–1629* (Cambridge: Cambridge University Press, 1995), p. 50; see also Elliott, 'Charitable "Intent"', pp. 163–6.

[43] Martin, *La police et reiglement*, pp. 33, 47, and the poem 'Charité Malade aux Riches Terriens' (unpaginated): 'Et vous ainsi simples gens miserables, | Changes de coeur, devenez charitables'; '... jamais n'ont perdu bataille, car l'aumône tient et bataille comme une lance forte contre notre ennemi'.

established their charitable foundation for poor Catholic girls in the year following the Saint Bartholomew's Day Massacre, in which the duke had played an active and bloody role. Madame de Dampierre became actively involved with Houel's 'academy of all [Catholic] piety and science',[44] possibly to dispel rumours of Protestant sympathies and atone for her husband's part in the Saint Bartholomew massacres.[45] Indeed, Houel's own treatises on his maison used similar rhetoric to that used in the documentation of the Nevers Foundation in which they wrote of 'these times so turbulent and full of heresies, divisions and impiety', which they hoped their 'perfection of Christian charity' might help to ease.[46]

Through his own charitable endeavour, Nicolas Houel had been employing charity as a weapon against poverty amongst orphaned boys of Paris since at least 1551, the year in which he wrote a will that left provisions for the orphans of the Enfants Rouges.[47] In his *Advertissement*, Houel, like Martin and the duke and duchess of Nevers, lamented the fact that 'the dangerous and pernicious effects of civil wars' had led to the abandonment of charity and left many people impoverished. It was the sight of such misery, he wrote, that had inspired his charitable endeavour in order to ease the suffering of his fellow Christians.[48] His treatise indicates that his 'pity and compassion' were shared by all the benefactors, including the 'very illustrious and charitable dame', Madame de Dampierre. Houel presented his *Maison de la Charité chrétienne* as a wholly Christian endeavour, one inextricably linked to the 'Catholic, Apostolic and Roman' church and with the approval and 'authority of the Holy Doctors of the Catholic Church', the cardinal de Bourbon providing letters patents proclaiming Houel's maison was 'agreeable and acceptable to God'.[49] The Nevers Foundation document also expressed the desire that all those involved with the charity be faithful to 'the Catholic Apostolic and Roman religion', an incontrovertible requirement declared repeatedly throughout the document.[50] Approval for their 'good and holy' charity came from the highest authority in the land, Pope Sixtus V, whose papal bull was included within the foundation document.[51] Jean Martin's own treatise included a statement from his tutors at the Faculty of Theology who testified to Martin

[44]   Houel, *Advertissement*, fol. Biir.
[45]   Diana Maury Robin, Anne R. Larsen and Carole Levin (eds), *Encyclopedia of Women in the Renaissance: Italy, France and England* (Santa Barbara, CA: ABC-CLIO, 2007), pp. 81–3.
[46]   *La Fondation faicte par Mes-seigneur et Dame*, pp. v, xxii; see also Elliott, 'Charitable "Intent"', pp. 159–82.
[47]   Warolin, 'Un testament authentique', pp. 331–41.
[48]   Houel, *Advertissement*, fols Aiiiiv–Aiiiir.
[49]   'Pardon octroie par Monseigneur de Reverendissime Cardinal de Bourbon, à la Maison de la Charité chrétienne, establie ès fauxbourg S. Marcel', in Houel, *Advertissement*, unpaginated.
[50]   *La Fondation faicte par Mes-seigneur et Dame*, pp. xxii, xxiii, xxv, xlii, xc, lxix.
[51]   *La Fondation faicte par Mes-seigneur et Dame*, p. lxxxv; see also Elliott, 'Charitable "Intent"', pp. 170–77.

being 'worthy and good' for sharing religious exhortations with his readers in an effort to promote 'this virtue of Charity'.[52] The rhetoric of Houel's language and the religious imagery in his treatises, particularly those associated with the maison, sought to emphasise the spiritual nature of his charitable endeavour. His treatises were designed to promote the maison as a legitimate Catholic charity to which true Christians, such as the royal family and Madame de Dampierre, could direct their patronage, gaining their heavenly salvation, as well as *publicly* aligning themselves during these 'dangerous' times to a high profile Christian charitable endeavour.

It was Houel's close connections with the royal court that enabled him to address his treatises on pharmacy and his maison to the highest royal figures in France, namely the kings Charles IX and his successor, Henri III, queen Louise de Lorraine and the queen regent, Catherine de Médicis, in his quest for patronage and financial support. Houel must have come to the attention of Catherine de Médicis sometime prior to his involvement in the work she commissioned from him in collaboration with court artist, Antoine Caron, *L'Histoire de la Reine Artémise*, published in 1562. In this work, Houel and Caron compared the classical widow Artémise, the exemplar of wise, female leadership, with France's very own widowed sovereign, Catherine. As Meredith Martin writes in her study *Dairy Queens*, 'Houel compared her [Catherine] to a gardener who, like Artemisia, had coaxed her nation back to life after a long and brutal winter' – an analogy that evoked the politically turbulent events of 1559–62.[53] Sheila ffolliott says that Artémise was 'the epitome of a non-threatening prototype, providing the perfect imagery for [Catherine] in her quest to maintain the French monarchy'.[54] Houel's efforts in this enterprise proved successful and provided him with a royal connection that enabled him to forge ahead with his plans for a school of pharmacy for orphaned boys.

Houel seemed to focus his pursuit of charity on the female members of the royal family, particularly Catherine de Médicis and her daughter-in-law, Louise de Lorraine, wife of Henri III. In his later treatises, particularly his 1586 treatise, *Les Mémoires et recherches de la dévotion, piété et charité des illustres roynes de France*, Houel depicted the ideal queen as, first, a charitable patron, then as the mother of heirs and lastly, one who encourages her husband in charitable giving. By taking this line, Houel was not advocating anything out of the ordinary, as his humanist contemporaries had advocated such a role for women in their own

---

[52]   Martin, *La police et reiglement*, p. iv; see also Elliott, 'Jean Martin', pp. 72–3.

[53]   Meredith Martin, *Dairy Queens: The Politics of Pastoral Architecture from Catherine de' Medici to Marie-Antoinette* (Cambridge, MA: Harvard University Press, 2011), p. 53.

[54]   Sheila ffolliott, 'Catherine de' Medici as Artemisia: Figuring the Powerful Widow in Early Modern Europe', in Margaret W. Ferguson, Maureen Quilligan and Nancy J. Vickers (eds), *Rewriting the Renaissance: The Discourses of Sexual Difference in Early Modern Europe* (Chicago: University of Chicago Press, 1986), p. 241; Warolin, 'Nicolas Houel et Michel Dusseau', pp. 325–6.

works.[55] The role of a queen was to be a mother to all her subjects, not just her heirs, and active participation in charitable endeavours was the best expression of her concern and care for all her 'children'. Houel's *Advertissement* was dedicated to France's other queen, Catherine's daughter-in-law, the 'very Christian, very illustrious and Charitable Princess Louise de Lorraine, Queen of France', whose 'happy reputation' was comparable to 'those heroic and charitable queens' of the past. Houel praised her 'zeal' for his maison and her 'exemplary virtue and holy conversation'.[56] In Plate 2 from *Le Manuscrit*, as well as images in *La Procession de la Reine Louise à l'Apothicairerie*, the queen is depicted as an active charitable patron participating in (sometimes) elaborate, highly public religious processions and visits to Houel's maison.[57] As the art historian Valérie Auclair notes, the imagery seen in the drawings from *La Procession* is highly idealised, with many of the buildings of the maison not actually having been constructed at this time.[58] However, Houel's treatises do suggest that the queen had visited the maison in a less elaborate fashion, which Auclair surmises was the inspiration behind the amazing *La Procession* drawings. Indeed, it is important to remember that Houel's primary motivation behind the composition of his literary and artistic works was to inspire within his audience 'the ardour of charity' and compassion for the city's orphans and *pauvres honteux*. His words and artwork were heavily imbued with easily recognisable imagery associated with the suffering of 'God's poor members', charity and heavenly salvation, which he hoped would inspire charity toward his maison.

In his 1586 treatise, dedicated to Catherine de Médicis, Houel sought to assure the queen mother and Louise de Lorraine, that their queenly duty was primarily to undertake and support charitable endeavours throughout the kingdom. As ffolliott writes, Houel sought to 'inform his potential benefactor about her time-honoured role while suggesting politely her proper future direction', namely to patronise his holy charitable endeavour.[59] Displaying the learnedness for which he was renowned, Houel again presented examples of charitable queens whom Catherine and Louise could emulate such as Judith of Bavaria, wife of Louis I, who, Houel wrote, 'with an honest generosity, ... gave her rings and jewels with all her effects, as dowries to help poor girls marry', and Marie of Brabant, second wife of Philip

---

[55] ffolliott, 'Ideal Queenly Patron', pp. 101, 104–5; Virginia Scott and Sara Sturm-Maddox, *Performance, Poetry and Politics on the Queen's Day: Catherine de Médicis and Pierre de Ronsard at Fontainebleau* (Aldershot: Ashgate, 2007), p. 49.

[56] Houel, *Advertissement*, fols Aiiv–Aiir: 'A très-Chrestienne, très illustre et charitable Princesse Loyse de Lorraine Roine de France. ... j'ose dire que vous estes parvenuë au comble de l'heureuse reputation, que meritent les Roynes heroïques et Charitables.'

[57] These images are also reproduced in Guiffrey, plates I–III, and Yates, *Astraea*, plates 1–10.

[58] Auclair (p. 44) also notes that there was no record of such a procession having taken place.

[59] ffolliott, 'Ideal Queenly Patron', p. 101.

II, who 'spent all her time in charitable endeavours'.[60] ffolliott remarks in her study that Houel also wrote of queens who encouraged their husbands into charitable patronage, specifically Charlotte de Savoie, second wife of Louis XI, who was behind his decision to build a hospital.[61] Houel was not advocating anything new, but simply drawing upon a trope of his fellow humanists, instructing and inspiring readers through the lives of notable exemplars from the past.[62]

In dedicating his treatises on the *Maison de la Charité chrétienne* to female patrons, Houel was not ignoring potential male benefactors. Within his treatises on the maison he addressed himself to male and female benefactors alike. Several of the images in *Le Manuscrit* and *La Procession* clearly depict female *and* male benefactors. In 'Le Bureau des Bienfaiteurs', male and female benefactors can be seen offering their donations to Houel and a plaque on the wall of the office reads '*Crains Dieu Honore le Roy Aime les Pauvres*' (Fear God, Honour the King, Love the Poor), an expression of traditional religious charitable doctrine (Plate 3).

In contrast, Houel's scientific treatises on pharmacy and medicine were predominantly addressed to male patrons as the sciences were deemed a masculine field of endeavour.[63] The rhetorical line, however, was the same. His 1573 treatise, *Traité de la theriaque et mithridat* was dedicated to 'the very Christian and Invincible King Charles IX' whom Houel likened to valiant leaders of the past, such as Hercules. Indeed, in the aftermath of the Saint Bartholomew's Day Massacre, Charles had medals forged depicting himself as Hercules to celebrate his crushing of the Protestants.[64] Houel utilised Charles's own representation of himself within his dedication and aligned himself with the Catholic faith by praising the king for 'embracing your faithful people' and punishing the 'rebels' (Protestants) who sought to stifle the country. Houel presents his 'small labour' as a tool with which the king can arm himself with medical knowledge and enhance his kingly attributes.[65] Houel repeated this trope in his other 1573 pharmaceutical treatise dedicated to the president of the Parlement of Paris, Christophle de Thou. Knowledge and learning were considered important tools for a governing man. Again, using a common trope of inspiration through historical example, Houel

---

[60]   Nicolas Houel, *Les Mémoires et recherches de la dévotion piété et charité des illustres roynes de France, ensemble les églises, monastères, hospitaux et collèges qu'elles ont fondez et édifiez en divers endroits de ce royaume* (Paris, 1586), quoted in ffolliott, 'Ideal Queenly Patron', pp. 102–3.

[61]   ffolliott, 'Ideal Queenly Patron', p. 104.

[62]   Elliott, 'Jean Martin', p. 81; ffolliott, 'Ideal Queenly Patron', p. 105.

[63]   Laurence Brockliss and Colin Jones, *The Medical World of Early Modern France* (Oxford: Clarendon Press, 1997), pp. 262–9; Susan Broomhall, *Women's Medical Work*, pp. 16–43.

[64]   Diefendorf, *Saint Bartholomew's Day Massacre*, p. 24.

[65]   Nicolas Houel, *Traité de la theriaque et mithridat, contenant plusieurs questions générales et particulières* (Paris: Jean de Bordeaux, 1573), pp. i–iiii; see also the 'Élégie de I. La Gessee, Mauvesionois, au roy très chrestien, Charles neusieme', which follows Houel's dedicatory epistle to the king.

wrote of the ancients 'toiling to embrace virtue [by] aspiring to grave things, useful and beneficial to the public'. He presented his treatise to President Thou, 'unworthy' though his language might be, because the knowledge he was imparting '[was] of such great usefulness' to the country, her governors and also, through Houel's medical knowledge, showed 'the goodness of God to his creatures'. Houel presented his plague treatise as an aid for both the civic and religious responsibilities of his readers, particularly to President Thou, Paris's leading secular governor.[66] Houel's pharmaceutical-themed treatises were a way in which to deliver compliments to potential patrons of his future charitable endeavours (the plans for his maison, no doubt, already fermenting), as well as participating in the flowering of his profession. By 1573, the profession of apothecary had successfully been established as a medical rather than a mercantile trade, with the skills, knowledge and expertise of France's apothecaries officially recognised by Paris's Faculty of Medicine and Parlement. A College of Apothecaries had been established in Montpellier in 1572. Like his professional contemporaries Thibault Lespleigney, Ambroise Paré and Michel Dusseau, Houel presented his French-language treatises as vital tools for the training and development of new practitioners.[67] For Houel, pharmaceutical knowledge was 'a friend of man' and a tool that could and should be charitably utilised for the benefit of all, a belief that would materialise within his vision for his *Maison de la Charité chrétienne*.

Within his pharmaceutical treatises, we can see Houel approaching his male dedicatees with the same Christian sentiment as in his maison treatises: utilising one's position, wealth and knowledge for the good of 'God's poor members'. Charity was an important aspect of one's Christian obligations and an important link between Heaven and Earth.[68] Indeed, Jean Martin wrote of the Christian's 'perpetual obligation' to God and his Church to promote 'this virtue of Charity'.[69] In *Le Manuscrit de la Maison*, Houel illustrated this idea with a depiction of Charity holding the key to Heaven and, shepherded by Hope and Faith, noble Catholic men and women seeking admittance by virtue of their earthly charitable lives, the inclusion of the image serving as a reminder of the Catholic doctrine of good works and heavenly rewards (Plate 4).

In his treatise on the Grand Bureau des Pauvres, Jean Martin talks about charity being the means by which the battle against the Protestants could be won, saying that for Charity to triumph, Christians must abandon their 'avaricious' ways that had caused Charity to 'sleep'. Houel also utilised this imagery in 'Le Couronnement de la Charité' (The Crowning of Charity). Charity is crowned victorious as she, aided by Death and the sword of God, crushes the earthly evils of avarice, vanity,

---

[66] 'Sonnet en faveur du premier president et de l'Autheur luy dediant son livre', in Houel, *Traité de la peste*, fols iii–v.

[67] Broomhall, *Women's Medical Work*, pp. 28–30; Warolin, 'Nicolas Houel et Michel Dusseau', p. 327.

[68] Mollat, pp. 42–5, 264; Pullan, p. viii.

[69] Martin, *La police et reiglement*, p. 73.

envy and corrupt earthly power beneath her feet.[70] In 'Visites aux Malheureux', this idea was again illustrated with Jesus beckoning the charitable heavenward to their salvation, while uncharitable Christians are chased into the fiery jaws of Hell.[71] Another image depicts the hellish damnation awaiting the rich man who squanders his wealth in selfish earthly pursuits and ignores the plight of his fellow man, naked and impoverished outside his own front door. The charitable man is seen being embraced by God, while Satan torments his unchristian counterpart who selfishly feasted while the poor starved (Plate 5).

The association of these religious concepts with Houel's maison was designed to depict the horrors of an unchristian, uncharitable life and illustrate how Houel's charitable endeavour was a worthy recipient of one's Christian charity and would lead to heavenly spiritual rewards more gratifying than immoral earthly pleasures. Houel himself is depicted in his office reading a holy scripture, indicated by the names 'Maria' and 'Jesus' on the book, watched over by an angel. In the background, under the earthly guidance of their teachers, the young orphan apprentices are at work making medicines and administering them to the *pauvres honteux* with God, represented in the top left corner by a blazing sun in which his name appears, watching over their activities, intended as a clear sign of heavenly approval for Houel's charitable endeavour (Plate 6).

Throughout this treatise, the visual imagery encapsulates the godliness and Catholicity of Houel's maison, and was designed to inspire compassion and 'the ardour of charity' within the hearts, or consciences of potential benefactors toward his *Maison de la Charité chrétienne*. Houel drew upon well-known religious imagery to position his charitable endeavour, in these 'dangerous and pernicious' times, as a tool with which to position the maison within the framework of Catholic charity. It was a tool he used in all his treatises, and very strongly so in those concerned with his maison. Following the floods in Paris of April 1579, Houel published a treatise in which he recounted the horrors of mothers 'charged with a multitude of small children' being overwhelmed by the floodwaters and the injuries sustained by his fellow Parisians. 'O God Almighty!' he cried, 'What a show!' He wrote of the distress of the 'poor little orphans [of] the house of Christian Charity … crying lamentations' and calmed only by the hospital's governor and priests leading them in prayers.[72] The residents and 'poor little orphaned children' sought consolation in their faith, which Houel believed resulted in a miracle for the hospital in that they were delivered from further losses.[73] Houel evokes these ideas of charity and faith as a universal salve for all ills: prayer saved the hospital from further destruction, faith bonded the inhabitants of the hospital during a crisis

---

[70]   'Le Couronnement de la Charité', in Houel, *Le Manuscrit de la Maison*, fol. 105; see also de Laborde, plate XXII.

[71]   'Visites aux Malheureux', in Houel, *Le Manuscrit de la Maison*, fol. 85; see also de Laborde, plate XVII.

[72]   Houel, *Ample discours*, fol. X.

[73]   Houel, *Ample discours*, fols XII–XIV.

and earthly relief for the flood victims was possible through charity, specifically Houel's charity.

Houel's establishment of the maison seems to have been inspired by his own spiritual beliefs and in pursuit of the charity needed to keep his charitable endeavour alive, he sought to demonstrate through words and images that his maison was a suitable *Catholic* charity through which Christians could actively, and publicly, demonstrate their own faith. And Houel was not just a man of words, for his personal religious convictions and compassion toward the poor fuelled his determination to realise his vision for the *Maison de la Charité chrétienne*. At the time of his death in 1587, he was reputed to have been on the brink of poverty having given his all, financially and physically to his charitable endeavour.[74] He did, as we would say today, put his money where his mouth is, demonstrating his belief in his charitable endeavour through words and deeds. Houel believed his medical knowledge was a divine gift through which 'the goodness of God to his creatures' was displayed and which should be utilised for the glory of God and the benefit of all mankind.[75] He drew upon this idea again in his *Advertissement*, expressing his hope that God would inspire Christians with means to look upon the maison and its young trainees as a religious institution of scientific *and* artistic learning, and emphasising his desire that his charitable endeavour should proclaim 'the glory of God' and provide 'relief for His poor members as recommended in the Holy Scriptures':[76]

> If it pleases the goodness and mercy of God to increase the welfare of the poor ... enlighten the king, the princes and lords and others filled with the zeal of God and love of neighbour to donate their property [to the maison] ... so it can be an academy of science *and piety*, all for the advancement of the glory of God, [and the] profit and decoration of the Republic.[77]

For his potential benefactors, Houel always drew upon this fundamental doctrine of the Catholic faith; that charity was an obligation for all and that the act of charity brought immediate earthly rewards for both benefactor and recipient, as well as

---

[74]   Guiffrey, p. 256.

[75]   'Épistle a Messire Christophle de Thou Chevalier Seigneur de cely Conseilier du Roy en son privé Conseil, et premier President en sa Court de Parlement à Paris' (1573), in Houel, *Traité de la peste*, unpaginated.

[76]   'A Très-Chrestienne, Très Illustre et Charitable Princesse Loyse de Lorraine Roine de France', in Houel, *Advertissement*, unpaginated.

[77]   Houel, *Advertissement*, sig. Biiv (emphasis added): 'Quand il plaira à la bonté et miséricorde de Dieu acroistre le bien de ceste pauvre maison, allumer ly Roy les princes et seigneurs et autres personnes remplis du zèle de Dieu et Charité du prochain à y aumosner de leurs biens, l'en y adjouster les sept Arts liberaux avec les autres disciplines et sciences jusque à langue grecque et hebraique, mesme les langues estrangeres: de sorte que ce sera une Académie de toute pieté et science, le tout pour l'advancement de la gloire de Dieu, prouffit et décoration de la République.'

heavenly rewards in the afterlife. In his pursuit of charity, Nicolas Houel presented his *Maison de la Charité chrétienne* as a charitable *religious* endeavour and thus a worthy recipient for the patronage and benevolence of Paris's Catholic citizens.

Conclusion

A visit to the website of the *Société d'Histoire de la Pharmacie* reveals the importance of Houel's legacy; he is considered the father of today's Faculty of Pharmacy in Paris.[78] While his *Maison de la Charité chrétienne* evolved from his original purpose almost immediately upon his death in 1587 (Henri IV established a hospice for poor invalid gentlemen there in 1598), Houel's legacy lived on.[79] Houel's fellow apothecary, Charles Audens, was his successor at the hospital *and* in marriage, marrying Houel's widow, Catherine de Vallée. He negotiated the relocation of Houel's school of pharmacy and the *Jardin des simples*. An *arrêt* of 10 September 1624 sought to protect these aspects of Houel's maison from Paris's Faculty of Medicine, which had designs upon the maison's land. At the time of the garden's actual relocation in 1626, Houel's apothecary garden contained over 1,000 species and it would form the basis of Paris's first botanical garden located between the streets Lourcine and l'Arbalète, which now forms part of Paris's *Muséum National d'Histoire Naturelle*. In 1905, a street in the vicinity of the gardens was renamed Rue Nicolas-Houël in his honour.[80] Dr Christian Warolin, one of the founders of the *Société d'Histoire de la Pharmacie*, has published three biographical papers on Houel, which corroborate the society's acknowledgement of his importance to their field. He states that Houel was as 'remarkable' as, and maybe even more than, his contemporaries Ambroise Paré and Bernard Palissy, whose treatises Houel's own works surpass 'in beauty and *generosity*'.[81] Indeed, his generosity of thought and spirit are evident throughout his works, especially within those concerned with his *Maison de la Charité chrétienne*.

Houel's vision for his *Maison de la Charité chrétienne* where young Parisian orphaned boys could receive spiritual guidance and training in a holy vocation may not have reached its full potential in practice, but in theory, his vision was beautifully and eloquently expressed. His manuscripts reveal a man of spiritual conviction who practised as he preached. His maison was competing against the other hospitals of Paris for charitable resources and trying to establish itself

---

[78]   'Nicolas Houel (1524?–1587)', available on the Société d'Histoire de la Pharmacie's website <http://www.shp-asso.org/index.php?PAGE=houel> [accessed 3 April 2013].

[79]   Depauw, pp. 11, 22. In the list of Parisian hospitals *c.* 1599, the Hôtel Lourcine is listed as 'accueil des gentilshommes invalides'.

[80]   Warolin, 'Nicolas Houel et Michel Dusseau', pp. 323, 327–8; Warolin, 'Un testament authentique', p. 331; Pierre Delaveau, René R. Paris and Geneviève Clair, 'The Museum of Materia Medica of Paris', *Journal of Ethnopharmacy*, 17 (1986), pp. 201–3.

[81]   Warolin, 'Nicolas Houel et Michel Dusseau', p. 320 (emphasis added).

during a period of great political, economic and religious turmoil. According to documentation from 8 May 1585, Houel had poured 2,000 écus of his own money into his charitable endeavour and was on the brink of poverty himself at the time of his death in late 1587.[82] He was a man who acted in practice as he encouraged his patrons and benefactors, his own life becoming an example of the selfless Christian charity he presented in his treatises. Houel was a man who utilised his professional connections for the benefit of his fellow Parisians and the 'ornament' of the city he clearly loved. Like his contemporary Jean Martin, Houel recognised the value of 'examples mov[ing] more than words' when attempting to inspire 'the ardour of charity' in his fellow Christians and persuade them to abandon their ways of 'little charity', as Martin put it, and show charitable compassion toward 'God's poor members'. He hoped his treatise would 'fan the fire of charity, so cold' and encourage his readers 'to serve God [and] to perform works of charity and mercy unto the poor'.[83] His evocative images of the royal family and members of the nobility actively engaged with his charitable endeavour demonstrated a purposeful employment of his professional connections, lending his cause credibility through association with the highest echelons of Parisian society. Most importantly, Houel succeeded in establishing the religious credentials of his *Maison de la Charité chrétienne*. His own religious conviction shone through in his treatises revealing a personal generosity of spirit and spiritual devotion that obviously inspired those who patronised the maison. Nicolas Houel and his *Maison de la Charité chrétienne* represent the spirit of the late sixteenth-century French charitable endeavour, using one's spiritual conviction to simultaneously alleviate the suffering of one's fellow Christians, fulfil Christian obligations of charity, and offer the means through which benefactors could publicly display their religious allegiance during a period of violent religious division.

---

[82] Guiffrey, p. 256.

[83] Martin, *La police et reiglement*, p. 39v; 'Salutaire Exhortation de l'Autheur', in Houel, *Ample discours*, fols III and IIII.

Chapter 9

'comme bons citoyens': Faith and Politics in the Poor Relief of Later Sixteenth-Century Gap

Susan Broomhall

In February 1567, representatives of the Huguenot consistory at Gap appeared before the town's poor relief bureau to agree with their Catholic counterparts in the confraternities and hospitals to contribute funds to the town's relief scheme. The funds, they concurred, would be shared equally among the town's poor, irrespective of faith, solely on the basis of need. In the context of civil wars which wracked France during the latter half of the sixteenth century, and which had caused much of the poverty and suffering that Gap faced then and for years to come, this was the culmination of a remarkable few months in the town's history and the triumph of a municipal strategy that sought political cohesion and dominance over ecclesiastical authorities, by inclusion of both faiths in its charitable endeavours. This action would, in time, instrumentalise poor relief in significant ways, making it both a reflection and instrument of changing faith, secular and ecclesiastical regimes in the years to come. In this chapter, I analyse the motivations and outcomes of charitable organisation at Gap in the changing contexts of the later sixteenth century during which the town lurched back and forth between Catholic and Huguenot supremacy, and consider what these motivations and their contexts would mean for those who sought assistance from successive bureaux.

Much work on poor relief in sixteenth-century France has necessarily examined those communities in which at least partial records have survived, leading to a wide range of studies of particular urban environments. These have highlighted the range of social, financial and spiritual challenges that communities faced, as well as the varied mechanisms by which they sought to relieve poverty, while tending to emphasise the distinctions between Catholic and Huguenot systems.[1] While

---

[1] Wilma J. Pugh, 'Social Welfare and the Edict of Nantes: Lyon and Nîmes', *French Historical Studies*, 8 (1974), 349–76; Natalie Zemon Davis, *Society and Culture*, esp. 'Poor Relief, Humanism, and Heresy', pp. 17–64; Raymond A. Mentzer, 'Organizational Endeavour and Charitable Impulse in Sixteenth-Century France: The Care of Protestant Nîmes', *French History*, 5 (1991), 1–29; Barbara Beckerman Davis, 'Reconstructing the Poor in early Sixteenth-Century Toulouse', *French History*, 7 (1993), 249–85; Matthew Koch, 'Poor Relief in Montauban, 1548 to 1629', *Proceedings of the Western Society*

these have identified distinct confessional practices, more recent scholarship, in particular on Huguenot relief, demonstrates how charitable measures were inflected by local contexts, and the rigidity associated with the Calvinist moral programme has been nuanced accordingly.[2] Within these studies, historians have occasionally noted the extent to which the ruling confessional administrators restricted relief to their co-religionists or extended its provision across whole populations. Poor relief became in such contexts a political and spiritual instrument, and a series of scholars has observed that rival relief measures, especially during the seventeenth century, could be used as tools to win converts or as indicative of mutual agreement to confessional coexistence.[3]

---

for French History, 23 (1996), 69–80; Daniel Hickey, *Local Hospitals in Ancien Régime France: Rationalization, Resistance, Renewal, 1530–1789* (Montreal, McGill-Queen's University Press, 1997); Martin Dinges, 'Self-Help and Reciprocity in Parish Assistance: Bordeaux in the Sixteenth and Seventeenth Centuries', in Peregrine Horden and Richard Smith (eds), *The Locus of Care: Families, Communities, Institutions and the Provision of Welfare since Antiquity* (London: Routledge, 1998), pp. 111–25; Colin Jones, 'Perspectives on Poor Relief, Health Care and the Counter-Reformation in France', in Ole Peter Grell, Andrew Cunningham with Jon Arrizabalaga (eds), *Health Care and Poor Relief in Counter-Reformation Europe* (London: Routledge, 1999), pp. 215–39; Martin Dinges, 'Health Care and Poor Relief in Regional Southern France in the Counter-Reformation', in ibid., pp. 240–79; Martin Dinges, 'Huguenot Poor Relief and Health Care in the Sixteenth and Seventeenth Centuries', in Raymond A. Mentzer and Andrew Spicer (eds), *Society and Culture in the Huguenot World, 1559–1685* (Cambridge, Cambridge University Press, 2002), pp. 157–74; Susan Broomhall, *Women's Medical Work*, pp. 71–95; Susan Broomhall, 'Identity and Life Narratives of the Poor in Late Sixteenth-Century Tours', *Renaissance Quarterly*, 57 (2004), 439–65; Susan Broomhall, 'Family and Household Limitation Strategies among the Sixteenth-Century Urban Poor', *French History*, 20.2 (2006), 121–37; Susan Broomhall, 'The Politics of Charitable Men', pp. 133–58; Susan Broomhall, 'Charitable Medicine: The Provision of Health Care in the Sixteenth Century Hôtel-Dieu de Paris', in Witold Konstanty Pietrzak and Magdalena Kozluk (eds), *Le Cabinet du curieux: culture, savoirs, religion de l'Antiquité à l'Ancien Régime* (Paris: H. Champion, 2013), pp. 145–60.

  [2]   Philip Conner, *Huguenot Heartland: Montauban and Southern French Calvinism during the Wars of Religion* (Aldershot: Ashgate, 2002); Philip Conner, 'Huguenot Identities During the Wars of Religion: The Churches of Le Mans and Montauban Compared', *Journal of Ecclesiastical History*, 54.1 (2003), 23–39; Glenn S. Sunshine, *Reforming French Protestantism: The Development of Huguenot Ecclesiastical Institutions, 1557–1572* (Kirksville, MO: Truman State University Press, 2003); Kevin C. Robbins, *City on the Ocean Sea: La Rochelle, 1530–1650: Urban Society, Religion, and Politics on the French Atlantic Frontier* (Leiden: Brill, 1997). On the relationship of the town council and consistory there, see chap. 3, pp. 136–7, and on charitable donations, pp. 164–73.

  [3]   Wilma J. Pugh, 'Catholics, Protestants, and Testamentary Charity in Seventeenth-Century Lyon and Nîmes', *French Historical Studies*, 11 (1980), 479–504; Dinges, 'Huguenot Poor Relief'; Timothy J. McHugh, 'Hospitals and Huguenots: Confessional Coexistence in Nîmes, 1629–85', *European History Quarterly*, 33 (2003), 5–27.

Gap's history seems to offer an opportunity to explore a different model of charitable endeavour in sixteenth-century France from those examined thus far, one in which Catholics and Huguenots worked together, albeit briefly, in the same committee to achieve outcomes for poor of both faiths.[4] It may serve as an example of grassroots 'commitment to public life as a shared moral endeavour' in a small regional environment, of the kind that Mark Greengrass has analysed in the national and royal political discourse from 1576 to 1584.[5] Recently, Penny Roberts has explored the challenges and contested discourse of governance in the later sixteenth century between local communities and the crown, as the latter sought to negotiate a lasting peaceful settlement between the two confessions within the French kingdom,[6] while Jérémie Foa has studied the work of the commissioners sent by the crown to enforce successive edicts of peace within the varied contexts of individual urban environments.[7] Both scholars emphasise the difficulty and the wide variety of solutions that were established to achieve peace across France.[8]

---

[4]   It was not the only case of its kind. For a number of years in the 1560s, Lyon's Aumône générale ceded places on its bureau to the Protestants and argued that funds should be shared between the poor according only to need. See Henri de Boissieu, 'L'Aumône-Générale sous la domination protestante', *Bulletin de la Société littéraire historique et archéologique de Lyon*, 3 (1908–09), 1–32. The evidence for the town council of Châlons-sur-Marne in 1567 also appears to show a willingness to support native Huguenots, although not strangers. See Mark W. Konnert, *Local Politics in the French Wars of Religion: The Towns of Champagne, the Duc de Guise, and the Catholic League, 1560–95* (Aldershot: Ashgate, 2006), p. 104. See also Mark W. Konnert, *Civic Agendas and Religious Passion: Châlons-sur-Marne during the French Wars of Religion, 1560–1594* (Kirksville, MO: Sixteenth Century Journal Publishers, 1997).

[5]   See Mark Greengrass, *Governing Passions: Peace and Reform in the French Kingdom, 1576–1585* (Oxford: Oxford University Press, 2007).

[6]   Most recently in Penny Roberts, *Peace and Authority during the French Religious Wars, c. 1560–1600* (Houndmills: Palgrave Macmillan, 2013).

[7]   Jérémie Foa, 'Making Peace: The Commissions for Enforcing the Pacification Edicts in the Reign of Charles IX (1560–1574)', *French History*, 18 (2004), 256–74; Jérémie Foa, '"Reconcilier les cueurs des subjects cy devant divisez": Les commissaires des édits de pacification au temps des premières guerres de Religion', in Lucien Bély (ed.), *Les Affrontements religieux en Europe* (Paris: Presses de l'Université Paris-Sorbonne, 2009), pp. 61–82.

[8]   See also the wider literature on coexistence, pluralism and multiconfessionalism, largely focused on the seventeenth century, Robert Sauzet, *Contre réforme et réforme catholique en Bas-Languedoc: le diocèse de Nîmes au XVIIe siècle* (Louvain: Nauwelaerts, 1979); Bernard Dompnier, *Venin de l'hérésie: images du protestantisme et combat catholique au XVIIe siècle* (Paris: Le Centurion, 1985); Elisabeth Labrousse, *'Une foi, une loi, un roi?': Essai sur la révocation de l'édit de Nantes* (Geneva: Labor et Fides, 1985); Gregory Hanlon, *Confession and Community in Seventeenth-Century France: Catholic and Protestant Coexistence in Aquitaine* (Philadelphia: University of Pennsylvania Press, 1993); Keith Cameron, Mark Greengrass and Penny Roberts (eds), *The Adventure of Religious Pluralism in Early Modern France* (Oxford: Peter Lang, 2000); Keith P. Luria, *Sacred*

Although particular charitable provisions could be secured for communities through the process of such negotiations, neither scholar discusses poor relief as a potential instrument of conciliatory coalition as it appears to have been, briefly, at Gap. This town's unusual charitable coalition came to pass as a result of a specific mix of political and religious tensions, which are the focus of the following section.

A Maelstrom of Municipal, Ecclesiastical and Spiritual Disputes

During the early 1560s, the consulate of Gap suffered a series of misfortunes that led to general dissatisfaction from Catholics and Huguenots alike and highlighted the weakness of its authority. Despite a series of early charters that provided exemption to Gap, in 1558 the town was named by the Etats de Dauphiné among those on the roll due to pay *tailles* and other charges of the province.[9] Complaints about the consuls from all sides, including the ecclesiastical authorities, led to the

---

Boundaries: Religious Coexistence and Conflict in Early-Modern France (Washington, DC: Catholic University of America Press, 2005); Richard Bonney and David J.B. Trim (eds), *Persecution and Pluralism: Calvinists and Religious Minorities in Early Modern Europe, 1550–1700* (Oxford: Peter Lang, 2006); Jérémie Foa, 'Quelque mots d'amour entre catholiques et protestants du Sud-ouest au temps des guerres de Religion', *Moreana*, 45.173 (2008), 29–40; Jérémie Foa, 'Retour à Lectoure: Un Pacte d'amitié entre catholiques et protestants au début du XVIIe siècle', in Fabien Salesse (ed.), *Le bon historian sait faire parler les silences: hommages à Thierry Wanegffelen* (Toulouse: Méridiennes, 2012), pp. 331–58. For Europe more broadly, see also Benjamin J. Kaplan, *Divided By Faith: Religious Conflict and the Practice of Toleration in Early Modern Europe* (Cambridge, MA: Belknap, 2007); Jesse Spohnholz, *The Tactics of Toleration: A Refugee Community in the Age of Religious War* (Newark: University of Delaware Press, 2011); Thomas Max Safley (ed.), *A Companion to Multiconfessionalism in the Early Modern World* (Leiden: Brill, 2011).

[9] Théodore Gautier, *Précis*, p. 68. For the Wars of Religion and Protestants in the Dauphiné region more broadly, see Jean-Denis Long, *La Réforme et les guerres de religion en Dauphiné de 1560 à l'Édit de Nantes (1598)* (Paris: Firmin Didot, 1856); Charles Charronnet, *Les Guerres de religion et la société protestante dans les Hautes-Alpes (1560–1789)* (Gap: P. Jouglard, 1861); Eugène Arnaud, *Histoire des protestants du Dauphiné aux XVIe, XVIIe et XVIIIe siècles*, 3 vols (Paris: Grasset, 1875–76), I (1875); Janine Garrison-Estèbe, *Protestants du Midi, 1559–1598* (Toulouse: Privat, 1980); Pierre Bolle, *Le Protestant dauphinois et la république des synodes à la veille de la Révocation* (Lyon: La Manufacture, 1985); Henry Heller, *The Conquest of Poverty: The Calvinist Revolt in Sixteenth Century France* (Leiden: Brill, 1986), esp. 'Protestantism on the Eve of the Religious Wars: The Revolt of Valence'; Gwenola de Rippert d'Alauzier, *Dauphiné protestant: regards sur les guerres de religion en Dauphiné au XVIe siècle, des prémices de la Réforme à l'Édit de Nantes* (Aubais: Musée du protestantisme dauphinois/Mémoires d'Oc éditions, 2006). On the specific taxation context of the province, see Llewain Scott van Doren, 'War Taxation, Institutional Change and Social Conflict in Provincial France: The Royal Taille in Dauphiné, 1494–1559', *Proceedings of the American Philosophical Society*, 121 (1977), 70–96; and Daniel Hickey, *Le Dauphiné devant la monarchie absolue.*

development of a new constitution of the community providing clarity as to the representation of citizens in the election and composition of the consulate. The *Règlement politique* of 1 February 1560 permitted a wide cross-section of Gap's male inhabitants to vote for the consuls and other officers of the community.[10] General council meetings were to be strictly attended by the elected officials, on pain of a 10 *sols* fine to the poor of Gap's Hôtel-Dieu, linking municipal endeavour to charity in ways common to many towns at this period.[11] The *Règlement* did not, however, clarify satisfactorily the relationship and hierarchy between Gap's bishop and the town, which would soon cause further challenges among the town's officiating bodies.[12] The cause of medical care for the less fortunate in the town was highlighted in the same year when an *arrêt* from the *cour de parlement* at Grenoble required the town's physicians to charge less for their services.[13] Some of the medical men implicated by this *arrêt*, Bernard de Cazeneufve, Jehan Jube and Bernard de Flandria, were among the longstanding civic elite of Gap, and had been already – and would be later again – both members of the consulate and engaged in the matter of the town's charitable services. By 1561 rioting had broken out among a large number of inhabitants who refused to pay a tax voted to help cover the debts of the town. The consulate in this instance would require the support of Parlement to manage the affair and maintain order.[14]

At the same period, differences of faith among Gap's inhabitants were reaching a crisis point. Dauphiné, the province in which Gap was situated, was a region considered a Huguenot stronghold.[15] In Gap, many of the most significant families of the city were adherents of the new faith.[16] Apart from its close proximity to Geneva, Gap had also hosted the polemical figure and persuasive preacher Guillaume Farel, whose family was from the local area. In 1561 he was the elderly minister of the Huguenot community, preaching just beyond the town walls.[17] Already in 1560, Huguenots had incited anger by burning down a series of crosses and other religious symbols from the Calvary constructed on the edge of the town.[18] Soon some were sufficiently emboldened to drive the parish of Sainte Collombe from their church which the Protestant community took over for services and for

---

Le procès des tailles et la perte des libertés provinciales 1540–1640 (Grenoble: Presse Universitaire de Grenoble, 1986).

[10] *Précis*, p. 68.

[11] *Précis*, p. 228; see also Arnaud, pp. 206–14.

[12] *Précis*, p. 69.

[13] *Précis*, p. 69.

[14] *Précis*, pp. 68, 70; Henry Heller, *Iron and Blood: Civil Wars in Sixteenth-Century France* (Montreal: McGill–Queen's University Press, 1991), p. 52.

[15] See references in n. 9.

[16] Charronnet, pp. 54–5.

[17] On Farel's earlier work, see Jason Zuidema and Theodore Van Raalte, *Early French Reform: The Theology and Spirituality of Guillaume Farel* (Farnham: Ashgate, 2011).

[18] *Précis*, p. 69.

Farel's public preaching.[19] This caused his detention by officials, possibly drawing even more attention to his cause. On 1 May 1562, the Huguenots briefly seized control of the town for a period of months, during which time Gabriel de Clermont, the Bishop of Gap since 1526, formally abjured Catholicism for the new religion, before the March 1563 Edict of Amboise brought a formal peace to Gap.[20]

Tensions between the faith communities, and between the municipal and ecclesiastical authorities, were, however, unresolved. External authorities, seeking to balance power between ecclesiastical and lay authorities, had instead increased antagonism that would linger through the later sixteenth century. In 1558, for example, the Parlement at Grenoble had determined that episcopal judicial officials could form a sentence in the matter of heresy, but the punishment was to be left to the royal judges.[21] The bishop was Lord of Gap and remained symbolically powerful although his real power in the town depended a great deal on the individual character (and evidently, also the faith) of the incumbent. Regarding municipal affairs, François de Scépeaux, maréchal de Vielleville, ordered commissioners to negotiate between the Catholics and Protestants in the hopes of finding a position of peace.[22] By April 1564, a new *règlement politique* was ratified by Parlement, substantially benefiting the minority, but powerful, Huguenot community, and likely reflecting the threat constituted by the strong Calvinist population in the areas directly surrounding Gap. Under the terms of this *règlement*, both Catholics and Huguenots would be eligible to vote in municipal elections. Executive power lay in the hands of the four popularly elected consuls, the first and third of whom were to be Catholic, and the second and fourth Huguenot. Of the 24 secular consulate positions, which were elected by the four new consuls and the four previous ones, 12 were allocated to former councillors but ten of the 14 new councillors were to be drawn from among the Reformed Church. Two final positions on the consulate were reserved for ecclesiastical members.[23] Such a confessional coalition among the consulate was not unique to Gap; a series of other south-eastern towns would make similar arrangements during the later sixteenth century, often, as Foa observes, under the guidance of the crown's commissioner.[24] Roberts has argued

---

[19]   *Précis*, p. 72. On Farel, see Arnaud, p. 88.

[20]   *Précis*, pp. 73–4; Charronnet, p. 31. For more on Gabriel de Clermont and his time in the See of Gap as both a Protestant and Catholic, see Joseph Bergin, *The Making of the French Episcopate, 1589–1661* (New Haven, CT: Yale University Press, 1996), pp. 338–9.

[21]   Charronnet, pp. 13–14.

[22]   On Vielleville's later work for the French crown in favour of the edicts of pacifications, see Jérémie Foa, 'La "pacification de la paix"? La mission du maréchal de Vielleville à Clermont en Auvergne (1570)', *Bulletin de la Société d'Histoire du Protestantisme*, 151 (2005), 231–64; and, more broadly, Roberts, chap. 7, 'Practicalities of Peace'.

[23]   Théodore Gautier, 'IIIe Lettre sur l'histoire de la ville de Gap (1563–1568)', *Revue du Dauphiné*, 3 (1838), 66–7; Charronnet, pp. 44–5.

[24]   See Foa, 'Making Peace', p. 267; Philip Benedict notes the same in *The Huguenot Population of France, 1600–1685: The Demographic Fate and Customs of a Religious*

that in nearby Valence too, representatives of both faiths were able to present a united front through their urban governance, in declarations of 'union and accord between the citizens', to protest against royal infringements of their liberties.[25] In Gap, this represented a significant gain of municipal power to the Huguenots who represented much less than half of the town's population.[26] These power-sharing arrangements did not put an end to aggression within the town though; sporadic violence saw the death of Antoine Rambaud, the local leader of the Protestants[27] and further deaths resulted from skirmishes surrounding the marriage celebrations of François de Bonne, sieur de Lesdiguières, in 1565.[28] The 1566 Edict of Moulins, however, encouraged the town's officials to renew attempts to work together, including through a focus on poor relief, for the edict had signalled that parishes were to care for their own poor and once again called upon lay officials to assume control of its organisation from ecclesiastical officials.[29]

The sources available to study the operation of Gap's poor relief in the immediately ensuing period are, unsurprisingly, far from regular during this time of considerable instability. A collection of deliberations from the bureau cover patchily the years 1566–73.[30] To deepen our knowledge of the period, however, are the surviving deliberations, or draft notes, of the town consulate, the *vibailli* and consuls, who worked and reported on the operation of assistance in place and comprised a civic elite, which, at various points, also participated as members of the bureau.[31] These documents shine some light on the period from 1570 to 1571 and 1572 to 1574 during which the Catholic majority held ascendency within the town, as well as for 1593 when Gap was under the control of the Huguenots. These texts also allow us to trace the use of language and the power of rhetoric,

---

Minority (Philadelphia: American Philosophical Society, 1991), p. 1.

[25]   Roberts, p. 139.

[26]   *Précis*, p. 74, n. 1. This *règlement* states that the Catholic population was 6000–7000 and Protestants some 200–300. Scholars have questioned whether these figures represent an error, perhaps for 2000–3000 instead. However, Gautier indicates that these figures are used repeatedly through that original document, lending credence to the notion that these were indeed the confessional proportions of the town, and thus making the decision to give almost half weighting to Huguenot representation within the consulate a significant gain.

[27]   *Précis*, p. 75.

[28]   *Précis*, pp. 75–6.

[29]   Susan E. Dinan, 'Motivations for Charity in Early Modern France', in Thomas Max Safley (ed.), *The Reformation of Charity: The Secular and the Religious in Early Modern Poor Relief* (Leiden: Brill, 2003), pp. 176–92 (p. 185).

[30]   A.D. Hautes-Alpes, 3 H suppl. 275 (formerly H suppl. 541), E.1.: Délibérations du bureau des pauvres de l'hôpital de Gap, 1566–1573.

[31]   A.D. Hautes-Alpes, Series BB. 9. Registre. Brouillon des délibérations de la ville de Gap, par 'Rambaudi, secrétaire de la communauté', 1570–71; BB. 10. Liasse. Extraicts des délibérations de la ville de Gap, 1572–74; BB. 11. Cahier. Délibérations 1593; BB. 12. Registre. 'Livre des conselz' de la ville de Gap, tenu par le notaire royale Gay, secrétaire. 19 August 1599–24 April 1601.

however codified in these genres, about charity through the voices of different leading men.[32] Such analysis may help to reveal contemporary notions of care, poverty and the poor which operated within and across faiths.

'l'unyon et concorde que doibt estre entre citoyens d'une mesme ville': A Charitable Endeavour, 1566–67

On Sunday 7 December 1566, a group of municipal and ecclesiastical officials met in the home of the *vibailli* and *juge présidial du Gapençois*, Benoît Olier.[33] The meeting was held at the request of Gap's councillors and with the intention of bringing together a committee to 'give regulation and order to poverty in Gap, its territories and parishes'.[34] Present was a series of religious and municipal leaders, from consuls, canons and lawyers to an ironmonger. The premier consul, Olivier Abon, emphasised the present crisis upon the town, particularly the high number of strangers. The decision was taken to form a bureau of twelve 'noteworthy people', to meet each Sunday at 1pm, which would include both secular, royal and Catholic ecclesiastical authorities, municipal leaders and members of the Huguenot community.[35] Four further men were elected as 'prosecutors … of poverty'.[36] This was a highly unusual composition for a relief bureau, both because of its mix of varied lay and ecclesiastical authorities at a time when most bureaux in France were increasingly secular and municipal, and because of its interfaith mix. The composition cannot simply be attributed to a small number of leaders available for such civic duty – Gap was a town estimated to have a population somewhere between 7,500 and 10,000 at this era.[37] Instead, the bureau seemed designed to incorporate the widest possible representation from the varied interest groups within the town, whether derived from a sense of reconciliation or for protection against criticisms and doubts about municipal authority that had been voiced vociferously in previous years.

At its first meeting on 15 December 1566, the bureau considered how it would support the poor and by what means. It was hoped that each pauper could be provided a pound and a half of bread each day,[38] the same amount the governors

---

[32]   In ways similar to those studies undertaken by Greengrass and Stefano Simiz (ed.), *La Parole publique en ville des Réformes à la Révolution* (Villeneuve d'Ascq: Presses Universitaires du Septentrion, 2012).

[33]   Charronnet (pp. 54–6) discusses the bureau briefly, principally for what it reveals about the state of organisation of the Huguenot community at this period.

[34]   A.D. Hautes-Alpes, 3 H suppl. 275, fol. 1r: 'fere reglementz et donner pollice sur la povrete dud gap ces terroyrs et parroisses.'

[35]   A.D. Hautes-Alpes, 3 H suppl. 275, fol. 1v: 'notables personnages.'

[36]   A.D. Hautes-Alpes, 3 H suppl. 275, fol. 2r: 'procureurs … de la povrete.'

[37]   See n. 26.

[38]   A.D. Hautes-Alpes, 3 H suppl. 275, fol. 2v.

at Lyon's Aumône Générale had concluded was required.[39] Actual delivery of the services proved more difficult, however. At a distribution at the St Dominique convent on 22 December, the three members administering the alms to those on the rolls discovered 'that there was still a great multitude of paupers not called up … unknown to the committee' and 'concluded that an order be sent to the poor … to be on the rolls and thus to receive alms'.[40] The volume of strangers to the town also prompted the bureau on 28 December to request that 'all poor strangers turn up tomorrow, after dinner, to have their names, surnames, place of origin and where they are living in Gap taken down, so as to be provided for'.[41] This rather generous policy was coupled with a more stringent order to 'imprison the poor who are found going about the gates'.[42] The bureau was true to its word, following up on individual cases in breach of the order where they were known. On 1 January 1567, a stranger not on the rolls was sent away and the man who had rented him lodgings ordered to discontinue, on pain of a 10 *livres* fine to the poor.[43] On 19 January, they reiterated their order to place any poor at the gates in prison.[44] The wife of one Anthoine Farel came before the bureau on 26 January to be investigated because 'despite having her pound of alms, she goes begging through the town'.[45] Control of the itinerant and begging poor, even at a cost to the town, was clearly preferable to the bureau, one measure to gain knowledge of newcomers and keep control over the latent hostilities that underlay urban life in Gap.

Coupled with these challenges of identifying and delivering sustenance to the poor was the issue of raising relief funds. Yet the bureau's decisions, seen broadly, appear generous, rather than suggesting urgent financial crisis. As one measure, the *vibailli* announced that he would write to the communities around Gap asking them to take back their poor, or to pay for them at a cost of one pound of bread a day (an amount less than the one and a half pound rations that the town was providing those same paupers). As to those paupers who did not have means to make the journey to their hometowns, the bureau would provide them with the 'passade', the traditional allowance of food and lodgings that was given

---

[39]   Davis, *Society and Culture*, p. 39.

[40]   A.D. Hautes-Alpes, 3 H suppl. 275, fol. 6r: 'quil y avoit encores grand multitude de povres non appelles … incoigneuz a la compagnie', 'ont concludz balher assignation ausd povres pour … estre au rolles et en apres recepvoyr laumosne.'

[41]   A.D. Hautes-Alpes, 3 H suppl. 275, fol. 11r: 'tout povre estrangier se treuve demain apres dyner pour estre prins leurs noms surnoms lieuz de leurs habitations et ou sont louges a la presente cite de Gap pour apres leur estre pourveu.'

[42]   A.D. Hautes-Alpes, 3 H suppl. 275, fol. 11r: 'emprisoner les povres quils treuveront allantz pour [par?] les portes.'

[43]   A.D. Hautes-Alpes, 3 H suppl. 275, fol. 12v.

[44]   A.D. Hautes-Alpes, 3 H suppl. 275, fol. 16v.

[45]   A.D. Hautes-Alpes, 3 H suppl. 275, fol. 18v: 'nonobstant sa lieure de lhaumosne va par la ville mendicant.'

to pilgrims.[46] At the bureau's 5 January meeting, the consul tasked with securing donations from the forest areas reported that he had been unable to construct a list of the wealthy inhabitants and that, in any case, 'the majority declared that they had no money to contribute ... they give what they can at the door'.[47] On 12 January, when the bureau heard 'that there was almost no one who wants to give', these communities were simply to be told to 'govern their own poor'.[48] While this left the problem of those paupers to their areas, it did not apply punitive measures or place wider contributing demands upon those forest-dwelling populations.

On the other hand, what this policy did make clear was that the poor were the responsibility of those directly around them. This was a decision that the committee articulated early on. At the committee's meeting of 15 December, one member had reported:

> that, yesterday, ... msr Jehan Rostaing, holding a meeting of leaders, before the lawyer mre Guilhe Puthod, as much in his own name as those of others of the so-called Religion, acted in the name of those on the mandate, to ask that donations made for those of the Religion, be distributed to the poor of the said so-called Religion.[49]

The bureau did not support this reasoning at all, and firmly and clearly stated in their deliberations their view 'that this was found strange and a beginning of division, more than of union; to which mandate the prosecutor of the town is opposed. On which it was concluded ... to make no division nor separation of religion'.[50] This belief was fundamental to the bureau's composition and would likewise be reflected in its operation. Indeed, nowhere was it clearer than in the order, made at the bureau meeting of 19 January, where the committee called upon the *sergent royal* to 'seize and imprison in person the wealthy neighbours' of Tonite, the widow of Thelme Mehère, of Treschastel, who was 'burdened with five

---

[46]   A.D. Hautes-Alpes, 3 H suppl. 275, fol. 14r.

[47]   A.D. Hautes-Alpes, 3 H suppl. 275, fol. 13r: 'La plus part ont declaire navoyr argent pour contribuer ... Ilz donnent aux portes ce quilz peuvent.'

[48]   A.D. Hautes-Alpes, 3 H suppl. 275, fol. 15v: 'que ne y a quasi persone que veullie doner', 'fere governer leurs povres.'

[49]   A.D. Hautes-Alpes, 3 H suppl. 275, fol. 3v: 'que du jour dhier a plaine audience episcopale de gap msr Jehan Rostaing tenant laudience des chiefz pardevant mre Guilhe Puthod advocat tant a son nom que des aultres de la Relligion pretendue a faict procure aulx nomes en la procuration pour exhiger les leyes faicts pour ceulx de la Relligion pour les distribuer aulx povres de lade pretendue Relligion.'

[50]   A.D. Hautes-Alpes, 3 H suppl. 275, fols 3v–4r: 'qua este treuve estrange et ung comencement de division plustost que de lunion A laquelle procuration le procureur de la ville sest oppose sur quoy a este concludz ... ne fere aulcune desparte ne division de Relligion.'

daughters', so as to provide her with three pounds of bread a day.[51] Proximity and commitment to each other as Gapençois, not faith, was key: charity was sought from those of means from the streets and houses directly around the very people who required it.

Indeed, the bureau acted promptly to demonstrate that it would expect both Catholic and Huguenot groups to share the burden of poor relief and to contribute accordingly. On 19 December, two members, the Catholic Raymond Juvenis and Huguenot Claude Brunet-Blocard were appointed to the task of organising 'street by street' contributions.[52] The heads of Gap's confraternities and hospitals would also be called upon to make known the donations made to their organisations that had been intended for the poor.[53] The bureau expected these to be made available to them to administer within the new poor relief structure. Several meetings later, when little had happened, the bureau agreed to ask 'those who are in charge of the confraternities' to attend their next meeting as well as the rector of the hospital of St Meins.[54] By 1 January 1567, they summoned Jeanne Marquis, whose now deceased husband had bought a vineyard from the Confraternity of Sainte Collombe, and on which she owed five years of arrears, on which they calculated a value for her to pay the bureau, including appreciation.[55] By 12 January, the bureau was also considering how to sell assets belonging to the confraternities 'for the greatest convenience and most profit to poverty'.[56] They concluded that 'the goods will be sold to the highest bidder, as the candleflame dies, on the understanding that the price in silver will be given as an annual pension, following the Ordonnance, to feed the poor'.[57] There was to be a sale out the front of the house of the *bailliage*, through the days of late January.[58]

Having first approached the longstanding Catholic organisations within the town, the bureau then tackled the matter of contributions from the Huguenots. On 27 December, the bureau considered a request from le Coiffard, 'so-called procurator of those of the so-called Reformed Religion' to distribute among his

---

[51]   A.D. Hautes-Alpes, 3 H suppl. 275, fol. 16v: 'saysir et emprisonner de leurs personnes les prochains voisins ayse', 'Tonite vefve a Thelme Mehere de Treschastel chargee de cinq filhes'.

[52]   A.D. Hautes-Alpes, 3 H suppl. 275, fol. 5v: 'de ruye en rue.'

[53]   A.D. Hautes-Alpes, 3 H suppl. 275, fols 6v–9r. See deliberations of 22 December.

[54]   A.D. Hautes-Alpes, 3 H suppl. 275, fol. 11v: 'ceulx qui ont charge des confrayries.'

[55]   A.D. Hautes-Alpes, 3 H suppl. 275, fols 12r–12v.

[56]   A.D. Hautes-Alpes, 3 H suppl. 275, fol. 14v: 'par plus grande comodite et plus de proffit de la povrete.'

[57]   A.D. Hautes-Alpes, 3 H suppl. 275, fol. 14v: 'le bien se peult vendre et sera vendu au plus offrant et dernier encharisseur a lestien de la chandelle soubz la qualite que le pris en argent quen porviendra sera balhe a pention annuelle suyvant lordonnance pour allimenter les povres.'

[58]   A.D. Hautes-Alpes, 3 H suppl. 275, fol. 16r, Deliberations of 19 January.

co-religionists the legacies from one Jean Fortune.[59] The bureau decided to take the advice of the consistory that would be meeting later that week.[60] Receiving no immediate answer, the bureau tasked 'those of the Religion, that is to say, sire Jacques Burle, Guillaume de Faure, and Claude Blocard' to ask the consistory to provide its response.[61] By 16 February, it was reported 'that those of the Religion are happy to transfer the donations, as long as there is agreement that their school master be paid from the funds'.[62] But the committee wanted clear confirmation direct from the consistory and decided that they should be called 'themselves to come and give their response'.[63] The following day, 'those of the new religion', Pierre Parat, Pierre Queyrel and Joseph Magna, responded.[64] To the request made to distribute equally among all the poor of Gap those donations that had been made by those of the reformed religion for their poor:

> They say, in order to show that they desire union and concord that must be between citizens of the same town, however much they have means to prevent it, that they are content and offer to make the said contribution of the donations.

However, the agreement was conditional:

> That it will be at the liberty of those of the consistory of the said Reformed Religion to name those who must attend from hereon the bureau of the poor from the said Religion, be they prosecutors, treasurers, controllers and other offices for poverty; and that they cannot take the principal of the donations but only the pensions which arise from these *deniers*.[65]

It was a clear staking of position. The representatives made clear that they held the power to refuse such a request but had decided for the greater good of the

---

[59]   A.D. Hautes-Alpes, 3 H suppl. 275, fol. 10v: 'soy disant procureur daulcuns de la Relligion pretendue Refforme.'

[60]   A.D. Hautes-Alpes, 3 H suppl. 275, fol. 10v.

[61]   A.D. Hautes-Alpes, 3 H suppl. 275, fol. 15v: 'ceux de la Relligion assavoyr sire Jacq Burle Guilhe du Faure et Claude Blocard.'

[62]   A.D. Hautes-Alpes, 3 H suppl. 275, fol. 23r: 'quilz de la Relligion sont comtens communiquer les leguatz avec pache que leurs mestres d'escolles soyt paye de ce.'

[63]   A.D. Hautes-Alpes, 3 H suppl. 275, fol. 23r: 'eulx-mesmes venir fere la response.'

[64]   A.D. Hautes-Alpes, 3 H suppl. 275, fol. 23v: 'ceulx de la novelle Relligion.'

[65]   A.D. Hautes-Alpes, 3 H suppl. 275, fol. 24r: 'disent pour monstrer que ilz desirent lunyon et concorde que doibt estre entre citoyens dune mesme ville combien ilz heussent moyen dempeycher quilz sont contens et offrent fere ladicte contribution desd legatz … a la condition quil sera a la liberte de ceulx du consistoyre de ladte Relligion Refforme de nommer ceulx qui debvent assister par cy apres par ladte Relligion audict bureau des povres soyent procureurs tresauriers contrerolleurs et aultres offices pour ladicte povrete que lon ne pourra prendre le fondz des sommes notables desd leguatz pies mes seullement les pentions qui sortiront desd deniers.'

town (or themselves) not to do so. In acquiescing, they had also gained a greater share of the bureau than they currently held, across a wider number of roles and positions. Moreover, they also made clear that they had not given up their key funds permanently to the bureau, but only the pensions arising from these.

The new poor relief bureau had commenced in Gap under the guise of charitable motivations, but it was clearly also a political measure by the civic elite to contain both the latent danger of paupers and strangers, as well as one which could secure the political co-operation of the town's other great menace, the Huguenots, through the consistent employment of irenicist rhetoric (and, perhaps, also irenicist beliefs of some individuals within it). However, the position taken by the Huguenot elders to contribute financial support to the Gap poor relief bureau on their terms reflected their growing power in the town. By the end of 1567, Huguenots had again taken control, when an influx of co-religionists from surrounding areas swept through the town, significantly damaging the cathedral. The *vibailli* had in the turmoil removed himself to nearby Serres, remaining there until his authority could be re-established.[66] Huguenot ascendency, though, proved short-lived. By 1570, the Catholic majority were back in charge of the town's key functions, including its poor relief, and in the next section I explore the confessionalising of charity that consequently occurred.

'tellement que puissions demeurer paisiblement et en paix': Catholicising Charity in the 1570s

From 1570, Gap's re-formed poor relief bureau took on a decidedly different persuasion from that which had struggled through the late 1560s. As the Catholic majority regained dominance within core civic operations, the relief bureau was to become increasingly partisan and the charitable endeavours it advocated distinctly Catholic in their orientation.

It was a consulate fearful of the threat of Huguenots that considered municipal affairs during this period. In late August 1570, the consulate met to discuss a response to the publication of the Edict of St Germain-en-Laye (8 August 1570). This edict had for the first time articulated provisions for specifically Huguenot hospital and charitable institutions.[67] They concluded 'not to let any *huguenaud* or *huguenaude* enter until those of the Religion are obedient, and let the Catholics enter and enjoy their goods in the places where they hold power'.[68] Despite strong resistance from members of the consulate, Huguenots were permitted to return to

---

[66] *Précis*, p. 76.

[67] Roberts, p. 37.

[68] A.D. Hautes-Alpes, BB. 9, fol. 36r: 'ne laisser entrer huguenaud ne huguenaude jusques ad ce que ceulx de la Relligion ayent obey et laisse entrer les catholiques et jouyr de leurs biens es lieux quilz tiennent en leur povoyr'.

their homes by September.[69] By the end of October, the consulate agreed to discuss with the governor the request of 'huguenot strangers who want to live in the town', determining that a roll would need to be made, and stipulating that no lodgings were to be rented to them until it was firmly decided.[70] Sixty soldiers were brought from nearby Embrun to secure order at the traditional St Martin's fair where the consulate determined that it 'is necessary to mount a good watch', because 'those of the Religion are threatening to create a disturbance at the time of the fair, to the extent that they are boasting about doing it'.[71] But it was an assertion of faith (and perhaps trust) that the fair went ahead. Then in February 1571, there were rumours that Vitalis, seigneur de Montfort en Provence, had come to enjoy his lands nearby:

> accompanied by a number of people of the so-called Religion that is called Reformed, and ... many of the said religion will come to Champsaur and other places, and there will be a great assembly of about 30 or 40, as they say, of the leaders.[72]

The consulate feared an attack on the town, from 'those of the said Religion of this town and other strangers who have come here' who were consorting together and swaggering about the town carrying swords, 'which could mean something sinister'.[73] They decided to report their fears to Humbert de Rosset, sieur de Prunières et de Rosset, the governor of Gap since 1568, seeking answers 'so we can live calmly and in peace'.[74] Rosset returned his answer: that the consulate 'must not show them their fear'.[75] A climate of distrust and fear pervaded the town.

However, the challenges of poverty and need were unchanged; in fact, they worsened after the conflicts of the previous few years. Billeted soldiers were added to the town's burden of care. In June, there were complaints in the consulate about the high number of 'Provençal stranger soldiers, who are not content with

---

[69]   *Précis*, p. 80.

[70]   A.D. Hautes-Alpes, BB. 9, fol. 43v: 'huguenaulx estrangiers qui veullent habiter a la ville.'

[71]   A.D. Hautes-Alpes, BB. 9, fols 44v, 46v: 'est necessaire de fere quelque bonne garde', 'ceulx de la Relligion font de grandz menasse de fere au temps de foyre quelques desordres de quoy se sont vante de le fere'.

[72]   A.D. Hautes-Alpes, BB. 9, fols 61v–62r: 'accompagne de quelque nombre de gens de la Relligion pretendue que ont dict Refformee, et ... seroyent venus beaucoup de ladite Relligion tant de champsaur que d'aultre part et y auroyt grande assemblée de trente ou quarante comme lon dit des chiefz.'

[73]   A.D. Hautes-Alpes, BB. 9, fol. 62r: 'ceulx de ladite Relligion deste ville et aultres estrangiers qui y sont y vont', 'que pourret signiffier chose sinistre.'

[74]   A.D. Hautes-Alpes, BB. 9, fol. 62r: 'tellement que puissions demeurer paisiblement et en paix.'

[75]   A.D. Hautes-Alpes, BB. 9, fols 64v–65r: 'quil ne falhoit leur monstrer avoyr crainte.'

their bread ration, so make themselves governors over their hosts'.[76] These were repeated later that month, when it was noted that the 'Provençals retained by Monsieur the governor and the assembly held by Monsieur *le vibailli* ... cause a lot of disorder for their hosts, despite being provided with a ration of bread and wine by them ... and the hosts complain about it ... Remonstration will be made with them to conduct themselves properly in their lodgings'.[77] By July, the consulate concluded that those who lodged the soldiers 'are required to feed them entirely, for the soldiers sell their rations and those of the Religion who have soldiers hardly care for them at all'.[78] Here was a clear resentment against the other community who were not doing their share. By January of the following year, the consulate concluded it must ask the soldiers to leave and collections were recommenced 'to provide for the poor'.[79] The situation was dire by April when the consulate concluded that it would not be able to pay its debts and taxes ordered by *lettres patentes* of the king in March: 'because of the poverty of the citizens, we have not been able to recover nor find the money'.[80]

When the relief bureau reconvened in early December 1571, it was in the context of 'urgent necessity'.[81] Having removed the billeted soldiers, the bureau decided that hosting might work just as well as a strategy for the town's poor. In its 16 December meeting, the committee concluded that those poor strangers who could not afford to leave because of their finances or injuries 'would be maintained at the expense of the hosts who have contravened the proclamations, and failing that, at the expense of the community'.[82] Thus, those who did not keep order would be punished by supporting the poor. This was followed by the drafting of a new roll with 'verification of the paupers who merit being lodged'.[83] By March, the bureau resolved that those who refused to obey by not providing bread as required, would be made to give double. But on 23 March, the issue again rose before the bureau, with 'several to whom the distribution of the poor had been

---

[76] A.D. Hautes-Alpes, BB. 9, fol. 24r: 'soudardz estrangiers provensaulx qui ne se contentent de pain de la monition ains se font gouverner aulx hostes.'

[77] A.D. Hautes-Alpes, BB. 9, fol. 26v: 'Prouvencaux rettenus par monsieur le gouverneur et la assemblee faicte par monsieur le vibaihi ... font beaucoup de desordres sus leurs hostes nonobstant quilz fornissent monition de pain et de vin ... et les hostes sen plaignent ... Leur fere remonstrer de se porter honestment aulx logis.'

[78] A.D. Hautes-Alpes, BB. 9, fol. 31r: 'sont contrainctz les norrir entierement car les souldardz vandent leur monition et ceulx de la Relligion qui on souldardz ne les gardent guere.'

[79] A.D. Hautes-Alpes, BB. 9, fol. 57v: 'pour subvenir a la povrete.'

[80] A.D. Hautes-Alpes, BB. 9, fol. 77v: 'causant la povrete des citoyens lons ne peut recovrer ni tru[v]er argent.'

[81] A.D. Hautes-Alpes, 3 H suppl. 275, fol. 25r: 'considere la hurgente necessite.'

[82] A.D. Hautes-Alpes, 3 H suppl. 275, fol. 28r: 'en seront portees aulx despens des hostes contravenantz aulx proclamations et a faulte diceulx aulx despens de la comune'.

[83] A.D. Hautes-Alpes, 3 H suppl. 275, fol. 28v: 'veriffication des povres que meritent destre loges.'

made, refusing them, not deigning to give them what is decreed'.[84] The bureau agreed that they would be made to comply or pursued 'by all means of justice' and even 'by seizing their bread from the oven'.[85] They would thus create a new kind of list, this time of the other end of the town's social spectrum, 'a roll of the refusers and the disobedient'.[86] This revealed further infractions, that 'there are several to whom the poor have been sent by the bureau, who have not wanted to receive them, and others who refused to feed them, having fed them for a few days, and then afterwards, sent them away and did not want to give them any food'.[87]

The 1571 bureau retained its mix of secular and ecclesiastical officials but no known Huguenots. Huguenot life was progressively pushed to the sidelines. Their weekly worship, since a 1571 *règlement*, had been confined to the small town of Chorges, four miles to the north of Gap.[88] After the Saint Bartholomew's Day Massacre of August 1572, which had not affected Gap too directly, the Governor of Dauphiné, Bertrand de Gordes, issued a series of orders in the interests of reconciliation in the latter months of the year. These offered Huguenots asylum in the town and restitution of their goods but refused them the right to preaching and assemblies 'to avoid similar troubles and inconveniences that have arisen previously from it' and pressured them to consider returning to the Catholic faith.[89]

By the time of the January 1573 records, the bureau had a noticeably stronger ecclesiastical composition and met in 'the high room of the house of the heirs of the late Monsieur Hugues de St-Marcel d'Avanson, in his lifetime the canon and *secrétain* of the church of Gap, where the said Lord Bishop now makes his residence'.[90] The Bishop, Pierre Paparin de Chaumont, was making his mark upon Gap quickly, having only staged his official entry into the town on 15 December 1572. Paparin had obtained the see after the formal, final resignation of professed Protestant, Gabriel de Clermont, who secured himself a comfortable pension through the transaction. Clermont wrote with some surprise that he should have

---

[84]   A.D. Hautes-Alpes, 3 H suppl. 275, fol. 30r: 'plusieurs a qui la distribution des povres a este faicte les reffusent les uns et les aultres ne daignent leur balher ce qua este ordone.'

[85]   A.D. Hautes-Alpes, 3 H suppl. 275, fol. 30v: 'par toutes voyes de justice', 'notament par saysie et prinse de leurs pains au four.'

[86]   A.D. Hautes-Alpes, 3 H suppl. 275, fol. 30v: 'du rolle des reffusantz et desobeissantz.'

[87]   A.D. Hautes-Alpes, 3 H suppl. 275, fol. X: 'il y a plusieurs a qui les povres ont este distribue par le bureau lesquelz ne les ont volleu recepvoyr et les aultres refusent de les allimenter les ayant allimente quelques jours et apres en ont renvoyes et ne leur veulhent balher aulcune norriture.'

[88]   Charronnet, pp. 64–7.

[89]   Charronnet, pp. 73–4: 'pour obvier à semblables maux et inconvénients qui en sont cy-devant advenus.'

[90]   A.D. Hautes-Alpes, 3 H suppl. 275, fol. 33r: 'la salle aulte de la maison des hoyrs de feu M. Hugues de sainct marcel davanson a son vivant chanoine et secrestain de lesglise de gap ou led. Sgr evesque faict sa residence.'

been asked to vacate his position 'purely because of religion',[91] a complaint that attests to something of the confessional and political spirit, and financial interests, that drove some portion of Gap's administrators at the period. Previously a soldier, Paparin was to provide a renewed Catholic fervour to Gap and to become intimately involved in the administration there.[92] The bureau renewed calls to deal with the town's poverty, this time enacting a new policy of expecting able-bodied poor to work for assistance. At the 25 January meeting, the bureau agreed that these recipients would be required to help clean the ruined cathedral (destroyed by the Huguenot incursion of late 1567) and for which funds for a new roof were being raised.[93] In addition to their bureau allowance, these paupers would also benefit from 'what will be given for God freely by the citizens having devotion to contribute. The Lord of Gap [Paparin] has given six charges of wine, which will be ... distributed to those who will work'.[94] Thus, the bureau's alms were now, for those who could assist Catholic endeavours, to be supplemented by additional contributions from the faithful and the Bishop. Neither Huguenot donors nor recipients were mentioned.

Paparin's presence in Gap proved to be an inflammatory one, causing tensions within the Catholic community about the relationship between ecclesiastical and secular governance.[95] On a later visit in October 1574, an attempt to assassinate the bishop was made. Shot in the leg, Paparin accused not Huguenots but rather the *vibailli* Benoît Olier, a leading Catholic noble, Etienne de Bonne, sieur d'Auriac, and no less than Gap's governor Balthasar de Combourcier, sieur du Monêtier, whom he saw as having become too closely aligned to the town's Huguenot population.[96] In May 1576, Paparin accused the councillors of rigging the municipal elections and furthering their friendships with the Huguenots, with the aim of limiting his own involvement in the town.[97] At this period, it was widely known that although Gap was under Catholic control, the Huguenots held most of the surrounding countryside. Indeed, the *lieutenant particulier au siege presidial de Gap*, Eynard Davin, had lamented in 1575 that there were few Catholic royalists in the region to execute the king's commands.[98] In these circumstances, a conciliatory policy towards the Huguenots may have been politically expedient as well as a continuation of traditional policy within Gap, but it was one which

---

[91] Bergin, pp. 338–9: 'pour le seul faict de la religion.'

[92] *Précis*, p. 232.

[93] A.D. Hautes-Alpes, 3 H suppl. 275, fol. 35v; and A.D. Hautes-Alpes, BB. 10, Deliberations of 28 December 1572 and 22 January 1573.

[94] A.D. Hautes-Alpes, 3 H suppl. 275, fol. 35v: 'ce que leur sera done pour dieu gratuitement pour les citoyens ayent devotion de donner. Ledicte Sgr de gap a done six charges vin qui sera done et distribue a ceulx qui travalheront.'

[95] Roberts, p. 141.

[96] *Précis*, pp. 86–7.

[97] *Précis*, p. 88.

[98] Gautier, 'Ve lettre sur l'histoire de la ville de Gap, (1575 à 1577)', *Revue du Dauphiné*, 4 (1838), 132.

angered the staunchly partisan Bishop who saw any reconciliation as building the power of the Huguenots. His recommendations to increase the forces at the city's wall was rejected by councillors as potentially provocative to Huguenots.[99] When, on the night of 2 January 1577, Huguenot forces did indeed capture the town, destroying not only the episcopal palace, chapter house, convents and churches, Paparin once again voiced his views that the Catholic councillors had not taken sufficient precautions to protect the town.[100]

Over the early 1570s, the bureau had shifted markedly both in composition and policy, in both aspects instrumentalised towards wider political and religious motivations. Initially during this period, poor relief had been oriented towards achieving the consulate's aim to keep the peace between Catholics and Protestants, requiring those who broke proclamations to shoulder a heavy burden of hosting the poor personally. However, in just a few years, the bureau had been reconstituted with a stronger representation of ecclesiastical officials and, at the same time, new mechanisms of relief developed that linked charitable assistance directly to the Catholic faithful, their place of worship and their visibility within the town. This phase of the welfare provision made use of poor relief, not to keep the peace, but to demarcate faith communities, driving a wedge between the town's inhabitants. It would inexorably achieve this aim, as Gap plunged once more into conflict in the late 1570s.

'unne bonne paix': Protestant Poor Relief in the 1590s

After 1577, apart from a brief incursion in 1590, Gap was held under Huguenot control until 1622. The town even played host to the Reformed Church national synod in 1603. Once Henri IV had ascended the throne, even Gap's divisive bishop, Paparin, reconciled – formally at least – with the new Huguenot leader, Lesdiguières, allowing him to resume his functions and powers within the town.[101] In the general assembly of August 1593, the next year for which consulate records exist, the *procureur de la ville* lamented how 'disunity at other times in this town has been the cause of a great deal of evil and loss' and celebrated that 'thanks be to God, at present the people are at peace, taking no offence in words or deeds. And to better maintain themselves in the future, Monseigneur de Diguières has deemed it good to have one and the other religion at peace'.[102] This may have painted

---

[99]   Charronnet, pp. 112–13.

[100]   Charronnet, on Paparin's dispute with the Governor, du Monêtier, chap. 6, pp. 106–9.

[101]   *Précis*, p. 233.

[102]   A.D. Hautes-Alpes, BB. 11. Cahier. Délibérations 1593, fol. [2r]: 'la dishugnion aultres fois a ceste ville a este cause de beaucoup de maux et pertes', 'dieu mercy a presant le peuple se contient en paix sans soffencer de faict ne de parolles et pour se mieulx entretenir a ladvenir, monseigneur desdiguieres truve bon de se tenir en paix lune et laultre religion.'

a rosier picture than Gap's fellow Catholics might have believed, but it was in any case a noticeable return to the peaceful rhetoric of the 1560s. Indeed, the *règlement politique* formalised in April 1601 returned to the confessional coalition in municipal entities created by the 1564 *règlement*. Once again, the *premier consul* was to be Catholic, the second Huguenot, and the two ecclesiastical members of the consulate were retained. Eleven further places were to be divided evenly between Catholics and Huguenots. Catholics were permitted processions as long as they did not trouble Huguenots in their practices. Charivari and youth abbeys were forbidden, but dances were allowed in private homes if owners were prepared to be held responsible for these.[103] The Catholic community had funds to build churches while the Huguenots could construct a dedicated temple.[104] Balancing the needs of soldiers and the poor remained a preoccupation of the town, with the assembly determining that contributions were to be collected 'by the soldiers, and distributed two thirds to them and the other third to the poor in the Hospital'.[105] It was hoped that collectively these measures would enjoin the whole community to act 'as good citizens' since 'it had pleased God to send us a good peace'.[106]

That a new period of *entente* was believed possible by Gap's citizenry may be suggested by some of the charitable business dealt with by the consulate into the new century. In September 1599, the canon of Montjeu appeared before the consuls regarding a pilgrimage to Nôtre-Dame d'Embrun, to ask the consulate 'to give something for the many paupers who will go, who have no means to live'.[107] The fact that no decision was recorded from the meeting or after suggests that the response was not favourable but it nonetheless spoke to the hopes of the Catholic community that a poor relief policy that embraced the differing traditions of charity might still be possible.[108] However, other items of business suggest that the Huguenots were slowly but surely asserting their control over what kind of charity would operate, and how. A discussion in January 1600 of the transaction then being negotiated between the chapter, bishop and the town about their rights and responsibilities noted in the records that consuls were to be given the power

---

[103] *Précis*, p. 105.

[104] A.D. Hautes-Alpes, BB. 11, fol. [2r]: 'tant par les fraictz des catholicques, par [pour] bastir lesglise que de ceux de la Relligion a continuer au temple et, pour employer a hevres piees tant dune part que daultre.'

[105] A.D. Hautes-Alpes, BB. 11, fol. [1v]: 'par des soldatz et distribué deux tiers a eulx et laultre, aux povres de l'Hospital.'

[106] A.D. Hautes-Alpes, BB. 11, fol. [2v]: 'comme bons citoyens', 'il a pleu à Dieu nous envoyer unne bonne paix'.

[107] A.D. Hautes-Alpes, BB. 12. Registre. 'Livre des conselz' de la ville de Gap, tenu par le notaire royale Gay, secrétaire. 19 August 1599–24 April 1601, fol. 58v: 'donner quelque choze pour beaucoup de povres que y iront, qui n'ont pas moyen de vivre.'

[108] Guillaume notes that this is one of the last references to this historic pilgrimage path. See Paul Guillaume (ed.), *Inventaire sommaire des Archives communales antérieures à 1790, vol. 1: Ville de Gap* (Gap: Imprimerie et Librairie Alpine, 1908), p. 64.

to replace the current *hospitallier*, ostensibly 'because he does not do his duty'[109] but signalling the Huguenot control over charitable organisation which would be thus gained.

All this demonstrates that, in the first decades under the Huguenot regime of Gap, poor relief continued to play an important role in signalling wider political and religious strategies and concepts. Here, the ideals and rhetoric of peace and harmony were foremost, although there was evidence of the Huguenots beginning slowly to assert dominance over the kinds of practices that would be supported and control over the mechanisms by which it would be delivered.

Conclusions

The later sixteenth century was a time of substantial instability in the Dauphiné region and in Gap itself. The poor and their needs were an issue that had the potential to bring together, and reinforce a vision of, the town's inhabitants as Gapençois to face a shared problem. Both faiths knew that their community members suffered indigence, both desired their comfort and sustenance, and both had wealthy adherents with capacity to shoulder parts of the burden. In its initial phases at least, the bureau appeared to aim for, and indeed achieve briefly, a politics of inclusion, not only of faiths but also of strangers – remarkable at a time when most communities firmly closed their doors on any to whom they could. It was also a strategic way for the consulate to gain some control over a dangerous and antagonistic population. As such, it was one of few urban projects about which a collaborative endeavour could potentially be formed, an ideal joint venture of confessional collaboration which – as municipal officials suggested – could attest to their attempts to uphold the cumulative peace edicts which flowed from afar, declaring through it their willingness to place faith, trust and hope in humanity of both persuasions. It was thus clearly an expedient political manoeuvre, which suited both Catholics and Huguenots alike, and, initially at least, allowed each a relative measure of power and security both within the governance of the city and socially among its citizenry.

Yet charity, its organisation and those it maintained, evidently also echoed the changing political control of Gap through its shifting confessionalisation over time. Certainly poor relief operated during this period as a way in which governance over the town could be asserted and signalled widely, but also as a source of social and spiritual power. As one confession, then the other, achieved political supremacy, if not dominance as the town's favoured persuasion, charity could become a potential mechanism to attract poor converts to a faith. This process of confessional assertion through poor relief may have happened more slowly in Gap than in nearby cities such as Lyon or Nîmes, but it did show progressive adjustments to the composition of the bureau, how funds would be allocated, in

---

[109]   A.D. Hautes-Alpes, BB. 12, fol. 79v: 'd'aultant qu'il ne faict poinct son debvoir.'

what activities, and to whom, that reflected the empowered confession's beliefs.[110] Poor relief was thus both a reflection and an instrument of political and spiritual projects, motivations that were not always easy to separate in Gap. The poor stood at some times to gain and at others to fall victims of these dual motivations, through these conflicts of physical spaces and material means, as well as of spiritual ideals, power plays and pragmatic practices. Gap's textual record suggests that the notion of poverty as a state needing amelioration altered little between faith regimes, but the same could not be said for definitions of the deserving, interpretation of their activities, or identification of those who should fund and deliver services; that is, precisely what was to be considered charity.

---

[110] Even so, when the sisters of St Joseph made an agreement between the consuls, the hospital administrators and Mother Jeanne Burdier to provide services in the hospital of Gap in September 1671, at a time when the town had returned to Catholic control, the act recognised that they were to 'admit and receive the poor of both religions'. See Marguerite Vacher, *Nuns Without Cloister: Sisters of St. Joseph in the Seventeenth and Eighteenth Centuries* (Lanham: University Press of America, 2010), p. 137, and also more generally for this period, Pierre Bolle (ed.), *Le Protestantisme en Dauphiné au XVIIe siècle: religion et vie quotidienne à Mens-en-Trièves, Die et Gap (1650–1685)* (Poët-Laval: Curandera, 1983).

Chapter 10

From France to England: Huguenot Charity in London

Susan Broomhall

Imagine that you see the wretched strangers,
Their babies at their backs, with their poor luggage,
Plodding to th' ports and coasts for transportation,
And that you sit as kings in your desires,
… whither would you go?
What country, by the nature of your error,
Should give you harbour? Go you to France or Flanders,
To any German province, Spain or Portugal,
Nay, anywhere that not adheres to England:
Why, you must needs be strangers. Would you be pleased
To find a nation of such barbarous temper
That breaking out in hideous violence
Would not afford you an abode on earth,
… What would you think
To be thus used? This is the strangers' case,
And this your mountainish inhumanity.[1]

Thus argued William Shakespeare through the voice of Sir Thomas More in his contribution to the jointly authored manuscript play of the same name at the turn of the seventeenth century.[2] Shakespeare was later to lodge in London with the Huguenot tire-maker Christopher Mountjoy.[3] Here he captured the local feelings that had awaited the early Huguenot refugees to London; that is, the fear of

---

[1]   BL, Harley MS 7368; *Sir Thomas More: By Anthony Munday and Others*, (ed.) Vittorio Gabrieli and Giorgio Melchiori, rev. edn (Manchester: Manchester University Press, 2000), II. 3, pp. 100–104.

[2]   The precise date of the play's composition is unclear, most likely in the period from 1591 to 1593, with revisions potentially as late as 1604. See *Sir Thomas More*, (eds) Gabrieli and Melchiori, and *Sir Thomas More*, original text by Anthony Munday and Henry Chettle, censored by Edmund Tilney, revised by Henry Chettle, Thomas Dekker, Thomas Heywood and William Shakespeare, (ed.) John Jowett (London: Arden Shakespeare, 2011).

[3]   On Shakespeare's contact with Huguenots, see E.A.J. Honigmann, 'Shakespeare, *Sir Thomas More* and Asylum Seekers', *Shakespeare Survey*, 57 (2004), 225–35.

economic competition and local merchants' lack of sympathy for their plight. Shakespeare, via More, compelled them to charity, visualising the needs of the 'wretched' and 'poor' strangers who sought assistance from the English.

The Dutch- and French-speaking refugees to London in the second half of the sixteenth century were ostensibly united by their shared religious beliefs. Escaping persecution in their homelands, they arrived in England with few possessions, to face restricted working opportunities and harsh regimes of taxation, Shakespeare's 'mountainish inhumanity'. In London, what united these new arrivals was not so much their faith (a form of Calvinism acceptable, if considered somewhat more stringent than the established Church in England), but instead their identity as strangers. It was their identities, legal and economic status, languages and cultures as much as the nuances of their religious practices that formed the bases for separation of the stranger Church communities in their new country. Dutch- and French-speaking communities each quickly formed separate groups in London, even though they continued to share close organisational and collegial ties with each other.

Accompanying liturgical and linguistically distinct practices within the stranger communities were also systems of social discipline and support. The stranger communities were not entitled to access English poor relief and, by the terms of their establishment, were required to provide entirely for their own poor. Those needs were indeed extensive and often different from those of the typical pauper familiar in their homelands. Even families of means in their localities of origin arrived without the majority of their possessions, many families were divided across the Channel, leaving partners and children in need of support both in London and on the continent, and working conditions were strictly limited. This chapter examines the poor relief of the French Huguenot community of Threadneedle Street, the oldest of the French-speaking communities established in London. It argues that the distinctive context of this Huguenot community's settlement altered the nature of the Church's poor relief, in its concerns, practices and challenges.

There are at least two distinct historiographies relevant to this chapter: analyses of Protestant poor relief and studies of the stranger communities in early modern England. In terms of the former, studies have been preoccupied with the extent to which distinct religious beliefs informed varied charitable and health care regimes in early modern Europe.[4] A range of studies has examined the particular role that

---

[4]   Ole Peter Grell, 'The Religious Duty of Care and the Social Need for Control in Early Modern Europe', *Historical Journal*, 39 (1996), 257–63; Ole Peter Grell and Andrew Cunningham (eds), *Health Care and Poor Relief in Protestant Europe, 1500–1700* (London: Routledge, 1997); Charles H. Parker, *The Reformation of Community Social Welfare and Calvinist Charity in Holland, 1572–1620* (Cambridge: Cambridge University Press, 1998); Ole Peter Grell, Andrew Cunningham and Jon Arrizabalaga (eds), *Health Care and Poor Relief in Counter-Reformation Europe* (London: Routledge, 1999); Timothy G. Fehler, *Poor Relief and Protestantism: The Evolution of Social Welfare in Sixteenth-Century*

Protestant poor relief played in establishing social control over communities – certainly something that was also at stake in the Threadneedle Street Church. Martin Dinges, for example, emphasises how 'poor relief contributed enormously in creating, re-creating and stabilising this particular confessional culture' which functioned through direct personal engagement, linked to family and household, and provided opportunities for a high degree of collective social control, 'a trait shared by minority cultures throughout early modern Europe'.[5]

At the same time, a rich historiography has developed around the stranger communities in England, in terms of their integration, religious beliefs, working practices, and cultural, religious and economic impact within England.[6] Historians have unanimously assessed the Churches' charitable practices favourably, indeed even admiringly. Generally, the Churches are seen to have eradicated begging and worked strenuously to create coherent communities.[7] For the most part, these conclusions have been reached from study of extensive late seventeenth- and early eighteenth-century poor relief, apprenticeship and charity school records

---

Emden (Aldershot: Ashgate, 1999); Claire Schen, *Charity and Lay Piety in Reformation London, 1500–1620* (Aldershot: Ashgate, 2002); Brian Pullan, 'Religion and the Rise of Poor Relief', *Journal of Early Modern History*, 4 (2000), 442–6; Thomas Max Safley (ed.), *The Reformation of Charity: The Secular and the Religious in Early Modern Europe* (Leiden: Brill, 2003).

[5]   Martin Dinges, 'Huguenot Poor Relief', pp. 157–74 (p. 174).

[6]   Among the more recent contributions are John Campbell, 'The Walloon Community in Canterbury, 1625–1649' (unpublished doctoral thesis, University of Wisconsin–Madison, 1970); Andrew Pettegree, *Foreign Protestant Communities in Sixteenth-Century London* (Oxford: Oxford University Press, 1986); Ole Peter Grell, *Dutch Calvinists in Early Stuart London: The Dutch Church in Austin Friars, 1603–1642* (Leiden: Brill, 1989); Marcel F. Backhouse, *The Flemish and Walloon Communities at Sandwich during the Reign of Elizabeth I (1561–1603)* (Brussels: Koninklijke Academie voor Wetenschappen, Letteren en Schone Kunsten, 1995); Randolph Vigne and Graham C. Gibbs (eds), *The Strangers' Progress: Integration and Disintegration of the Huguenot and Walloon Refugee Community, 1567–1889: Essays in Memory of Irene Scouloudi* (London: Huguenot Society, 1995); Ole Peter Grell, *Calvinist Exiles in Tudor and Stuart England* (Aldershot: Ashgate, 1996); Andrew Spicer, *The French-Speaking Reformed Community and their Church in Southampton, 1567–c. 1620* (London: Huguenot Society, 1997); Robin D. Gwynn, *Huguenot Heritage: The History and Contribution of the Huguenots in Britain* (1995; Brighton: Sussex Academic Press, 2001); Randolph Vigne and Charles Littleton (eds), *From Strangers to Citizens: The Integration of Immigrant Communities in Britain, Ireland and Colonial America, 1550–1750* (Brighton: Sussex Academic Press, 2001); Lien Bich Luu, *Immigrants and the Industries of London, 1500–1700* (Aldershot: Ashgate, 2005); Nigel Goose and Lien Luu (eds), *Immigrants in Tudor and Early Stuart England* (Brighton: Sussex Academic Press, 2005); Anne Dunan-Page (ed.), *The Religious Culture of the Huguenots, 1660–1750* (Aldershot: Ashgate, 2006).

[7]   See Campbell, chap. 4; and Gwynn, pp. 137–9.

of the London Churches, including those of Threadneedle Street.[8] These studies suggest that the French Churches were well organised in their charity, that people strongly identified with the Church, and created a coherent and disciplined internal community of their own.[9] As Eileen Barrett has argued, 'Huguenot sources of poor relief provided a long-term, reliable, safety net until such time as the migrant had become part of the English community'.[10] Randolph Vigne even claims: 'Perhaps the experiences of persecution and exile and a sense of duty to Almighty God who had preserved them inspired those Huguenots with a stronger sympathy for the poor and needy than was common among the native English or French at home.'[11] Such views are pervasive even for earlier periods. Andrew Pettegree, examining the foreign Protestant Churches in sixteenth-century London, also praises the 'heroic effort' 'required to maintain the social provision of the community at an adequate level'.[12] Paul Slack has suggested that hospital reforms which occurred during the reign of Edward VI may have been inspired by the poor relief available in the stranger communities.[13] In sum, the current historiography suggests that poor relief was well organised, and functioned to create a coherent and supportive community in a foreign location that was a model to the native population.

The Threadneedle Street Church was the oldest of the French Huguenot Churches in England. It was first established after Edward VI granted a charter to 'Germans and the strangers … who have been persecuted and banished from their own countries' in 1550.[14] The Coetus, a general Church council that met

---

[8]   See 'Tracing your poor Huguenot ancestors in London Huguenot records', a guide to seventeenth-, eighteenth- and nineteenth-century Huguenot poor relief documentation provided by The Huguenot Society of Great Britain and Ireland, which can be viewed as a PDF from the 'Family History' page <http://www.huguenotsociety.org.uk/family.html>; Eileen Barrett, 'Poor Relief in Hanoverian London: Assistance to Widows in the Period 1735–1750' (unpublished master's thesis, Massey University, 1997).

[9]   William C. Waller, 'Early Huguenot Friendly Societies', *Proceedings of the Huguenot Society of London*, 6 (1898–1901), 201–35; C.F.A. Marmoy, 'L'Entraide des réfugiés français en Angleterre', *Bulletin de la Société de l'histoire du protestantisme français*, 115 (1969), 591–604; Randolph Vigne, '*Dominus Providebit*: Huguenot Commitment to Poor Relief in England', in Dunan-Page (ed.), *Religious Culture of the Huguenots*, pp. 69–86.

[10]   Eileen Barrett, 'Huguenot integration in late 17th- and 18th-Century London: Insights from the records of the French Church and some relief agencies', in Vigne and Littleton (eds), *From Strangers to Citizens*, pp. 375–82 (p. 381).

[11]   Vigne, p. 86.

[12]   Pettegree, p. 206.

[13]   Paul Slack, 'Hospitals, Workhouses and the Relief of the Poor in Early Modern London', in Grell and Cunningham (eds), *Health Care and Poor Relief*, pp. 234–51.

[14]   *Actes 1*, p. xii. For a detailed history of the Threadneedle Street Church, see Baron Fernand de Schickler, *Les Églises du Refuge en Angleterre*, 3 vols (Paris: Fischbacher, 1892); George B. Beeman, 'Sites and History of the French Churches of London', *Proceedings of the Huguenot Society of London*, 8 (1905–08), 13–59; and George B. Beeman, 'The Early History of the Strangers' Church, 1550–61', *Proceedings of the Huguenot Society of London*, 15 (1935), 261–82.

monthly, united the French, Flemish and Italian Protestant Churches in London.[15] The French Church, whose community was comprised of French-speaking refugees from northern France and the Low Countries, largely followed the Genevan Calvinist example. The church at Austin Friars had been reserved for the strangers' shared use but the Chapel of St Anthony in Threadneedle Street was leased by the dean and canons of Windsor to the French Church in October 1550 because Austin Friars was not ready for use. Austin Friars would later become the home of the Dutch community.[16] After the death of Edward, the communities were disbanded and many returned to the continent. However with the ascension of Elizabeth to the throne, Jan Utenhove, Martin Micronius and Peter de Loene returned to the city to re-establish the French Church in 1559. Edmund Grindal, Bishop of London, greatly supported the stranger Churches and became, as bishop of the diocese, their official superintendant.[17] By 1560, the Church began to order itself, electing elders and deacons in July of that year.[18]

In this chapter, I analyse a set of records that do not appear to have been studied closely in the context of Huguenot poor relief.[19] These are the remaining acts of the consistory of Threadneedle Street, which run in several sequences covering the period June 1560 to September 1561, April 1564 to December 1565, then June 1571 to September 1577.[20] These acts deal largely with a range of disciplinary offences for which members of the community were brought before the elders – from quarrels and fighting, drunken, immoral and blasphemous behaviour, marital squabbles and adultery, to irregular betrothals and marriages.[21] They recorded not

---

[15]   *Actes 1*, p. xiii.

[16]   *Actes 1*, p. xiii; see also Andrew Spicer, '"A Place of Refuge and Sanctuary of a Holy Temple": Exile Communities and the Stranger Churches', in Goose and Luu (eds), *Immigrants*, pp. 91–109 (pp. 92–3).

[17]   *Actes 1*, p. xiv; see also Patrick Collinson, *Godly People: Essays on English Protestantism and Puritanism* (London: Hambledon, 1983), esp. 'Calvinism with an Anglican Face: The Stranger Churches in Early Elizabethan London', pp. 213–44.

[18]   *Actes 1*, p. xvi.

[19]   With the exception of the analysis of Pettegree, pp. 210–14.

[20]   *Actes 1*; and *Actes 2*.

[21]   On comparative Huguenot social disciplining in France, see Raymond A. Mentzer, '*Disciplina nervus ecclesiae*: The Calvinist Reform of Morals', *Sixteenth Century Journal*, 18 (1987), 89–116; Raymond A. Mentzer, 'Le Consistoire et la pacification du monde rural', *Bulletin de la Société de l'histoire du protestantisme français*, 135 (1989), 373–89; Raymond A. Mentzer, 'Ecclesiastical Discipline and Communal Reorganization among the Protestants of Southern France', *European History Quarterly*, 21 (1991), 163–83; Raymond A. Mentzer (ed.), *Sin and the Calvinists: Morals Control and the Consistory in Reformed Tradition* (Kirksville, MO: Truman State University Press, 1994); Raymond A. Mentzer, 'Morals and Moral Regulation in Protestant France', *Journal of Interdisciplinary History*, 31 (2000), 1–20; Raymond A. Mentzer, 'La Place et le rôle des femmes dans les églises réformées', *Archives de sciences sociales des religions*, 46.113 (2001), 119–32. Dinges questions the efficacy of Calvinist moral reform through poor relief funding though, in

only offences and punishments (including payment of fines which contributed to the poor relief fund), but frequently also the voices of those brought before the consistory and debates among the elders themselves. Among the range of matters addressed were exceptional demands for assistance from community members and foreign Churches as well as the struggles of the deacons and elders to raise and secure funds for poor relief. What emerges from these records are both divergent visions of charity among the consistory and community members, and certainly a different practice from those seen in contemporary Huguenot communities in France or the Threadneedle Street congregation at a later period.[22] While archives of the distribution of funds such as those from the later period suggest cohesion and smooth organisation of the assistance system, the consistory's early acts highlight concerns among the deaconate and elders about debts, debates about the rightful subjects or amounts of relief, investigations for the misuse of funds, irregular and false claims on the relief fund, and the unwillingness of community members to contribute adequately.

These records suggest a different analysis of the Threadneedle Street Huguenot community's practice of charity in the early years of its operation, years in which what united French strangers to London was not so much their conscious choice to remain in the fold of French Calvinist practices as their social and financial status as impecunious foreigners and outsiders in London. The Church provided an important network for strangers to the city and security for those who had not received letters of denization, or could not do so.[23] However, in the early years, many new arrivals came before the elders for investigation because of their attempts to integrate into the wider London community, marrying English or other foreign partners outside the Threadneedle Street community (which the elders actively discouraged). The English would eventually be forbidden from attending the Church's worship as a means to reduce opportunities for interaction outside the stranger community.[24] Likewise, people who wished to join English congregations were prevented from doing so unless they could produce written certification of approval from the French minister. A letter was issued from the Bishop of London

---

Martin Dinges, 'Frühneuzeitliche Armenfürsorge als Sozialdisziplinierung? Probleme mit einem Konzept', *Geschichte und Gesellschaft*, 17 (1991), 5–29.

[22]   For studies of contemporary Huguenot charitable provisions, see Wilma J. Pugh, 'Social Welfare', 349–76; Wilma J. Pugh, 'Catholics, Protestants', 479–504; Martin Dinges, 'L'Assistance paroissiale à Bordeaux à la fin du XVIIe siècle. L'exemple du consistoire protestant (1660–1670)', *Histoire, Economie et Société*, 5 (1986), 475–507; Raymond A. Mentzer, 'Organizational Endeavour', 1–29; Matthew Koch, 'Poor Relief in Montauban', 69–80; Kevin C. Robbins, *City on the Ocean Sea*, chap. 3; Martin Dinges, 'Self-Help and Reciprocity', pp. 111–25.

[23]   *Actes 1*, p. xiv. Their legal position was precarious because of the non-confirmation of the charter by Elizabeth, see ibid., p. xv. Denization provided a means for foreigners to enjoy some of the rights of native-born subjects. A denizen could purchase – though not inherit – property, but could not vote, as could a citizen.

[24]   *Actes 2*, pp. vii–viii.

in 1565 instructing clergy of this, at the insistence of the French Church elders.[25] By the 1570s, when a fresh wave of immigrants reached England after the violent events in France, widespread fears among locals that the immigrants were not all victims of religious persecution but sought better economic situations in which to pursue their livelihood began to be more prominently voiced. The acts showed the elders' pursuit of several members investigated for 'papist practices' which may have fuelled such fears (although there were often extenuating circumstances that explained some of the actions).[26] In that decade and the 1580s, as Lien Luu has argued, a series of further restrictions to the social, legal and economic rights of strangers may have made them ever more reliant on the support of their Churches.[27] Later immigrants and those who chose to remain in the bosom of the French Huguenot community by the late seventeenth and early eighteenth century thus did so in a different context from these earlier arrivals and this, I argue, affected their perceptions of charity provided by the Church and perhaps also their willingness to support it in the early years of its establishment.

Recipients of Charity and their Responses

As no relief was available to the strangers within the English system, it was the duty of the deacons to gather and distribute the monies dedicated to the needy, to prisoners and the sick, as well as to visit them and have them under their care.[28] The list of those to whom the Church provided care was extensive. At times, it reached well beyond their own membership, as in 1565 when the sum of £10 was lent to the Dutch Church at Austin Friars after the plague epidemic of the early 1560s had wrought havoc with their community and funds.[29]

As to the poor fund managed by the deacons, money was given for a range of reasons, either as regular maintenance or lent or given in larger sums for a specific purpose. In 1573, for example, the deacons spent around £15 a month on doles to about 50 needy widows, orphans, disabled or elderly men, as well as some £70

---

[25]   *Actes 1*, pp. xxvi–xxvii.

[26]   For example, a cohort of the community was investigated for papal practices just after the 1572 massacre. Oakley describes some of the community as 'rather timid martyrs for their faith' (*Actes 2*, p. viii) citing these cases in which members were reported to the elders for having worn crosses and participating in Catholic activities. Those 'offences' appear to have taken place in France which suggests they may have been survival strategies at the time of the massacre as much as evidence of a return to the Catholic faith. See ibid., p. 96.

[27]   For analysis of the rights of aliens which declined in the 1570s and 1580s, see Lien Luu, 'Natural-Born versus Stranger-Born Subjects: Aliens and their Status in Elizabethan London', in Goose and Luu (eds), *Immigrants*, pp. 57–75.

[28]   Cited in *Actes 1*, p. xvii, in the Church's *Discipline or Book of Order of the Reformed Churches in France*, written in 1675.

[29]   Pettegree, pp. 206–9; and *Actes 2*, p. 112.

in extraordinary payments.[30] Those funds allocated for a specific or extraordinary purpose were those most likely to be debated and their resolution recorded in the consistory minutes, although from time to time, queries concerning expenditure brought to light more regular practices of poor relief. For example, in November 1572, the consistory queried the 'excessive price that has to be paid for the burial of our poor'.[31] The minister, Robert Cousin, was to accompany one of the deacons to find one Monsieur Sampson, 'with an extract setting out the expenditure for the poor these last three or four years and to see if it was not possible to give some order to them'.[32]

Others were exceptional cases among the needy of the congregation. In September 1564, the consistory became concerned with the case of the child of Pierre Caillou, whose mother, now the wife of Pierre le Sage, had absconded. A letter received by the consistory asked 'if there was not a way to save the goods of the poor child'. Minister Cousin was accordingly sent to investigate and seek the advice of the magistrate Dr Strange.[33] Hugues Serreau from Valenciennes, his wife Antoinette Gigot from Maastricht and their two children were reported to the consistory in October 1565 as 'in the streets and none will take them in'. This was 'a very great pity' but they reported also that 'it is said that the person [Serreau] is so well known to be of evil conversation that no one wants to meddle and he goes from Church to Church'. This couple had earlier come before the consistory when they had admitted that they were living together out of wedlock in 1560. Nonetheless, the consistory resolved to provide six shillings for bread and to help them to find lodgings.[34] Such cases reflected common kinds of challenges that the poor faced across Europe.

Some cases of need within the Threadneedle Street community were, however, a function of their refugee experiences or status as aliens. In November 1560, the consistory approved 10 shillings to buttonmaker Mychel Blanq to assist him in going to seek his wife, whom he had left ill in Biannes.[35] In May 1565, Thomas des Camps was loaned 10 shillings for payment to secure his letters of denization,

---

[30]   Pettegree (p. 211) has analysed French Church, MS 194, a single volume covering fourteen months of the deacons' 1573 accounts.

[31]   *Actes 2*, p. 93: 'Sur le pris excessif que faut paier pour la sepulture de noz povres.'

[32]   *Actes 2*, p. 93: 'aveq ung extrait declarant par parties la despense faitte pour les povres depuis trois ou quatre ans et adviser avecq luy sil ne serroit possible d'y faire donner quelque ordre.'

[33]   *Actes 1*, p. 76: 'sil ny auroit point de moyen de sauuer le bien du poure enfant.'

[34]   *Actes 1*, p. 119: 'quil sont par les Rues que nulz ne les veult loger, disant que cest fort grand pitie et quil seroit bon dy adviser on leur dit que le personage est sy bien Congnu de mauuais conuersation que on ne se vollut mesler et que ce quil alloit ainsy deglise en Eglise.' Case continues p. 120. For the 1560 case, see *Actes 1*, p. 20.

[35]   *Actes 1*, p. 17.

a costly and cumbersome process.[36] Assistance could also be in kind, as it was for Nicholas le Roy, who in November 1565:

> recommended his daughter Ezabeau and her husband, newly come from Metz and as poor as Job, begging the Church to give them some assistance for he could not. Decided to give them some silver tissue in the name of the Church to make buttons, which is their trade.[37]

Many families were divided across the Channel by illness, work opportunities and other circumstances. Much of the consistory's labour was engaged in disentangling complex, often illicit relationships that had emerged in the absence of kin, pre-existing partners and Church oversight. Thus, it was logical that the Church elders should be keen to support, as best they could, the reunion of both community and ministers' families by their funds.

Indeed, the consistory was required to keep an eye on either side of the Channel in order to regulate the behaviour of its congregation. In May 1577, Jehan Prouvost came before the consistory for refusing to acquiesce to the advice of the company to instruct his poor wife and children to join him in England. Instead, his wife, 'in great poverty and misery', had been obliged to go to the Magdelaine charity hospital in Rouen for support. The elders were annoyed; Prouvost 'ought to have summoned his wife or at least written and sent her some money'.[38] The consistory again instructed him to 'do his duty to bring her to this country'.[39]

In addition to its own congregation which included some 1,700 souls by 1571, in that year, the company took part in campaigns to support 'the needs of many poor families newly arrived here, newcomers from the Churches of Germany, France and the Low Countries', clearly not all of whom would ever become members of their own French-speaking community.[40] At the same time, the consistory discussed fund-raising for fellow confessional communities on the continent including 'the extreme necessity of the great number of poor people taking refuge at Wesel' as had been announced by a letter from the Church in Wesel seeking their aid:

---

[36]   *Actes 1*, p. 109. See Luu ('Natural-Born versus Stranger-Born Subjects', pp. 60–61) on the decline in denization during Elizabeth's reign.

[37]   *Actes 1*, p. 121; translation by Johnston, p. xxi: 'recomandy sa fille Ezabeau et son mary quy estoient Revenu de metz, et sy tres poure que Job priant que leglise leur volut faire quelque assistence, car luy na pas le pouuoir De les asister, Il fut advise que on leur feroit auoir vng papier de soye au nom de leglise pour faire des boutins quy est vng de leur mestier.'

[38]   *Actes 2*, p. 201: 'en grande povreté et miserie', 'quil la debvoit aller querir ou pour le moins escripre et luy envoyer quelque argent'.

[39]   *Actes 2*, p. 201: 'de faire son debvoir de la faire venir en ce pays.'

[40]   *Actes 2*, p. vii.

The majority are comprised of poor artisans who have no means to work in the bombazine trade and the cost of wheat is very high, begging to be helped to pass the coming winter more easily from collections that might be made among the French and Low Countries refugee Churches in the English realm.[41]

The consistory considered their plight worthy and debated a number of ways to raise funds to support these groups as well as their own congregation.

In fact, it was not just across the Channel that the consistory extended its gaze: oversight was also required of the interactions of community members with the wider English population. Thus, the widow of Augustin Marlorat was investigated by the consistory in March 1576, for having presented a request through an Englishman to the Bishop of London for assistance for the five children with which she was burdened, although the consistory claimed none were with her, and further, that she had not declared this assistance when also claiming from the Threadneedle Street poor funds. Marlorat retorted in turn to the elders, deacons and ministers that when an opportunity had arisen to present her case to the bishop she had had no intention of rejecting it, especially:

> given that they [the consistory] took no account of her and she had not been assisted as her status required and that she had found such ingratitude in this place that she had debated returning to France, where, although there were still infidels, there were at least some people of more charity than there were here. She was happy to declare this to the company. As to her children, it was true that after the death of her husband, five children remained in her care, but two had since died, but she still had care of the three living.[42]

Marlorat went on; she declared that she had done nothing wrong in presenting her request for assistance and took the opportunity to offer her opinion, as the consistory acts committed only rather vaguely to paper, on 'several other things'. The consistory were stunned; to her accusation of ingratitude, they noted that she

---

[41]   *Actes 2*, p. 28: 'la necessité de beaucoup de povres familles Icy refugies de nouveau venans des eglises dAllemaigne, France et Pays Bas', 'lextreme necessite du grand nombre des povres gens Refugiez a Wesel suyvant lavertissement fait a la compagnie par lettres de leglise dudyt Wesel dont la pluspart dicelle est composee de povres artisans que les moiens pour les ouvraiges de bonbasins defaillent et la cherete de bled fort grande (supplie destre aydee et secourue pour passer plus aysement lhyver prochain) Des collectes quy se pouront faire par les eglises franchoises du Pays Bas Refugiees en ce Royaulme dAngleterre'.

[42]   *Actes 2*, p. 178: 'voyant que lon ne tenoit compte delle et quelle nestoit pas subvenue comme sa qualite le requeroit et quelle trouvoit si grande ingratitude en ce lieu quelle avoit deslibere de se retirer en France laquelle verroit si encore les infideles elle trouveroit point quelques gens de plus charite quil ny avoit Icy ce quelle voulloit bien dire et declarer en ceste Compaignee et quant au nombre de ses enffans quil estoit veritable que apres le decez de son mary elle estoit demeuree chargee de cinq enffans dont deux estoient decedez. Et en avoit encor troyz vivant dont elle debvoit bien avoir soing', 'et plusieurs autres propos'.

had been provided, indeed remained provided, with 13 shillings each week. They demanded that she recognise her fault. But Marlorat left unrepentant, even after being threatened that she would not be received at communion. The consistory made note that it would send two of the elders after her in the hopes of making her recognise her fault. A week later, they reported back that Marlorat still would not admit the error of her ways and advised that another member should be sent to speak to her before the next communion.[43] He too was unsuccessful when he returned to the consistory a week later,[44] but finally, in December that year, the widow Marlorat appeared, ostensibly repentant before the consistory, declaring her 'fault about the confusion of the ecclesiastical order' although she maintained that 'she found it very strange that one made such grief, it being such a little thing to have received or been offered money'.[45]

The widow Marlorat was by no means the only recipient of the Church's aid who was less than impressed with what was offered. Many of those who now received its assistance had not, it seems, been exposed to the stark realities of pauper relief as recipients before their sojourn to London. But the consistory was keen to defend the assistance it offered as fair and reasonable relative to its capacity. Thus, in December 1560, the consistory summoned Jehan du Mont before them to answer to the charge that he had written to compatriots in Antwerp to complain that 'the Church had left him in need and dying of hunger'. Perhaps du Mont wrote in dramatic tones about his plight abroad to those in his homelands in the hopes of further support. In fact, the consistory showed that it had been paying him two shillings a week at the time in question. Du Mont confessed 'his great fault and his great ingratitude to have blamed the Church falsely' and he was ordered to write to Antwerp to correct his earlier claims.[46] However Thierry de Lespine, who came before the consistory in October 1574, was not to be so easily reconciled. He complained that the deacons had called him a thief at the temple 'and that the deacons were not worthy men to have left him in need' as they had. The company replied 'that the word thief was said because if you take the alms of the poor without having need of it you would be a thief'. Furthermore, they claimed that, while they had not assisted him in his illness, as soon as the deacons had been aware of his situation, they had not left him in need as he claimed. Finally, they

---

[43] *Actes 2*, p. 179.

[44] *Actes 2*, p. 180.

[45] *Actes 2*, p. 186: 'sa faulte de la confusion de lordre ecclesiastique', 'quelle trouve bien estrange quon estime cela tant grief estant sy petit chose come davoir receu ou on luy a offert de Largent.' The case of Marlorat is not dissimilar to the vocal objections that other Huguenot community members, women among them, raised when brought before the consistory. See Susan Broomhall, *Women and Religion in Sixteenth-Century France* (Houndmills: Palgrave, 2006), pp. 39–44.

[46] *Actes 1*, p. 17: 'que leglise le Laissoit auoir dissette et mourir de faim', 'sa grande faulte et sa grande ingratitude, de blasmer ainsy leglise a tort'.

chastised him for having abstained from communion for so long, 'upon which he left without being reconciled'.[47]

Refugee ministers were also among those who complained about the resources allocated to them. More than once they claimed the fund set aside for their needs was less than sufficient, and complained that reserve monies should be released for their assistance. The elders however argued that 'some portion of the money was reserved for future needs but that [otherwise] they distributed it to the needy refugees of France, ministers as well as others, as per the donors' requests'.[48] One minister also objected before the consistory in March 1573 to the fact that ministers had to approach the deacons to receive their funds 'like beggars before the table of the deacons' and had even been told several times to go learn a trade.[49] The following month, they requested that instead 'the deacons ought to bring the money to the homes of the ministers who are being assisted, without them having to come to ask and make them wait at a shop as has happened'.[50] Refugee ministers again demanded that 'the subvention be handled with discretion so that they are not required to come begging at the table of the deacons', 'that their names are not found among the ordinary poor but written apart on a separate paper', and that two worthy deacons ought to be delegated to 'have charge of the donations intended for the ministers, and to dispense them with honour and to better enquire into their needs'.[51] The extant accounts of 1573 demonstrate that some 60 newly arrived ministers were maintained in their separate account, amounting to as much as £20 a month – a larger sum than that provided for the ordinary relief of the needy.[52]

In sum, the ministers, elders and deacons faced difficulties in providing relief at levels that were satisfactory to all concerned, partly due to a shortage of funds and also because they sought to cover so many different groups both within and beyond the congregation. Additionally, however, vocal dissatisfaction stemmed from the fact that the status of those who sought support in London encompassed a far wider group of recipients than those who would have received assistance in

---

[47]   *Actes 2*, p. 145: 'que les diacres nestoient point gens de bien de lavoir laissé en necessité', 'que mot de larron avoit esté dict en telle sorte que sy vous prenies laumosne des povres sans en avoir necessité vous series larron', 'sur ce, sest party sans se reconsilier'.

[48]   *Actes 2*, p. 106. 'que la Compagnie trouve bon de reserver quelque portion dudyt argent pour la necessite future mais quon le distriburoit aux necessiteuz refugies de France tant ministres qu'autres comme le vouloir des donateurs est.'

[49]   *Actes 2*, p. 111: 'comme mendiants devant la table des diacres.'

[50]   *Actes 2*, p. 112: 'que les diacres vueillent porter largent aux maisons des ministres qui sont assistes sans les faire venue querir et les faire targer a une bouticle comme on a fait.'

[51]   *Actes 2*, p. 112: 'que la subvention leur soit faicte avec honneur quilz ne soient plus tenus de venir mendier a la table des dyacres', 'que leur noms ne soient point trouves entre les povres ordinaries mais quon en tienne ung papier a part et extraordinaire', 'pour avoir la charge des donnations qui se pourront faire pour les ministres, et leur dispenser avec honneur et pour mieux senquerir de leurs necessites'.

[52]   Pettegree, p. 211.

their communities of origin. Their high and likely unrealistic expectations simply could not be met. Moreover, these needy recipients were not prepared to accept the limited offers of assistance meekly. Instead, they complained directly to the consistory, to loved ones and friends at home, and to the English from whom they hoped also to gain support as they sought to establish new relationships and networks in London.

While pauper agency and notions of 'negotiation' have been widely discussed in the scholarship of poverty, the degree to which paupers could meaningfully resist the dominant views of those from whom they sought relief is still much debated.[53] Certainly, some of the needy members of the Threadneedle Street Church did not hesitate to complain in ways that appear distinct from those who more generally received relief in England at this time. The finances of these Calvinists might not have crossed the Channel but, for some, a strong sense of their previous elevated social status and concomitant expectations, real or imagined, had. Moreover, the analyses of Martin Dinges on the Calvinist community of Bordeaux in the later seventeenth century has emphasised how the consistory there utilised minimal relief payments as a means to encourage thrift, work ethics and a sense of self-help within a community network instilling bonds of reciprocity.[54] Here, some within the Church appear to have manoeuvred and sought out other options in what might have been, in other contexts, praised as self-help. But as strangers in London, the elders demanded strong discipline within the community for the sake of its reputation in the city, and could not afford to support paupers with such small amounts that they would develop strategies of survival that exposed them to the view of hostile Londoners. Thus, the issuing of funds to needy members had to function as a means to maintain obedience and to prevent members from looking for support outside the social network of the Church in the wider community of London.

---

[53]   Within a far wider literature, see, for example, Steve Hindle's articulation of negotiations in the context of the settled poor in England's rural parishes, *On the Parish?.* On men and women's ability to negotiate positive narratives about their social identities while applying for relief funding in sixteenth-century France, see Susan Broomhall, 'Identity and Life', 439–65. For similar approaches using early nineteenth-century pauper letters, see Thomas Sokoll, 'Negotiating a Living: Essex Pauper Letters from London, 1800–1834', *International Review of Social History*, 45, Supplement 8 (2000), 19–46; S. King, '"Stop this overwhelming torment of destiny": Negotiating Financial Aid at Times of Sickness under the English Old Poor Law, 1800–1840', *Bulletin of the History of Medicine*, 79 (2005), 228–60; and David R. Green, *Pauper Capital: London and the Poor Law, 1790–1870* (Aldershot: Ashgate, 2010), esp. chap. 5, 'Negotiating Relief: Pauper Encounters with the Poor Law'.

[54]   See Dinges, 'Self-Help and Reciprocity'.

The Desire for Charity and the Struggle for Donations

Monthly figures for 1573 suggest that the Church was spending annually just under £500 in welfare payments, a sizeable sum. Yet it is important to note that almost half this amount was spent on support for ministers while the remaining fund which was set aside for the poor was also drawn upon to cover church repairs. The internal community was not a wealthy one. Amounts received were never large, as Elsie Johnston has calculated, rarely more than £20 a month in the early years.[55] One-off donations, as will be shown below, would be critical, and the generation of sufficient funds to support the charitable work of the Church would become a preoccupation of the deacons and elders.

Funds were collected in a variety of ways. Collections were made at the church door at services and the monthly communion, bringing in about £10 to £12 monthly to the coffers of the poor fund.[56] Some of those summoned to the elders were required to pay fines as a result of their misdemeanours. For example, in December 1560, George Brem, servant to Artus Lardenois, agreed to pay three shillings to his master for treatment to an injury to his finger as well as three for the poor of the Church, as punishment for a violent quarrel between them.[57] Others, however, were critical of the way the elders discharged their duties. In August and September 1571, Robert de Chaleur and his wife were investigated several times and Chaleur required to pay 20 shillings for his alleged misdemeanours. Chaleur was then subsequently summoned as to whether he had said to one elder, Bodelay, that the company 'plunders the poor to maintain the unjust' and to the minister Robert Cousin, 'You have put a man as elder in St Martin to trouble the poor people.'[58] Chaleur explained that Bodelay had asked him for money for the ministers. He admitted that he had replied: 'No, no. I do not want to pay so that you can act against me. You frisk the poor to maintain the cause of the unjust.'[59] It was almost a year later before Chaleur finally agreed to admit his fault and become reconciled once more with the Church, perhaps realising that he could not afford to operate independently of the community as a stranger in London. He confessed that he had falsely accused the elders of fleecing the good and innocent for the company's own unjust causes.[60]

A further source of funds was in donations to the Church's poor made in testaments and bequests. This required the close attention of the elders and

---

[55] *Actes 1*, p. xxi.

[56] Pettegree, pp. 211–12.

[57] *Actes 1*, p. 20.

[58] *Actes 2*, p. 11: 'nous fouillons les povres pour maintenir les Iniques'; p. 16: 'Vous aves mis ung homme pour ancien en St. Martin pour troubler les povres gens.'

[59] *Actes 2*, p. 16: 'non non Je ne veux point payer pour proceder contre moy vous foules les povres pour maintenir la cause des Iniques.'

[60] *Actes 2*, p. 78: 'que on fouloit les bons et innocens pour maintenir la cause des iniques et injustes.'

deacons to ensure that the Church received its rightful share of such donations from the executors of wills. Guillaume Nourry was investigated in September 1564 for falsifying his account to deny the poor fund of some 20 marks from a will of which he was executor. When he appeared before the consistory in March to admit his fault, minister Cousin could barely contain his annoyance, 'that he had been very badly used in this affair and that he was very offended about it as well as others in the company'.[61] In November 1574, a Guillaume Nonray came before the consistory to explain why he had sold furniture which belonged to his father-in-law Guillaume des Aulnois, the proceeds of which had been destined for the poor.[62]

It was not only community members whom the elders were required to investigate. When the first elders of the Church were elected in 1560, at least one had to publicly confess first to his fault in retaining part of a legacy left to the poor.[63] Simon Persy was accused of having retained £8 intended for the poor from the testament of Nicolas Lor Bateur. He confessed to his fault 'that he had not discharged his office as he should have'.[64] Likewise, one of the eight deacons, Guillaume Maubert, also admitted (upon investigation) to have failed to disburse a legacy to the poor before he was accepted into the deaconate.[65]

Funds were accounted for publicly each month at the consistory meetings. As early as 24 February 1560, Jehan Rock noted on behalf of the deacons not only their observation 'that alms are cooling every day' but also their fears 'that it was because they rendered their accounts publicly before the people who, seeing that there is enough money in the fund, might restrain from giving so liberally'.[66] He wondered 'if it might not be good *not* to reveal all to the knowledge of the people when they render their aforesaid account'.[67] Rock pointed out that there had been some unusually large expenses in the previous period that 'if they put them in the accounts before the people, there will be cause to make them whisper'. However, the deacons' views were rejected by the ministers and elders who argued that their best course was to:

> proceed rightly and roundly and hide nothing from the people, for if it was done outside the meeting, that would create even greater cause for whispers. And as to

---

[61]   *Actes 1*, p. 104: 'quil auoit fort mal besognes en ladyte affaire et quil en estoit fort offense et pareillement plusieurs de la Compaignie.' Previous records of this case on pp. 75, 77–8 and 104–5.

[62]   *Actes 2*, p. 148.

[63]   *Actes 1*, p. xvi.

[64]   *Actes 1*, p. 5: 'quil nauoit pont exercier son office comme il debuoit.'

[65]   *Actes 1*, p. 5.

[66]   *Actes 1*, p. 31: 'que les amôsnes se Refroident Journellement.'

[67]   *Actes 1*, p. 31: 'quil craindent que ce ne soit a cause que quant il Rendent leur Compte publiquement deuant le peuple quant il voient quil ya argent asses en la bourse. que cela ne soit cause de les Retenire sy de doner Sy liberalment', 'sil ne seroit point bon de ne point donner tout chosse a cognoistre au peuple quant il Rendent leur dyt Compte'(my italics).

the extraordinary expenses, those who whisper will have no reason to do so and
should sooner praise God who aided us in our great necessity.[68]

The company also took more innovative strategies to raise their poor relief funds
than simply carefully accounting. Calvin had allowed that money could be lent out
for interest in some circumstances and on 1 November 1565, the company resolved
to take this option to raise funds by loaning a portion.[69] The clerk recorded that '25
pounds had been taken from the funds of the deacons to put into the hands of some
of the elders, to make a profit for the benefit of the Church of which I promise to
give for love of the poor five shillings a month in profit'.[70]

Apart from their own poor, successive waves of immigrants and calls for
assistance from overseas confessional allies also placed pressure on the funds
of the Church. In July 1571, the consistory agreed that there would be need for
renewed weekly collections as the 'number of the poor was still large and they
were coming daily'.[71] By October, the deacons reported that the funds for the
poor had fallen into arrears to the sum of £30. Coupled with their own strained
resources, weekly house-by-house collections were to be re-instigated, with a
deacon and elder assigned in each district to 'ask at each house what it might please
the willing to contribute'.[72] Sharing the burden of the support required was another
strategy that the French Church enacted to distribute the financial load. In addition
to discussing their own deacons' house-by-house collection, at the meeting of 21
November 1571, the consistory decided to send a copy of the Wesel Church's
letter 'in which they ask for assistance from the Churches which are in our land
for the maintenance of their poor' to the other stranger Churches.[73] By December
1571, it was evident that weekly collections had been less than successful when
the deacons advised that the poor fund was by then in arrears to the sum of £60.[74]
The Church was in need of some alternative strategies to voluntary charity among
its membership.

---

[68]   *Actes 1*, p. 31: 'sy on les met en Compte Deuant le peuple, ce sera occasion de les
faire murmurer', 'le plus beau et le plus net, est de cheminer droitement et Rondement et
ne Riens cacher au peuple, car sy cela venoit Dehors ce seroit encoire plus grande occasion
de murmurer. Et quant aux despens dextraordinaires, ceulx qui murmurent nauront aucune
Raison en cela ains auront plus tost De louer dieu qui nous secoure en nostre grande
necessitez'.

[69]   *Actes 1*, p. xxi.

[70]   *Actes 1*, p. 121: 'on retireroit hors de la bourse des diacres 25 lib' pour metre entre
les mains de qualques des Anciens pour les faire prouffiter au prouffit de leglise dont Je
promis en donner pour lamour des poures v s' pour moys de prouffit.'

[71]   *Actes 2*, p. 2: 'le nombre des pouvres est encoire grand et y en vient Journellement.'

[72]   *Actes 2*, p. 34: 'demander par les masons ce quil plaira aux volontaires de contribuer
ou de donner pour une fois.'

[73]   *Actes 2*, p. 36: 'demandant assistance aux eglises quy sont en ce pays pour
lentrenement de leurs povres.'

[74]   *Actes 2*, p. 40.

Open accountability remained an important mainstay of the Church's charitable practice. On 21 December 1571, the minister des Roches gave 'a long remonstrance ... concerning the needs which pressure us at the moment because of the great number of poor which increases daily'.[75] He recommended that at the audit of each deacon's account of their district, a minister and six elders should be present to supervise as well as an additional man selected at their discretion from the district 'so that they see both how and to whom the alms are distributed'.[76] This person from the district was to be changed at each audit 'so that several see and understand the affairs of the poor'.[77] This would ensure that those contributing could be confident that their funds were appropriately disbursed. Moreover, ministers should take it in turns to audit the deacons' accounts after the communion service each Sunday. This was accepted and became a regular feature of the Church's practice from 25 February 1572.[78] Clearly it was warranted as, from time to time, deacons themselves came before the consistory to be investigated for misuse of the funds. In December 1572, Guerard Clergies or Clergé appeared before the consistory for having 'made an error and badly conducted himself in his charge to the detriment of the poor'.[79] At a second meeting in January 1573, after hearing the evidence of his fellow deacons, Clergé finally confessed to having misappropriated more than once the funds for the poor that had been placed in his care.[80]

The organisation of collections quickly became formalised and systematised. Weekly collections among the people within their districts were soon a regular feature but their proceeds could hardly be termed satisfactory, with the extant 1573 accounts suggesting that deacons gathered an average of about £10 a month through such activities.[81] However, at the meeting of 16 December 1571, the consistory called for elders to identify the 'names of those most significant and zealous for charity on their rolls' so that they could be asked to provide extra funds for the 'poor people who are coming from Germany, as well as France and the Low Countries'. In addition, they hoped to 'ask their advice as to means by which they can assist them'.[82] On the 21st, the consistory discussed a list of those

---

[75]　*Actes 2*, p. 47: 'une longue remonstrance par Monsieur des Roches aus convoques touchant la necessite laquelle nous presse pour le present a cause du grandt nombre de povres qui augment tous les jours.'

[76]　*Actes 2*, p. 48: 'affin quilz voient comment et a quy laumonse se distribue.'

[77]　*Actes 2*, p. 48: 'affin que plusieurs voient et entendent les affaires des povres.'

[78]　*Actes 2*, pp. 65–6.

[79]　*Actes 2*, p. 100: 'avoit faict faulte et sestoit mal porte en sa charge au prejudice des povres.'

[80]　*Actes 2*, p. 100.

[81]　Pettegree, p. 212.

[82]　*Actes 2*, p. 44: 'les nons dauchuns des plus notables et affectiones a charité extres de leurs rolles', 'tant de povres gens qui viennent tant dAlemaigne que de Franche que du Pais Bas tous desnues', 'pour leur demander conseil confort et avis pareillement ausy les moiens par lesquels on y polra subvenir'.

considered particularly 'capable of contributing'[83] and included 'widows with means' who were to be visited by the deacons in their homes.[84] On 26 December 1571, the elders, ministers and deacons decided to delay targeting specific community members for six weeks or two months because 'need … could be very great and more pressing still than it is at present because the height of winter is yet to come'.[85] In the meantime, the congregation was to be exhorted from the pulpit the following Sunday 'so that those who have already promised will not delay in paying and those who are called prepare themselves to do their duty'.[86] On 21 February 1572, the deacons asked the consistory to name a day for the 'capable' to be called forth.[87]

It seems that the consistory's strategy of targeted donations met with initial success. In March 1574, Jacques Hagoubert agreed to lend the Church £50 to top up the poor funds, to be re-paid within three months. Targeted calls were re-employed in April of 1574, where the acts recorded that 'next Tuesday some 25 to 30 of the most significant people will be called to attend the temple in the morning after the service so as to be together advised about the matter of the poor, the fund for which is greatly in arrears and to remonstrate to them the need to find means for it'.[88] However, two weeks later, the acts recorded the disappointment of the consistory about 'the small number of those who were convened there'. The company determined thus that the matter should go before the entire congregation, to be:

> declared to the people from the pulpit next Sunday as at the meeting it was suggested by a good number of the people that everyone was needed to help and that they should tax consciences each week so that each should give according to his means.[89]

The notable few who had turned up were clearly in favour of distributing the charitable burden more widely!

---

[83]   *Actes 2*, p. 47: 'quon trouver a cappables pour ladicte contribution', 'quant aus vefues qui ont les moiens on ira a leurs maisons'.

[84]   *Actes 2*, p. 48: 'quant aus vefues qui ont les moiens on ira a leurs maisons.'

[85]   *Actes 2*, p. 48: 'pour leur remonstrer la necessite qui alhors polra estre plus grande et plus pregnante que pour le present a cause du destroit de l'hyver quy est encore a passer.'

[86]   *Actes 2*, p. 48: 'affin que ceulx qui ont desia promis ne different a paier et que seulx qui sont a convoquer se preparent a faire leur debvoir.'

[87]   *Actes 2*, p. 65.

[88]   *Actes 2*, p. 135: 'mardy prochain seront appellez quelques xxv ou xxx personnes des plus notables pour se trouver au temple le matin appres le presche affin dadviser par ensemble pour le faict des povres la bourse desquels est du beaucop a larriere et que leur remonstrant le necessite est besong de trouver les moyens.'

[89]   *Actes 2*, p. 135: 'le petit nombre de ceulz quy y furent convocquez', 'Que le meilleur moien estoit de declarer au peuple en chayre le dimanche suyvant comment en lassemblee dugne bonne partie du peuple avoit este advisé quil estoit besoing que chacun y aydast et quil se taxast en conscience par sepmaine a donner chascun selons sa portee'.

Finally, a much-needed source of funds in their hour of need came from the Church's official supervisor, the Bishop of London. The exceptional events of 1572, with the bloody Saint Bartholomew's Day Massacre in August, saw a further influx of refugees from France. This brought the French-speaking stranger congregations particularly to the attention of the English. On 24 December 1572, the acts recorded the Bishop's generous donation of some £320 given to the stranger Churches both 'because of his care and charity to the poor strangers' and because of 'the poor ministers and other French refugees in this country since the last troubles and massacres of France'.[90] Less successful though were appeals to the Queen. Not only had she never officially ratified Edward VI's acceptance of the stranger communities, but she declined to flame internal tensions among the English population by acceding to the collective stranger Churches' request, made by the Coetus through the Bishop of London, that the poor of their communities be allowed the right to open their workshops, exceptionally, through the winter of 1572.[91]

Clearly there were challenges to the accumulation of a sizeable resource of poor relief funds that were in part a consequence of the congregation's restricted economic conditions. Additionally, though, it appears that not all the congregation felt that their donations were well spent by the company. They were not afraid to tell the consistory as much, and resisted contributing as far as they could. Even those considered most generous among the community quickly grew tired of the heightened burden placed upon them, and rejected the targeted call for their aid, either by refusing to attend to hear the company's remonstrance, or by suggesting that it be put to the whole congregation instead.

Conclusions

Huguenot notions and practices of charity were necessarily altered by displacement to England. The acts of the consistory from these early years of the Threadneedle Street Church's foundation highlight the extensive ambition of the Church's early ministers, elders and deacons, as Andrew Pettegree has argued, to provide for a wide range of their confessional brethren, both in London and on the continent. Equally, their practices of assistance echoed the expectation of concomitant social discipline among community members that was seen in other contemporary Protestant communities and with which they were familiar from their homelands. Indeed, it seems likely that the fears of the local population to the alien presence

---

[90] *Actes 2*, p. 100: 'par sa sollicitude et charite envers les povres estrangers', 'les povres ministres et autre francoys refugiez en ce pais depuys les derniers troubles et massacres de France'.

[91] *Actes 2*, pp. 54–5. Aliens were only allowed closed workshops, which did not provide them the opportunity to display their goods directly to the public. See Luu, 'Natural-Born versus Stranger-Born Subjects', p. 64.

in London made the consistory more determined to demonstrate the exemplary behaviour of their congregation.

However, the acts also revealed considerable dissention in the early years from a congregation who did not necessarily envisage the Church as their primary network in London, as it would become for many by the next century. Some appeared to look upon the Church as more akin to a French-speaking financial interest group that could offer them assistance in times of need, but they did not submit readily to the strict religious discipline of the consistory. Some certainly saw themselves as needy and requiring support in their new country, but perhaps not necessarily as 'the poor' in the conventional conceptualisation of recipients of charity. If many finally confessed their fault and were reconciled to the control of the consistory, this was for most as much a sound economic and social strategy, which ensured a mechanism for support as a stranger in London, as it was evidence of zeal for Calvinist moral values. As the acts demonstrate, a good number were prepared to reject vocally the consistory's right to govern their actions, to prevent them from seeking help beyond the Church if the opportunity arose, or to control their own notions of charitable donation.

PART II
The Material Record

Chapter 11

'An ancient box': *The Queen v. Robert Wortley and John Allen* (1846); or, A History of the English Parochial Poor Box *c.* 1547

Nicholas Dean Brodie

Robert Wortley and John Allen had a canny advocate. Prosecuted for having entered the parish church of Oundle, Northamptonshire, and stolen a poor box, at the 1846 Northampton Assizes the defendants were acquitted by a jury of breaking and entering the church (most likely on the basis that the church was unlocked). When they were found guilty of theft their lawyer then objected with a series of procedural and legal arguments centring on the poor box. The judge reserved immediate judgement, with arguments presented at the Queen's Bench before nine judges.[1] For the historian of late medieval and early modern charity, the nineteenth-century theft of a poor box provides a fascinating insight into how old poor boxes were placed, used, and understood in the nineteenth-century English parish church. But the trial also highlights wider problems in understanding the history of the early modern English parish poor box, and raises methodological questions about exploring medieval and early modern constructions of 'charity'.

In the first instance, the case provides a description of what by 1846 was a 'very ancient box'. It was:

> firmly fixed by two screws at the back to the outside of a pew in the centre aisle of the church, and a third screw at the bottom to a supporter beneath; and over the box was an ancient board, with the inscription painted thereon, 'Remember the Poor'. There were two locks to the box but no evidence was given to shew in whose custody the keys of such locks were kept; nor was there any evidence that the money had ever been taken out by the churchwardens, or any other person, for the purpose of being distributed, although it was proved that both silver and copper had from time to time been dropped into the box.[2]

That the custody of the keys and the extraction of the money were legally unproved (that is, not presented as evidence by the prosecution), was central to the lawyer's defence argument, which pointed to problems with the form of the

---

[1]   E.W. Cox (ed.), *Reports of Cases in Criminal Law Argued and Determined in all the Courts of England and Ireland, vol. 2, 1846–1848* (London: J. Crockford, 1848), pp. 32–5; the box has since disappeared.

[2]   Cox (ed.), *Reports of Cases*, pp. 32–3.

original indictment. The box, he argued, 'was fixed to the freehold of the church', therefore a 'fixture', and was as such not covered by the indictment in accordance with the appropriate statute. He similarly argued that the indictment identified the theft as being of property owned by named individuals, rather than by the title of their office or collective designation (churchwardens, vicar and parishioners), and therefore not in the appropriate form. Ultimately these arguments about the wording of the indictments were unsuccessful. But he also challenged the legal ownership of the box, arguing that it could not be the property of the churchwardens, and also that this particular box did not belong to the parish church. These arguments, despite failing to save Robert Wortley and John Allen from being sentenced to transportation, encapsulate perfectly problems to be had when interpreting the English parish poor box's early modern past.

'no part of the churchwardens' duty'[3]: The Parish Poor Box in Liturgy and Statute 1536–1846

Historians have tended to be a little confused about how parish poor boxes fitted in the scheme of the sixteenth-century parish church, a fact that this author and McIntosh have both recently noted.[4] The confusion seems to stem from a misreading of relevant statute law. This has been coupled with a tendency on the part of historians of poor relief to see the poor box principally as an agent of 'poor relief' rather than 'charity', a theme to which we shall shortly return. And it also derives from a conflation of different sorts of boxes under a single heading.

A courtroom exchange between the lawyer (Flood) and the judge (Tindal, C.J.) in the Wortley and Allen case highlights a number of these issues and is worth quoting at some length:

> *Flood.* – ... the box and the money could not be the property of the churchwardens; churchwardens have not necessarily any property in things found in the church, unless they are things with which they have some concern in the discharge of their duties as churchwardens. ...

> TINDAL, C. J. – Why do you say that it is no part of the churchwardens' duty to fix boxes in the church? The statute 27 Hy. 8, c. 25, expressly requires a poor-box to be kept in the church; and one of the canons (Can. 84) directs the churchwardens to keep a strong chest, to which there were to be three keys. Suppose the churchwardens have done their duty, and put the box there?

---

    [3]   Cox (ed.), *Reports of Cases*, p. 35.
    [4]   N.D. Brodie, 'Beggary, Vagabondage', pp. 238, 246–65; Margery K. McIntosh, *Poor Relief in England*, p. 108.

> *Flood.* – This box had only two keys; and the offertory-money was not put into it; but ... [Flood here returns to his argument about the form of the indictment].[5]

A couple of themes immediately stand out. In 1846 the relationship between churchwardens, parish churches and poor boxes was at least arguable at law. The arguments rested on laws passed centuries earlier. There clearly was not a strong contemporary custom of poor boxes in English parish churches in the nineteenth century sufficient to automatically negate the lawyer's argument. Poor box ownership *was* a matter for Queen's Bench. That this was so was driven in part by another element of nineteenth-century practice illustrated by the trial, which is the frequent absence of poor boxes in parish churches. This is a theme echoed in other nineteenth-century commentary on poor boxes in English parish churches. For example, in the same year that Wortley and Allen faced the Northampton Assizes, G.A. Poole's section on 'The Alms-Chest' in his volume on *Churches: Their Structure, Arrangement, and Decoration* (1846) asserted three points of direct relevance here: 1) the alms chest was required by the 84th Canon (1604); 2) prior provision for an alms chest was made by *27 Hen.VIII.c.25* (1536); and 3) 'yet so little respect is shown to this Canon, that one may have visited many churches, and perhaps all the churches in many districts, and not seen a single alms chest'.[6] One wonders if Chief Justice Tindal held a copy at the time of the trial.

Yet both Poole and Tindal were wrong. There was no explicit requirement in *27 Hen.VIII.c.25* (1536) that churches have an alms chest or a poor box. That Act provided for a weekly collection on behalf of the poor where boxes *could* be part of the collection mechanism:

> gathering and procuring of suche charitable and voluntarie almes of the good christen people within the same with boxes evry sonday holy day and other festival day or otherwise amonge them selffes.[7]

Besides apparently being optional, these 'boxes' were clearly meant to mean portable collection boxes of a sort similar to that utilised in a collection scheme in Rouen from 1534:

> one is to carry a dish or plate, and a box with two keys, the other a piece of paper on which are to be recorded gifts in kind.[8]

---

[5]   Cox (ed.), *Reports of Cases*, p. 35.

[6]   G.A. Poole, *Churches: Their Structure, Arrangement, and Decoration* (London, 1846), pp. 94–5.

[7]   27 Henry VIII, c.25.4, see *Statutes of the Realm*, 9 vols (London, 1810–28), III: 1509/10–1545 (1817), 559.

[8]   F.R. Salter (ed.), *Some Early Tracts*, p. 115.

Portable alms boxes were probably common in the early sixteenth century.[9] These were useful tools for garnering alms on behalf of another person or institution: keys could act to insure against skimming by unscrupulous collectors, and coin slots performed a similar function against donors.

Moreover, portable and stationary poor boxes were not mutually exclusive within any given collection system. Again the example of Rouen is instructive. Not only did it use portable poor boxes for direct collecting, it also featured stationary poor boxes placed 'at every church door, and at all the doors of public buildings', and then centralised all of the collected money from all of these boxes into yet another box with three locks and administered by the city.[10] This highlights that understanding any given early modern 'poor box' is a highly context-dependent activity. There are important distinctions between boxes that are portable or stationary; and those that are for donation or principally for secure storage.

The Henrician statute *27 Hen.VIII.c.25* (1536) did provide for how the collected money was to be stored, stating it:

> shalbe kept in the comen coffre or boxe standing in the Churche of evry parisshe, or els it shalbe committed unto the hands and safe custodie of any other such good and substanciall trustie man as they can agree upon.[11]

This was an explicit reference to the parish chest where other parish records were kept, not to a particular receptacle for money gathered for the poor.

Nothing in the 1536 statute conforms to an alms chest of the 84th Canon, which states explicitly what we now generally think of as a parish's 'poor box':

> The Churchwardens shall provide and have, … a strong Chest, with a hole in the upper part thereof, to be provided at the charge of the parish (if there be none such already provided), having three keys … which Chest they shall set and fasten in the most convenient place, to the intent the Parishioners may put into it their alms for their poor neighbours.[12]

The box stolen from Oundle is certainly closer to that of the Canon than that of the statute, even if it lacked the correct number of keys. The Canon's poor box is stationary, and designed for the explicit purposes of receiving and storing money for the poor.

Yet in looking for the original requirement that English parishes have a multi-locked poor box, fastened in place, and with a slot in the top, the Chief Justice

---

[9]   For an example, see 'Proceedings at Meetings of the Royal Archaeological Institute', *Archaeological Journal*, 27 (1870), 134–46 (pp. 140–41).

[10]   Salter (ed.), *Some Early Tracts*, pp. 115–16.

[11]   27 Henry VIII, c.25.18, see *Statutes of the Realm*, III, 561.

[12]   C.H. Davis (ed.), *The English Church Canons of 1604: With Historical Introduction* (London: Sweet, 1869), p. 80.

overlooked the pivotal moment in English poor box history: the Royal Injunctions of 1547. According to these, each parish was to have had:

> a strong chest, with a hole in the upper part therof, to be provided at the cost and charge of the parish, having three keys, whereof one shall remain in the custody of the parson, vicar, or curate, and the other two in the custody of the churchwardens or any other two honest men to be appointed by the parish from year to year.[13]

Practically verbatim, the 1604 Canon's poor box was clearly modelled on that of 1547 with two important changes, the first being the addition of a provision of exemption from the duty to install a poor box if one was 'already provided'. The second change concerns the placement of the box within the church.

So if we identify the English 'parish poor box' as a stationary, multi-locked receptacle, which was capable of receiving donations from parishioners directly through a hole, then it is a product of the 1547 Royal Injunctions. This fact is borne out by parish records, where a number of parishes can be seen to have tried to conform to the new requirements. This can be seen in churchwardens' accounts, church inventories and testamentary bequests, all of which seem to indicate that from 1547 onwards, the poor box was certainly a much more common part of the English parish church.[14] Some records are particularly clear. In the London parish of St Andrew Hubbard in Eastcheap the churchwardens 'paid for an alms box' and also 'paid for writing the table over the alms box' in 1547/8.[15] St Petrock's parish in Exeter purchased 'a cofer wt loks' according to the 1547/8 account, which is a little less clear, but is most probably a poor box.[16] McIntosh's survey of parish records indicates that about twenty-nine per cent of parishes surveyed show evidence of poor boxes installed or extant in the period following 1547.[17]

Yet, just as the case seems resolved, interpretative tensions between prescriptive sources and documented materiality unsettle any too confident assertion that 1547 marks the start of the English parish poor box. From the 1567 visitation records of the diocese of York, we can see the evidentiary problems clearly. A number of parishes simply did not have a poor box; others had poor boxes 'without locks' or 'no key' or 'not sufficient'.[18] So some parishes simply did not install poor boxes, others had poor boxes that did not conform to requirements. The same issues apply

---

[13] P.L. Hughes and J.F. Larkin (eds), *Tudor Royal Proclamations*, no. 287, p. 401.

[14] Brodie, pp. 246–65.

[15] C. Burgess (ed.), *The Church Records of St Andrew Hubbard, Eastcheap, c. 1450–c. 1570* (London: London Record Society, 1999), p. 161.

[16] Cornwall and Devonshire Record Office, EDRO/PW 2, fol. 113.

[17] McIntosh, *Poor Relief in England*, pp. 132–3.

[18] J.S. Purvis (ed.), *Tudor Parish Documents in the Diocese of York: A Selection* (Cambridge: Cambridge University Press, 1948), pp. 29–34.

to the broader picture of England in 1547: are the records indicative of installation or repair?

Firstly, in a few cases, there is evidence that some parishes had something akin to a parish poor box prior to 1547, so it is perhaps reasonable to assume some continuity. The London parish of St Mary at Hill had an 'Almes box' prior to the 1520s.[19] Yet, come the 1547/8 account, the churchwardens made no mention of purchasing a poor box, presumably because they already had one.[20] The survival patterns of English churchwardens' accounts do not allow for great confidence in asserting the general picture in the decades and centuries prior to the mid-sixteenth century. Further to this, we need to be aware that in the late medieval church it was not uncommon to have an alms box that was not necessarily for the poor, or was for a purpose external to the church, for instance a poor box for a nearby hospital. The Oundle box seems to be a box of this last sort. These could easily be converted into a parish poor box without necessitating much effort, and therefore diminishing the likelihood of poor boxes being documented, even where circumstances for the production of documentation existed.

Secondly, within the same sorts of parish records that indicate poor boxes from 1547 onwards, there are occasional hints that such poor boxes may have already existed and were only being made to conform to the specific requirements of the Royal Injunctions. The Churchwardens of St Michael Spurriergate in York noted in 1547 they 'paid for two hyng lokes to the chyst off the poor folkes'.[21] There is no mention of the purchase of a poor box. In this instance, the churchwardens held onto money from the sale of the sacrament light 'to be put into the puyre folks chyst', suggesting it might have been new, but in other cases there is no clear indication this was the case. Then again, their poor box could have been out of commission while two extra locks were added to an extant one-lock poor box. In St Ewan's, Bristol, the churchwardens 'paid for puttinge iij lockes on the coffer for the poor people and dressing the same', highlighting how it is the purchase of keys and locks that tends to dominate churchwarden recording of poor boxes in 1547 and the years immediately following.[22] This focus on locks, and the common appearance of poor boxes in churchwardens' accounts in 1547–48 as a destination of parish money from the sale of church furnishings, suggests *conforming* rather than *installing*, something that may have been the case in many English parishes.

---

[19]   H. Littlehales (ed.), *The Medieval Records of a London City Church*, EETS o.s. 125 and 128 (London: Kegan Paul, Trench, Trübner, 1904–05), part 1, pp. 295, 304. Interestingly, the same parish hints at early parish collecting for the poor, albeit not necessarily weekly (ibid., part 1, pp. 284, 299).

[20]   Littlehales (ed.), *Medieval Records*, part 2, pp. 385–8.

[21]   C.C. Webb (ed.), *The Churchwardens' Accounts of St Michael, Spurriergate, York 1518–1548, vol. 2: 1538–1548* (York: University of York, 1997), p. 330.

[22]   B.R. Masters and E. Ralph (eds), *The Church Book of St. Ewen's, Bristol 1454–1584* (London and Ashford: Bristol and Gloucestershire Archaeological Society, 1967), p. 184.

However, the 1567 visitation of York should caution against too readily accepting widespread poor boxes pre-1547. Remember that many parishes lacked poor boxes, particularly those that were rural and poor. The parish of Holme was reported as having 'no pore mens boxe for that ther parishe is pore and nothing to put into the same'.[23] Yet a sensitive reading of the source material certainly cannot rule out earlier poor boxes and in fact often suggests their presence, especially in larger, urban parishes. Either way, the notion of conformity being the main concern is furthered by the connection between the poor box and the wider religious instructions of the Royal Injunctions and other changes discernible in English parishes.[24]

It seems that the historians most interested in poor boxes have been historians of poor relief, and that has meant they have not always seen the poor box in its religious and liturgical context. The 1547 Royal Injunctions are nothing if not concerned with religion and liturgy. Of the poor box's placement it said:

> Which chest you shall set and fasten near unto the high altar, to the intent the parishioners should put into it their oblation and alms for their poor neighbours.[25]

The intention behind this placement becomes a little clearer when read in connection with the introduction of the first *Book of Common Prayer* in 1549. In the late medieval Mass, during the offertory, the laity could make a voluntary (and probably quite public) offering towards the cost of the bread and wine prior to consecration.[26] A similar offering by the laity was retained in the new Protestant Communion Service of 1549, but the focus shifted. A rubric in the *Book of Common Prayer* instructed the laity that:

> In the meane time, whyles the Clerkes do syng the Offertory, so many as are disposed, shall offer unto the poore mennes boxe euery one accordynge to his habilitie and charitable mynde.[27]

Here we can see the poor box in its liturgical setting, something suggested by the location stipulated in the 1547 Royal Injunctions and the wider changes in church

---

[23] Purvis (ed.), *Tudor Parish Documents*, p. 29.

[24] Brodie, pp. 246–65. For a detailed appreciation of wider changes to the parochial fabric, see K. Fincham and N. Tyacke, *Altars Restored: The Changing Face of English Religious Worship, 1547–c. 1700* (Oxford: Oxford University Press, 2007).

[25] Hughes and Larkin (eds), *Tudor Royal Proclamations*, I, no. 287, p. 401.

[26] T.F. Simmons (ed.), *The Lay Folks Mass Book*, EETS o.s. 71 (London: Trübner, 1879), p. 22.

[27] *The First Prayer-Book of King Edward VI* (London: Griffith, Farran, Okedent, Welsh, 1888), p. 200.

arrangements stipulated at the same time.[28] This can also be seen in churchwardens' accounts like that of St Ewen's in Bristol, where the poor box is only mentioned in the 1547/8 account after 'takeinge downe the tabernacles with the Images', the application of 'lyme' and shortly before 'takeinge downe the Roode and the reste of the Images'.[29] The poor box is quite literally in the middle of significant ecclesiological changes to the interior of the church.

That some connection was intended between these service-based donations and the weekly poor relief system developed in mid-Tudor England seems likely, but it is important to note that in a strict statutory sense the poor box never featured as a collection mechanism nor as an explicitly designated receptacle for the weekly rates that were supposed to have been gathered from 1552 onwards.[30] McIntosh has indicated that some parishes were instructed to use the poor boxes for storing collected rates,[31] and it is highly likely that many others did use their poor boxes this way anyway; but, from a conceptual standpoint, in 1552 statutory rates for the poor and the parish poor box parted ways.

In 1552 the statute *5&6 Edw.VI.c.2* detailed how collections for the poor were to be administered, and did not stipulate that poor boxes were the receptacles of gathered funds.[32] The simple reason was that the alms were gathered and distributed weekly, and the idea of a receptacle was redundant, as the funds were held by the collectors. With echoes of *27 Hen.VIII.c.25* (1536), it indicated that surplus funds at the end of a collector's term of office go to 'the common Chest of the Churche or in some other safe place', confirming that collectors held custody of the funds for the short term, and that the poor box was not explicitly intended for regular storage of the parish poor rate. That this is so is furthered by the one explicit mention in *5&6 Edw.VI.c.2* of 'the Allmes boxe of the poore': it was the receptacle for fines levied on collectors who refused or failed to duly execute their office.[33] It is rather unlikely that carefully worded statutes would confuse the 'comon boxe' with the parish poor box; besides, a fine to the poor box was a fine to a separate fund from that administered by the person so fined.

Ironically, however, within the English Communion Service the poor box did become the receptacle of gathered alms from 1552 onwards. Whereas previously congregants placed any offering in the poor box near the altar, the 1552 *Book of Common Prayer* stipulated that:

---

[28] Hughes and Larkin (eds), *Tudor Royal Proclamations*, I, no. 287, p. 401. The details about the poor box placement followed immediately after a section about making shrines 'extinct', ordering the removal of artwork 'so that there remain no memory of the same', and requiring 'a comely and honest pulpit to be set in a convenient place'.

[29] Masters and Ralph (eds), *Church Book of St. Ewen's*, pp. 183–4.

[30] Brodie, pp. 257–63; 5&6 Edward VI, c.2, *Statutes of the Realm*, IV: 1547–1624 (1819), 131.

[31] McIntosh, *Poor Relief in England*, pp. 129–30.

[32] 5&6 Edward VI, c.2, *Statutes of the Realm*, IV, 131–2.

[33] 5&6 Edward VI, c.2.3, *Statutes of the Realm*, IV, 131.

the Churchwardens, or some other by them appoynted, [shall] gather the deuocion of the people, and put the same into the poore mens boxe.[34]

That there may have been practical overlap with parish collections is certainly possible, although far from certain, and the statutory regulations would suggest this was not intended to be the case. Conceptually, the offertory was still a moment for voluntary almsgiving, but the poor box itself became less central to the liturgical action. It was still the ultimate destination for the alms, but the act of giving was through intermediaries, and a prayer of thanks was offered after these alms were collected and presented if any had been offered.[35] The act of giving was retained, but the poor box itself was no longer quite so essential to the performance of the liturgy. This formula was retained in the Elizabethan *Book of Common Prayer* of 1558–59 and that of 1604.[36]

These secondary changes to the English Communion Service encouraged a rearrangement of the location of the poor box within the church. From 1552 the altar was to have been replaced with a communion table, and thus in the Canon of 1604 the poor box was to be 'in the most convenient place' rather than close to the altar.[37] Just as the requirement that poor boxes be installed from 1547 is discernible in parish records, so is the waning of its importance from 1552 also apparent in churchwardens' accounts that lack mentions of poor boxes after 1547/8.

In 1662, when the order of the Communion Service was again revised, the collection of alms was retained but the alms were to be gathered 'in a decent Basin, to be provided by the Parish for that purpose; and [the collectors were to] reverently bring it to the Priest, who shall humbly present and place it upon the holy Table'.[38] The poor box was no longer a part of the English church liturgy, although nominally still required by the 84th Canon. This change, perhaps in response to a general lack of poor boxes (and also liturgically reconnecting the alms more explicitly with the communion), explains the relative unfamiliarity the nineteenth-century judiciary had with the parish poor box. After an awkward century (1547–1662) when poor boxes were theoretically required but apparently not always used, it had been two centuries since poor boxes were integrated into the regular act of worship by the time Wortley and Allen pinched one from a pew.

---

[34]   *The Second Prayer-Book of King Edward VI* (London: Griffith, Farran, Okedent, Welsh, 1900), p. 96.

[35]   Again pointing to a divide between liturgical and statutory collections, as the latter were certainly expected to have been undertaken, whereas the liturgical collections were clearly optional.

[36]   *The Prayer-Book of Queen Elizabeth* (London: Griffith, Farran, Okedent, Welsh, 1890), p. 162; *The Book of Common Prayer, King James Anno 1604* (London: Pickering, 1844), p. T2.

[37]   Davis (ed.), *English Church Canons*, p. 80.

[38]   *The Book of Common Prayer, And Administration of the Sacraments* (London, 1681), sig. Oii.

'a very ancient box'[39]: Re-Thinking Poor Boxes and Early Modern Charity

The theft of the Oundle poor box was a defining moment in the lives of Robert Wortley and John Allen. For the historian looking at the period before the Oundle theft it is possible to see a trend leading to Wortley's eventual conviction. On at least two previous occasions he had been convicted: in 1838 he had committed 'Robbery, with violence'; and, in 1841, assault.[40] Here we have a history of criminality that may go some way to explaining both the action of stealing a poor box, and the judiciary's obvious desire to see the conviction upheld. The pre-trial history of the younger and more commonly named Allen is less clear. What prompted the 24-year-old to join Wortley is unclear and likely to remain so. Post-trial, the reverse is true. Wortley seems to disappear from the documentary record; whereas Allen can be charted from the Northampton Assizes to Sydney on the convict ship *Randolph*, arriving in the antipodes in 1849.[41] For these men, their trial for the theft of the poor box at Oundle is possibly the best-documented single activity of their lives.

As already seen, a similar scenario exists for the English parish poor box in the wake of the 1547 Royal Injunctions. There were clear instructions, soon followed by discernible activity in some parish records that appear to relate to those instructions. Yet, despite its limited historical visibility, the English parish poor box can still be a useful tool for tackling larger questions about early modern charity. The requirement from 1547 that every English parish church have a poor box helps centre notions of continuity and change, theory and practice, activity and evidence. So too, using the poor box to explore the separation of the liturgical charity and statutory welfare from 1552, a theological construction of 'charity' can be better situated against tangential and to some extent anachronistic concepts such as 'poor relief' or 'welfare'.

These problems can be addressed by asking about the early modern English parish poor box a series of questions concerning its origins, ideological context and continued usage.

Where Did the Idea of a Parish Poor Box Come From?

In a word: antiquity. Broadly speaking, the concept of a communal fund for the relief of the poor manifested as a box into which money was put and held and

---

[39]   Cox (ed.), *Reports of Cases*, p. 32.

[40]   TNA, Home Office: Criminal Registers, Middlesex and Home Office: County of Northampton Register of all persons charged with Indictable Offences at the Assizes and Sessions held within the County during the Year 1838, fol. 52v; County of Northampton Register of all persons charged with Indictable Offences at the Assizes and Sessions held within the County during the Year 1841, fol. 365v.

[41]   State Records Authority of New South Wales, Musters and other papers relating to convict ships, Series CGS 1155, Reels 2417–28, *Randolph* 1849, p. 15.

from which the poor were supported could be said to have biblical origins, if not a perfect biblical analogy. Looking first at form, in the Second Temple in Jerusalem, the presence of an alms-receptacle where people made offerings is most clearly and famously articulated in the story of the Widow's mite detailed in the Gospels of Mark and Luke.[42] The Jewish Talmud further contextualises this story and its setting, where in the Court of Women the receptacles for the offerings were shaped like horns or trumpets, probably designed to ensure alms offered stayed offered.[43] Yet, while some of this money could be given to the poor, it was not exclusively for them, and therefore in concept is not quite a 'poor box'. The Temple did have a more specifically poor-relieving element in the Quiet Chamber, where 'God-fearing people would place money secretly in the Quiet Chamber, and poor relatives of people of good class would discreetly support themselves from it'.[44] Unlike later poor boxes, however, this was a situation where money could be donated individually and taken by personal discretion.

A managed fund for the specific relief of the poor has a biblical analogy in the Pauline collection for the Christians in Jerusalem, but this does not help greatly illuminate the history of the poor box as such.[45] It bears some conceptual analogy to the traditional tithe for the poor detailed in Deuteronomy, although Paul was keen to stress it as a voluntary gift, and it was apparently a response to a particular crisis rather than a permanent structural mechanism.[46] Yet the tithe was a long-standing tradition of communal concern for the poor, managed by and centred on the Temple. This notion was adopted by Christian theology and church law and can be seen explicitly reiterated into the medieval period in the Western Church.[47] Yet if conceptually closer to a 'poor box' than that of the treasury horns, here it is the form that is lacking.

For our purpose, charting the individual twists and turns of archaic poor box evolution is less important, however, than recognition of a monotheistic charitable milieu in the late antique and medieval world that influenced Western European Christian poor box development and context. The famed Dead Sea Scrolls, for instance, contain rules outlining a monthly collection for the poor, orphaned, aged and sick of the Essene community.[48] Early Christianity was deeply and particularly concerned with giving alms to the poor. According to the Gospel of

---

[42]   Mark 12. 42; Luke 21. 2.

[43]   Mo'ed Sheqalim (6, 1), Middoth (2, 5), in N. Solomon (ed.), *The Talmud: A Selection* (London: Penguin, 2009), p. 190; J.M. Lundquist, *The Temple of Jerusalem: Past, Present, and Future* (Westport: Praeger, 2008), pp. 190, 685; note what this means for Matthew 6. 2.

[44]   Mo'ed Sheqalim (5, 6), in Solomon (ed.), *Talmud: A Selection*, p. 190.

[45]   Romans 15. 25–9; I Corinthians 16. 1–4; II Corinthians 8. 1–6; Galatians 2. 10.

[46]   Deuteronomy 14. 28–9, 26. 12.

[47]   B. Tierney, *Medieval Poor Law*, pp. 78–9.

[48]   G. Vermes (ed.), *The Complete Dead Sea Scrolls in English*, rev. edn (London: Penguin, 2011), p. 145.

John, Judas could be misconstrued by the Apostles as going to give money to the poor when he was going to betray Jesus, simply because he 'had the common purse' which, presumably, was regularly so deployed.[49] The Apostles appointed deacons to conduct charity on behalf of the community.[50] A few centuries later and St Augustine's church had a poor box named the 'Quadriga', a four-horsed chariot 'to sweep the alms of the faithful'.[51] His contemporary, St John Chrysostom, provided instructions to the effect that Christians should put alms chests in the houses in which they prayed and make donations prior to commencing prayer.[52]

Talmudic Judaism and Islam shared with Christianity similar notions of worship-centred charitable apparatuses. The Baba Bathra details a 'charity treasury', collectors and distributors amongst Jews and for the wider community.[53] In medieval Egypt this framework can be seen operating in conjunction with a poor box specifically for orphans, a reminder that the poor box was not an exclusively Christian concept.[54] Almsgiving ('zakāt') is, of course, one of the five pillars of Islam, and so mosques naturally became centres of charitable exchange. In medieval Syria the appropriateness of having alms boxes in mosques was questioned by some commentators, but this nonetheless highlights their sometime presence.[55]

So in a general sense the poor box of the late medieval and early modern English parish would have been familiar to a wider cultural context of the first and early second millennia AD. But if we are to situate the poor box properly within a wider discourse about charity in the immediately pre-Reformation period, then before we move to examine the poor boxes of that period we need to appreciate that the 'poor box' was a specialised sub-set of 'alms box', because charity was and is a concept with broader application than poor relief.

Nonetheless, boxes identifiable as principally for the poor are discernible in Western Europe in a variety of forms prior to the Reformation, even sharing many aspects of the Reformation format instituted in England in 1547. Poor boxes could be an alms-gathering mechanism for communities of lepers, as was the case in Gaywood in Norfolk, where their alms box has a three-keyed security system.[56] There were guild-managed poor boxes strategically placed around the city of

---

[49]   John 13. 29.

[50]   Acts 6. 1–6.

[51]   Peter Brown, *Through the Eye of a Needle: Wealth, the Fall of Rome, and the Making of Christianity in the West, 350–550 AD* (Princeton, NJ: Princeton University Press, 2012), p. 86.

[52]   J. Maxwell, 'Lay Piety in the Sermons of John Chrysostom', in D. Krueger (ed.), *Byzantine Christianity* (Minneapolis: Augsburg Fortress, 2010), pp. 19–38 (p. 24).

[53]   I. Epstein (ed.) and Maurice Simon (trans.), *Babylonian Talmud, Tractate Baba Bathra*, fol. 8v, available online at <http://www.come-and-hear.com/bababathra/bababathra_8.html>.

[54]   M.R. Cohen, *Poverty and Charity in the Jewish Community*, p. 205.

[55]   D. Talmon-Heller, *Islamic Piety in Medieval Syria: Mosques, Cemeteries and Sermons under the Zangids and Ayyūbids, 1146–1260* (Leiden: Brill, 2007), p. 53, n. 121.

[56]   Carol Rawcliffe, *Leprosy*, p. 331.

Florence by the early fifteenth century, labelled with appropriate injunctions to passers-by to 'Give alms for the poor and needy sick'.[57] In the Netherlands, many guilds appear to have established poor boxes in the fifteenth century, and continued to maintain their own poor boxes well into the Reformation period with no discernible difference between the Catholic or Protestant-dominated guilds when it came to the presence or otherwise of poor boxes.[58]

Poor boxes often featured in continental poor relief schemes of the early to mid-sixteenth century, both Protestant and Catholic.[59] Historians are divided on the issue of confessional difference and poor relief, and on the degrees of continuities and discontinuities in practice and conceptualisation. This will be addressed in more depth shortly, as bearing on the wider connection between poor boxes and charity. Suffice for now to note that town schemes like those of Wittenberg (1520–22), Nürnberg (1522), Leisnig (1523), Bruges (1526), Ypres (1531) and Rouen (1534) all prescribed poor box usage, located at or within churches.[60]

The first and third of these plans were authored by Luther, and it seems the Lutheran model of a poor box influenced the later English one most explicitly. In Wittenberg he proposed a three-keyed poor box, which was apparently made at the town's expense in early 1521.[61] This was associated with the introduction of a weekly collection.[62] Similarly, in Leisnig Luther coupled the notion of a 'common chest' with collection boxes.[63] One of these collection boxes was to be a poor box, again connected with a regular collection:

> alms … for the upkeep of the poor when our parish is gathered together in God's house, shall be put at once in such a box and applied to such a use.[64]

That the 1547 Royal Injunctions were influenced to some extent by this seems likely.

Indeed there is a very strong suggestion in a surviving draft parliamentary bill that the idea of requiring that poor boxes be placed in English churches was being

---

[57]   Edgcumbe Staley, *The Guilds of Florence* (London: Methuen, 1906), p. 548.

[58]   B. De Munck, 'Fiscalizing Solidarity (From Below)', in E. Van Nederveen and G. Vermeesch (eds), *Serving the Urban Community: The Rise of Public Facilities in the Low Countries* (Amsterdam: Aksant, 2009), pp. 168–93 (p. 178).

[59]   Brodie, pp. 259–62.

[60]   C. Lindberg, '"There Should Be No Beggars"', 313–34 (pp. 322–3, 326–7); H.J. Grimm, 'Luther's Contribution to Sixteenth-Century Organization of Poor Relief', *Archives for Reformation History*, 61 (1970), 222–34 (pp. 226, 230); Salter (ed.), *Some Early Tracts*, pp. 26, 86–7, 115–16; William Marshall, *The forme and maner of subue[n] tion or helping for pore people deuysed and practysed i[n] the cytie of Hypres in Flaunders, whiche forme is auctorised by the Emperour, [and] approued by the facultie of diuinitie in Paris* (London: Thomas Godfray, 1535), pp. C.11–C.12.

[61]   Lindberg, pp. 326–7.

[62]   Lindberg, p. 327.

[63]   Salter (ed.), *Some Early Tracts*, p. 87.

[64]   Salter (ed.), *Some Early Tracts*, p. 87.

considered by 1535. Although not passed into law at that time, and situated within a wider funding mechanism for public works, the draft bill's construction of a parish alms box is strikingly similar to that of 1547:

> that in evry churche wher [appointed ...] shalbe set up in some part of the churche before the sacrament there as nygh as can be reasonably devysed a chest to receive such Almes as shalbe geven ..., And evry chest to have thre keyes[65]

So it turns out that Chief Justice Tindall was almost correct, a sort of poor box was considered in 1535, but abandoned in favour of the more general provisions of *27 Hen.VIII.c.25*; and it was not only to relieve the poor, but to make them work.[66] Against this we should, however, not dismiss the codification and refinement of some extant practices both in reforming continental churches and in England. In Ypres, the 1531 scheme required churches to 'set a boxe wherin euery man shall put prtuely what he wyll', which was a 'comen boxe for poore men', and it was specifically noted of these that they were to be 'after the olde maner'.[67] This could be intended to refer to Biblical precedent, but as already noted, there is not an exact Scriptural model. More likely it is a reference to medieval church poor boxes. The pre-1520s 'Almes box', and also 'money gayderd ffor the powr peple', in St Mary at Hill in London, pre-dated both Reformation-era boxes and the Royal Injunctions' poor boxes.[68] In a recent study of late medieval English poverty and poor relief Dyer re-discovered the bishop of Worcester's 1451 instructions that churchwardens of his diocese should collect funds for the poor of each parish.[69] Dyer suggested that 'this practice should not be assumed to have been confined to one diocese'.[70] Close examination of this bishop's instruction to his diocese is very telling of how sixteenth-century 'innovations' frequently modelled extant or earlier practices that suffer from poor documentation and thus may appear to be novel.[71] Three times each year the Worcester diocese's churchwardens were to have taken a collection for the poor from their assembled parishioners. The funds were then publicly counted and placed either 'in manibus dictorum

---

[65]   BL, MS Royal 18 C vi, fols 8r–8v.

[66]   BL, MS Royal 18 C vi, fols 8r–8v, 20r–20v. It is worth noting that in addition to this collection box, the same document proposed another box which 'shalbe called thalmes box', which had two keys and was for the money which was to be distributed to the poor. For more on this plan and the legislation of the 1530s see N. Brodie, 'Reassessing 27 Henry VIII, c.25 and Tudor Welfare: Changes and Continuities in Context', *Parergon*, 31 (2014), 111-36.

[67]   Marshall, *The forme and maner of subue[n]tion or helping for pore people*, pp. C.11–C.12.

[68]   Littlehales (ed.), *Medieval Records*, part 1, pp. 284, 295, 299, 304.

[69]   C. Dyer, 'Poverty and its Relief', 41–78 (p. 73).

[70]   Dyer, p. 73.

[71]   R.M. Haines, 'Bishop Carpenter's Injunctions to the Diocese of Worcester in 1451', *Bulletin of the Institute of Historical Research*, 40 (1967), 203–7 (p. 206).

gardianorum' (in the Churchwarden's hands) or in a 'communi pixide' (common box).[72] It is strikingly similar to the 1536 parish collection model, and may go a long way to explaining why the institution of those collections met with so little contemporary commentary.

Poor boxes are at the heart of a methodological tension between instructive or prescriptive source materials, absences of or in documentation, and the discernment and characterisation of change in the late medieval and early modern past.[73] Their apparent prominence in mid-sixteenth-century 'welfare reform' is in part both a documentary and disciplinary construct. English collections and poor boxes of various sorts definitely pre-date Luther's *Ninety-five Theses*, and in many instances pre-date Luther. Even Luther's scheme for Wittenberg was about refocusing the community's traditional charitable collections. Luther wrote that what was 'heretofore ... for the benefit of the hospital, from now on is to be used for all infirm and needy persons in the congregation', what was only done at weddings was to be done weekly.[74] Thus even Luther was looking at the late medieval context, not any Biblical precedents. In that particular case the poor box may have been newly made, but the collections associated with it were not. Any difference between Protestant and Catholic poor boxes is likely therefore to be found not in their presence, but rather in their use, and even then, most likely only in relatively nuanced ways.

Was the Idea of a Parish Poor Box Exclusively Reformist/Protestant?

Having a long tradition, the idea of a poor box, even a parish poor box, was not new to the sixteenth century. It was not a Lutheran invention. For both Catholics and Protestants, where poor boxes existed, they survived changes to church furnishing. Both Catholic and Protestant welfare reformers often encouraged poor box installation if they were lacking. Regardless of sectarian position, the poor box never seems to have been an object of theological scorn.

Yet there is something particular about the way that Protestant reformers integrated poor boxes within their churches, which tells us something about changing constructions of charity. To appreciate this, however, it is first necessary to discriminate two ways of looking at the concept of 'charity', and the poor box enables us to look closely at the two meanings in tandem. One is that most commonly meant by historians interested in charity, by which is meant charity the transferable noun, the thing given. Charity is routinely used in this sense as a catch-all concept for what would more accurately be described as poor relief

---

[72]   Haines, p. 206.

[73]   The same is true of urban and parish collections generally. See N. Brodie, '"The names of all the poore people": Corporate and Parish Relief in Exeter, 1560s-1570s', in Scott (ed.), *Experiences of Poverty*, pp. 107-131.

[74]   Lindberg, p. 327.

or welfare.[75] This is a somewhat anachronistic use in the medieval context. What historians tend to parse as 'charity' in this sense is often in primary documentation referred to as 'alms', 'offerings', 'donations', 'gifts'. Where 'charity' does appear in primary documentation in this setting as gift or alms it frequently does so in an adjectival sense: 'charitable alms'.

The Christian construction of the concept 'charity' is broader than gifts or alms, and this held true for the late medieval period's use of the term.[76] Charting the transmission of the language of the Gospels is a simplistic but effective means of cutting to the heart of this concept, and a simplified version runs that the Greek '*agape*' was translated as the Latin '*caritas*', which is generally translated into English in the twenty-first century as 'love'. This is something that can be felt, can be possessed, and can be given, but unlike the narrower modern construction, cannot be lost in the giving. Historians have been aware of this, certainly, but as Brodman has recently noted, the anachronistic focus on welfare or poor relief has often led scholars to overlook the broader applications of late medieval 'charity' when understood on its own terms.[77] Focusing through the lens of the poor box can add to this by helping us to appreciate how we got from that earlier and broader construction to the narrower modern one.

A good illustration of this construction of charity can be found in a series of sermons closely linked to the English poor box. The first of these was published in 1547 in a compilation of 'official' homilies that the Edwardian government ordered to be read in churches in England.[78] Charity was described clearly as 'to love God … also, to love every man'.[79] This is still the sense of the concept as detailed in the Gospels and articulated by St Augustine. In the 'second part of the sermon of Charitee', the concern with definition moved to application. Here 'charity' was construed as having two 'offices': the first of which was to 'cherish good and innocent men'.[80] Interestingly none of the longstanding medieval theological treatments of giving alms and discriminating between recipients is

---

[75]   See for example C. Jones, 'Some Recent Trends in the History of Charity', in M. Daunton (ed.), *Charity, Self-Interest and Welfare in the English Past* (London and New York: Taylor and Francis, 1996), pp. 51–63, and other contributions to the same volume.

[76]   John Augustine Ryan, 'Charity and Charities', in *Catholic Encyclopedia, vol. 3* (New York: Robert Appleton, 1913), online at <http://www.newadvent.org/cathen/03592a. htm>; J.W. Brodman, *Charity and Religion*, p. 3, see also chap. 1, pp. 9–44.

[77]   Brodman, pp. 1–8.

[78]   [Thomas Cranmer?], *Certayne sermons, or homilies, appointed by the Kynges Maiestie, to be declared and redde, by all persones, vycares, or curates, euery Sonday in their churches, where they haue cure* (London: Edward Whitchurch, 1547); it was also reprinted in 1551: Thomas Cranmer, *Certain sermones, or homelies, appoincted by the kynges Maiestue, to bee declared and read, by all persones, vicars, or curates, euery Sondaie in their churches, wheir thei haue cure* (London: Richard Grafton, 1551).

[79]   *Certayne sermons, or homilies* (1547), sig. Kiii.

[80]   *Certayne sermons, or homilies* (1547), sig. Liiv.

even obliquely noted.[81] More curiously, despite something of a historiographical obsession with the idea that this was a period that saw increasing discrimination about almsgiving, there is nothing really said in this homily about almsgiving at all.[82]

The second part of the sermon was principally about the second office of charity, which was 'to rebuke, correct, and punishe vice'.[83] This was further elaborated at length, first in terms of how 'every loving father correcteth his natural sonne', and then by noting the duties of preachers and magistrats to this effect. This corrective aspect of charity awaits more detailed historical unpacking, but Augustine, in his sermon on the first letter of St John, was fairly clear:

> Do not think that you love your son when you do not strike him, or that you love your son when you do not discipline him, or that you love your neighbour when you do not correct him: That is not charity but weakness. Let your charity be fervent to correct, to amend. If behaviour is good, take delight in it; if wicked, let it be amended, corrected.[84]

So traditional and persistent was this dual-office construction of charity that when England returned to Catholicism under Mary, and a new 'official' homily book was produced, the sermon of charity remained verbatim in the new collection.[85] The same was true for a subsequent Elizabethan 'official' homily book.[86]

Noting that the English parish poor box was nominally installed in the same year as this homily was introduced we can see that the introduction of a parish poor box was not intended to mark a major shift in the overall construction of charity. It does, however, point to a new catechetical focus on and about charitable

---

[81]   Brodman, pp. 9–32; see also E. Buhrer, 'From *Caritas* to Charity: How Loving God Became Giving Alms', in C. Kosso and A. Scott (eds), *Poverty and Prosperity in the Middle Ages and Renaissance* (Turnhout: Brepols, 2012), pp. 113–28.

[82]   This helps to affirm McIntosh's assertion (*Poor Relief in England*, p. 295) that the much-held idea of a period-specific or ideologically-specific increase in the degree of discrimination about almsgiving has little evidentiary support.

[83]   *Certayne sermons, or homilies* (1547), sig. Liiv.

[84]   *Augustine of Hippo: Selected Writings*, (ed.) M.T. Clark (Mahwah, NJ: Paulist Press, 1984), pp. 306–7.

[85]   Edmund Bonner, *Homelies sette forth by the righte reuerende father in God, Edmunde Byshop of London, not onely promised before in his booke, intitled, A necessary doctrine, but also now of late adioyned, and added thereunto, to be read within his diocese of London, of all persons, vicars, and curates, vnto theyr parishioners, vpon sondayes, & holydayes* (London: John Cawodde, 1555), fols 21v–27r.

[86]   *Certayne sermons appointed by the Quenes Maistie, to be declared and read, by all persones, vicars, and curates, euery Sondaye and holy daye in thery churches: and by her Graces aduyse perused & ouer sene, for the better vnderstandyng of the simple people: newly imprinted in partes accordynge as is mencioned in the booke of commune prayers* (London: R.I., 1559).

admonition. There were English homiletic precedents that cited Augustine's example of correcting children even before the Norman Conquest, and in many ways the very essence of much preaching was a clerical response to this charitable imperative.[87] Almsgiving was routinely advocated as a means of countering greed, for example, and so the homily itself was an act of charity on the part of the preacher.[88] Yet considering that the 1547 homily was introduced into a cultural setting with considerable homiletic material addressing duties towards the poor, the spiritual benefits of almsgiving, the poverty of Christ and exemplary acts of charity in the hagiographical tradition, the absence of a specific discussion of charitable compassion or mercy is remarkable. When combined with an extended elaboration of the duty to correct and punish, the seemingly orthodox homily points to the imposition of a forceful logic of loving rule. Although not new in itself, the greater emphasis on magisterial charitable admonition justified reformation to and within each parish, and provided an ideological framework for assisting collaboration and condemning opposition. This same logic of reform worked to support counter-reform, explaining why it also appealed to the Marian restoration, and the Elizabethan settlement.

When read in connection with the nominal installation of poor boxes in 1547, however, the homily of the same year was also clearly intended to help facilitate a shift in contemporary understandings and practices associated with the first portion of the definition of charity (love of God) and of the first office of charity (care for man). The Royal Injunctions could not have been clearer. Priests were to:

> declar[e] unto them [the parishioners], whereas heretofore they have been diligent to bestow much substance, otherwise than God commanded, upon pardons, pilgrimages, trentals, decking of images, offerings of candles, giving to friars, and upon other like blind devotions, they ought at this time to be much more ready to help the poor and needy; knowing that to relieve the poor is a true worshipping of God, required upon pain of everlasting damnation; and that also whatsoever is given for their comfort is given to Christ himself.[89]

Thus the poor box seems to have been used explicitly as a tool for narrowing a wider construction of love of God and love of neighbour, that is, a medieval construction of *caritas*. God could no longer be loved by images and candles. The poor box was also an instrument for focusing other Protestant concerns such as the idea of voluntary poverty (giving to friars), or for promoting a Lutheran sense of justification by faith (pardons, pilgrimages, etc.). Yet this was not

[87]   For Ælfric quoting Augustine, see S. Irvine (ed.), *Old English Homilies from MS Bodley 343*, EETS o.s. 302 (Oxford: Oxford University Press, 1993), p. 44.

[88]   For example, see Stephen Morrison (ed.), *A Late Fifteenth-Century Dominical Sermon Cycle Edited from Bodleian Library MS E MUSAEO 180 and Other Manuscripts*, vol. 1, EETS o.s. 337 (Oxford: Oxford University Press, 2012), p. 139.

[89]   Hughes and Larkin (eds), *Tudor Royal Proclamations*, i, no. 287, p. 401.

quite justification by faith alone, as almsgiving was still 'required upon pain of everlasting damnation', curiously retaining something of the sense of good works.

The early modern parish poor box can therefore be thought of as a useful reforming device, and so naturally it was those who undertook the most reforming that seemed to use it the most. It was a little more Protestant perhaps, but belonged to the reforming milieu of the sixteenth century fairly generally. It was a means of redirecting attention, a change of charity by degree, rather than abandoning the wider conceptual framework. Yet if not exactly marking the precise genesis of a modern construction of charity or definite terminus of the old construction, then we can at least see in the 1547 poor box an indicator of a shift, one where love of God and care for humanity was increasingly to be expressed only in coinage given 'in charity' to the poor.

Why Did the Parish Poor Box Not Remain a Feature of Statutory Parish Relief?

The premise of this question is slightly problematic, because of course the poor box did remain a feature of statutory poor relief, but it was a very minor one, and only for a brief period. As a repository of fines the English parish poor box nominally played a continued role in the structure of the English legal system beyond the liturgical abandonment of the poor box as a primary agent of collection in 1552. According to the provisions of *5&6 Edw.VI.c.2* (1552), a person refusing to be a collector of money for the poor was to forfeit 'twentie shillings to the Allmes box of the poore'.[90] This was a formula retained in 1555, but from 1563 the wording of the statutes abandoned any specific reference to the poor box.[91]

So, while the poor box was seemingly contemplated as corresponding with early forms of parish collecting, it did not specifically feature in the legislation concerned with administering weekly rates for the poor as a part of the collection mechanism. And while being briefly used to fine collectors (possibly further suggesting the box was intended to be a separate fund), the poor box also dropped out of the nominally 'poor relief' legislation entirely. The probable answer to why this may have been so again draws our attention to a potential shift in contemporary constructions of the concept of charity.

Examining medieval theological treatment of the first office of charity (relief for the poor or almsgiving), Tierney noted how medieval theologians were concerned with two aspects of this: firstly, the effect of giving alms on the donor;

---

[90] 5&6 Edward VI, c.2.3, *Statutes of the Realm*, IV, 131; this provision was retained in 1555 with a doubling of the fine: 2&3 Philip & Mary, c.5.3, *Statutes of the Realm*, IV, 280.

[91] 5 Elizabeth I, c.3.3, *Statutes of the Realm*, IV, 411: in 1563, however, the levied fines were to be divided between the churchwardens and 'to thuse and relief of the Poore of the said P[ar]ishe'. This maintained a parochial poor relief focus, but was not explicitly connected to the repository of liturgical collection funds. In 1572, the collector refusing office was subject to a 40s. fine 'to the use of the Poore of the same Place'. See 14 Elizabeth I, c.5.19, *Statutes of the Realm*, IV, 594.

and, secondly, the effect of the alms upon the receiver.[92] While Protestant reformers were not alone in devising mechanisms to reduce beggary or for demanding that people did not live idly by begging, Protestant objections against voluntary poverty made giving alms directly to beggars problematical as each transaction required a judgement of sorts upon the prospective recipient.[93] A poor box resolved this by enabling a person to give alms to 'the poor', while leaving the judgement of recipients to an intermediary. This is not uniquely Protestant, but as with the poor box as a tool of reform, it is easy to see how it might have appealed more to a Protestant charitable ethic.

As already noted, the 1547 English parish poor box explicitly served this purpose of facilitating almsgiving and channelling it to appropriate causes. Yet there is another aspect of the theological background to charity that the poor box can help illuminate: the development of a statutory system of relief itself. Traditionally charity was demanded of the individual and of the Church, both separately and jointly. Very early poor boxes helped the church fulfil this corporate responsibility, but with the conversion of Constantine and the establishment and growth of an institutional church, new mechanisms developed to allow the Church to perform its charitable duties. Tithes, benefactions and other income would support the clergy, and from this a portion was supposed to be used to manifest the Church's care of humanity, and of the poor particularly.[94] Tierney noted how in England this notion was reiterated at a provincial council in 1281, illustrating the perpetuation of the concept of Church responsibility for the poor at the parish level.[95] Yet Tierney also argued that this was disrupted by the process of alienation of Church incomes, particularly to monasteries, who then nominally took on a greater share of the responsibility for the poor.[96]

Despite a traditional downplaying of the amount of charitable output by English monasteries prior to the dissolutions, it is now clear that the monasteries, hospitals and priories of England certainly did provide a significant amount of poor relief.[97] Thus it is true that the development of a statutory system of poor relief was partly driven by a need to replace lost welfare apparatuses, and it is no coincidence that the first statute to that effect (1536) was passed in the same session of Parliament that commenced the first major wave of dissolutions.[98] Beyond the issue of economic need, however, dissolving the monasteries could be argued to

---

[92]   Tierney, p. 49.

[93]   Grimm, p. 225.

[94]   Tierney, p. 78.

[95]   Tierney, pp. 78–9.

[96]   Tierney, p. 79.

[97]   Neil S. Rushton, 'Monastic Charitable Provision', 9–44; Neil S. Rushton and W. Sigle-Rushton, 'Monastic Poor Relief', 193–217; and N.S. Rushton's chapter in this volume, Chapter 6.

[98]   Brodie, pp. 299–302.

have returned the theological charitable imperative of the Church back more fully into the hands of the parish.

A broader argument can be made that the Royal Supremacy and the dissolution of the monasteries together saw a shift in charitable imperative from Church to the new Church-State. So, between 1535 and 1552, weekly collections, poor boxes and liturgical collections developed in tandem to address poor relief. While welfare reform could be said to have been focused on 'order', the development of a state charitable apparatus that had both poor relief and punishment and was frequently centred on the parish and worship, could equally be said to be grounded in a traditional construction of medieval *caritas*. This had always been the responsibility of governors, certainly, but the disestablishment of parts of the church and the establishment of a state church perhaps amplified this sense of responsibility. That the proposed alms box of 1535 was in fact not one, but two boxes highlights this nicely. There was to have been a three-keyed donation box 'to receive such Almes as shalbe geven', and another different box 'called thalmes box', which was a two-keyed repository for money to have been given to the poor.[99] A donation box supplemented a wider charitable programme of cherishing and punishing, clearly stipulated by Henry VIII in a preamble that said 'charitie requyreth that some waie be taken to helpe and socour them that be in such necessite and also to prevent that other shall not herafter fall into like mysery'.[100] Similarly, this seems to have been the intention of the poor box between 1547 and 1552.

But by 1547 a principle of weekly collections for the poor was already established by *27 Hen.VIII.c.25* (1536) which did not necessarily involve a poor box, and was not exclusively focused on the parish. The 1547 poor box was not so much a new development from a welfare standpoint as an attempted regression to a parochial and divine-service-centred form of charitable almsgiving. This was preserved in the liturgy of the Church of England, but the urban-parochial weekly rates that were re-established in 1552 made no use of an alms box for the purposes of collection, and continued undisturbed by the return to Catholicism under Mary, or the renewed Protestantism of Elizabeth I. It seems that the adoption of statutory welfare in 1536 can mark a major shift from 'sacramental' to 'secular' charity in terms of charitable responsibility more than attitude, and then only with the benefit of hindsight and a willingness to see Henry VIII's and Edward VI's regimes as 'secular'. Either way, the broad construction of the notion of charity remained relatively stable.

Yet hints that charity would come to be seen principally as a thing rather than a relational attitude are increasingly evident in the sixteenth century. In 1572 the legislation that regulated weekly collections for the poor ceased referring to the gathered money as 'charitable alms' as it had previously done, and it removed bishops from the process of eliciting money from recalcitrant or unwilling

---

[99] BL, MS Royal 18 C vi, fols 8r–8v, 20r–20v.
[100] BL, MS Royal 18 C vi, fols 2–2v.

contributors as had been the procedure previously.[101] According to the statute of 1552, collectors were annually to 'gentellie aske and demaunde of everie man and woman what they of their charitie wilbe contented to give wekelie'.[102] By 1572 they were to 'by their good discretions taxe and assesse all and every the Inhabitaunts'.[103] The 1572 statute did, however, refer to the collections as 'charitable Worcke' and to the collection as 'charitable a Deede' when providing for putting non-contributors in gaol, but in 1601 the language of that portion of the statute had dropped the 'charitable' part also.[104] Traditionally, poor relief historians have seen in all of this an increasing compulsion to contribute to these collections, but this author has elsewhere argued that it most likely reflects procedural changes in the legislation itself, particularly those that bear on the parish no longer being the unit of collection in 1572.[105] It also points to a growing conceptual division between the still 'charitable' individual liturgical almsgiving, and the state provision for and reform of the poor funded by weekly rates. At least in the language of statute law, 'charity' gradually ceased to be associated with what was fed into this system.

A Final Donation

The absence of a strong contemporary culture of poor box usage, which led the Queen's Bench of 1846 to discuss the origin and ownership of the poor box at Oundle, stemmed from a combination of factors. In 1547 many parishes dutifully established poor boxes, or made existing poor boxes conform to regulations. Many parishes, however, clearly did not do so. In 1549, the idea of congregants directly putting money into poor boxes during divine service was used to narrow the construction of charitable almsgiving, but in 1552 whatever poor boxes existed were relegated to repositories for those in-service collections. In the same year, statutory collections were re-established with clear mechanisms that did not involve poor box use. When the revised liturgy of 1662 replaced poor boxes with basins, it probably at least partly reflects a reality that poor boxes were insufficiently common and thus indicates what may have been happening in many parishes anyway.

This still leaves us with the problem of the 84th Canon of 1604. Why, when poor boxes were clearly no longer central to the liturgy and apparently often lacking, would they be required of English parishes? The answer may rest on the theology of charity in a broadly Protestant sense: a Protestant ethic of charity, if you will. Essentially, the presence of a poor box was not purely about almsgiving as such, or

---

[101]   14 Elizabeth I, c.5.16, *Statutes of the Realm*, IV, 590–98.
[102]   5&6 Edward VI, c.2.2, *Statutes of the Realm*, IV, 131.
[103]   14 Elizabeth I, c.5.16, *Statutes of the Realm*, IV, 593.
[104]   14 Elizabeth I, c.5.21, *Statutes of the Realm*, IV, 594; 43 Elizabeth I, c.2.2, *Statutes of the Realm,* IV, 963.
[105]   Brodie, pp. 283–4.

correcting vice, although both were charitable tasks. Rather, it was charity as love of God, which, for many reformers, could not be expressed by certain things or in certain ways. A prominent poor box was supposed to be a visual argument against images, pardons, pilgrimages, candles and so on.

But the new logic of poor box placement and use should not be uncritically considered a determinant of new presence or prior absence. After all, in the late sixteenth century, Portuguese Catholics established contact with Christians living in Kerala on the west coast of India, closely paralleling the timing of the 84th Canon. At the Synod of Diamper (1599) that sought to establish communion between the Indian Christians and the Catholic Church, one of the decrees issued concerned poor boxes. The decree reveals the existence of poor boxes, confirming an ancient continuity in Christian practice, but also that poor boxes needed closer attention because they were subject to robbery.[106] Perhaps the Oundle box's inscription to 'Remember the Poor', apparently common amongst the few surviving ancient poor boxes, would have been better served by another scriptural imperative: 'Thou shalt not steal.'

---

[106] M. Geddes (ed.), *The History of the Church of Malabar* (London: Smith, Walford, 1694), p. 372.

Chapter 12

Hearing the Poor: Experiencing the Sounds of Charity in Early Modern England

Dolly MacKinnon

There were near 800 boys and girls, so decently clad, cleanly lodged, so wholesomely fed, so admirably taught ... They sung a psalm before they sat down to supper in the Great Hall to an organ which played all the time with such a cheerful harmony that it seemed to me a vision of angels.[1]

John Evelyn, Christ's Hospital, 10 March 1687

This chapter focuses on the sounds of thanksgiving offered up by the poor to the ears of audiences in early modern England, through an analysis of the surviving musical print psalm settings specifically composed for charitable institutions. In contrast to the traditional image of fundraising for poor charitable institutions typified by professional composers and musicians from the eighteenth century, and the omission by historians of any analysis of the sounds of thanksgiving, I want to consider these printed musical psalm settings as an alternative perspective on the sorts of sounds the poor made in early modern society. Focusing on England in the seventeenth century, this chapter shows that while the sounds of the poor through charity psalms became more pronounced in the Protestant nation during the mid-seventeenth century, this tradition also reflected a continuity in the public demonstrations of London charity dating back to the fourteenth century, well before the English Reformation.

Yet the experience from the perspective of the poor remains the least explored aspect of early modern poverty and the most elusive, apart from the ground-breaking forays into this realm by Patricia Crawford, Stephanie Tarbin, Janette Bright, Gillian Clark and John Styles.[2] So rather than turning our gaze towards 'charity', what I propose to do here is retune our ears to hear the significance of

---

[1] John Evelyn, cited in Susi Jeans, 'The Easter Psalms', 45–60 (pp. 54–5).

[2] Patricia Crawford, *Parents of Poor Children 1580–1800* (Oxford: Oxford University Press, 2010); Stephanie Tarbin, 'Caring for Poor and Fatherless Children in London, *c.* 1350–1550', *Journal of the History of Childhood and Youth*, 3 (2010), 391–410; John Styles, *Threads of Feeling: The London Foundling Hospital's Textile Tokens, 1740–1770* (London: Foundling Hospital Museum, 2010); Janette Bright and Gillian Clark, *An Introduction to the Tokens at the Foundling Museum* (London: Foundling Hospital Museum, 2011).

these psalms sung by the poor as part of their role in the public acts of reciprocity that accompanied charitable giving, and that required their vocal articulation of gratitude. I then seek to tease out evidence of the aspects of these sounds of charity recorded in contemporary accounts, concentrating on seventeenth-century experiences of the poor children involved in musical thanksgiving with the intention of prompting new charitable acts. I offer a new trajectory, on the auditory realm of charitable practices both experienced and generated by the poor and heard across early modern cities and towns in seventeenth-century Protestant England. This chapter also demonstrates that the sounds of charity are not a unique element of English charity, but a feature of early modern Europe.

Historiography of the Forms of English Charity

The substantial existing research on charity in England has elucidated our understandings of the poor in medieval and early modern urban and, to a lesser extent, rural settings, by outlining the processes of charitable giving through the practicalities of governance and administration, as well as individual donor motivations. Much has been written about medieval and early modern English charity, with the leading works in the field including those by W.K. Jordan, Miri Rubin, P.H. Cullum and Steve Hindle.[3] These works have largely set the orthodox theoretical and practical trajectories of the studies that followed. More recently, innovative scholarship utilising new sources in terms of material culture demonstrates that there is a cultural and sensory landscape of charity that also needs to be considered. For the medieval period the work by Sheila Sweetinburgh, my own work for early modern rural English charity clothing and John Styles, Janette Bright and Gillian Clark's work on the textile tokens from the eighteenth-century London Foundling Hospital, all demonstrate that useful new sources for examining charitable activities also lie beyond administrative and economic accounts of charitable distributions.[4] Acts of charity, redolent with reciprocity,

---

[3]   For example, see the works of W.K. Jordan, *The Charities of Rural England 1480–1660: The Aspirations and Achievements of the Rural Society* (London: Allen and Unwin, 1961); Miri Rubin, *Charity and Community*; P.H. Cullum, '"And hir name was Charities": Charitable Giving by and for Women in Late Medieval Yorkshire', in P.J.P. Goldberg (ed.), *Women in Medieval English Society* (Stroud: Sutton, 1997), pp. 182–211; Sara Mendelson and Patricia Crawford, *Women in Early Modern England* (Oxford: Clarendon Press, 1998); and Steve Hindle, *On the Parish?*.

[4]   Sheila Sweetinburgh, 'Clothing the Naked' pp. 109–22; Dolly MacKinnon, '"Charity is worth it when it looks that good": Rural Women and Bequests of Clothing in Early Modern England', in Stephanie Tarbin and Susan Broomhall (eds), *Women, Identities and Communities in Early Modern Europe* (Aldershot: Ashgate, 2008), pp. 79–93; Styles; Bright and Clark; Dolly MacKinnon, 'Charitable Bodies: Clothing as Charity in Early-Modern England', in Megan Cassidy-Welch and Peter Sherlock (eds), *Practices of Gender in Late Medieval and Early Modern Europe* (Turnhout: Brepols, 2008), pp. 235–59.

were not performed in silence by either the benefactors or the recipients. Therefore the existing historiography needs to be expanded to include a range of historical sources that move beyond the confines of just the textual.

Until recently, the best-known event for fundraising endeavours for orphans was George Frideric Handel's *Messiah* (1741), an oratorio based on a biblical story with the text set in English, performed during Lent, a time when the opera houses were shut and the singers and musicians were not in paid employment. Given the prevalence of opera audiences keen to avail themselves of any source of recitative, aria and chorus, biblical stories presented to them as oratorios offered a suitable alternative form of music which they could listen to with a clear conscience. Therefore Handel's oratorio raised considerable funds for Foundling Hospitals in the eighteenth century.[5] But Handel was one in a long line of musicians connected with and employed by the City of London charitable institutions that used music not only as a fundraiser for the poor, but also as a form of spiritual employment in the godly education of orphans. For example, in the sixteenth and seventeenth centuries the thanksgiving musical performances and fundraising concerts had traditionally utilised the skills of the young charitable charges and the music masters of Christ's Hospital. In 1560, Henry Machyn described how, on:

> The third day of April went unto St Mary Spital unto the sermon all the masters and rulers and schoolmasters and mistresses and all the children, both men and women children, all in blue coats and wenches in blue frocks and with escutcheons embroidered on their sleeves with the arms of London and red capes. And so two and two together. And every man in his place and office. And so at the hospital was made of timber and covered with canvas and sets one above another, for all the children sit one above another like steps. And after through London.[6]

The same year he also made note of the musical sounds he heard:

> The seventeenth day of March did preach at Paul's Cross Veron, parson of St. Martin at Ludgate. And there was my lord mayor and the masters, the aldermen,

---

[5]   This musical association is a feature of the Foundling Hospital Museum Exhibition in London today.

[6]   'The iij day of aprełł whent vnto saynt mare spytyłł onto yᵉ sermon ałł yᵉ masterſ & rularſ & skollmasturſ & mastoreſ & ałł yᵉ chylderyn boyth men & vomen chylderyn ałł in plue cot{s} & wēssyſ in blue ffrokeſ & wᵗ skoychyonſ in brodered on ther sleuyſ wᵗ yᵉ armeſ of london & red capeſ & so ij & ij geder & evere man in yſ plasse & offeſ & so at yᵉ spyttyłł waſ mad of tymbur & coverd wᵗ canueſ & set{s} on a boyſſ a nodur for ałł yᵉ chylderyn syttyn on a boyſſ a nodur lyke stepeſ & aft- thrug london', cited in *A London Provisioner's Chronicle, 1550–1563, by Henry Machyn: Manuscript, Transcription, and Modernization*, (eds) Richard W. Bailey, Marilyn Miller and Colette Moore, fol. 17r, online edition hosted by Michigan Publishing at <http://quod.lib.umich.edu/m/machyn> [accessed 3 January 2013].

with many more people. And after the sermon had ended, they sang, all old and young, a psalm in meter, the tune of Geneva-wise.[7]

Young and old voices were raised as one by the steady, regular metre of Reformed Protestantism, where the psalm was designed to include and unite the godly. Therefore the children's singing was intended to fulfil this primary aim. The quality of the children's singing would have been favourable when compared with the variable attempts of parish psalm singing reflected in contemporary accounts which describe such efforts as 'uncouth and discordant': 'what whinning, toting, yelling, or screeking there is in many country Congregations'.[8] As Christopher Marsh points out, 'psalm singing was almost wholly a spiritual exercise', therefore the actual quality of the sounds produced was incidental to the primary motivation for singing.[9]

Opportunities for analysis lie not only in the realm of material culture (including musical instruments), but also in the evidence of the sonorous and auditory realms that survive in printed musical psalm settings issued by charitable institutions, together with the reception histories of these performances found in the diary accounts of audience members. Only the printed settings intended for the purposes of fundraising for the four Royal Hospitals in London survive: St Thomas's Hospital, Christ's Hospital, Bridewell and St Bartholomew's Hospital. The practice of providing printed psalm settings only ceased in 1863. Tackling the traces of the ways in which the poor, in singing, experienced these collective sounds of charity, and audiences responded to the effect of these group performances of the sounds of piety, then forms the basis of this analysis. My intention is to demonstrate how the godly sounds of music were understood to provide a vehicle through which God could reach the souls of individual women, men and children from every level of early modern society. Music was understood to be especially efficacious when used with orphaned children as it could reform and redeem the soul, by bringing those deemed spiritually lost back into the fold of Christian worship.[10] Music formed part of the provisions of a godly household,

---

[7]   'The xvij day of marche dyd pryche at powll{s} cross veron psun off sant marttenſ att ludgatt & ther waſ my lord mare & ye masturſ yᵉ altthermen wᵗ mony more pepull & aft-yᵉ Smon done they songe all old & yonge a ssalme in myter yᵉ tune of genevay wayſ', cited in *London Provisioner's Chronicle*, (eds) Bailey, Miller and Moore, fol. 120v.

[8]   Christopher Marsh, *Music and Society in Early Modern England* (Cambridge: Cambridge University Press, 2010), pp. 419–20.

[9]   Marsh, p. 419.

[10]   The link between music's power to influence body and soul is discussed in the following works: Penelope Gouk, 'Music, Melancholy, and Medical Spirits in Early Modern Thought', in Peregrine Horden (ed.), *Music as Medicine: The History of Music Therapy since Antiquity* (Aldershot: Ashgate, 2000), pp. 173–94; Dolly MacKinnon, '"The Trustworthy Agency of the Eyes": Reading Images of Music and Madness in Historical Context', *Health and History*, 5.2 (2003), 123–49 (esp. pp. 129–31); Marsh, p. 447.

where the charitable institution acted as a surrogate father in the model of the godly patriarchal household.[11]

Early Modern European Precedents for the Use of Music and Charity

What little work has been done hitherto on the function of music in charitable institutions is to be found in musicological studies, individual institutional histories and local or national accounts of charitable practices before the Reformation period. This compartmentalisation of historical analysis has created studies that adhere to a sharp break before or after the Reformation in English historiography regarding charitable practices. Any study of music and charity then slips between the traditional disciplinary silos that render certain sources such as musical compositions and performances the domain of musicology, while charity remains the preserve of historical inquiry. Musicology also uses artificial categorisations of music such as classical (also termed art music) or popular music, creating, much as in literature, a canon of musical works that then ranks certain classical works and certain individual composers as important, and a similar canon for popular music considered separately.

Most recently the historian Christopher Marsh has, for early modern England, demonstrated the power and prevalence of different forms of music and their functions in early modern society, showing that music was to be found everywhere in society. In his study, Marsh broke the overriding dominance of the musicological tradition of researching only art music found in the court, church and elite homes, to the exclusion of the popular music of the streets.[12] Samuel Pepys's ballad collection, for example, shows an eclectic musical reality ranging from the sacred to the profane, something not reflected in academic categorisations. My own work on music-making in the Scottish elite households identified and analysed valuable yet under-utilised sources such as music manuscripts, evidence of household musicians, material culture including wall paintings and musical instruments showing signs of wear from use, to demonstrate the role of music tutors in family music-making within early modern Scottish households after the Scottish Reformation in 1560.[13]

---

[11]   Robert Clever and John Dod, *A Godly Forme of Household Government: for the Ordering of Private Families According to the direction of God's Word* (London: T. Mann, 1630), p. vi; Anon., *Festival Hymns for the Use of the Blew and Green Coat Boys, of the Charity-School [Reading]* (Reading: David Kinnier, 1723); Marsh, p. 447.

[12]   Marsh, pp. 1–31.

[13]   Dolly MacKinnon, "'I now have a book of songs of her writing": Scottish Families, Orality, Literacy and the Transmission of Musical Culture *c*. 1500–*c*. 1800', in Elizabeth Ewan and Janay Nugent (eds), *Finding the Family in Medieval and Early Modern Scotland* (Aldershot: Ashgate, 2008), pp. 35–48.

It is important to remember that music's purpose and function for both the Protestant and Roman Catholic churches was to promote spiritual benefit and engagement, even though the forms of music used by each differed vastly. Intimate performances of religious music within the household became either a way of supporting the Protestant Reformation, or an act of agency for some by reclaiming at least a domestic place for Roman Catholicism. Cheryl Nixon's analysis of eighteenth-century Scottish daily accounts of Protestant orphans' activities also found these involved 'reading, writing, arithmetic, religious singing, and memorising the catechism'.[14]

The historiography for early modern Europe regarding the sounds generated by the poor in both Roman Catholic and Protestant contexts is far richer than that for England, and offers examples of practices that have resonances in English contexts not yet explored. Joel Francis Harrington's study of foundlings, orphans and juvenile criminals in early modern Germany (or the German lands) identified the Protestant preoccupation with reforming the 'immorality on the streets' that emanated from orphaned girls and boys 'singing "shameless" and "worldly" songs"'.[15] The rehabilitation of orphans once inside the institutions actively involved music making. For Roman Catholic Italy, Nicholas Terpstra examined the practice of orphaned boys singing at important religious festivals at shrines, as well as at funeral processions, important rites of passage within early modern Roman Catholic society.[16] During the eighteenth century, the composer Antonio Vivaldi (the red priest) was *Maestro di violino* at the *Pio Ospedale della Pietà*, the orphanage for girls in Venice, and the works by Vivaldi we are all familiar with today were composed for, and ably performed by, these poor female orphan musicians. These concerts, like all public performances by the children of charitable institutions, raised much-needed funds, but also reflected a spiritual dimension, where piety, conformity and a reformation of the character through music was attainable. These performances additionally demonstrated the musical accomplishments of these young women, skills that were thought to improve their marriage and employment prospects.[17]

---

[14]   Cheryl Nixon, *The Orphan in Eighteenth-Century Law and Literature: Estate, Blood, and Body* (Farnham: Ashgate, 2011), pp. 245–6.

[15]   Joel Francis Harrington, *The Unwanted Child: The Fate of Foundlings, Orphans, and Juvenile Criminals in Early Modern Germany* (Chicago: University of Chicago Press, 2009), pp. 141–2.

[16]   Nicholas Terpstra, *Abandoned Children of the Italian Renaissance: Orphan Care in Florence and Bologna* (Baltimore, MD: Johns Hopkins University Press, 2005).

[17]   Jane L. Baldauf-Berdes, 'Anna Maria della Pietà: The Woman Musician of Venice Personified', in Susan C. Cook and Judy S. Tsou (eds), *Cecilia Reclaimed: Feminist Perspectives on Gender and Music* (Urbana: University of Illinois Press, 1994), pp. 134–55; Nixon, pp. 245–6.

Psalms, Protestantism and Early Modern English Charity

As Stephanie Tarbin has concluded in the context of medieval and early modern London, and citing the work of Marjorie K. McIntosh, 'the origins of the sixteenth-century developments in welfare' were to be found in the 'practices of local communities dating back to the fourteenth and fifteenth centuries'.[18] What is more, as Tarbin highlights, it was the 'compulsory contributions and parochial administration of charity' that 'were the distinctive features of the evolving national system of poor relief in England'.[19] Those distinctive features for Protestant English charity after 1558 also incorporated the modified ancient practices of Roman Catholic charitable giving – both as individual acts as well as collective acts – reconfigured into the ongoing reformation of the Protestant national charitable project. Yet common to both Roman Catholic and Protestant communities within the war-torn early modern Europe of the seventeenth century was the institutional care of poor and destitute children. Early modern Roman Catholic and Protestant institutions alike set out to care for orphaned poor children and were united in their realisation of the potential benefits of providing religious education to their charges, and regularly providing musical performances to local communities in order to fill their institutional coffers.

Beliefs about the power of music were prevalent. For example, Robert Burton in *The Anatomy of Melancholy* (1621) professed that different types of music had healing properties, and when prescribed in moderation for ailments such as melancholy could provide a soothing atmosphere, or equally, an unsuitable atmosphere.[20] The Church recognised the power of music, severely frowning upon the effects of popular music, but also utilising psalms as a vehicle through which to reach the soul. As Christopher Marsh has demonstrated, 'between 1560 and 1600, a succession of moralists and godly authors warned that music could all too easily become the servant of Satan, corrupting and destroying the minds of listeners'.[21] As I have written elsewhere, this was only possible because of the ongoing belief that music has the power to enter the ear and effect a change, either for good or evil, in the listener.[22] Peregrine Horden has demonstrated that in writings from antiquity, as well as from the medieval and early modern worlds, music was understood to

---

[18] Marjorie K. McIntosh, 'Local Responses', 209–45; Tarbin, pp. 391–410.

[19] Tarbin, pp. 391–410.

[20] Robert Burton, *The Anatomy of Melancholy*, (eds) Nicolas Kiessling, Thomas Faulkner and Rhonda Blair, 3 vols (Oxford: Clarendon Press, 1990), II, 112–16.

[21] Marsh, p. 33.

[22] MacKinnon, '"The Trustworthy Agency of the Eyes"', pp. 123–49 (esp. pp. 129–30); Dolly MacKinnon, '"Poor Senseless Bess, Clothed in her Rags and Folly": Early Modern Women, Madness, and Song in Seventeenth-Century England', *Parergon*, 18.3 (2001), 119–51; Dolly MacKinnon, 'Music, Madness, and the Body: Symptom and Cure', in Sander L. Gilman (ed.), *Mind and Body in the History of Psychiatry*, Special Issue of *History of Psychiatry*, 17.1 (2006), 9–21.

be medicinal when combined with prayer, and could combat Satan's influence, as the often cited and well-known examples from antiquity and the Bible, such as David and Saul, attest.[23] Martin West, quoting a passage in the *Timaeus*, shows how Plato demonstrates that 'different kinds of music' affected the 'emotions and the character of the listener'. Hence, in education it was imperative to use only the right kinds of music, in this instance the specific modes of the Dorian and Phrygian, to ensure a spiritual harmony: 'Attunement … having motions akin to the circuits in our soul, has been given by the Muses to the intelligent user of the arts not for mindless pleasure, as is fashionable to assume, but as an aid to bringing our soul-circuit, when it has got out of tune, into order and harmony with itself.'[24] These understandings of the interaction of the music of the spheres dominated early modern thought. If music was used on God's errand then it was also recognised as capable of great effects, as an anonymous eighteenth-century Scottish writer observed, reworking his reading of Romans 10. 17 and Galatians 3. 2–5 towards the power of music as he understood it: 'Hearing is the sense of diseypline & inlet of faith. Faith cometh by hearing + hearing be the word of God whither read[,] spoken or sung.'[25]

The utilisation of music by institutions, and more specifically musical performances by their young charges, could elicit charitable donations from individuals within society. As Susi Jeans observed in the case of the Christ's Hospital psalms sung by poor children as 'part of the Easter Ceremonies of the City of London', this tradition dates back to the fourteenth century.[26] The musical performances accompanied the five sermons preached over Easter at the two different locations of St Paul's Cross and Spital Cross within London. The Good Friday sermon preached at St Paul's Cross was on the topic of Christ's Passion. The three sermons at Spital Cross centred on the topic of the Resurrection and were preached on Easter Monday, Tuesday and Wednesday respectively. The fifth and final sermon preached at St Paul's Cross offering a summation of the preceding four sermons was preached on the Sunday after Easter.[27] The Christ's Hospital

---

[23]   King James Bible (1611), 1 Samuel 16. 23; Peregrine Horden (ed.), *Music as Medicine: The History of Music Therapy since Antiquity* (Aldershot: Ashgate, 2000), pp. 1–4, 43–50, 103–8, 147–53.

[24]   Martin West, 'Music Therapy in Antiquity', in Horden (ed.), *Music as Medicine*, pp. 51–68 (p. 59).

[25]   MacKinnon, '"I have now a book of songs of her writing"', p. 43, citing National Archives Scotland GD18/4015 manuscript 'On musick agst reading …', 1709, reproduced by permission of Sir Robert Clerk Penicuik, Bt; King James Bible (1611), Romans 10. 17: 'So then faith *cometh* by hearing and hearing by the word of God'; Galatians 3. 2–5: 'This only would I learn of you, Received ye the Spirit by the works of law, or by the hearing of faith?'

[26]   Jeans, p. 46.

[27]   Jeans, p. 46.

children sang at the Spital Cross during the seventeenth century in the open air, as the old Priory of St Mary Spital was no longer standing by the sixteenth century.[28]

Audiences responded positively to these performances held on feast days, at funerals or at special commemorative concerts, and the sights and sounds of reformed godly children loosened the purse strings of many a benefactor. As Mark Michael Smith has concluded in his recent work *Sensing the Past*, in the 'early modern period sound increasingly mediated and helped inform ideas about class, identity and nationalism'.[29] To Smith's list, I would add piety and charity. Within early modern Europe more broadly, as well as England more specifically, the religious tensions that erupted into civil-religious wars were as much to do with the sounds (words and music) of worship as they were to do with the rituals and visual codes of theological adherence to certain forms of Protestantism or Reformed Catholicism after the Reformation that broke unevenly across Europe and the British Isles.[30] That musical charity forms part of this is an important point to raise here.

Experiencing the Sounds of Charity

In the remainder of this chapter, I consider why it was that certain forms of music were understood in the early modern world to have a spiritual and physical efficacy for both performers and audiences. Here the experience of charity by the poor has an auditory component, something that is missing from the existing literature on early modern English charity. Printed musical psalm settings proclaimed the good works of the charitable institutions' endeavours towards the poor. They also demonstrated the pious effects not only on those deserving poor girls and boys who sang those psalms, but also on those audiences that listened to and heard the music.

Instead of using readily available printed common psalm tunes, where the same piece of music was used to accompany multiple psalm texts, the charitable institutions set their texts to original musical compositions that were similar in form to the common tune with a new piece commissioned most years.[31] In addition to the financial gains from selling the single printed sheets of words and music, these

---

[28]   Jeans, p. 46.

[29]   Mark Michael Smith, *Sensing the Past: Seeing, Hearing, and Smelling, Tasting and Touching History* (Berkeley: University of California Press, 2007), p. 48.

[30]   Dolly MacKinnon, 'From "Shameless" and "worldly songs" to a "vocal tribute" to "Sing their Praises": The Contested Soundscapes of Early Modern Poor Children', unpublished paper presented at Philippa Maddern and Stephanie Tarbin (convenors), Material Worlds of Childhood Symposium, The University of Western Australia, 2012.

[31]   Common tunes were published in England by Thomas Sternhold and John Hopkins in *The Whole Book of Psalms* (London: John Day, 1562) from 1562 onwards, and these tunes were based on earlier Genevan settings. To accommodate particular English tastes new common tunes were developed; for a discussion of this, see Marsh, pp. 412–13.

ephemeral psalm settings also demonstrated the effects of music on the soul, the collective ability of music to instil order and obedience in these orphaned children and the power of collective singing to act as a form of individual redemption, where ungodly children proved redeemable.

What emerged, then, was the poor, not simply acting and singing as puppets at the behest of their institutional and individual benefactors in order to raise funds for the institution, but also demonstrating their agency and musical abilities. The children's collective singing in unison demonstrated their compliance and obedience within the institutional establishment that fulfilled the role of surrogate father. This performance also demonstrated a reformation of character in which the ungodly and ungoverned children were integrated back into an ordered and godly society. Their performance of thanksgiving and gratitude was reflected in the texts they sang and through the steady and simple harmonic structure of the psalm's musical setting they vocalised. These performances also had an emotional resonance, positive, negative or a combination of the two, triggered by memory and music-making for those performers involved; and, in turn, these pious sounds may have elicited emotional responses from some potential benefactors in the audience. For example, in 1687 on hearing the Christ's Hospital children, John Evelyn described his response to their performance in terms of his sense of 'the cheerful harmony' and the sight of the orphaned children appearing as a 'vision of angels'.[32] The emotional effect on Evelyn of children performing the charity thanksgiving psalms was achieved by their ability to learn a series of musical skills that may well have been beyond the musical abilities of many of their social superiors in the audience. To all intents and purposes these children were redeemed, as in Evelyn's 'vision of angels'. This no doubt carried a particular cachet and confirmed for some of the audience a perception of godly music as having a divine quality and the power to work miracles on the spiritual and physical well-being of the person. Contemporaries understood that different sorts of music caused different effects on the performer or listener. John Playford commented on the appropriateness of 'Psalms of Prayer and Confession, to solme grave Flat tunes' and 'Psalms of Thanksgiving and Praise, to lively cheerful Sharp Tunes'.[33] For example, a hymn sung in the early eighteenth century in commemoration of the benefactors and founders of the Reading Charity School of 'Blew and Green Coats' had the children proclaiming:

> In Garb distinguish'd, let us joyn
> In Symphony and Hymns Divine!
> To Sing their Praises and prepare
> To follow them whose Badge, we wear.[34]

---

[32]   John Evelyn, cited in Jeans, p. 55.

[33]   John Playford, *Whole Book of Psalms*, preface, cited in Marsh, p. 419.

[34]   Anon., *Festival Hymns for the Use of the Blew and Green Coat Boys*, p. 6; MacKinnon, 'Charitable Bodies', p. 255.

Poor children who were fatherless, even if their mother still lived, were understood to be all the more deprived and to be pitied. Therefore, orphaned children who raised their voices in song were publicly affirming that these charitable institutions had provided them with a model of a godly family, with the administrative paternalistic institution acting as a saviour and surrogate father for the orphaned children.[35] Their voices sang 'In joyful Songs, Let ORPHANS pay, | Their vocal Tribute to this Day; | which does, while they Obedient live, | The fatherless a Father give'.[36] The reciprocity involved the obedience owed by a child to the father of the godly household, and implicit in this public performance is the children's tribute to the institutional patriarchal symbol that sponsored their spiritual and corporal welfare.

Most often the printed words, but not the music, survive for many early modern ballads and psalms, making the performance of the printed musical psalm no longer possible. Yet the tangible printed and manuscript music for some of the charity psalms of thanksgiving performances are extant. These surviving examples of printed ephemera relating to the Easter services for the City of London provide another important recoverable aspect of the performances of charity and reciprocity, one the existing historiography has not recognised. The more ornate printed psalms were also accompanied by a printed account of the state of the four institutions: Christ's Hospital, St Thomas's Hospital, Bridewell and St Bartholomew's Hospital.[37] Susi Jeans suggests that those printed broadsheets with both the psalm and the annual account can be attributed to the Easter Monday service.[38] For example, for Christ's Hospital London, printed psalms (words and music) were published from as early as 1610 for a period of over 250 years.[39] We know that in 1676 William Godbid was paid £14 4s. for the 'Printing of the Spittle Psalmes', and that in 1680 the Hospital paid for '16 Reame [480 sheets per ream] of paper for the Spittle Psalmes' which Jeans calculates was enough to print '7,680 Easter Psalms'.[40] Allowing that some of these Psalm sheets would have been handed gratis to some of the audience members, the majority of sheets represented a large potential income considering the quantity printed. Here the performance of charity moved beyond the confines of the Easter service performances at St Paul's Cross and Spital Cross into the godly homes of early modern urban and rural England, as the printed Psalm sheets could be purchased and carried into households near and far. In 1560, Henry Machyn recorded that over 20,000 attended the service at Spital Cross that was held in the open air.[41] In this way, the

---

[35] MacKinnon, 'Charitable Bodies', p. 256.

[36] Anon., *Festival Hymns*, p. 13; MacKinnon, 'Charitable Bodies', p. 255.

[37] Jeans, p. 50.

[38] Jeans, p. 50.

[39] Jeans, p. 46.

[40] Jeans, p. 55.

[41] Jeans, p. 47.

reformation of orphaned children enabled the godly poor to act as a model of piety for other early modern individuals, including children, within households.

Poor children's musical performances, then, form another substantial and integral feature, not only of the effects of a gift of charity, but also of the educational opportunities (including music and musicianship) offered to poor children with the ultimate aim of reclaiming orphaned children as godly and employable members of the early modern communities within society. Reformed Protestant societies targeted the vice and immorality to be heard from the mouths of orphans and the poor in the streets of cities, towns and villages, aiming to replace this ungodly noise with suitable sounds of piety.[42] Poor children were considered redeemable. The sounds of pious music-making emanating from the vocal chords of these orphaned children combated the lascivious, corrupting and far-reaching sounds of popular music that ravaged the soul. The poor, and poor children especially, needed to hear godly sounds, for as one seventeenth-century pamphlet lamented, the main problem was that 'Bawdy Ballads, or an idle Song are these idle peoples greatest paines, where they make many more idle then themselves, and there I leave these idle people, who might be better imployed, if they were better looked unto'.[43] Singing bawdy ballads was also a way for the poor, including children, to earn money through busking. Philip Stubbes in 1583 considered most forms of popular music were 'inticements to wantoness and sin'.[44] Suitable godly alternatives were needed to combat ungodly sounds.

What is also not recognised fully in the existing literature regarding the poor is that the provision of a musical education offered yet another potential employment avenue for certain poor children, especially those who were blind. In early modern cultural histories of music both Christopher Marsh and I have identified that some poor children were being taught to read and write 'pricksonge' (musical notation), as well as learning to sing or play a musical instrument, while others were offered other trades.[45] Many institutions, both urban and rural, offered poor children education in the skills of reading and writing, with the aim of providing them with yet another useful form of training that would render them self-sufficient and capable of regular employment. For example, the 1557 Ordinances and Rules for the Hospitals for the City of London indicated, for those children admitted, 'that suche of the children as be pregnant and very apt to learning, be reserved and kept in the grammar-schole, in the hope of preferment to the Vniversities; where they may be vertuously educated, and in time become learned and good members in

---

42   MacKinnon, 'From "Shameless" and "worldly songs"'.

43   M.S., *The Poore Orphans Court, or Orphans Cry* (London, 1636), fols Br–Bv.

44   Philip Stubbes, *The Anatomie of Abuses* (London: John Kingston for Richard Jones, 1583), preface, cited in Marsh, p. 32.

45   Dolly MacKinnon, 'From Monarch to Milkmaid: Women and Musical Literacy in Britain 1500–1800', unpublished paper, 24th National Conference of the Musicological Society of Australia, The University of Melbourne, April 2001 (available open access at Academia.edu.au); Marsh, p. 9.

the commonweale'.[46] That music was part of this process is indicated by the fact that the children at Christ's Hospital were being taught music, as the Hospital had employed 'a teacher of Pricksonge' from as early as 1553, the year after Edward VI founded the four London Hospitals: St Thomas's Hospital, Christ's Hospital, Bridewell and St Bartholomew's Hospital.[47] According to Marsh, by the seventeenth century, for example, at Christ's Hospital, London, 'precise arrangements varied under the influence of new masters and successive benefactors ... [and] a small minority of the young inmates were taught to read music and play instruments, while the majority of children learned to sing'.[48] Early modern understandings of music's ability to move the spirit and reform the child were clear. As Susi Jeans elaborates, the endowments for the musical teaching at Christ's Hospital came from Robert Dow, a wealthy London merchant who left funds in an indenture dated 7 February 1609 specifically for the musical education of the poor.[49] The year after this endowment, the first surviving printed psalm setting (words and music) appeared on the London streets. What is more, Dow provided £80 to fund the purchase of virginals and a bass viol, and the maintenance of those instruments for the instruction of three or four children at Christ's Hospital.[50]

Christ's Hospital's most successful recipient of a musical education, and Dow's bequests, was the child Thomas Brewer (1611–60). Brewer, since his admission in *c*. 1614 at the age of three, had been an inmate and received his entire education until 1626 under the auspices of Christ's Hospital. The music masters at this time were Thomas Ravenscroft and John Farrant. In 1626, Brewer was 'apprenticed to Thomas Warner'.[51] In 1638, Brewer returned as the 'song-schoolmaster' at Christ's Hospital remaining until 1641, when he was discharged for marrying, which was in breach of his employment terms as Dow's bequest required music masters to be bachelors. Brewer was also dismissed for 'various misdemeanours' he had committed.[52] After 1641 he earned his keep by ably teaching members of the gentry to play the viol, and also composing songs, some of which survive

---

[46]   *Memoranda, References and Documents Relating to the Royal Hospitals of the City of London* (London: Arthur Taylor, for the Committee of Common Council, 1836), p. 90.

[47]   Tarbin, pp. 391–410.

[48]   Marsh, p. 9.

[49]   *Further Report of the Commissioners for Inquiring concerning Charities* (London: H.M.S.O., 1840), pp. 109–10.

[50]   Jeans, p. 48.

[51]   Julia Gasper, 'Brewer, Thomas (1611–*c*. 1660)', *Oxford Dictionary of National Biography* (Oxford: Oxford University Press, 2004), online edition at <http://www.oxforddnb.com> [accessed 28 December 2012] (hereafter *DNB*); MacKinnon, '"I now have a book of songs of her writing"', pp. 35–48; Ian Spink, 'Brewer, Thomas', *Grove Music Online. Oxford Music Online* (Oxford: Oxford University Press) online at <http://www.oxfordmusiconline.com> [accessed 28 December 2012].

[52]   Spink.

copied into the music books of his educational charges.[53] Working in the Norfolk household of Sir Nicholas Lestrange, he was described by his employer:

> Thom: Brewer, my Mus: servant, through his Pronenesse to good-Fellowshippe, having attaind to a very Rich and Rubicund Nose; being reproved by a Friend for his too frequent use of strong Drinkes and Sacke; as very Pernicious to that Distemper and Inflammation in his Nose – Nay, faith, says he, if it will not endure sacke, it's no Nose for me.[54]

Brewer's liking for 'strong Drinkes and Sacke' clearly sat at odds with the godly intentions of his institutional upbringing, but it may also hint at an endeavour on his part to mask the trauma of his early childhood institutional life. We cannot be certain what prompted Brewer to drink, if indeed this account is accurate, but childhood trauma is one emotional response that we must also be alert to, even if the evidence for this is beyond recovery.

Among Brewer's array of compositions appear 'both instrumental and vocal music, including six fantasias for four viols, seven catches, six songs, twenty-eight airs for four parts, and two psalm settings written for the choir of Christ's Hospital to perform on Easter Monday and Tuesday'.[55] The melodies for Brewer's psalms were 'published singly' in 1641, because, as Susi Jeans observed, they were intended for two of the three separate services held on the Easter Monday or Tuesday and Wednesday.[56] One 'Psalm of thanksgiving' for Christ's Hospital set to music by Brewer was published in the second edition of *The divine services and anthems usually sung in the cathedrals and collegiate choires in the Church of England* (1664) by the clergyman James Clifford (1622–98).[57] I have not seen a copy of this work so it is unclear whether this is only the text, or text with the psalm melody.

Brewer was one of at least 12 music masters known to have been employed by Christ's Hospital London during the seventeenth century: John Farrant (fl. 1610–34); Thomas Ravenscroft (fl. 1618–22) and Thomas Pearce filled the position during Farrant's temporary seven-year retirement; Henry Semper (fl. 1636); Richard Watkins (fl. 1636); Thomas Brewer (fl. 1638–41); John Williams (died in 1654); a gap during the Protectorates of Oliver and Richard Cromwell where no suitable unmarried master could be found; Richard Price (fl. 1659–75); John Moss (1675); John Curtis (fl. 1675/6–1687/8); Richard Brown (1688–97); and John Barrett (1698–1718). We also have some insights into the musical education

---

53   Gasper; MacKinnon, "'I now have a book of songs of her writing'", pp. 35–48; Spink.

54   Spink, citing BL, Harley MS 6395, 'Merry passages and Jests'.

55   Gasper; Spink; MacKinnon, "'I now have a book of songs of her writing'", pp. 35–48.

56   Jeans, pp. 45–60.

57   W.B. Squire, 'Clifford, James (*bap.* 1622, *d.* 1698)', rev. Peter Lynan, *DNB*.

and provisions available during the seventeenth century. For example, John Farrant gifted 'eight Synginge Books and an Organ Book bound in parchment' on 1 October 1622, and Dow funded his salary increase from £4 to £16 and then to £20 for the musical education of 10 to 12 children.[58] William Parker provided the bequest for a salary of £10 for the organist at Christ's Hospital in 1615/16. By 1659 no musical instruments were in use, and so more had to be purchased. In 1661, the music master Richard Price was required at the Hospital every day: from seven to eleven in the morning and from one to five each afternoon, however, the children were only required to practise on two days each week.[59] The activity of singing fulfilled the function of music's perceived ability through words and harmony to replicate God's divine order and universal harmony.

The text to be set for the thanksgiving psalms was given to the music masters; we read that 'the Usher of the Grammarschool' was to 'deliver the Spital Psalm to Mr. Curtis, so that it could be set in time for Easter'.[60] Robert Brown, who was the first music master to have his name actually printed upon the 'Thanksgiving Psalms', was adamant that it was 'of absolute necessity for a true performance of ye Antems sung by the children' that the Hospital organ be repaired because 'its pitch [is] so sharp and so much above the reach of the children's voices that it causes in them an unnaturall squealing, whenever they endeavour to reache a high note'.[61] Yet a healthy self-interest also drove Brown's request for the urgent repair of the organ, for it inhibited his playing and did not permit 'that mastery of freedom that might otherwise [be] expected from him'.[62] Brown's settings demanded a high level of musical proficiency, as in the case of the Psalm for 1694 that contained three variations on a ground requiring the children to sing complex rhythms.[63]

The experience of these poor children within the institution could also be a much darker and even brutal one. Whether Brewer's drinking was a form of self-medication to combat childhood trauma is something we can never know. What we do know is that violence was a feature of institutional life. Richard Watkins the music master was dismissed because he hit children, as 'the print from his fingers has been seene on one of the children's cheeks', and because he had used ropes and 'crabstickes'.[64] John Curtis was sacked from his position as music master 'because he frequently used the Children of this Hospital with inhumane and barbarous severities, instead of moderate correction'.[65] Some of the children's musical performances, then, were performed under duress, and music and the memory of the rehearsals may have elicited darker emotional responses from

---

[58] Jeans, pp. 48, 51.
[59] Christ's Hospital, Committee Books, 1649–61 and 1661–77, cited in Jeans, p. 53.
[60] Jeans, p. 54, citing Samuel Pepys.
[61] Christ's Hospital Committee Book, 1687–98, cited in Jeans, p. 56.
[62] Jeans, p. 56.
[63] Jeans, p. 55.
[64] Jeans, p. 52.
[65] Christ's Hospital, Court Books, 1677–89, cited in Jeans, p. 55.

individual children that sat at odds with the broader institutional and remedial intent of musical education and performance.

Children's Performance of Charity

The printed psalms of thanksgiving therefore provide a rare insight into the practicalities of sounding pious. These performances were a demonstration of social cohesion, reintegration, godly harmony and the gendered order of society. The performances drew clear distinctions between the child performers and the audience, creating inbuilt dynamics during the performance by alternating between solo children's voices and then combined children and adult voices. Inbuilt *piano* and *forte* dynamics were to be found in these settings through the use of the different timbres between children's voices (collectively or singly) and adult voices. The musical abilities of the child singers must have influenced this, and young boys' unbroken voices singing in supplication to their benefactors would have had a powerful emotional impact on many of the assembled audience. The instructions indicating the antiphonal component of the singing were printed onto the sheet complete with text and music, and were available for sale at these annual thanksgiving Easter services. For example, in 1610 the 'Psalm of thanksgiving' sung at the 'Munday' service during Easter at Saint Mary Spitalfields 'for their founders and benefactors' prescribed the performance sequence thus: 'These two lines are to be sung by one or two of the Children, and then repeated by the people and all the Children.'[66] The solo voices sang: 'Regard O Lord from heaven above, accept the hartie prayse, | which Children render for the love thou shewest to them always.'[67] The quality of the children's voices available to the music master enabled the most proficient and/or the musical favourites to be selected.

This opening refrain is sung twice, using just the musical resources of the children and people present to create the inbuilt timbral dynamics. The combined audience and children's voices then sang the remainder of the verse, as the following tabulation demonstrates:

VERSE 1
A [Chorus] Opening two lines (solo for one or two children)
A [Chorus] Opening two lines repeated (all children and people present)
B Remaining six lines of verse (all children and people present)

VERSE 2
A [Chorus] Opening two lines (solo for one or two children)

---

[66] *A psalme of thanksgiving, to be sung by the children of Christ's Hospitall, on Munday in the Easter holy dayes, at Saint Mary Spittle, for their founders and benefactors Anno Domini 1610* (London: Printed by E. Allde for W., 1610).

[67] *A psalme of thanksgiving* (1610).

A [Chorus] Opening two lines repeated (all children and people present)
B Remaining six lines of verse (all children and people present)

VERSE 3
A [Chorus] Opening two lines (solo for one or two children)
A [Chorus] Opening two lines repeated (all children and people present)
B Remaining six lines of verse (all children and people present)

Here the cohesion of a godly society is audibly demonstrated, through the pious words and sounds the children utter. These fatherless children are reintegrated into the community of the assembled congregation, and redeemed from the life of vice and neglect that occurs when children are left to their own devices on the city streets.

The printed Psalm text and music for 1643 also contains instruction for the children's choir.[68] 'This Chorus is to be sung by *all* the Children, and repeated after every Verse.' Children's voices sang out to 'Rise Orphans, raise your Voyce in praise of God, for Patrones kind, | For bounteous Citizens from whom, we daily favour finde'.[69] Once again the reciprocity of the musical abilities of these poor children is reflected in this articulation of their performance practice, which in turn is intended to reaffirm the expected ongoing charitable giving of the audience participants.

The 1628 Psalm lists no instructions for performance, but does indicate the sections of Chorus and Verse.[70] Here the performance practice instructions may no longer be necessary, as the practice was well established. From 1673, and still in 1686, the printed music and text for the Psalm of thanksgiving indicates that the children were to sing on three separate occasions on Easter Monday, Tuesday and Wednesday, and the broadsheet indicated which printed verses were to be performed on each of the days, with the children performing as a group and then combining with the assembled congregation.[71] This practice was listed as 'according to ancient custom', and furthermore, the 1686 Psalm indicated that

---

[68]   *A psalme of thanks-giving to be sung by the children of Christs Hospitall, on Munday in the Easter Holy dayes, at Christ Church, for their founders and benefactors* (London: Printed by R.O. & G.D., 1643).

[69]   *A psalme of thanks-giving* (1643).

[70]   *A psalme of thankes-giving, to be sung by the children of Christs Hospitall, on Munday in Easter holy dayes, at Saint Maries Spittle, for their founders and benefactors* (London: Printed by Eliz. Allde, 1628).

[71]   *A psalm of thanksgiving, to be sung by the children of Christs-Hospital, on Monday, Tuesday, and Wednesday in Easter holy-days (according to ancient custom) at St. Mary Spittle, for their founders and benefactors* (London: Printed by William Godbid, 1673); *A psalm of thanksgiving, to be sung by the children of Christs-Hospital, on Monday, Tuesday, and Wednesday in Easter week, (according to ancient custom) at St. Mary Spittle, for their founders and benefactors* (London: Printed by Miles Flesher, 1686).

the musical setting was for 'A 3 Voc. Cantus, Primus and Bassus'.[72] One psalm copy includes the annotation of the date '5 Aprill. 1686' and also the word 'gratis' indicating this was not a copy that was sold, but in fact given to a member of the congregation who attended the services. The copy for the 1676 printed Psalm also includes the three different verse settings, and includes the annotation that 'This is the first that Mr Courtis their Organist made', and under that last stave of music, there is inscribed 'Dr Chr. Gibbons'.[73] The Psalm of 1688 indicates that the text was 'set to musick by Ric. Brown' and the annotation reveals this was another 'gratis' copy dated '16 Aprill. 1688'.[74] The printed Psalm from 1689 also included the name of the composer, 'Mr. Richard Brown Master of the Music Boys'.[75]

Conclusion

In his bequests to Christ's Hospital London, Dow not only left a musical legacy, but also gifted the provision of gloves, both to the 'singing children' valued at 6d. a pair, and for the music master at 8d. a pair.[76] The singers therefore represented both the sights and sounds of Dow's charity, for which they articulated their vocal gratitude in song. What this chapter has attempted to do is demonstrate that in addition to the provision of charity clothing and accommodation for the poor, poor children were required to participate and perform in musical acts of thanksgiving. The large number of extant printed psalms demonstrates the orchestration of these performances. These analyses of material culture collectively test the reality of continuity and change regarding charitable practices in English material culture across the break of the Reformation and into the seventeenth century, something Sharon Farmer has analysed for early modern Europe elsewhere in this volume.[77] By utilising these new sources in innovative ways and by cutting across discipline boundaries and restrictions, we can reveal the early modern customs of the sounds of charity, which accompanied the clothing doles that dressed the poor. By doing so we create a more complete and complex rendering of the sounds and sights/sites of charitable performances in the early modern world.

---

[72] *A psalm of thanksgiving* (1686).

[73] *A psalm of thanksgiving, to be sung by the children of Christs-Hospital, on Monday, Tuesday, and Wednesday in Easter holy-days, (according to ancient custom) at St. Mary Spittle, for their founders and benefactors* (London: Printed by William Godbid, 1676).

[74] *A psalm of thanksgiving, to be sung by the children of Christs-Hospital, on Monday, Tuesday, and Wednesday in Easter-week, (according to ancient custom) for their founders and benefactors* (London: Printed by Miles Flesher, 1688).

[75] *A psalm of thanksgiving to be sung by the children of Christ's Hospital, on Monday, Tuesday, and Wednesday in Easter-week (according to ancient custom) for their founders and benefactors* ([London]: Printed by E. Jones, for John Carr and Samuel Scot, 1689).

[76] Jeans, p. 48.

[77] See Farmer, Chapter 2 in this volume.

Chapter 13

Remembering the Poor: Signs of Charity in Late Medieval Images and Texts

Anne M. Scott

In an earlier study on treatment of the medieval poor, I expressed the view that, 'although devout and compassionate people took steps to alleviate suffering, elimination of the state of poverty was not on the medieval agenda. From the study of wills and the foundation of charitable institutions, it is evident that the poor were structural to society'.[1] This is not a new idea. In his work that is in many ways the bedrock of studies on medieval poverty in Europe, Michel Mollat wrote:

> Not until the Renaissance and Reformation, when contemporaries began to feel ashamed at the sight of people living in a state considered unworthy of human beings, did anyone dream of eradicating [poverty].[2]

I want to pursue this idea that the medieval poor are structural to society, in what Mark R. Cohen calls the 'dyadic relationship' of poverty and charity,[3] by teasing out the potential contradiction that, while the poor are systemic to society, their worst problems arise from being largely ignorable within that society.[4] They are ignorable within a society that places importance on material things; the poor have no material benefits to offer such a society. But they are systemic within a society that acknowledges a duty of care between human beings, for they offer themselves as objects of neediness, giving people the opportunity to indulge a charitable impulse to relieve need. These are not two different societies, but the same one, for materialistic societies measure need in material terms, and relieve it in material ways. Yet needs are emotional and spiritual, too, as Peter Brown suggests in an essay 'Remembering the Poor and the Aesthetic of Society': 'hunger and exposure were only the "presenting symptoms" of a deeper misery. Put bluntly, the heart of the problem was that the poor were eminently forgettable persons'.[5]

---

[1]   Anne M. Scott, *'Piers Plowman'*, p. 39.
[2]   Michel Mollat, *The Poor in the Middle Ages*, p. 1.
[3]   Mark R. Cohen, 'Introduction: Poverty and Charity in Past Times', *Journal of Interdisciplinary History*, 35 (2005), 347–60 (p. 360).
[4]   This is an idea developed by Peter Brown, 'Remembering the Poor', 513–22.
[5]   Brown, p. 519.

Brown works through a theory that earlier societies, in particular that of late antique Rome, placed an emphasis on maintaining a good society, and in order to preserve what he calls 'the aesthetic of society', attended to the needs of the poor, for to neglect the poor would be to create an ugly society.[6] In applying this theory to medieval and early modern societies, Brown asks why the poor matter in the first place, and answers that 'the poor challenged the memory like God. They were scarcely visible creatures who, nonetheless, should not be forgotten'.[7] These ideas resonate with my research into ways in which poverty, the poor and the pauper are represented in visual and literary imagery, for the pauper has a deep need to be noticed and remembered, but society often prefers to treat 'the poor' as a generic category to be 'dealt with' and then dropped out of mind.

In this concluding chapter, I shall examine whether the manner in which charity towards the pauper is portrayed in visual and textual imagery helps us to understand anything about the nature and purpose of charity as understood in late medieval and early modern Europe. Four basic types of poor present themselves through these images: those recognised among their neighbours as people who have their own identity and, at the same time, act as the image of Christ; those who are summoned into being more distantly within emblematic instances of charity, or as occasions of charity; those who are seen as a social evil; and those who are poor but assert their right to reasonable recompense for their work – they ask due payment, not gratuitous gifts. Each of these categories corresponds to one or more instances in the case studies of the preceding chapters. To recognise them helps to nuance our understanding of the experience of charity between individual paupers and donors, and between the generic faceless poor and administrators.

In many respects, poverty and charity are perceived as concepts that go together almost without question. Late medieval English poetry, plays and sermon literature often carry the implicit understanding that poverty is a state that brings people close to God, and that charity towards the poor is a way of gaining salvation for the donor. These two ideas are so widely discussed by cultural historians and literary critics that they have become truisms,[8] and my research into both visual and textual imagery equally suggests that a set of well-worn themes recurs in material artefact and in literature. The way they are repeated might imply, to the twenty-first-century mind, that notions of charity as applied to the poor have become standardised – a lingua franca, or an interpretive code that fits the poor

---

[6] Brown, p. 515: 'This "aesthetic of society" amounted to a sharp sense of what constituted a good society and what constituted an ugly society, namely, one that neglected the poor or treated them inappropriately.'

[7] Brown, p. 520.

[8] The Special Issue of *Journal of Interdisciplinary History*, 35.3 (2005), *Poverty and Charity: Judaism, Christianity, and Islam*, contains several articles that reiterate the teaching. A recent overview of literature in this field, much of which promotes these concepts, can be found in Anne M. Scott, 'Experiences of Poverty', in Anne M. Scott (ed.), *Experiences of Poverty*, pp. 1–15.

into predetermined categories, and prescribes set ways of dealing with them, precluding other ways of considering the poor, and dulling the perception of issues that need to be addressed. To the medieval mind this might not have been quite the case, and to grasp this, it is important to understand something of the way medieval theories of memory work. In this context, it is not strange that medieval images of the poor come through to us in what appear to be tropes, for, as Mary Carruthers explains, tropes are the building blocks of memory, from which new ideas and thoughts are 'invented'. The English word 'invent' is cognate with the Latin *inventio*, which can be translated as 'finding', as used in the modern word 'inventory'. Additionally, it can mean 'invent', the making of something new. Mary Carruthers explains:

> Because crafting memories also involved crafting the images in which those memories were carried and conducted, the artifice of memory was also, necessarily, an art of making various sorts of pictures: pictures in the mind, to be sure, but with close, symbiotic relationships to actual images and words that someone had seen or read or heard – or smelled or tasted or touched, for all the senses ... were cultivated in the monastic craft of remembering.[9]

The task of remembering the poor is, then, assisted by the existence of images which place the poor in predictable, because familiar, positions. This would suggest that the way the poor are depicted in text and visual image is symptomatic of the way they are understood by their contemporaries. What I shall aim to do is to discover whether, in medieval text or extant visual image, what appears to be a trope can be taken further.

My literary focus will be on the work of the late medieval poet, Hoccleve, precisely because his view of the relationship between charity and the poor moves away from standard imagery and language even while building upon it. In his *Regiment of Princes, Prologue*, Hoccleve 'invents' a poor bedesman, as a man dependent upon the charity of others for his basic sustenance, in this adopting a well-known trope; but he endows him with an identity, a history, and independence in handling his own life situation. In this respect, Hoccleve creates a new figure who carries in himself all the recognisable features of a poor man in need of charitable aid, but expresses the independence and individuality that feature in so many of the poor people considered in the preceding chapters. I shall elaborate on this literary image towards the end of my chapter; at this point I want to introduce the idea that, for Hoccleve, the condition of poverty is only remotely linked to charity; instead, he conceives the problem of the poor in terms of their forgettability, or even their deliberate occlusion, an idea in tune with that of Peter Brown, introduced above.[10]

---

[9] Mary Carruthers, *The Craft of Thought: Meditation, Rhetoric, and the Making of Images, 400–1200* (Cambridge: Cambridge University Press, 2000), p. 10.
[10] Brown, pp. 513–22.

Brown suggests that the medieval and early modern reiteration of St Paul's injunction: 'Remember the poor'[11] is necessary precisely because the poor, by the nature of their condition, are likely to become invisible to the powerful and the non-poor. The poetry of Hoccleve, in which he gives serious consideration to the forgotten poor, is written in the form of petition to named, influential, contemporary figures. The petitionary genre is hard to ignore, and Hoccleve uses this public form to bring to the attention of his readers – for example, the future king and influential court ladies – individual poor people whose needs are both monetary and emotional. Hoccleve understands the damage done to a society in which the poor are not remembered, in this foreshadowing in the fifteenth century arguments made by Brown in the twenty-first:

> Paul's injunction to "remember the poor" (Galatians 2. 10) and its equivalents in Jewish and Muslim societies warned about far more than a lapse of memory. It pointed to a brutal act of social excision the reverberations of which would not be confined to the narrow corridor where rich and poor met through the working of charitable institutions.[12]

The reciprocity of need and charity practised between poor and non-poor endorses what Brown calls a 'profoundly integrative activity' for society. Hoccleve fully understands the workings of a good society, but before examining the relationship of his poetry to Brown's 'aesthetic of society', I want to consider the implications of this reciprocity as evidenced in some of the visual artefacts and literary texts that reflect the aesthetic of a society in which 'charity was not only prudent but also beautiful'.[13]

The 'beauty' of a society that relates its care of the poor to charity which is, in itself, an expression of love for God, is still materially visible in extant public art and artefacts which would have been accessible to and enjoyed by both the medieval poor and the non-poor. Church ornament preserves representations of beggars, cripples and hungry people in wall paintings,[14] stained glass windows, stone sculpture, wood carvings, particularly misericords[15] and bench ends

---

[11] Galatians 2. 10.

[12] Brown, p. 519.

[13] Brown, p. 518.

[14] Anne Marshall, 'Medieval Wall Painting in the English Parish Church: A Developing Catalogue', available online at <http://www.paintedchurch.org/> [accessed 21 December 2012]; Roger Rosewell, *Medieval Wall Paintings in English and Welsh Churches* (Woodbridge: Boydell and Brewer, 2012).

[15] Carvings, often exquisitely detailed, found on the underside of choir stalls seats. A useful introduction to these can be found in Paulette Elaine Baron, *Mercy and the Misericord in Late Medieval England: Cathedral Theology and Architecture* (Lewiston, NY: Edwin Mellen, 2009); G.L. Remnant, *A Catalogue of Misericords in Great Britain* (Oxford: Clarendon Press, 1969) has a useful introductory essay by M.D. Anderson; see also Paul Hardwick, *English Medieval Misericords: The Margins of Meaning* (Woodbridge: Boydell,

(Plate 7).[16] The most frequent occurrences of the poor and needy in manuscript illumination of prayer books and presentation volumes,[17] as well as in church ornament, are found in association with the Seven Corporal Works of Mercy, and with a particular range of popular saints whose lives are narrated in the *Legenda Aurea*.[18] Numerous images survive, dating from the early to late Middle Ages, of St Martin who gives half his cloak to a beggar (Plate 9), St Elizabeth of Hungary who gives food to the starving[19] and St Nicholas who dowers three maidens, or restores life to three murdered and pickled boys. In specific regions we find representations of local, patronal saints like St Radegund who is depicted as assisting the needy in a stunningly preserved set of windows in Poitiers, France,[20] and Saint Sulpice le Pieux sculpted in stone relief ministering to sick, maimed and lame petitioners in Favières, France (Plate 8). French manuscripts often represent St Louis ministering to the poor,[21] and there are extant images of prisoners being freed by St Leonard, particularly plentiful in Germany.[22] In some manuscripts Christ is pictured giving food to the hungry or sight to the blind, implicitly identifying himself with those

---

2011), for an up-to-date appraisal of misericords within modern scholarship. Hardwick assures me that he has found very few images of the poor (private correspondence).

[16]   The stalls in this ancient collegial church of Champeaux date from 1522. (Church Guide literature on site).

[17]   Books of Hours and Psalters – the latter particularly common in England.

[18]   Jacobi a Voragine, *Legenda Aurea*, (ed.) Th. Graesse (Leipzig: Librariae Arnoldianae, 1850); also widely read in Middle English as the *Gilte Legende*, (ed.) Richard Hamer, 3 vols, EETS o.s. 327, 328, 339 (Oxford; New York: Oxford University Press, 2006–12).

[19]   For example, Pierpont Morgan Library, MS M.88, fol. 21v, which shows a giant-sized Elizabeth sheltering a crowd of diminutive paupers under her mantle; viewable at <http://www.flickr.com/photos/icaimagedatabase/4951819797/in/set-72157624741045625> [accessed 20 February 2014].

[20]   Church of St Croix, Poitiers, France. Radegund was traditionally revered as a saint who cared for the needy. Her biographer tells us how – like a new Martha, with a love of active life – she shrank from no disease, not even from leprosy. Fortunatus, *Vita*, chap. 26, quoted in 'St Radegund and the Nunnery at Poitiers', Lina Eckenstein, *Woman Under Monasticism: Chapters on Saint-Lore and Convent Life between A.D. 500 and A.D. 1500* (Cambridge: Cambridge University Press, 1896) p. 496, available online at <http://digital.library.wisc.edu/1711.dl/History.EckenWoman> [accessed 4 February 2014], see note 21.

[21]   See, for example, the exquisite sequence of images in the hours of Jeanne d'Evreux, The Hours of Jeanne d'Evreux, *c.* 1324–28, New York, The Metropolitan Museum of Art, The Cloisters Collection, 1954 (54.1.2). These are discussed in detail by Gerald Guest, 'A Discourse on the Poor: The Hours of Jeanne d'Evreux', *Viator*, 26 (1995), 153–80.

[22]   For example, BL, Yates Thompson 3, fol. 269v, available online at <http://www.bl.uk/catalogues/illuminatedmanuscripts/ILLUMINBig.ASP?size=big&IllID=34730> [accessed 20 February 2014]. For a recent study of these images, see Megan Cassidy-Welch, 'Images of Incarceration in Late-Medieval Art', in G. Kratzmann (ed.), *Imagination, Books and Community in Medieval Europe* (Melbourne: Macmillan Art Publishing/State Library of Victoria, 2009), pp. 190–5.

who perform such charitable works, and in one sixteenth-century French book, he identifies himself with the poor overtly, as he carries his cross assisted by a selection of the conventional gospel categories of poor: the blind, lame, widows, orphans and mendicants (Plate 10).[23] The association of these poor people with the suffering Christ reinforces in allegorical form the role of the poor as favoured by God. It also fixes them in their socio-economic state as necessary recipients of Christ's mercy and as object lessons to those using the prayer book, reminding them that they are called to emulate Christ.

These are what I have referred to above as the poor 'summoned into being … within emblematic instances of charity', and the repetitiveness of all these images suggests that the artists and those who commissioned their work placed at least as much emphasis on the spiritual benefit to be gained by the charitable giver as on the relieving of suffering for the poor person. The presence of the poor within an image demonstrates the often-heroic generosity of the non-poor without indicating anything specific about the poor beyond the obvious need that makes a relationship between poor victim and non-poor sponsor.[24] Already marginalised within society by being poor, the socio-economically poor, when they are present in a visual image, are frequently portrayed as smaller than or at least subordinate to the non-poor person in the image, hinting that they are like dependent children who need to come under the mantle of the powerful heavenly patron.[25] The poor persons are formulaic. St Martin's beggar customarily appears in medieval representations as an almost totally naked cripple, wonderfully setting off the munificent gesture of the wealthy and splendidly robed saint (Plate 9). Martin rides high on a horse; the beggar stoops in a suppliant position below. The works of mercy, seen spectacularly preserved on the walls of St Peter and St Paul's church, Pickering, Yorkshire, depict the poor cared for by better-off citizens in a religious context which links care of the poor with salvation for the donor at domesday.[26] Images of the parable of Dives and Lazarus depict the stark contrast between rich and poor, and form a warning to the rich to use their wealth to benefit the poor, without suggesting that

---

[23]   Huntington Library, HM 1088, fols 225v–226, accessible online in the Digital Scriptorium, <http://dpg.lib.berkeley.edu/webdb/dsheh/heh_brf?CallNumber=HM+1088> [accessed 4 February 2014]. Gospel categories of the needy derived from Luke 14. 21.

[24]   Kenneth Wolf (*The Poverty of Riches*) has developed this idea provocatively, suggesting that the impulse towards poverty in St Francis's life had the effect of reducing the socio-economic poor to a condition where, not only did they suffer materially, but, because their poverty was involuntary, they were deprived of the spiritual benefits accruing to those who voluntarily left all to follow Christ.

[25]   The Pierpont Morgan image of St Elizabeth of Hungary is a striking example of this. See n. 20 above.

[26]   These images are reproduced in Kate Giles, 'Marking Time? A fifteenth-century liturgical calendar in the wall paintings of Pickering parish church, North Yorkshire', *Church Archaeology*, (2000), 42–51. A PDF of the document, with images, is accessible online through the White Rose Research Online <http://eprints.whiterose.ac.uk/910/> [accessed 18 February 2014].

they attempt to eliminate poverty.[27] The viewer can infer that, while the presence of the poor is necessary to highlight the saintliness of a Martin or an Elizabeth, it is equally clear that the saint, whose life and deeds are commemorated in the image, confers significance on poverty, suffered by the poor as a generic group.

In relating these findings to Brown's question: 'why do the poor matter?', a complex of responses emerges which can be illustrated by the image of St Sulpice in the parish church of Favières, Essonne, France (Plate 8). The medieval sculpture of Sulpice le Pieux[28] ministering to the needy is, in itself, an artefact of beauty that presents a visual reminder of leadership within society. The saintly bishop stands in juxtaposition to the petitioning beggars and sick people, close to him both in the image and within the heart of the community, the parish church. In this prime location, the image perpetuates the memory of the saint and of the needy, a visual exemplum reminding the parish community that, not only are the poor always with us, but that we are bound to them in a relationship of mutuality. The poor, in this case, matter because, to use Brown's terms again, the society in which they can be cared for at this level of leadership within the community, is 'a "beautiful" rather than an "ugly" society'.[29] Such images fulfil the often-quoted saying of Caesarius of Arles: 'If nobody were poor, nobody could give alms and nobody could receive remission of his sins,'[30] and further underline the structural nature of poverty. We can say that because of the poor, society is blessed in being able to gaze on uplifting visual images of Christlike mercy; and the material evidence that remains visible in the hospitals, almshouses, poor boxes,[31] stained glass windows and wall paintings surviving from the Middle Ages, makes tangible the intangible virtues of human generosity and altruism that contribute to making society 'beautiful'.

But are the poor, as Brown suggests, invisible? The very fact of their representation in the material images suggests that they are not so, although both they and the non-poor who are shown giving them aid are anonymous. If not invisible, then, the poor are nonetheless, to quote Brown again, forgettable: 'The poor challenged the memory like God. They were scarcely visible creatures who, nonetheless, should not be forgotten.'[32] The visual images accentuate, not just the importance of the poor themselves, but the whole ethical fabric of society in which

---

[27]   Several images of this are accessible online, including BL, Yates Thompson 5, fol. 70v, Dives and Lazarus, <http://www.bl.uk/catalogues/illuminatedmanuscripts/ILLUMIN. ASP?Size=mid&IllID=484> [accessed 24 March 2014].

[28]   The church of Saint-Sulpice-de-Favières dates from the twelfth and thirteenth centuries. There is no information available on the dating of the sculpture, but it appears medieval.

[29]   Brown, p. 518.

[30]   *Sancti Caesarii Arelatensis Sermones, vol. i*, (ed.) G. Morin (Turnhout: Brepols, 1953), p. 112, epistle 25, quoted by Ludo J.R. Milis, *Angelic Monks and Earthly Men: Monasticism and its Meaning to Medieval Society* (Woodbridge: Boydell, 1992), p. 55. See a similar comment about St Eligius, quoted by Young, Chapter 4 in this volume, p. 110.

[31]   For poor boxes, see Brodie, Chapter 11 in this volume.

[32]   Brown, p. 520.

care for the needy becomes a gauge of society's moral health, something that is particularly obvious in sequences of the works of mercy, ubiquitously found in wall-painting, tapestry, sculpture and manuscript illumination. These works of mercy, based on Matthew's eschatological account of what Christ will say at the Last Judgement, Matt. 25. 35–7, had become a blueprint of how to treat the poor, and appear repeatedly in text and image throughout the Middle Ages: to feed the hungry, give drink to the thirsty, to harbour the harbourless, clothe the naked, visit the sick, visit the imprisoned and bury the dead are the works presented as the *sine qua non* of salvation.

Of the multitude of available examples portraying the works of mercy, I select University of Leeds, Special Collections, Brotherton MS 7, a Low Countries manuscript, illuminated in Utrecht *c.* 1500. Written in what the catalogue used to call Netherlandish, but now refers to as Dutch, this manuscript comprises the hours of Eternal Wisdom, the hours of the Holy Spirit, the hours of the Holy Cross, the hours of the Blessed Virgin and the hours of All Saints.[33] It is about the size of an A5 book, easy to handle, designed for personal prayer. In addition to eight full-page miniatures, there are border sequences illustrating typology between events in the Old and New Testaments, the life of the Virgin, the Passion of Christ, a series of saints, and, over several folios appears a sequence of tiny but masterly marginal illustrations of the Seven Corporal Works of Mercy.[34]

It is clear that the manuscript is, in itself, a richly produced article. The gold leaf, of which there is abundance, is thick and lustrous, and the illuminations are of a high quality.[35] The portraits of the man and woman (fol. 17v) whom one must deem to have been the original owners show them to be gentry. All the more poignant, then, is the direct involvement of well-to-do people as well as those of more humble status in the practice of the works of mercy. A well-accoutred young man leads a prisoner away from his captor, holding him by the hand in a welcoming, encouraging gesture, fulfilling the obligation to shelter the homeless as well as to visit the imprisoned (fol. 50v). A compassionate woman offers bread in front of her elegant townhouse to a beggar whose wooden limb disappears off the page, as if to suggest a fuller scene of which this is but a limited view. In the same street scene, another woman wearing an imposing headdress holds a naked child by the arm, yet stares out of the page beyond the immediate scene of activity

---

[33]   University of Leeds, Special Collections catalogue, online at <https://ludos.leeds. ac.uk:443/R/-?func=dbin-jump-full&object_id=77721&silo_library=GEN01>.

[34]   Leeds, Brotherton Collection, MS 7, fols 44r, 46v, 48v, 50v, 52v, 54v, 57r.

[35]   All the images from this manuscript have been digitised and are freely accessible in the Leeds University Library's Digital Objects, Medieval Manuscripts collection, <http:// ludos.leeds.ac.uk:1801/webclient/DeliveryManager?application=DIGITOOL-3&owner =resourcediscovery&custom_att_2=simple_viewer&pid=77721> [accessed 6 February 2014]. The catalogue attributes the marginal illuminations to the Master of the Adair Hours, and most of the miniatures, including those employing gold leaf, to the Master of the Dark eyes. See n. 32.

with a contemplative gaze, and points to the text which asks the Holy Spirit to fill the hearts of the faithful with grace, as if to suggest the grace both needed to perform acts of charity, and gained by carrying them out (Plate 11, fol. 52v). Other more humble-looking people carrying baskets participate in the scene, and may have already conducted their own charitable giving. The men who offer clothing to the naked are themselves opulently dressed in fur-lined mantles (Plate 12, fol. 46v), and the woman who holds out a garment to the naked man does so with a wide gesture that suggests generosity. Standing above her, as he does, with his arms outstretched, this man resembles the figure of Christ to be seen on a crucifix, whom the woman, in what seems to be a visionary moment, recognises as needing her act of charity.

The artist is at pains to illustrate, through detail of both external and internal architecture, the contemporary local context in which the works of mercy are performed. He creates an urban environment, which today looks recognisably Dutch, in which people engage in works of charity towards the poor as part of their daily lives. These citizens are not leaving such soul-saving activities until the hour of death; neither are they delegating the practice of caring for the needy to a church or parish institution; they are performing the acts themselves towards a variety of poor and needy people whom the illustrations show to be local individuals, not generic poor. The practice of charity here depicted represents the approach of the non-poor towards their needy neighbours who appear in suppliant, dependent and passive modes. It may be that the reciprocal benefit is unequal; for, even in the act of caring for the needy, the rich gain spiritual benefit, while the poor gain what medieval religious thought considered to be inferior: worldly goods.[36] The marginal illustrations are tiny snapshots of moments in the daily life of urban Low Countries citizens, and, in their position in a book of hours, serve as focal points for the kind of meditation encouraged by the *Devotio Moderna*, whose influence on this book of hours is strong.[37] It is inevitable, then, that the poor and needy will be viewed, in such a context, as an aid to the spiritual advancement of the non-poor who are using the book. Yet the representation of one poor man in a Christlike pose suggests a depth of significance for the local pauper, since the image implies that Christ has identified himself with him, and by extension, all the needy neighbours who are depicted in the images.

Remembering the poor according to the requirements of the works of mercy certainly translated from what was seen in images to practical good works. Elsewhere in this volume, Philippa Maddern gives hard evidence for conscious

---

[36] Wolf, p. 5.

[37] This fourteenth-century religious reform movement, whose influence continued far into the sixteenth century, encouraged people to follow a simple spiritual life, imitating Christ, developing a life of prayer and meditation, and practising good works according to simple Gospel precepts. Its founder, Geert Grote, placed great stress on pious reading, prayer and writing.

awareness of the works of mercy by testators in Norwich,[38] in this following the seminal studies of Cullum and Goldberg who pointed out that, mindful of the need to save their souls by giving to the poor in whom Christ is represented, some late medieval people made a point of structuring their wills to ensure that, when they went to meet their maker, they had very recently fulfilled the works of mercy. Examples from the English city of York in the late fourteenth and fifteenth centuries illustrate this vividly.[39] Thomas Bracebridge (d. 1437), made provision for a thousand farthing loaves to be distributed to the poor: feeding the hungry; Agnes Elvelay (d. 1395), left four quarters of malt and one of grain: this would be made into ale for the thirsty. Richard Carlell's widow, Agnes, was requested to give food and drink to five poor men or women every Sunday for a year following his death. Similarly with clothing, lengths of cloth, pairs of shoes and shirts were distributed; Richard Wartere (d. 1466), provided one hundred gowns and shirts for the poor, who were enjoined to say twenty-five psalters of St Mary for his soul. The particular injunction to receive the stranger and to visit the sick was fulfilled by various acts of endowment, from small ones, like Cecily Giry's provision of three feather beds to be kept in her guesthouse for the hospitality of the poor, to more substantial ones like that of John Burden (d. 1400), who left half the residue of his goods to St Leonard's hospital, which had beds for over two hundred sick and poor. Bequests to prisoners held at York Castle, on Ousebridge, and in the archbishop's prison satisfied the sixth of the gospel precepts – though less frequently than bequests to the poor at large. The burial of the dead, the one work not based on the Gospel text, is most often fulfilled by the testators' concern that their own bodies should receive a proper burial, with provision of funds to this end.

Some wills are specific in designating bequests to identified individuals, but more often, as in the will of the singlewoman, Philippa Russell, the bequests are linked to the locality or parish, rather than to a particular person. Though not excessively wealthy, Philippa Russell made generous provision for the poor in her will of 1458 with the stipulation that they should pray for her soul:[40]

> Also I leave 20 marks sterling (£13 6s. 8d.) to be distributed by the sound discretion of my underwritten executors among the poor prisoners in the prisons of Newgate, Ludgate, Fleet, Marshalsea, the King's Bench and the Abbot of Westminster's [prison] of convicted clerks, and also among the sick and other weak and poor people in hospitals within and outside the city of London … to pray especially for my soul.[41]

---

[38]   See Maddern, Chapter 5 in this volume, pp. 81, 96, 100–101.

[39]   All examples taken from P.H. Cullum and P.J.P. Goldberg, 'Charitable Provision', 24–39.

[40]   Judith M. Bennett and Christopher Whittick, 'Philippa Russell', 251–69.

[41]   Bennett and Whittick, p. 262.

Philippa also left money to aid the marriages of poor maidens in two city wards, to support the fraternities of the drapers and brewers, and to provide coal to be distributed among the poor of Walbrook Ward for seven years after her death. Her will is not unusual in this. The care is concrete but, nonetheless, the textual record of this care is couched in terms that link the poor with the salvation of the donor's soul, attaching a symbolic value to the provisions for clothing the naked, giving shelter to the homeless and feeding the hungry. The practical value of the dole is undeniable, but, as Maddern deduces, and I have surmised elsewhere,[42] the funeral doles cannot have been anything more than intermittent respite for the poor who qualified. None of this is news to students of poverty and charity, yet the tenor of anonymity surrounding bequests like these, repeated in wills throughout the late medieval period, does suggest a certain invisibility of the individual poor person, whose identity is lost within the generic terms – poor men and women, sick and poor, poor maidens, prisoners.

A potentially more serious submerging of identity comes through in imagery that depicts the disreputable and vicious poor, a topos as widespread as that of the Christlike poor, and equally powerful in stereotyping the poor within their estate. Axel Bolvig quotes instances of wall paintings in which two cripples who, on the face of it look poor, are actually evil men.[43] This is clear from their position in the procession of Christ carrying his cross, since one leads the procession dancing and blaring on a trumpet, and the other brandishes a stick to torment Christ; further iconographical hints that they represent evil are that they have lost their feet,[44] and wear striped or parti-coloured hose, all recognised signs of vice.[45] Far from being identified with Christ, and the community charity such identification stimulates, these are poor and outcast. Some French texts, such as the *Roman de la Rose*[46] or *La Voie de Povreté ou de Richesse*,[47] present the allegorical figure of Poverty as representing a state that is vicious. In the *Roman*, the dwelling place of Fortune is on a high mountain; one side of the house is a mansion, rich and gorgeous,

---

[42]   Scott, *'Piers Plowman'*, p. 141.

[43]   For a brief discussion and reproduction of these images, see Axel Bolvig, 'What Does Poverty Look Like?', in Gerhard Jaritz (ed.), *The Sign Languages of Poverty* (Vienna: Verlag der Österreichischen Akademie der Wissenschaften, 2007), pp. 165–76.

[44]   According to Bolvig, loss of a foot is a sign of viciousness, though he adduces no reference for this. It may be connected with the practice of maiming and laming children mentioned in several texts, including *Piers Plowman*, as mentioned below.

[45]   Ruth Mellinkoff, *Outcasts: Signs of Otherness in Northern European Art of the Late Middle Ages* (Berkeley: University of California Press, 1993), pp. 20–21.

[46]   Guillaume de Lorris and Jean de Meun, *Le Roman de la Rose*, (ed.) Ernest Langlois, 5 vols (Paris: Librairie de Firmin-Didot, 1920), (trans.) Charles Dahlberg (Princeton, NJ: Princeton University Press, 1971).

[47]   Jean Bruyant, 'La Voie de Povreté ou de Richesse', in Georgina E. Brereton and Janet M. Ferrier (eds), *Le mesnagier de Paris* (Paris: Librairie Générale Française, 1994), pp. 814–37.

while the other is a hovel, horrifically poor and wretched.[48] Here, Poverty has nothing to do with virtue, and is as prone to sinful misery as the excessive wealth provided by Fortune. *La Voie de Povreté ou de Richesse* represents Poverty as the vicious companion to Sloth.[49] In English works, Langland presents graphic images of the slothful and vicious poor who maim their children in order to beg more effectively;[50] and Robert Mannyng presents at least one exemplum in which the poor are idle, raucous and vicious beggars who bask in the sun, their hats on their chests, cunning enough to win a loaf of bread from a rich man, and smart enough to sell on a kirtel received as charity.[51] While the vicious or undeserving poor have exercised the minds of lawmakers, both ecclesiastical and civil, from Roman times through to the present day, the language of the statutes in fourteenth-century England and France did nothing to help improve the lot of the poor, and much to punish them. Implications of criminality come through in a clause which states that:

> because many sturdy beggars, so long as they can live by begging for alms, refuse to labour, living in idleness and sin and sometimes by thefts and other crimes, no man, under the aforesaid penalty of imprisonment, shall presume under colour of pity or alms to give anything to such as shall be able profitably to labour, or to cherish them in their sloth, so that they may be compelled to labour for the necessaries of life.[52]

This language, as has been noted by others writing in this volume,[53] associates the poor with crime, and further ordinances regularly forbade citizens to give shelter or aid to any poor who were not part of the neighbourhood, and were therefore not known as individuals. Marjorie McIntosh gives examples of such regulatory control,[54] and even as late as the seventeenth century, as Lesley Silvester informs us, Norwich emptied its Bridewell of the homeless in order to turn the building into a place of correction. All these associated ideas and representations contribute

---

48   *Le Roman de la Rose*, II, ll. 6079–6118.

49   A full discussion of poverty as vice, not virtue, can be found in my chapter: '*Le Chastel de Labour, La Voie de Povreté ou de Richesse* and a Luxury Book, Widener 1, Free Library of Philadelphia', in Scott (ed.), *Experiences of Poverty*, pp. 253–77 (pp. 257–60).

50   William Langland, *Piers Plowman: A Parallel-text Edition of the A, B, C and Z Versions*, (ed.) A.V.C. Schmidt (London; New York: Longman, 1995–2008), C.IX, 152–79.

51   Robert Mannyng of Brunne, *Handlyng Synne*, (ed.) Idelle Sullens (Binghamton, NY: Medieval and Renaissance Texts and Studies, 1983), pp. 140–43, ll. 5581–6; ll. 5591–622; ll. 5697–710. Young, Chapter 4 in this volume, p. 72, mentions this widely known exemplum in connection with usury, a further hint that these poor are vicious.

52   From the 1349 Ordinance of Labourers, in *Statutes of the Realm*, 307–8. See Rushton, Chapter 6 in this volume, p. 106, n. 4, for original Latin text.

53   See Farmer, Chapter 2, pp. 30, 40–41; Rushton, Chapter 6, pp. 106–107; and Silvester, Chapter 7, pp. 142–4, in this volume.

54   Marjorie K. McIntosh, *Controlling Misbehavior*, pp. 23–45.

to making the poor, to use another of Brown's terms, 'eminently forgettable persons',[55] for, if the poor are as evil as the visual imagery and language used about them suggests, then it becomes legitimate for people to consider them as a generic mass, and ignore them. Known individuals are hard to ignore, but a criminalised group can be safely forgotten.

It is this loss of identity experienced by the poor in not being remembered that the late medieval poet, Thomas Hoccleve, confronts in his poem *The Regiment of Princes*.[56] Hoccleve wrote his poetry in court circles, since he was both Clerk of the Privy Seal and courtly poet, serving under four kings through turbulent times, from *c.* 1387 to 1425/6.[57] In his poetry, Hoccleve presents himself as the petitioner who depends on the goodwill of his employers for his livelihood, and it is perhaps not wholly ironic that many of Hoccleve's poems should be a masterly form of petition, since his official employment at the Privy Seal involved him in writing out petitions for others, the form of which has been preserved in the formulary he assembled for succeeding scribes to follow.[58] Much of Hoccleve's poetry evinces a deep spirituality, and all of it adheres to a strong ethical code derived from Christianity. It is the more surprising, then, to find that, when he writes about a duty of care for the poor, he does not invoke a notion of Christian charity. Instead, Hoccleve identifies the needs of sections of the community as something that should be relieved as a matter of justice – and, in Peter Brown's terms, as a matter of self-interest for the good order of society. This is evident particularly in the *Regiment of Princes*, a traditional 'Mirror for Princes', written as homage and advice for Prince Henry, shortly before the death of his father, and his subsequent accession as Henry V of England.[59]

The long Prologue to the *Regiment of Princes*[60] is framed as a dialogue between the persona of the poet, Hoccleve, and an old man, containing much information that scholars take to be autobiographical.[61] It must be remembered that the figure

---

[55] Brown, p. 519.

[56] *Thomas Hoccleve 'The Regiment of Princes'*, (ed.) Charles R. Blyth (Kalamazoo, MI: Medieval Institute Publications, 1999) (hereafter *Regiment of Princes*).

[57] For a succinct account of Hoccleve's life, see J.A. Burrow, *Thomas Hoccleve* (Aldershot: Ashgate/Variorum, 1994).

[58] E.-J.Y. Bentley (ed.), 'The Formulary of Thomas Hoccleve' (unpublished doctoral thesis, Emory University, 1965), a complete edition of BL, MS Additional 24062. For commentary, see Ethan Knapp, *The Bureaucratic Muse: Thomas Hoccleve and the Literature of Late Medieval England* (Philadelphia: Pennsylvania State University Press, 2001).

[59] For the tradition of advice literature, see Judith Ferster, *Fictions of Advice: The Literature and Politics of Counsel in Late Medieval England* (Philadelphia: University of Pennsylvania Press, 1996); and Nicholas Perkins, *Hoccleve's Regiment of Princes: Counsel and Constraint* (Cambridge: D.S. Brewer, 2001).

[60] The Prologue runs to 2016 lines out of a total of 5459 lines.

[61] J.A. Burrow, 'Autobiographical Poetry in the Middle Ages: The Case of Thomas Hoccleve', *Proceedings of the British Academy*, 68 (1982), 389–412; Anne M. Scott,

of Hoccleve in this poem is a fictive persona; Hoccleve the clerk would have been far from destitute when he retired from service. Yet Hoccleve the poet knows that even a king – Richard II – can fall from prosperity and be consigned to death. This understanding gives poignancy to his emotional outcry against the poverty he fears will take him into a state of deathlike privation from all he values and holds dear. These anxieties, expressed in regard to the prospect of old-age poverty for himself, are pressed into the service of his argument that all those who labour should, in justice, be recompensed and not allowed to drift into old age and death, forgotten by the successful and strong.

Ranging over a wide number of social issues, the Prologue touches on three that are relevant to my argument here. The first is Hoccleve's expressed fear of poverty, not primarily because it will bring him physical hardship, but because it is a state akin to death. Brown outlines such a situation:

> But hunger and exposure were only the "presenting symptoms" of a deeper misery. Put bluntly, the heart of the problem was that the poor were eminently forgettable persons. In many different ways, they lost access to the networks that had lodged them in the memory of their fellows. Lacking the support of family and neighbors, the poor were on their own, floating into the vast world of the unremembered. This slippage into oblivion is strikingly evident in Jewish Midrash of the book of Proverbs, in which statements on the need to respect the poor are attached to the need to respect the dead. Ultimately helpless, the dead also depended entirely on the capacity of others to remember them. The dead represented the furthest pole of oblivion toward which the poor already drifted.[62]

This passage bears striking resemblances to the opening of Hoccleve's Prologue, in which he describes his poetic persona as unable to sleep through anxiety over what he sees as an inevitable fall from prosperity, using the recent fall of King Richard II in 1399 as an object lesson. He considers the troubles, not only of the king, but of other fallen nobles; then he turns to those of middling rank – 'mene estat' – but finds as little security – 'seuretee' – in their position. Finally he recognises that, ironically, the only thing to depend upon is poverty, lower than which none can fall, for the next and inevitable step from poverty is death, a fate inevitable for all:

Me fil to mynde how that nat longe agoo	I remembered
Fortunes strook doun thraste estat rial	royal
Into mescheef, and I took heede also	
Of many anothir lord that hadde a fal.	

'Thomas Hoccleve's Selves Apart', in Ronald Bedford, Lloyd Davis and Philippa Kelly (eds), *Early Modern Autobiography: Theories, Genres, Practices* (Ann Arbor: University of Michigan Press, 2006), pp. 89–103.

   [62]   Brown, p. 519.

In mene estat eek sikirnesse at al	safety
Ne saw I noon, but I sy atte laste	
Wher seuretee for to abyde hir caste.	security
In poore estat shee pighte hir pavyloun	pitched her tent
To kevere hir fro the storm of descendynge	shelter
For shee kneew no lower descencion	
Sauf oonly deeth, fro which no wight lyvynge	except; living creature
Deffende him may; and thus in my musynge	
I destitut was of joie and good hope,	
And to myn ese nothyng cowde I grope.	for my relief; grasp[63]

In the course of the Prologue, Hoccleve explains why he fears he will fall: as an employee of the Crown, his payment is often severely in arrears, and he suffers anxiety because, if he finds it hard to secure his payment while he is active in court, once retired he is likely to be forgotten, and inevitably sink into poverty:

"For syn that I now in myn age greene,	vigorous
And beynge in court, with greet peyne unnethe	effort; with difficulty
Am paid, in elde and out of court, I weene,	old age; imagine
My purs for that may be a ferthyng shethe;	holder for a farthing
Lo, fadir myn, this dullith me to dethe.	stuns
Now God helpe al, for but he me socoure,	unless; aid
My future yeeres lyk been to be soure."	are likely[64]

In this, Hoccleve implies that invisibility is one of his greatest fears, but he does not invoke charity as a palliative; instead he is adamant that, as a matter of justice, having worked all his life for the crown, he should be reliably supported in his old age.

He takes this idea further in considering the scandal of old soldiers who have fought in the wars in France being left to fend for themselves in old age, instead of receiving compensation for loyal service. Far from invoking the ideal of giving to the poor in order to store up heavenly – and perhaps earthly – reward,[65] Hoccleve suggests that one very good reason to remember these poor knights is a kind of self-interest, since only by making sure the poor are noticed and cared for will others – in this case knights who were once hearty and young but have now outgrown their usefulness – be assured of being looked after in their turn:

"Knyghthode, awake! Thow sleepist to longe;

---

[63] *Regiment of Princes*, ll. 22–35.

[64] *Regiment of Princes*, ll. 834–40.

[65] See Young, Chapter 4, pp. 76–8 in this volume, on the concept that charity on earth was sometimes believed to lead to a hundredfold reward, to be measured in earthly gain.

Thy brothir, see, ny dieth for mescheef;	misfortune
Awake and reewe upon his peynes stronge.	feel pity for; severe
If thow heeraftir come unto swich preef,	test
Thow wilt ful sore thriste aftir releef;	long for
Thow art nat seur what that thee shal befalle.	certain
Welthe is ful slipir; be waar lest thow falle.	slippery

"Thow that yclomben art in hy honoures,	you who have climbed
And hast this worldes welthe at thy devys,	at your pleasure
And bathist now in youthes lusty floures;	
Be waar, rede I, thow standist on the ys.	advise; ice
It hath been seen, as weleful and as wys	fortunate; wise
As thow han slide; and thow that no pitee	
On othir folk hast, who shal reewe on thee?[66]	

This is an intergenerational compact of the kind alluded to in Scripture: 'Son, support the old age of thy father, and grieve him not in his life | And if his understanding fail, have patience with him, and despise him not when thou art in thy strength.'[67] It is nothing to do with the notion of supererogatory charity that leaves it up to the donor to decide, voluntarily, on the provision of care for the needy. That charity is motivated by a belief in the rightness of religious charity, and performed for the benefit of the donor's soul. Hoccleve is much more concerned that poverty should be avoided in the first place, and his motivation springs from a concept of society in which due account is taken of service rendered, whether within the immediate family or the wider community.

The old man of the poem is living proof of the kind of 'death in poverty' that Hoccleve fears. Not quite a beggar, the old man recognises that his present poverty obliterates the identity he once had as a strong and wealthy young man, and accepts his state as a punishment for the sins of his youth, many of which are those that Hoccleve, in earlier poems, accuses himself of committing – reckless spending, extravagant clothes, high living – all sins of excess conventionally pilloried in sermons and moral treatises of the time.[68] In this, he might be considered one of the disreputable poor, the kind whose poverty is brought upon themselves by sin, much as portrayed in the French poem, *La Voie de Povreté ou de Richesse,*[69] where residence in the hovel of Dame Poverty represents the conclusion of a life of sloth,

---

[66]   *Regiment of Princes*, ll. 897–910.

[67]   Sirach 3. 14–15: 'Son, support the old age of thy father, and grieve him not in his life; And if his understanding fail, have patience with him, and despise him not when thou art in thy strength: for the relieving of the father shall not be forgotten.'

[68]   For this see, in particular, 'La mal règle de Thomas Hoccleve', in *Hoccleve's Works, the Minor Poems*, EETS e.s. 61, 73 (Oxford: Oxford University Press, n.d.), pp. 25–39.

[69]   For full commentary on this, see Scott, '*Le Chastel de Labour*', pp. 253–77.

whereas hard and honest work leads to 'the life of worldly happiness, security and virtue that is made possible by attaining to *Richesse*':[70]

"Whyler, my sone, tolde I nat to thee	
What habundance in yowthe I hadde of good?	
And how me blente so prosperitee	blinded
That what God was I nothyng undirstood?	
But ay whil that I in my welthe stood,	
Aftir my flesshly lust my lyf I ledde,	in pursuit of
And of His wreche nothyng I me dredde.	vengeance
"And as I seide, He smoot me with the strook	
Of povert, in which I continue yit,	
Whos smert my good blood first so sore sook,	blood (humour); sucked
Or that I was aqweyntid wel with it,	
That ny it hadde reft fro me my wit.	
But sythen, thanke I God, in pacience	since then
I have it take and shal for myn offense."	accepted; shall [accept] [71]

My final point on reading Hoccleve's text is that the old man and Hoccleve himself both appear in the situation of suppliants. Like the lowly-positioned beggar who petitions St Martin who sits high on his horse, a diminutive Hoccleve kneels before the tall prince who will become his king (Plate 13). Hoccleve, though, is not asking for a gift of charity, but patronage in recompense for the book that contains his poem of advice for the prince. This advice represents a contract between prince and poet,[72] with the image of the presentation acting as a lasting visual reminder of their mutual relationship. It encapsulates the good graces of the prince towards his subject together with the benefit to him and to society when he heeds the advice contained in the book created and penned by the poet. For Hoccleve, the book is his insurance against a life of poverty which, to him, would be like death.

Conclusion

Thomas Hoccleve's work is an example of textual material that challenges the often repeated idea that eradication of poverty was not something to be pursued in medieval Europe, and that the practice of giving charitable aid in many ways perpetuated the condition of poverty. Hoccleve's poor man may be invisible to those who lead the life of wealth as he once did, but he does not depend on charitable assistance, any more than the *leprosi* who, we learn from Stemmle, to a

---

[70] Scott, '*Le Chastel de Labour*', p. 277.
[71] *Regiment of Princes*, ll. 1317–1330.
[72] See Ferster, pp. 146–7.

large extent took charge of their own lives once they had joined the leprosarium.[73] Having accepted his poverty as due punishment for his former sins, the old man has a new identity, as a self-professed poor bedesman, one of those whom Maddern mentions in her chapter.[74] In return for the basic necessities of life, the old man prays for his benefactors, in this rendering a service, much as the young choristers of Christ's Hospital performed a service by their singing, as Dolly MacKinnon explains.[75] In different ways, the poor who appear in visual images are seen to be offering important services. Martin's sanctity is forever captured in the image of sharing his cloak with the beggar who, himself, stands forever as the efficient cause of Martin's sainthood. Such reciprocity between donor and recipient moves the relationship on from that of benefactor giving a needy suppliant charitable aid, to a condition of equal value where reward is given for acknowledged and valued service to the benefit of society.

---

[73]   Stemmle, Chapter 4 in this volume.
[74]   Maddern, Chapter 5 in this volume, pp. 81, 91–93, 100–102.
[75]   MacKinnon, Chapter 12 in this volume.

Select Bibliography

Adam, Paul, *La vie paroissiale en France au XIVe siècle* (Paris: Sirey, 1964).

Aladjidi, Priscille, 'Les Espaces du don au Moyen Âge: l'exemple de la charité princière', in *Construction de l'espace au Moyen Âge: pratiques et représentations* (Paris: Publications de la Sorbonne, 2007), pp. 349–56.

——, *Le Roi père des pauvres: France XIIIe–XVe siècles* (Rennes: Presses Universitaires de Rennes, 2009).

Amsler, Mark, 'Poverty as a Mobile Signifier: Waldensians, Lollards, *Dives and Pauper*', in Anne M. Scott (ed.), *Experiences of Poverty in Late Medieval and Early Modern England and France* (Farnham: Ashgate, 2012), pp. 227–51.

Appleby, Andrew A., 'Grain Prices and Subsistence Crises in England and France, 1590–1740', *Journal of Economic History*, 39 (1979), 870–82.

Arnaud, Eugène, *Histoire des protestants du Dauphiné aux XVIe, XVIIe et XVIIIe siècles*, 3 vols (Paris: Grasset, 1875).

Arrizabalaga, Jon, John Henderson and Roger French, *The Great Pox: The French Disease in Renaissance Europe* (New Haven, CT: Yale University Press, 1997).

Aston, Margaret, '"Caim's Castles": Poverty, Politics and Disendowment', in Barrie Dobson (ed.), *The Church, Politics and Patronage in the Fifteenth Century* (Gloucester: Sutton, 1984), pp. 45–81.

Auclair, Valérie, 'Un logis pour l'âme des rois. Nicolas Houel (ça. 1520–ça. 1587) et les dessins de procession à la maison de la Charité chrétienne pour la famille royale', in Isabelle de Conihout, Jean-François Maillard and Guy Poirier (eds), *Henri III mécène des arts, des sciences et des lettres* (Paris: Presses de l'Université Paris-Sorbonne, 2006), pp. 39–54.

Avril, Joseph, 'Le IIIe concile du Latran et les communautés des lépreux', *Révue Mabillon,* 60 (1981), 21–76.

Babelon, Jean-Pierre, *Nouvelle Histoire de Paris: Paris au XVIe siècle* (Paris: Hachette, 1986).

Backhouse, Marcel F., *The Flemish and Walloon Communities at Sandwich during the Reign of Elizabeth I (1561–1603)* (Brussels: Koninklijke Academie voor Wetenschappen, Letteren en Schone Kunsten, 1995).

Balau, Sylvain, *Les Sources de l'histoire de Liège au Moyen-Âge; étude critique* (Brussels: H. Lamertin, 1903).

Baldauf-Berdes, Jane L., 'Anna Maria della Pietà: The Woman Musician of Venice Personified', in Susan C. Cook and Judy S. Tsou (eds), *Cecilia Reclaimed: Feminist Perspectives on Gender and Music* (Urbana: University of Illinois Press, 1994), pp. 134–55.

Baldwin, John W., *Masters, Princes and Merchants: The Social Views of Peter the Chanter and His Circle*, 2 vols (Princeton, NJ: Princeton University Press, 1970).

Bardsley, Sandy, 'Women's Work Reconsidered: Gender and Wage Differentiation in Late Medieval England', *Past & Present*, 165 (1999), 3–29.

Baron, Paulette Elaine, *Mercy and the Misericord in Late Medieval England: Cathedral Theology and Architecture* (Lewiston, NY: Edwin Mellen, 2009).

Barrett, Eileen, 'Poor Relief in Hanoverian London: Assistance to Widows in the Period 1735–1750' (unpublished master's thesis, Massey University, 1997).

——,'Huguenot integration in late 17th- and 18th-Century London: Insights from the records of the French Church and some relief agencies', in Vigne and Littleton (eds), *From Strangers to Citizens*, pp. 375–82

Barringer, Christopher, 'The Changing Face of Norwich', in Carole Rawcliffe and Richard Wilson, with Christine Clark (eds), *Norwich Since 1550* (London and New York: Hambledon and London, 2004), pp. 1–34.

Baskerville, Geoffrey, *English Monks and the Suppression of the Monasteries* (London: Cape, 1937).

Baulant, Micheline and Jean Meuvret, *Prix des céréales extraits de la Mercuriale de Paris (1520–1698)*, 2 vols (Paris: S.E.V.P.E.N., 1960–62).

Bearman, Peter S. and Glenn Deane, 'The Structure of Opportunity: Middle-Class Mobility in England, 1548–1689', *American Journal of Sociology*, 98 (1992), 30–66.

Beecheno, F.R., 'The Sucklings' House at Norwich', *Norfolk and Norwich Archaeological Society*, 20 (1921), 158–78.

Beeman, George B., 'Sites and History of the French Churches of London', *Proceedings of the Huguenot Society of London*, 8 (1905–08), 13–59.

——, 'The Early History of the Strangers' Church, 1550–61', *Proceedings of the Huguenot Society of London*, 15 (1935), 261–82.

Beier, A.L., *The Problem of the Poor in Tudor and Early Stuart England* (London: Routledge, 1983).

——, *Masterless Men: The Vagrancy Problem in England 1560–1640* (London: Methuen, 1985).

——, '"A New Serfdom": Labor Laws, Vagrancy Statutes, and Labor Discipline in England, 1350–1800', in A.L. Beier and Paul Ocobock (eds), *Cast Out: Vagrancy and Homelessness in Global and Historical Perspective* (Athens: Ohio University Press, 2008).

Benedict, Philip, *The Huguenot Population of France, 1600–1685: The Demographic Fate and Customs of a Religious Minority* (Philadelphia: American Philosophical Society, 1991).

Bennett, Judith M., 'Conviviality and Charity in Medieval and Early Modern England', *Past & Present*, 134 (1992), 19–41.

—— and Christopher Whittick, 'Philippa Russell and the Wills of London's Late Medieval Singlewomen', *London Journal*, 32 (2007), 251–69.

Bergin, Joseph, *Cardinal de la Rochefoucauld: Leadership and Reform in the French Church* (New Haven, CT: Yale University Press, 1987).

——, *The Making of the French Episcopate, 1589–1661* (New Haven, CT: Yale University Press, 1996).

Bériac-Lainé, Françoise, *Histoire des lépreux au moyen-âge: une société d'exclus* (Paris: Éditions Imago, 1988).

Bertrand, Paul, *Commerce avec Dame Pauvreté: structures et fonctions des couvents mendiants à Liège, XIIIe–XIVe siècles* (Geneva: Droz, 2004).

Biraben, Jean-Noël, *Les Hommes et la peste en France et dans les pays européens et méditerranéens*, 2 vols (Paris-La Haye: Mouton, 1976).

Bird, Jessalynn, 'Medicine for Body and Soul: Jacques de Vitry's Sermons to Hospitallers and their Charges', in Peter Biller and Joseph Ziegler (eds), *Religion and Medicine in the Middle Ages* (Woodbridge: York Medieval Press/ Boydell, 2001), pp. 91–108.

Black, J. William, 'From Martin Bucer to Richard Baxter: "Discipline" and Reformation in Sixteenth- and Seventeenth-century England', *Church History*, 70 (2001), 644–73.

Blomefield, Francis, *An Essay Towards a Topographical History of the County of Norfolk*, 11 vols (London: William Miller, 1805–10).

Boissieu, Henri de, 'L'Aumône-Générale sous la domination protestante', *Bulletin de la Société littéraire historique et archéologique de Lyon*, 3 (1908–09), 1–32.

Bolle, Pierre, *Le Protestant dauphinois et la république des synodes à la veille de la Révocation* (Lyon: La Manufacture, 1985).

—— (ed.), *Le Protestantisme en Dauphiné au XVIIe siècle: religion et vie quotidienne à Mens-en-Trièves, Die et Gap (1650–1685)* (Poët-Laval: Curandera, 1983).

Bolvig, Axel, 'What Does Poverty Look Like?', in Gerhard Jaritz (ed.), *The Sign Languages of Poverty* (Vienna: Verlag der Österreichischen Akademie der Wissenschaften, 2007), pp. 165–76.

Bonney, Richard and David J.B. Trim (eds), *Persecution and Pluralism: Calvinists and Religious Minorities in Early Modern Europe, 1550–1700* (Oxford: Peter Lang, 2006)

Borradori, Piera, *Mourir au monde: les lépreux dans le pays de Vaud, XIIIe–XVIIe siècle* (Lausanne: Université de Lausanne, Faculté des lettres, Section d'histoire, 1992).

Bos, Agnès, 'Les Archives des fabriques parisiennes à la fin du Moyen Âge et à l'époque moderne', *Bibliothèque de l'École des Chartes*, 156 (1998), 369–405.

Bourgeois, Albert, *Psychologie collective et institutions charitables. Lépreux et maladreries du Pas-de-Calais (Xe–XVIIIe siècles)* (Arras: Commission départementale des monuments historiques du Pas-de-Calais, 1972).

Bove, Boris, *Dominer la ville: prévôts des marchands et échevins parisiens de 1260 à 1350* (Paris: Éditions du Comité des travaux historiques et scientifiques, 2004).

Bowler, Kate, *Blessed: A History of the American Prosperity Gospel* (Oxford: Oxford University Press, 2013).

Braekman, W.L., 'A Middle English Didactic Poem on the Works of Mercy', *Neuphilologische Mitteilungen*, 79 (1978), 145–51.

Braid, Robert, '"Et non ultra": politiques royales du travail en Europe occidentale au XIVe siècle', *Bibliothèque de l'École des Chartes*, 161 (2003), 437–91.

Brassine, J., 'Une source du livre II des "miracula sancti Trudonis"', in *Bulletin de la Société d'art et d'histoire du diocèse de Liège*, 26 (1935), 39–52.

Brémond, Claude, Jacques Le Goff and Jean-Claude Schmitt, *L''Exemplum'* (Turnhout: Brepols, 1982).

Brenner, Elma, 'Recent Perspectives on Leprosy in Medieval Western Europe', *History Compass*, 8 (2010), 388–406.

Bright, Janette and Gillian Clark, *An Introduction to the Tokens at the Foundling Museum* (London: Foundling Hospital Museum, 2011).

Brockliss, Laurence and Colin Jones, *The Medical World of Early Modern France* (Oxford: Clarendon Press, 1997).

Brodie, Nicholas Dean, 'Beggary, Vagabondage and Poor Relief: English Statutes in the Urban Context, 1495–1572' (unpublished doctoral thesis, University of Tasmania, 2010).

Brodman, James William, *Charity and Welfare: Hospitals and the Poor in Medieval Catalonia* (Philadelphia: University of Pennsylvania Press, 1998).

——, *Charity and Religion in Medieval Europe* (Washington, DC: Catholic University of America Press, 2009).

Brody, Saul, *The Disease of the Soul: Leprosy in Medieval Literature* (Ithaca, NY: Cornell University Press, 1974).

Broomhall, Susan, *Women's Medical Work in Early Modern France* (Manchester: Manchester University Press, 2004).

——, 'Identity and Life Narratives of the Poor in Late Sixteenth-Century Tours', *Renaissance Quarterly*, 57 (2004), 439–65.

——, *Women and Religion in Sixteenth-Century France* (Houndmills: Palgrave, 2006).

——, 'Family and Household Limitation Strategies among the Sixteenth-Century Urban Poor', *French History*, 20.2 (2006), 121–37.

——, 'The Politics of Charitable Men: Governing Poverty in Sixteenth-Century Paris', in Anne M. Scott (ed.), *Experiences of Poverty in Late Medieval and Early Modern England and France* (Farnham: Ashgate, 2012), pp. 133–58.

——, 'Charitable Medicine: The Provision of Health Care in the Sixteenth Century Hôtel-Dieu de Paris', in Witold Konstanty Pietrzak and Magdalena Kozluk (eds), *Le Cabinet du curieux: culture, savoirs, religion de l'Antiquité à l'Ancien Régime* (Paris: H. Champion, 2013), pp. 145–60.

Brown, Peter, 'Remembering the Poor and the Aesthetic of Society', *Journal of Interdisciplinary History*, 35 (2005), 513–22.

——, *Through the Eye of a Needle: Wealth, the Fall of Rome, and the Making of Christianity in the West, 350–550 AD* (Princeton, NJ: Princeton University Press, 2012).

Buhrer, E., 'From *Caritas* to Charity: How Loving God Became Giving Alms', in C. Kosso and A. Scott (eds), *Poverty and Prosperity in the Middle Ages and Renaissance* (Turnhout: Brepols, 2012), pp. 113–28.

Burgess, Clive, '"By Quick and by Dead": Wills and Pious Provision in Late Medieval Bristol', *English Historical Review*, 102 (1987), 837–58.

——, 'A Service for the Dead: The Form and Function of the Anniversary in Late Medieval Bristol', *Transactions of the Bristol and Gloucestershire Archaeological Society*, 105 (1987), 183–211.

——, 'Late Medieval Wills and Pious Convention: Testamentary Evidence Reconsidered', in Michael A. Hicks (ed.), *Profit, Piety and the Professions in Later Medieval England* (Stroud: Sutton, 1990), pp. 14–33.

——, '"An Afterlife in Memory": Commemoration and its Effects in a Late-Medieval Parish', in Peter Clarke and Tony Claydon (eds), *The Church, the Afterlife and the Fate of the Soul* (Woodbridge: Boydell/Ecclesiastical History Society, 2009), pp. 196–217.

Burrow, J.A., 'Autobiographical Poetry in the Middle Ages: The Case of Thomas Hoccleve', *Proceedings of the British Academy*, 68 (1982), 389–412.

——, *Thomas Hoccleve* (Aldershot: Ashgate/Variorum, 1994).

Cahen, Léon, *Le Grand Bureau des Pauvres de Paris au milieu du XVIIIe siècle* (Paris: Société nouvelle de librairie et d'édition, 1904).

Cameron, Keith, Mark Greengrass and Penny Roberts (eds), *The Adventure of Religious Pluralism in Early Modern France* (Oxford: Peter Lang, 2000).

Campbell, B.M.S., J.A. Galloway, D. Keene and M. Murphy, *A Medieval Capital and its Grain Supply: Agrarian Production and Distribution in the London Region c. 1300* (London: Institute of British Geographers, 1993).

Campbell, John, 'The Walloon Community in Canterbury, 1625–1649' (unpublished doctoral thesis, University of Wisconsin–Madison, 1970).

Carlton, Charles, with Robert L. Woods, Mary L. Robertson and Joseph S. Block (eds), *State, Sovereigns and Society in Early Modern England: Essays in Honour of A.J. Slavin* (New York: St Martin's Press, 1998).

Carruthers, Mary, *The Craft of Thought: Meditation, Rhetoric, and the Making of Images, 400–1200* (Cambridge: Cambridge University Press, 2000).

Cassidy-Welch, Megan, 'Images of Incarceration in Late-Medieval Art', in G. Kratzmann (ed.), *Imagination, Books and Community in Medieval Europe* (Melbourne: MacMillan Art Publishing/State Library of Victoria, 2009).

Catá Backer, Larry, 'Medieval Poor Law in Twentieth-Century America: Looking Back Towards a General Theory of American Poor Relief', *Case Western Reserve Law Review*, 44 (1995), 871–1041.

Cavallo, Sandra, *Charity and Power in Early Modern Italy: Benefactors and Their Motives in Turin, 1541–1789* (Cambridge: Cambridge University Press, 1995).

Charronnet, Charles, *Les Guerres de religion et la société protestante dans les Hautes-Alpes (1560–1789)* (Gap: P. Jouglard, 1861)

Chaunu, Pierre, *La Mort à Paris, XVIe, XVIIe et XVIIIe siècles* (Paris: Fayard, 1978).

Cipolla, Carlo M., *Before the Industrial Revolution: European Society and Economy, 1000–1700* (London: Methuen, 1981).

Cohen, Esther, 'Vagabondage à Paris au XIVe siècle', *Le Moyen Âge*, 88 (1982), 293–313.

Cohen, Mark R., *Poverty and Charity in the Jewish Community of Medieval Egypt* (Princeton, NJ: Princeton University Press, 2005).

——, 'Introduction: Poverty and Charity in Past Times', *Journal of Interdisciplinary History*, 35 (2005), 347–60.

—— (ed.), *Poverty and Charity: Judaism, Christianity, and Islam*, Special Issue, *Journal of Interdisciplinary History*, 35.3 (2005).

Collinson, Patrick, 'The Reformer and the Archbishop: Martin Bucer and an English Bucerian', *Journal of Religious History*, 6 (1971), 305–30.

——, *Godly People: Essays on English Protestantism and Puritanism* (London: Hambledon, 1983).

——, 'Puritanism and the Poor', in Rosemary Horrocks and Sarah Rees Jones (eds), *Pragmatic Utopias: Ideals and Communities, 1200–1630* (Cambridge: Cambridge University Press, 2001), pp. 242–58.

—— and John Craig (eds), *The Reformation in English Towns 1500–1640* (New York: St Martin's Press, 1998).

Connally, Michael, 'Les "Bonnes Femmes" de Paris: des communautés religieuses dans une société urbaine du bas moyen âge' (unpublished doctoral thesis, Université de Lyon, 2003).

Conner, Philip, *Huguenot Heartland: Montauban and Southern French Calvinism during the Wars of Religion* (Aldershot: Ashgate, 2002).

——, 'Huguenot Identities During the Wars of Religion: The Churches of Le Mans and Montauban Compared', *Journal of Ecclesiastical History*, 54.1 (2003), 23–39.

Constant, G., 'Les Registres de marguilliers', *Revue de l'histoire de l'église de France*, 103 (1938), 170–83.

Courtenay, William J., 'Token Coinage and the Administration of Poor Relief during the Late Middle Ages', *Journal of Interdisciplinary History*, 3 (1972), 275–95.

Coyecque, E., *L'Hôtel-Dieu de Paris au Moyen Âge, histoire et documents*, 2 vols (Paris: H. Champion, 1889–91).

Crawford, Patricia, *Parents of Poor Children 1580–1800* (Oxford: Oxford University Press, 2010).

Cullum, P.H., '"And hir name was Charities": Charitable Giving by and for Women in Late Medieval Yorkshire', in P.J.P. Goldberg (ed.), *Women in Medieval English Society* (Stroud: Sutton, 1997), pp. 182–211.

——, '"For pore people harberles": What Was the Function of the Maisonsdieu?', in Dorothy J. Clayton, Richard G. Davies and Peter McNiven (eds), *Trade, Devotion and Governance; Papers in Later Medieval History* (Stroud: Sutton, 1994), pp. 36–54.

—— and P.J.P. Goldberg, 'Charitable Provision in Late Medieval York: "To the Praise of God and the Use of the Poor"', *Northern History*, 29 (1993), 24–39.

Davies, C.S.L., 'Popular Religion and the Pilgrimage of Grace', in Anthony Fletcher and John Stevenson (eds), *Order and Disorder in Early Modern England* (Cambridge: Cambridge University Press, 1985), pp. 58–91.

Davis, Adam, 'The Economic Power of a Hospital in Thirteenth-Century Provins', in Katherine Jansen, Guy Geltner and Anne E. Lester (eds), *Center and Periphery: Studies on Power in the Medieval World in Honor of William Chester Jordan* (Leiden: Brill, 2013), pp. 121–34.

Davis, Barbara Beckerman, 'Reconstructing the Poor in Early Sixteenth-Century Toulouse', *French History*, 7 (1993), 249–85.

Davis, James, *Medieval Market Morality: Life, Law and Ethics in the English Marketplace, 1200–1500* (Cambridge: Cambridge University Press, 2012).

Davis, Natalie Zemon, *Society and Culture in Early Modern France* (Stanford: Polity, 1987).

Dawson, J.D., 'Richard FitzRalph and the Fourteenth-Century Poverty Controversies', *Journal of Ecclesiastical History*, 34 (1983), 315–44.

de Laborde, Alexandre, *Un philanthrope au XVIe siècle: Nicolas Houel, fondateur de la Maison de la Charité chrétienne* (Paris: La Société des bibliophiles françois, 1937).

de la Selle, Xavier, *Le Service des âmes à la cour: confesseurs et aumôniers des rois de France du XIIIe au XVe siècle* (Paris: École des Chartes, 1995).

De Munck, B., 'Fiscalizing Solidarity (From Below)', in E. Van Nederveen and G. Vermeesch (eds), *Serving the Urban Community: The Rise of Public Facilities in the Low Countries* (Amsterdam: Aksant, 2009), pp. 168–93.

de Spiegeler, Pierre, *Les Hôpitaux et l'assistance à Liège: Xe–XVe siècles: aspects institutionnels et sociaux* (Paris: Les Belles Lettres, 1987).

Dean, Trevor, *Crime in Medieval Europe* (Harlow: Longman, 2001).

Delaveau, Pierre, René R. Paris and Geneviève Clair, 'The Museum of Materia Medica of Paris', *Journal of Ethnopharmacy*, 17 (1986), 201–3.

Delmaire, Bernard, 'Hôpitaux urbains et hôpitaux ruraux en Artois entre le XIIe et le XIVe siècle', *Histoire médiévale et archéologie*, 17 (2004), 221–40.

Denis, Émile, *Sainte Julienne et Cornillon: étude historique* (Liège: Printing Co. Société Anonyme, 1927).

Depauw, Jacques, 'L'Assistance a Paris à la fin du XVIe siècle', *Bulletin Société Française d'Histoire des Hôpitaux*, 59 (1989), 10–24.

Despy, Georges, 'Le Temporal de l'abbaye d'Hélécine au XIIe siècle: un piège pour les Norbertins', *Revue du Nord*, 72 (1990), 427–41.

——, 'Franchises urbains et rurales: les ducs de Brabant et l'ancien comté de Brugeron aux XIIe et XIIIe siècles', in Jean-Marie Duvosquel and Erik Thoen (eds), *Peasants and Townsmen in Medieval Europe: Studia in honorem Adriaan Verhulst* (Gent: Snoek-Ducaju and Zoon, 1995), pp. 631–49.

Dickens, A.G., 'An Elizabethan Defender of the Monasteries', *Church Quarterly Review*, 130 (1940), 236–62.

——, *The English Reformation* (London: Batsford, 1964).

Diefendorf, Barbara B., *Paris City Councillors in the Sixteenth Century: The Politics of Patrimony* (Princeton, NJ: Princeton University Press, 1983).

——, *The Saint Bartholomew's Day Massacre: A Brief History with Documents* (Boston: Bedford/St Martin's Press, 2009).

Dinan, Susan E., 'Motivations for Charity in Early Modern France', in Thomas Max Safley (ed.), *The Reformation of Charity: The Secular and the Religious in Early Modern Poor Relief* (Leiden: Brill, 2003), pp. 176–92.

Dinges, Martin, 'L'Assistance paroissiale à Bordeaux à la fin du XVIIe siècle. L'exemple du consistoire protestant (1660–1670)', *Histoire, Économie et Société*, 5 (1986), 475–507.

——, 'Frühneuzeitliche Armenfürsorge als Sozialdisziplinierung? Probleme mit einem Konzept', *Geschichte und Gesellschaft*, 17 (1991), 5–29.

——, 'Self-Help and Reciprocity in Parish Assistance: Bordeaux in the Sixteenth and Seventeenth Centuries', in Peregrine Horden and Richard Smith (eds), *The Locus of Care: Families, Communities, Institutions and the Provision of Welfare since Antiquity* (London: Routledge, 1998), pp. 111–25.

——, 'Huguenot Poor Relief and Health Care in the Sixteenth and Seventeenth Centuries', in Raymond A. Mentzer and Andrew Spicer (eds), *Society and Culture in the Huguenot World, 1559–1685* (Cambridge: Cambridge University Press, 2002), pp. 157–74.

Dompnier, Bernard, *Venin de l'hérésie: images du protestantisme et combat catholique au XVIIe siècle* (Paris: Le Centurion, 1985).

Duffy, Eamon, *The Voices of Morebath: Reformation and Rebellion in an English Village* (New Haven, CT: Yale University Press, 2001).

Dunan-Page, Anne (ed.), *The Religious Culture of the Huguenots, 1660–1750* (Aldershot: Ashgate, 2006).

Dyer, Christopher, *Standards of Living in the Later Middle Ages: Social Change in England c. 1200–1520* (Cambridge: Cambridge University Press, 1989).

——, 'Work Ethics in the Fourteenth Century', in James Bothwell, P.J.P. Goldberg and W.M. Ormrod (eds), *The Problem of Labour in Fourteenth-Century England* (Woodbridge: York Medieval Press/Boydell, 2000), pp. 21–41.

——, 'Poverty and its Relief in Late Medieval England', *Past & Present*, 216 (2012), 41–78.

Elliott, Lisa Keane, 'Jean Martin, Governor of the *Grand Bureau des Pauvres*, on Charity and the Civic Duty of Governing Men in Paris, circa 1580', in Susan Broomhall and Jacqueline Van Gent (eds), *Governing Masculinities in the Early Modern Period* (Farnham: Ashgate, 2011), pp. 65–83.

——, 'Charitable "Intent" in Late Sixteenth-Century France: The Nevers Foundation and Single Poor Catholic Girls', in Anne M. Scott (ed.), *Experiences of Poverty in Late Medieval and Early Modern England and France* (Farnham: Ashgate, 2012), pp. 159–82.

Ellis, Hastings, 'The Contributions of Martin Bucer to the Reformation', *Harvard Theological Review*, 24 (1931), 29–42.

Evans, John Thadewald, 'The Political Elite of Norwich, 1620–1690: Patterns of Recruitment and the Impact of National Affairs' (unpublished doctoral thesis, Stanford University, 1971).

Farmer, Sharon, 'Persuasive Voices: Clerical Images of Medieval Wives', *Speculum*, 61 (1986), 517–43.

——, *Surviving Poverty in Medieval Paris: Gender, Ideology, and the Daily Lives of the Poor* (Ithaca, NY: Cornell University Press, 2002).

——, 'Manual Labor, Begging and Conflicting Gender Expectation in Thirteenth-Century Paris', in Sharon Farmer and Carol Braun Pasternack (eds), *Gender and Difference in the Middle Ages* (Minneapolis: University of Minnesota Press, 2003), pp. 261–87.

——, 'The Leper in the Master Bedroom: Thinking Through a Thirteenth-Century Exemplum', in Rosalynn Voaden and Diane Wolfthal (eds), *Framing the Family: Narrative and Representation in the Medieval and Early Modern Periods* (Tempe, AZ: Arizona Center for Medieval and Renaissance Studies, 2005), pp. 79–100.

——, 'Charity: A Deaf Mute's Story', in Miri Rubin (ed.), *Medieval Christianity in Practice* (Princeton, NJ: Princeton University Press, 2009), pp. 203–7.

Fehler, Timothy G., *Poor Relief and Protestantism: The Evolution of Social Welfare in Sixteenth-Century Emden* (Aldershot: Ashgate, 1999).

Ferster, Judith, *Fictions of Advice: The Literature and Politics of Counsel in Late Medieval England* (Philadelphia: University of Pennsylvania Press, 1996).

Fideler, Paul A., 'Poverty, Policy and Providence: The Tudors and the Poor', in Paul A. Fideler and T.F. Mayer (eds), *Political Thought and the Tudor Commonwealth: Deep Structure, Discourse and Disguise* (London: Routledge, 1992), pp. 194–222.

——, '*Societas*, *Civitas* and Early Elizabethan Poor Relief', in Charles Carlton with Robert L. Woods, Mary L. Robertson and Joseph S. Block (eds), *State, Sovereigns and Society in Early Modern England: Essays in Honour of A.J. Slavin* (New York: St Martin's Press, 1998), pp. 59–69.

——, *Social Welfare in Pre-Industrial England* (Basingstoke and New York: Palgrave Macmillan, 2006).

Fincham, K. and N. Tyacke, *Altars Restored: The Changing Face of English Religious Worship, 1547–c. 1700* (Oxford: Oxford University Press, 2007).

Fletcher, Anthony and John Stevenson (eds), *Order and Disorder in Early Modern England* (Cambridge: Cambridge University Press, 1985).

Fosseyeux, Marcel, *L'Assistance parisienne au milieu du XVIe siècle* (Paris, 1916).

——, 'Les Premiers Budgets municipaux d'assistance: la taxe des pauvres au XVIe siècle', *Revue d'histoire de l'église de France*, 20 (1934), 407–32.

French, Katherine, *The People of the Parish: Community Life in a Late Medieval English Diocese* (Philadelphia: University of Pennsylvania Press, 2000).

Gager, Kristin Elizabeth, *Blood Ties and Fictive Ties: Adoption and Family Life in Early Modern France* (Princeton, NJ: Princeton University Press, 1996).

Garrison-Estèbe, Janine, *Protestants du Midi, 1559–1598* (Toulouse: Privat, 1980).

Gautier, Théodore, 'IIIe Lettre sur l'histoire de la ville de Gap (1563–1568)', *Revue de Dauphiné*, 3 (1838), 65–85.

——, *Précis de l'histoire de la ville de Gap* (Gap: Alfred Allier, 1844).

Geremek, Bronisław, 'La Lutte contre le vagabondage à Paris aux XIVe et XVe siècles', in Luigi di Rosa (ed.), *Ricerche storiche ed economiche in memoria di Corrado Barbagallo* (Naples: Edizioni scientifiche italiane, 1970), pp. 213–36.

——, 'Criminalité, vagabondage, paupérisme: la marginalité à l'aube des temps modernes', *Revue d'histoire moderne et contemporaine*, 21 (1974), 347–51.

——, *The Margins of Society in Late Medieval Paris*, (trans.) Jean Birrell (Cambridge: Cambridge University Press, 1987).

——, *Poverty: A History*, (trans.) Agnieszka Kolakowska (Oxford: Blackwell, 1994).

Gibbs, Gary, 'New Duties for the Parish Community in Tudor England', in Katherine French, Gary Gibbs and Beat A. Kümin (eds), *The Parish in English Life, 1400–1600* (Manchester: Manchester University Press, 1997), pp. 163–77.

Gilbert, Émile, *La Pharmacie à travers les siècles: antiquité, moyen âge, temps modernes* (Toulouse: Vialelle et Cie, 1886).

Gonthier, Nicole, *Lyon et ses pauvres au Moyen Âge (1350–1500)* (Lyon: Éditions L'Hermès, 1978).

Goose, Nigel and Lien Luu (eds), *Immigrants in Tudor and Early Stuart England* (Brighton: Sussex Academic Press, 2005).

Green, David R., *Pauper Capital: London and the Poor Law, 1790–1870* (Aldershot: Ashgate, 2010).

Greengrass, Mark, *Governing Passions: Peace and Reform in the French Kingdom, 1576–1585* (Oxford: Oxford University Press, 2007).

Grell, Ole Peter, *Dutch Calvinists in Early Stuart London: The Dutch Church in Austin Friars, 1603–1642* (Leiden: Brill, 1989).

——, *Calvinist Exiles in Tudor and Stuart England* (Aldershot: Ashgate, 1996).

——, 'The Religious Duty of Care and the Social Need for Control in Early Modern Europe', *Historical Journal*, 39 (1996), 257–63.

—— and Andrew Cunningham (eds), *Health Care and Poor Relief in Protestant Europe, 1500–1700* (London: Routledge, 1997).

——, Andrew Cunningham and Jon Arrizabalaga (eds), *Health Care and Poor Relief in Counter-Reformation Europe* (London: Routledge, 1999).

Grimm, H.J., 'Luther's Contribution to Sixteenth-Century Organization of Poor Relief', *Archives for Reformation History*, 61 (1970).

Guest, Gerald, 'A Discourse on the Poor: The Hours of Jeanne d'Evreux', *Viator*, 26 (1995), 153–80.

Guiffrey, Jules, *Nicolas Houel, apothicaire parisien fondateur de la Maison de la Charité chrétienne et premier auteur de la Tenture d'Artémise* (Paris: H. Champion, 1898).

Guillaume, Paul (ed.), *Inventaire sommaire des Archives communales antérieures à 1790, vol. 1: Ville de Gap* (Gap: Imprimerie et Librairie Alpine, 1908).

Gutton, Jean-Pierre, *La Société et les pauvres en Europe, XVIe–XVIIIe siècles* (Paris: Presses Universitaires de France, 1974).

Gwynn, Robin D., *Huguenot Heritage: The History and Contribution of the Huguenots in Britain*, 2nd edn (Brighton: Sussex Academic Press, 2001).

Haigh, Christopher, *The Last Days of the Lancashire Monasteries and the Pilgrimage of Grace* (Manchester: Manchester University Press/Chetham Society, 1969).

——, *Reformation and Resistance in Tudor Lancashire* (Cambridge: Cambridge University Press, 1975).

Haines, R.M., 'Bishop Carpenter's Injunctions to the Diocese of Worcester in 1451', *Bulletin of the Institute of Historical Research*, 40 (1967), 203–7.

Hanlon, Gregory, *Confession and Community in Seventeenth-Century France: Catholic and Protestant Coexistence in Aquitaine* (Philadelphia: University of Pennsylvania Press, 1993).

Hardwick, Paul, *English Medieval Misericords: The Margins of Meaning* (Woodbridge: Boydell, 2011).

Harrington, Joel Francis, *The Unwanted Child: The Fate of Foundlings, Orphans, and Juvenile Criminals in Early Modern Germany* (Chicago: University of Chicago Press, 2009).

Harris, Tim, *The Politics of the Excluded, c. 1500–1850* (Basingstoke: Palgrave, 2001).

Harrison, Milmon F., *Righteous Riches: The Word of Faith Movements in Contemporary African-American Religion* (Oxford: Oxford University Press, 2005).

Harriss, G.L., *Cardinal Beaufort: A Study in Lancastrian Ascendancy and Decline* (Oxford: Clarendon Press, 1988).

Harvey, Barbara, *Westminster Abbey and its Estates in the Middle Ages* (Oxford: Clarendon Press, 1977).

——, *Living and Dying in England 1100–1540: The Monastic Experience* (Oxford: Oxford University Press, 1993).

Hatcher, John, 'England in the Aftermath of the Black Death', *Past & Present*, 144 (1994), 3–35.

——, 'The Great Slump of the Mid-Fifteenth Century', in Richard Britnell and John Hatcher (eds), *Progress and Problems in Medieval England* (Cambridge: Cambridge University Press, 1996), pp. 237–72.

——, 'Women's Work Reconsidered: Gender and Wage Differentiation in Late Medieval England', *Past & Present*, 173 (2001), 191–8.

Heal, Felicity, *Hospitality in Early Modern England* (New York: Oxford University Press, 1990).

Heath, Peter, 'Urban Piety in the Later Middle Ages: The Evidence of Hull Wills', in R.B. Dobson (ed.), *The Church, Politics and Patronage in the Fifteenth Century* (Gloucester: Sutton, 1984), pp. 209–34.

Heller, Henry, *The Conquest of Poverty: The Calvinist Revolt in Sixteenth Century France* (Leiden: Brill, 1986).

Henderson, John, *Piety and Charity in Late Medieval Florence* (Chicago: University of Chicago Press, 1994).

——, *The Renaissance Hospital*: *Healing the Body and Healing the Soul* (New Haven, CT: Yale University Press, 2006).

Hickey, Daniel, *Local Hospitals in Ancien Régime France: Rationalization, Resistance, Renewal, 1530–1789* (Montreal: McGill–Queen's University Press, 1997).

Hindle, Steve, *The State and Social Change in Early Modern England, c. 1550–1640* (Basingstoke: Macmillan, 2000).

——, *On the Parish? The Micro-Politics of Poor Relief in Rural England, c. 1550–1750* (Oxford: Oxford University Press, 2004).

Holt, Mack P., *The French Wars of Religion, 1562–1629* (Cambridge: Cambridge University Press, 1995).

Horden, Peregrine (ed.), *Music as Medicine: The History of Music Therapy since Antiquity* (Aldershot: Ashgate, 2000).

Horrocks, Rosemary and Sarah Rees Jones (eds), *Pragmatic Utopias: Ideals and Communities, 1200–1630* (Cambridge: Cambridge University Press, 2001).

Houston, Rab, 'Vagrants and Society in Early Modern England', *Cambridge Anthropology*, 6 (1980), 18–32.

Hoyle, R.W., 'Agrarian Agitation in Mid-Sixteenth-Century Norfolk: A Petition of 1553', *Historical Journal*, 44 (2001), 223–38.

Hufton, Olwen, *The Poor of Eighteenth-Century France, 1750–1789* (Oxford: Clarendon Press, 1974).

Imbert, Jean, *Histoire des hôpitaux en France* (Toulouse: Privat, 1982).

——, *Le Droit hospitalier de l'Ancien Régime* (Paris: Presses Universitaires de France, 1993).

Jeans, Susi, 'The Easter Psalms of Christ's Hospital', *Proceedings of the Royal Musical Association*, 88 (1961–62), 45–60.

Jéhanno, Christine, 'La Réforme de l'Hôtel-Dieu de Paris à la fin du Moyen Âge: remise en ordre nécessaire ou réforme monastique imposée à l'hôpital?', *Revue du Nord*, hors série, collection histoire, 22 (2008), 67–88.

Jones, C., 'Some Recent Trends in the History of Charity', in M. Daunton (ed.), *Charity, Self-Interest and Welfare in the English Past* (London and New York: Taylor and Francis, 1996), pp. 51–63.

Jones, W.R.D., *The Tudor Commonwealth 1529–1559* (London: Athlone, 1970).

Jordan, Wilbur K., *Philanthropy in England 1480–1660* (London: Routledge, 1959).

——, *The Charities of Rural England 1480–1660: The Aspirations and Achievements of the Rural Society* (London: Allen and Unwin, 1961).

Jütte, Robert, *Poverty and Deviance in Early Modern Europe* (Cambridge: Cambridge University Press, 1994).

Kamen, Henry, *Early Modern European Society* (London and New York: Routledge, 2000).

Kaplan, Benjamin J., *Divided by Faith*: *Religious Conflict and the Practice of Toleration in Early Modern Europe* (Cambridge, MA: Belknap, 2007).

Kaye, Joel, *Economy and Nature in the Fourteenth Century: Money, Market Exchange, and the Emergence of Scientific Thought* (Cambridge: Cambridge University Press, 1998).

____, *A History of Balance, 1250-1375: The Emergence of a New Model of Equilibrium and its Impact on Thought* (Cambridge: Cambridge University Press, 2014).

Kelly, Thomas J., *Thorns on the Tudor Rose: Monks, Rogues, Vagabonds and Sturdy Beggars* (Jackson: University Press of Mississippi, 1977).

King, S., '"Stop this overwhelming torment of destiny": Negotiating Financial Aid at Times of Sickness under the English Old Poor Law, 1800–1840', *Bulletin of the History of Medicine*, 79 (2005), 228–60.

Kinney, Arthur F. (ed.), *Rogues, Vagabonds and Sturdy Beggars* (Amherst: University of Massachusetts Press, 1990).

Knowles, David, *The Monastic Orders in England*, (Cambridge: Cambridge University Press, 1949).

——, *Religious Orders*, 3 vols (Cambridge: Cambridge University Press, 1979).

Koch, Matthew, 'Poor Relief in Montauban, 1548 to 1629', *Proceedings of the Western Society for French History*, 23 (1996), 69–80.

Konnert, Mark W., *Civic Agendas and Religious Passion: Châlons-sur-Marne during the French Wars of Religion, 1560–1594* (Kirksville, MO: Sixteenth Century Journal Publishers, 1997).

——, *Local Politics in the French Wars of Religion: The Towns of Champagne, the Duc de Guise, and the Catholic League, 1560–95* (Aldershot: Ashgate, 2006). .

Kümin, Beat A., *The Shaping of a Community: The Rise and Reformation of the English Parish, c. 1400–1560* (Brookfield, VT: Scolar Press, 1996).

Kupper, Jean-Louis, *Liège et l'église imperiale, XIe–XIIe siècles* (Paris: Société d'Édition 'Les Belles Lettres', 1981).

Labrousse, Elisabeth, *'Une foi, une loi, un roi?': Essai sur la révocation de l'édit de Nantes* (Geneva: Labor et Fides, 1985).

Ladurie, Emmanuel Le Roy, *Montaillou: The Promised Land of Error*, (trans.) Barbara Bray (New York: Vintage Books, 1979).

Langholm, Odd, *Economics in the Medieval Schools: Wealth, Exchange, Value, Money and Usury According to the Paris Theological Tradition, 1200–1350* (Leiden: Brill, 1992).

Le Blévec, Daniel, *La Part du pauvre: l'assistance dans les pays du Bas-Rhône du XIIe au milieu du XVe siècle*, 2 vols (Rome: École française de Rome, 2000).

Le Goff, Jacques, *The Birth of Purgatory*, (trans.) Arthur Goldhammer (Chicago: University of Chicago Press, 1984).

Le Grand, Léon, *Les Béguines de Paris* (Paris, 1893).

——, *Les Quinze-Vingts: depuis leurs fondation jusqu'à leur translation au faubourg Saint-Antoine. XIIIe–XVIIIe siècles*, 2 vols (Paris, 1886–87).

——, *Les Maisons-Dieu et léproseries du diocèse de Paris au milieu du XIVe siècle* (Paris, 1898).

——, *Statuts d'hôtels-dieu et de léproseries: recueil de textes du XIIe au XIVe siècle* (Paris, 1901).

Le Roux de Lincy, Antoine, 'Hugues Aubriot, prévôt de Paris sous Charles V, 1367–1381', *Bibliothèque de l'École des Chartes*, 23 (1862), 173–213.

Lindberg, Carter, '"There Should Be No Beggars Among Christians": Karlstadt, Luther, and the Origins of Protestant Poor Relief', *Church History*, 46 (1977), 313–34.

——, *Beyond Charity: Reformation Initiatives for the Poor* (Minneapolis: Augsburg Fortress, 1993).

Lis, Catharina and Hugo Soly, *Poverty and Capitalism in Pre-Industrial Europe*, (trans.) James Coonan (Hassocks: Harvester, 1979).

Little, Lester, 'Pride Goes before Avarice: Social Change and the Vices in Latin Christendom', *American Historical Review*, 76 (1971), 16–49.

Loach, Jennifer and Robert Tittler (eds), *The Mid-Tudor Polity c. 1540–1560* (London: Macmillan, 1980).

Long, Jean-Denis, *La Réforme et les guerres de religion en Dauphiné de 1560 à l'Édit de Nantes (1598)* (Paris: Firmin Didot, 1856).

Lundquist, J.M., *The Temple of Jerusalem: Past, Present, and Future* (Westport: Praeger, 2008).

Luria, Keith P., *Sacred Boundaries: Religious Coexistence and Conflict in Early-Modern France* (Washington, DC: Catholic University of America Press, 2005).

Luu, Lien Bich, *Immigrants and the Industries of London, 1500–1700* (Aldershot: Ashgate, 2005).

MacKay, Dorothy-Louise, *Les Hôpitaux et la charité à Paris au XIIIe siècle* (Paris: E. Champion, 1923).

MacKinnon, Dolly, '"Poor Senseless Bess, Clothed in her Rags and Folly": Early Modern Women, Madness, and Song in Seventeenth-Century England', *Parergon*, 18.3 (2001), 119–51.

——, '"The Trustworthy Agency of the Eyes": Reading Images of Music and Madness in Historical Context', *Health and History*, 5.2 (2003), 123–49.

——, 'Music, Madness, and the Body: Symptom and Cure', in Sander L. Gilman (ed.), *Mind and Body in the History of Psychiatry*, Special Issue of *History of Psychiatry*, 17.1 (2006), 9–21.

——, '"Charity is worth it when it looks that good": Rural Women and Bequests of Clothing in Early Modern England', in Stephanie Tarbin and Susan Broomhall (eds), *Women, Identities and Communities in Early Modern Europe* (Aldershot: Ashgate, 2008), pp. 79–93.

——, '"I now have a book of songs of her writing": Scottish Families, Orality, Literacy and the Transmission of Musical Culture c. 1500–c. 1800', in Elizabeth Ewan and Janay Nugent (eds), *Finding the Family in Medieval and Early Modern Scotland* (Aldershot: Ashgate, 2008), pp. 35–48.

——, 'Charitable Bodies: Clothing as Charity in Early-Modern England', in Megan Cassidy-Welch and Peter Sherlock (eds), *Practices of Gender in Late Medieval and Early Modern Europe* (Turnhout: Brepols, 2008), pp. 235–59.

Maddern, Philippa, '"Oppressed by Utter Poverty": Survival Strategies for Single Mothers and their Children in Late Medieval England', in Anne M. Scott (ed.), *Experiences of Poverty in Late Medieval and Early Modern England and France* (Farnham: Ashgate, 2012), pp. 41–62.

——, 'Order and Disorder', in Carole Rawcliffe and Richard Wilson (eds), *Medieval Norwich* (London: Continuum, 2004), pp. 189–212.

Marmoy, C.F.A., 'L'Entraide des réfugiés français en Angleterre', *Bulletin de la Société de l'histoire du protestantisme français*, 115 (1969), 591–604.

Marsh, Christopher, *Music and Society in Early Modern England* (Cambridge: Cambridge University Press, 2010).

Martin, Meredith, *Dairy Queens: The Politics of Pastoral Architecture from Catherine de' Medici to Marie-Antoinette* (Cambridge, MA: Harvard University Press, 2011).

Maxwell, J., 'Lay Piety in the Sermons of John Chrysostom', in D. Krueger (ed.), *Byzantine Christianity* (Minneapolis: Augsburg Fortress, 2010), pp. 19–38.

McClendon, Muriel C., '"Against God's Word": Government, Religion and the Crisis of Authority in Early Reformation Norwich', *Sixteenth Century Journal*, 25 (1994), 353–69.

——, *The Quiet Reformation* (Stanford: Stanford University Press, 1999).

McHugh, Timothy J., 'Hospitals and Huguenots: Confessional Coexistence in Nîmes, 1629–85', *European History Quarterly*, 33 (2003), 5–27.

——, *Hospital Politics in Seventeenth-Century France: The Crown, Urban Elites and the Poor* (Aldershot: Ashgate, 2007).

McIntosh, Marjorie K., 'Local Responses to the Poor in Late Medieval and Tudor England', *Continuity and Change*, 3 (1988), 209–45.

——, *Controlling Misbehavior in England, 1370–1600* (Cambridge; New York: Cambridge University Press, 1998).

——, 'Poverty, Charity and Coercion in Elizabethan England', *Journal of Interdisciplinary History*, 35 (2005), 457–79.

——, *Poor Relief in England, 1350–1600* (Cambridge: Cambridge University Press, 2012).

Mellinkoff, Ruth, *Outcasts: Signs of Otherness in Northern European Art of the Late Middle Ages* (Berkeley: University of California Press, 1993).

Mendelson, Sara and Patricia Crawford, *Women in Early Modern England* (Oxford: Clarendon Press, 1998).

Mentzer, Raymond A., '*Disciplina nervus ecclesiae*: The Calvinist Reform of Morals', *Sixteenth Century Journal*, 18 (1987), 89–116.

——, 'Le Consistoire et la pacification du monde rural', *Bulletin de la Société de l'histoire du protestantisme français*, 135 (1989), 373–89.

——, 'Ecclesiastical Discipline and Communal Reorganization among the Protestants of Southern France', *European History Quarterly*, 21 (1991), 163–83.

——, 'Organizational Endeavour and Charitable Impulse in Sixteenth-Century France: The Care of Protestant Nîmes', *French History*, 5 (1991), 1–29.

—— (ed.), *Sin and the Calvinists: Morals Control and the Consistory in Reformed Tradition* (Kirksville, MO: Truman State University Press, 1994).

Mesmin (McDougall), Simone C., 'Waleran, Count of Meulan and the Leper Hospital of S. Gilles de Pont-Audemer', *Annales de Normandie*, 32 (1982), 3–19.

——, 'Du Comté la Commune: la léproserie de Saint-Gilles de Pont-Audemer', *Annales de Normandie*, 37 (1987), 235–68.

Meurgey de Tupigny, Jacques, *Histoire de la paroisse Saint-Jacques-de-la-Boucherie* (Paris: H. Champion, 1926).

Michielse, H.C.M. and Robert van Krieken, 'Policing the Poor: J.L. Vives and the Sixteenth-Century Origins of Modern Social Administration', *Social Service Review*, 64 (1990), 1–21.

Milis, Ludo J.R., *Angelic Monks and Earthly Men: Monasticism and its Meaning to Medieval Society* (Woodbridge: Boydell, 1992).

Moisa, Maria A., 'Fourteenth-Century Preachers' Views of the Poor: Class or Status Group?', in R. Samuel and G.S. Jones (eds), *Culture, Ideology and Politics* (London: Routledge & Kegan Paul, 1982), pp. 160–75.

Mollat, Michel, *Les Pauvres au Moyen Âge: étude sociale* (Paris: Hachette, 1978).

——, *The Poor in the Middle Ages: An Essay in Social History*, (trans.) Arthur Goldhammer (New Haven, CT: Yale University Press, 1986).

Moore, R.I., *The Birth of Popular Heresy* (London: Arnold, 1975; Toronto: University of Toronto Press/Medieval Academy of America, 1995).

Muldrew, Craig, *The Economy of Obligation: The Culture of Credit and Social Relations in Early Modern England* (New York: St Martin's Press, 1998).

Muskett, Joseph James (ed.), *Suffolk Manorial Families: Being the County Visitations and Other Pedigrees* (Exeter: William Pollard, 1894–1908).

Newhauser, Richard, 'The Love of Money as Deadly Sin and Deadly Disease', in Jörg O. Fichte, Karl Heinz Göller and Bernhard Schimmelpfennig (eds), *Zusammenhänge, Einflüsse, Wirkungen. Kongressakten zum ersten Symposium des Mediävistenverbandes in Tübingen, 1984* (Berlin: de Gruyter, 1986), pp. 315–26.

——, *The Early History of Greed: The Sin of Avarice in Early Medieval Thought and Literature* (Cambridge: Cambridge University Press, 2000).

Nixon, Cheryl, *The Orphan in Eighteenth-Century Law and Literature: Estate, Blood, and Body* (Farnham: Ashgate, 2011).

O'Tool, Mark P., 'Caring for the Blind in Medieval Paris: Life at the Quinze-Vingts 1250–1430' (unpublished doctoral thesis: University of California, Santa Barbara, 2007).

——, 'The *povres avugles* of the Hospital of the Quinze-Vingts', in Meredith Cohen and Justine Firnhaber-Baker (eds), *Difference and Identity in Francia and Medieval France* (Farnham: Ashgate, 2010), pp. 157–74.

Orth, Myra Dickman, 'Francis du Moulin and the Journal of Louise de Savoy', *Sixteenth Century Journal*, 13 (1982), 55–66.

Otis, Leah L., 'Municipal Wet Nurses in Fifteenth-Century Montpellier', in Barbara Hanawalt (ed.), *Women and Work in Pre-Industrial Europe* (Bloomington: University of Indiana Press, 1986), pp. 83–93.

Palliser, D.M. (ed.), *The Cambridge Urban History of Britain, vol. 1: 600–1540* (Cambridge: Cambridge University Press, 2000).

Parker, Charles H., *The Reformation of Community Social Welfare and Calvinist Charity in Holland, 1572–1620* (Cambridge: Cambridge University Press, 1998).

Parturier, Louis, *L'Assistance à Paris sous l'Ancien Régime et pendant la Révolution* (Paris: Larose, 1897; Geneva: Mégariotis Reprints, 1978).

Pelling, Margaret, *The Common Lot: Sickness, Medical Occupations and the Urban Poor in Early Modern England* (London and New York: Longman, 1998).

Perkins, Nicholas, *Hoccleve's 'Regiment of Princes': Counsel and Constraint* (Cambridge: D.S. Brewer, 2001).

Persoons, Ernest, Walter de Keyzer, Marleen Forrier and Michel van der Eycken, *La Lèpre dans les Pays-Bas (XIIe–XVIIIe siècles)* (Brussels: Archives Générales du Royaume, 2000).

Pettegree, Andrew, *Foreign Protestant Communities in Sixteenth-Century London* (Oxford: Oxford University Press, 1986).

Planchon, M.G., 'Les Jardins des apothicaires de Paris', *Journal de pharmacie et de chimie*, 25 (1893), 289–98.

Poole, G.A., *Churches: Their Structure, Arrangement, and Decoration* (London, 1846).

Poos, L.R., *A Rural Society after the Black Death: Essex 1350–1525* (Cambridge: Cambridge University Press, 1991).

—— (ed.), *Lower Ecclesiastical Jurisdiction in Late-Medieval England: The Courts of the Dean and Chapter of Lincoln, 1336–1349, and the Deanery of Wisbech, 1458–1484* (Oxford: British Academy/Oxford University Press, 2001).

Pound, John, 'An Elizabethan Census of the Poor: The Treatment of Vagrancy in Norwich, 1570–1580', *University of Birmingham Historical Journal*, 7 (1962), 135–61.

——, *Tudor and Stuart Norwich* (Chichester: Phillimore, 1988).

——, 'Government to 1660', in Carole Rawcliffe and Richard Wilson, with Christine Clark (eds), *Norwich Since 1550* (London and New York: Hambledon and London, 2004), pp. 35–61.

Pugh, Wilma J., 'Social Welfare and the Edict of Nantes: Lyon and Nîmes', *French Historical Studies*, 8 (1974), 349–76.

——, 'Catholics, Protestants, and Testamentary Charity in Seventeenth-Century Lyon and Nîmes', *French Historical Studies*, 11 (1980), 479–504.

Pullan, Brian, *Rich and Poor in Renaissance Venice* (Cambridge, MA: Harvard University Press, 1971).

——, 'Religion and the Rise of Poor Relief', *Journal of Early Modern History*, 4 (2000), 442–6.

Ramsey, Matthew, 'Poor Relief and Medical Assistance in 18th and 19th Century Paris', in Ole Peter Grell, Andrew Cunningham and Robert Jütte (eds), *Health Care and Poor Relief in 18th and 19th Century Northern Europe* (Aldershot: Ashgate, 2002), pp. 280–308.

Rawcliffe, Carole, *Medicine for the Soul: The Life, Death and Resurrection of an English Medieval Hospital: St Giles's, Norwich, c. 1249–1550* (Stroud: Sutton, 1999).

——, *Leprosy in Medieval England* (Woodbridge: Boydell, 2006).

—— and Richard Wilson (eds), *Medieval Norwich* (London and New York: Hambledon and London, 2004).

—— and Richard Wilson, with Christine Clark (eds), *Norwich Since 1550* (London and New York: Hambledon and London, 2004).

Reynolds, Matthew, *Godly Reformers and their Opponents in Early Modern England: Religion in Norwich c. 1560–1643* (Woodbridge: Boydell, 2005).

Richards, Peter, *The Medieval Leper and His Northern Heirs* (Woodbridge; Rochester: D.S. Brewer, 2000).

Rippert d'Alauzier, Gwenola de, *Dauphiné protestant: regards sur les guerres de religion en Dauphiné au XVIe siècle, des prémices de la Réforme à l'Édit de Nantes* (Aubais: Musée du protestantisme dauphinois/Mémoires d'Oc éditions, 2006).

Robbins, Kevin C., *City on the Ocean Sea: La Rochelle, 1530–1650: Urban Society, Religion, and Politics on the French Atlantic Frontier, 1530–1650* (Leiden: Brill, 1997).

Roberts, Penny, *Peace and Authority during the French Religious Wars, c. 1560–1600* (Houndmills: Palgrave Macmillan, 2013).

Robin, Diana Maury, Anne R. Larsen and Carole Levin (eds), *Encyclopedia of Women in the Renaissance: Italy, France and England* (Santa Barbara, CA: ABC-CLIO, 2007).

Rosenthal, Joel T., *The Purchase of Paradise: Gift Giving and the Aristocracy, 1307–1485* (London: Routledge & Kegan Paul, 1972).

Rubin, Miri, *Charity and Community in Medieval Cambridge* (Cambridge and New York: Cambridge University Press, 1987).

Rudd, David Paul, 'The Involuntary Poor in English Religious Writings from the Late Middle Ages to 1600' (unpublished doctoral thesis, Lancaster University, 1992).

Ruelle, Pierre (ed.), *Les Congés d'Arras: Jean Bodel, Baude Fastoul, Adam de la Halle* (Brussels: Presses Universitaires de Bruxelles, 1965).

Ruiz, Teofilo F., *From Heaven to Earth: The Reordering of Castilian Society, 1150–1350* (Princeton, NJ: Princeton University Press, 2004).

Rushton, Neil S., 'Monastic Charitable Provision in Tudor England: Quantifying and Qualifying Poor Relief in the Early Sixteenth Century', *Continuity and Change*, 16 (2001), 9–44.

——, 'Monastic Charitable Provision in Late Medieval England, *c.* 1260–1540' (unpublished doctoral thesis, Cambridge, 2002).

——, 'Spatial Aspects of the Almonry Site and the Changing Priorities of Poor Relief at Westminster Abbey *c*. 1290–1540', *Architectural History*, 45 (2002), 66–91.

—— and W. Sigle-Rushton, 'Monastic Poor Relief in Sixteenth-Century England', *Journal of Interdisciplinary History*, 32 (2001), 193–216.

Sabra, Adam, *Poverty and Charity in Medieval Islam: Mamluk Egypt, 1250–1517* (Cambridge: Cambridge University Press, 2000).

Safley, Thomas Max (ed.), *The Reformation of Charity: The Secular and the Religious in Early Modern Europe* (Leiden: Brill, 2003).

—— (ed.), *A Companion to Multiconfessionalism in the Early Modern World* (Leiden: Brill, 2011).

Saunier, Annie, 'Gros vérolés à l'Hôtel-Dieu de Paris en 1508', *Bulletin d'information de la Société de démographie historique*, 8 (1973), 5–10.

Sauzet, Robert, *Contre réforme et réforme catholique en Bas-Languedoc: le diocèse de Nîmes au XVIIe siècle* (Louvain: Nauwelaerts, 1979).

Savine, Alexander, *English Monasteries on the Eve of the Dissolution*, (ed.) Paul Vinogradoff (Oxford: Clarendon Press, 1909).

Scase, Wendy, *'Piers Plowman' and the New Anti-Clericalism* (Cambridge: Cambridge University Press, 1989).

Schen, Claire, *Charity and Lay Piety in Reformation London, 1500–1620* (Aldershot: Ashgate, 2002).

Schervish, Paul G., 'Why the Wealthy Give: Factors which Mobilize Philanthropy among High Net-Worth Individuals', in Adrian Sargeant and Walter Wymer (eds), *The Routledge Companion to Nonprofit Marketing* (London and New York: Routledge, 2008), pp. 165–81.

Schickler, Fernand de, *Les Églises du Refuge en Angleterre*, 3 vols (Paris: Fischbacher, 1892).

Scott, Anne M., *'Piers Plowman' and the Poor* (Dublin: Four Courts Press, 2004).

——, *'Le Chastel de Labour, La Voie de Povreté ou de Richesse* and a Luxury Book, Widener 1, Free Library of Philadelphia', in Anne M. Scott (ed.), *Experiences of Poverty in Late Medieval and Early Modern England and France* (Farnham: Ashgate, 2012), pp. 253–77.

—— (ed.), *Experiences of Poverty in Late Medieval and Early Modern England and France* (Farnham: Ashgate, 2012).

——, 'Thomas Hoccleve's Selves Apart', in Ronald Bedford, Lloyd Davis and Philippa Kelly (eds), *Early Modern Autobiography: Theories, Genres, Practices* (Ann Arbor: University of Michigan Press, 2006), pp. 89–103.

Scott, Virginia and Sara Sturm-Maddox, *Performance, Poetry and Politics on the Queen's Day: Catherine de Médicis and Pierre de Ronsard at Fontainebleau* (Aldershot: Ashgate, 2007).

Siena, Kevin (ed.), *Sins of the Flesh: Responding to Sexual Disease in Early Modern Europe* (Toronto: University of Toronto Press, 2005).

Silber, Ilana F., 'Monasticism and the Protestant Ethic: Asceticism, Rationality and Wealth in the Medieval West', *Journal of British Sociology*, 44 (1993), 103–22.

——, 'Gift-Giving in the Great Traditions: The Case of Donations to Monasteries in the Medieval West', *Archives Européenes de Sociologie*, 36 (1995), 209–43.

Silvester, Lesley, '"hav dwelt here ever. No alms. Veri pore": Life Experiences of the Poor in Sixteenth-Century Norwich – A Longitudinal Study' (unpublished doctoral thesis, The University of Western Australia, 2013).

Simiz, Stefano (ed.), *La Parole publique en ville des Réformes à la Révolution* (Villeneuve d'Ascq: Presses Universitaires du Septentrion, 2012).

Simons, Walter, *Cities of Ladies: Beguine Communities in the Medieval Low Countries, 1200–1565* (Philadelphia: University of Pennsylvania Press, 2001).

Slack, Paul, 'Social Policy and the Constraints of Government 1547–58', in Jennifer Loach and Robert Tittler (eds), *The Mid-Tudor Polity c. 1540–1560* (London: Macmillan, 1980).

——, *The Impact of Plague in Tudor and Stuart England* (London: Routledge & Kegan Paul, 1985).

——, *Poverty and Policy in Tudor and Stuart England* (London and New York: Longman, 1988).

——, *The English Poor Law 1531–1782* (Basingstoke: Macmillan, 1990).

——, *From Reformation to Improvement* (Oxford: Clarendon Press, 1999).

Smith, Mark Michael, *Sensing the Past: Seeing, Hearing, and Smelling, Tasting and Touching History* (Berkeley: University of California Press, 2007).

Snape, R.H., *English Monastic Finances in the Later Middle Ages* (Cambridge: Cambridge University Press, 1926).

Sokoll, Thomas, 'Negotiating a Living: Essex Pauper Letters from London, 1800–1834', *International Review of Social History*, 45, Supplement 8 (2000), 19–46.

Spicer, Andrew, *The French-Speaking Reformed Community and their Church in Southampton, 1567–c. 1620* (London: Huguenot Society, 1997).

Spohnholz, Jesse, *The Tactics of Toleration: A Refugee Community in the Age of Religious War* (Newark: University of Delaware Press, 2011).

Spufford, Margaret, 'Puritanism and Social Control?', in Anthony Fletcher and John Stevenson (eds), *Order and Disorder in Early Modern England* (Cambridge: Cambridge University Press, 1985), pp. 41–57.

Staley, Edgcumbe, *The Guilds of Florence* (London: Methuen, 1906).

Styles, John, *Threads of Feeling: The London Foundling Hospital's Textile Tokens, 1740–1770* (London: Foundling Hospital Museum, 2010).

Sunshine, Glenn S., *Reforming French Protestantism: The Development of Huguenot Ecclesiastical Institutions, 1557–1572* (Kirksville, MO: Truman State University Press, 2003).

Swanson, R.N., *Indulgences in Late Medieval England: Passports to Paradise?* (Cambridge: Cambridge University Press, 2007).

Sweetinburgh, Sheila, 'Clothing the Naked in Late Medieval East Kent', in Catherine Richardson (ed.), *Clothing Culture, 1350–1650* (Aldershot: Ashgate, 2004), pp. 109–22.

Swietek, Francis R., 'The Alms Repaid a Hundredfold: A New Latin Version of a Popular *Exemplum*', *Fabula*, 17 (1976), 169–81.

Talmon-Heller, D., *Islamic Piety in Medieval Syria: Mosques, Cemeteries and Sermons under the Zangids and Ayyūbids, 1146–1260* (Leiden: Brill, 2007).

Tanner, Norman P., *The Church in Late Medieval Norwich 1370–1532* (Toronto: Pontifical Institute of Mediaeval Studies, 1984).

Tarbin, Stephanie, 'Caring for Poor and Fatherless Children in London, *c.* 1350–1550', *Journal of the History of Childhood and Youth*, 3 (2010), 391–410.

Terpstra, Nicholas, *Lay Confraternities and Civic Religion in Renaissance Bologna* (Cambridge: Cambridge University Press, 1995).

——, *Abandoned Children of the Italian Renaissance: Orphan Care in Florence and Bologna* (Baltimore, MD: Johns Hopkins University Press, 2005).

——, *Cultures of Charity: Women, Politics, and the Reform of Poor Relief in Renaissance Italy* (Cambridge, MA: Harvard University Press, 2013).

Thomson, J.A.F., 'Piety and Charity in Late Medieval London', *Journal of Ecclesiastical History*, 16.2 (1965), 178–95.

Tierney, Brian, 'The Decretists and the "Deserving Poor"', *Comparative Studies in Society and History*, 1 (1958–59), 360–73.

——, *Medieval Poor Law: A Sketch of Canonical Theory and Its Application in England* (Berkeley: University of California Press, 1959).

Tits-Dieuaide, M.-J., 'Les Tables des pauvres dans les anciennes principautés belges au moyen âge', *Tidjschift voor Geschiedenis*, 88 (1975), 562–83.

Tittler, Robert, 'Reformation, Resources and Authority in English Towns: An Overview', in Patrick Collinson and John Craig (eds), *The Reformation in English Towns 1500–1640* (New York: St Martin's Press, 1998).

Todd, Margo, *Christian Humanism and the Puritan Social Order* (Cambridge: Cambridge University Press, 1987).

Touati, François-Olivier, *Maladie et société au Moyen Âge. La Lèpre, les lépreux et les léproseries dans la province ecclésiastique de Sens jusqu'au milieu du XIVe siècle* (Paris-Brussels: De Boeck Université, 1998).

——, 'Contagion and Leprosy: Myth, Ideas, and Evolution in Medieval Minds and Society', in Lawrence I. Conrad and D. Wujastyk (eds), *Contagion: Perspectives from Pre-Modern Societies* (Aldershot: Ashgate, 2000), pp. 79–201.

Traver, Andrew G., 'William of Saint-Amour's Two Disputed Questions *De quantitate eleemosynae* and *De valido mendicante*', *Archives d'histoire doctrinale et littéraire du moyen-âge*, 62 (1995), 295–342.

Tubach, Frederic C., *Index Exemplorum: A Handbook of Medieval Religious Tales* (Helsinki: Suomalainen Tiedeakatemia, 1969).

Tuttle, Virginia G., 'Bosch's Image of Poverty', *Art Bulletin*, 63 (1981), 88–95.

Vacher, Marguerite, *Nuns Without Cloister: Sisters of St. Joseph in the Seventeenth and Eighteenth Centuries* (Lanham: University Press of America, 2010).

VanderSchaaf, Mark E., 'Archbishop Parker's Efforts Toward a Bucerian Discipline in the Church of England', *Sixteenth Century Journal*, 8 (1977), 85–103.

Vigne, Randolph and Graham C. Gibbs (eds), *The Strangers' Progress: Integration and Disintegration of the Huguenot and Walloon Refugee Community, 1567–1889: Essays in Memory of Irene Scouloudi* (London: Huguenot Society, 1995).

Vigne, Randolph and Charles Littleton (eds), *From Strangers to Citizens: The Integration of Immigrant Communities in Britain, Ireland and Colonial America, 1550–1750* (Brighton: Sussex Academic Press, 2001).

von Moos, Peter, 'L'*Exemplum* et les *Exempla* des Prêcheurs', in Jacques Berlioz and Marie Anne Polo de Beaulieu (eds), *Les 'Exempla' médiévaux: Nouvelles perspectives* (Paris: H. Champion, 1998), pp. 67–81.

Waller, William C., 'Early Huguenot Friendly Societies', *Proceedings of the Huguenot Society of London*, 6 (1898–1901), 201–35.

Warolin, Christian, 'Un testament authentique de Nicolas Houel (5 septembre 1551)', *Revue d'histoire de la pharmacie*, 82 (1994), 331–41.

——, 'Trois contrats passés avec Nicolas Houel, intendant et gouverneur de la Maison de la Charité chrétienne en 1586', *Revue d'histoire de la pharmacie*, 86 (1998), 63–6.

——, 'Nicolas Houel et Michel Dusseau, apothicaires à Paris au XVIe siècle', *Revue d'histoire de la pharmacie*, 88 (2000), 319–36.

Warren, Anne K., *Anchorites and their Patrons in Medieval England* (Berkeley: University of California Press, 1985).

Watkins, Carl, 'Providence, Experience and Doubt in Medieval England', in Yola Bataski, Subha Mukherji and Jan-Melissa Schramm (eds), *Fictions of Knowledge: Fact, Evidence, Doubt* (Houndmills: Palgrave Macmillan, 2012), pp. 40–60.

Webb, Sydney and Beatrice Webb, *English Poor Law History: The Old Poor Law* (London: Longmans, Green, 1927; repr. Camden, CN: Archon, 1963).

Wei, Ian P., *Intellectual Culture in Medieval Paris: Theologians and the University c. 1100–1330* (Cambridge: Cambridge University Press, 2012).

West, Martin, 'Music Therapy in Antiquity', in Peregrine Horden (ed.), *Music as Medicine: The History of Music Therapy since Antiquity* (Aldershot: Ashgate, 2000), pp. 51–68.

Weston, Robert, 'Whooping Cough: A Brief History to the 19th Century', *Canadian Society for the History of Medicine*, 29 (2012), 329–49.

Weygand, Zina, *The Blind in French Society from the Middle Ages to the Century of Louis Braille*, (trans.) Emily-Jane Cohen (Stanford: Stanford University Press, 2009).

Witters, Willibrord, 'Pauvres et pauvreté dans les coutumes monastiques du Moyen Âge', in Michel Mollat (ed.), *Études sur l'histoire de la pauvreté*, 2 vols (Paris: Publications de la Sorbonne, 1974), I, 177–215.

Wolf, Kenneth Baxter, *The Poverty of Riches: St. Francis of Assisi Reconsidered* (Oxford; New York: Oxford University Press, 2003).

Wood, Diana, *Medieval Economic Thought* (Cambridge: Cambridge University Press, 2002).

Woodward, G.W.O., *The Dissolution of the Monasteries* (London: Pitkin, 1966).

Wright, D.F. (ed.), *Martin Bucer: Reforming Church and Community* (Cambridge: Cambridge University Press, 1994).

Wrightson, Keith, *English Society 1580–1680* (London: Routledge, 2003).

Youings, Joyce, *Sixteenth-Century England* (Harmondsworth: Penguin, 1984).

Young, Spencer E., *Scholarly Community at the Early University of Paris: Theologians, Education and Society, 1215–1248* (Cambridge: Cambridge University Press, 2014).

Zuidema, Jason and Theodore Van Raalte, *Early French Reform: The Theology and Spirituality of Guillaume Farel* (Farnham: Ashgate, 2011).

Index